Introduction to Clinical Psychology

Introduction to Clinical Psychology

Alan S. Bellack

Department of Psychology
University of Pittsburgh

Michel Hersen

Western Psychiatric
Institute and Clinic
University of Pittsburgh
School of Medicine

New York   Oxford
OXFORD UNIVERSITY PRESS
1980

Copyright © 1980 by Oxford University Press, Inc.

Library of Congress Cataloging in Publication Data
Bellack, Alan S
  Introduction to clinical psychology.
  Bibliography: p.
  Includes index.
  1. Clinical psychology. 2. Psychological tests.
3. Personality assessment. 4. Psychotherapy.
I. Hersen, Michel, joint author. II. Title.
[DNLM: 1. Psychology, Clinical. WM105 B435i]
RC467.B438   661.8′9   79-15430
ISBN 0-19-502641-1

Printed in the United States of America

To our parents

Preface

We have had two goals in preparing this book. *First,* we attempted to convey some of our excitement about the field of clinical psychology. Of course, as a textbook rather than a novel, this excitement must be construed in a figural rather than a literal sense. While we have not presented "sexy" anecdotes, we have tried to describe what psychologists do, how they approach their activities, and how they evaluate them. Much of the excitement about the field stems from the tremendous variety of activities clinical psychologists engage in, the social import of those activities, and the dynamism of applied research (i.e., developing and evaluating new clinical procedures). There are few professions which afford the opportunity to engage in such a diversity of activities (e.g., clinical practice, teaching, research, consultation), *and* also experience the personal satisfaction of providing help to others. Whether through direct clinical service and teaching, or indirectly through applied research accomplishments, clinical psychology is a service oriented profession.

Our *second* goal was to provide an empirical picture of the field. We consider clinical psychology to be an applied *scientific* discipline. While clinical intuition and self-appraisal can be valuable sources of information, we ultimately must rely on research to adequately understand behavior and evaluate clinical techniques. Hence, we have endeavored to follow descriptions of the predominant techniques and orientations with up-to-date research reviews. It will quickly become apparent that some popular procedures have ample empirical support while others do not. Some are even contraindicated by the research literature. The reader should not be dismayed by this state of affairs. Rather, he or she should be encouraged by the rapid development and change in the field. Clinical psychology really only began after World War II, and there is much work yet to be done. This is part of the stimulus for our excitement.

Many people have contributed to this book in either a direct or indirect fashion. Our faculty mentors at the Pennsylvania State University (Alan S. Bellack) and the State University of New York at Buffalo (Michel Hersen) played a critical role in shaping our careers and attitudes about clinical psychology, and thus helped to shape this book. More recently, the challenging questions of many students and colleagues have stimulated continual study and reappraisal of our ideas. We wish to express our great appreciation to our wives and children for sacrificing their many evenings and weekends during which time we worked on the manuscript. We are grateful to Marcus Boggs for his constant encouragement, high expectations, and positive feedback. Finally, we are indebted to Mary Newell and Lauretta Guerin for their good humor, patience, and hard work in producing the typed copy of the manuscript.

Pittsburgh   Alan S. Bellack
April, 1979   Michel Hersen

Contents

Introduction to Clinical Psychology

CHAPTER ONE

Introduction

The field of psychology had its beginning in 1879, when the first psychology laboratory was opened by Wilhelm Wundt. Clinical psychology, primarily an applied subdivision of the field, is even newer. While the term was used as early as 1896 (by Witmer), clinical psychology really blossomed as a profession only after World War II. In thirty-five years it has grown from a poor stepchild of scientific psychology and psychiatry to one of the premier learned professions. In terms of their numbers, their abilities, and the diversity of their roles, clinical psychologists have established themselves as an independent and uniquely skilled discipline. Clinical psychologists have made important scientific contributions to our understanding of human behavior and our ability to change it. They work in universities, schools, mental health centers and clinics, hospitals, business and industry, government, labor unions, prisons, and in the private practice of psychotherapy. In all these settings and roles, they can be found in positions of leadership and in the forefront of efforts to increase human dignity and improve the quality of life.

This chapter is an introduction to the field of clinical psychology. First, we will describe what clinical psychology is and what clinical psychologists do. We will then provide a brief history of the field. Basic to this is the "scientist-professional" model, which has dominated the field since World War II. Criticisms of this model and alternatives will also be examined. The uniqueness of clinical psychology stems from the special training of prospective psychologists. We describe typical training programs and include sample curricula. Internship training, with examples, will then be described. Finally, we will briefly consider postdoctoral training and continuing professional development.

What Is Clinical Psychology?

"Clinical psychology is an applied science in which the principles of psychology are utilized to understand and help alleviate human problems." This somewhat terse statement provides a thumbnail sketch of the field. Like all such brief portraits, it does not do justice to its subject. No single statement could adequately account for the field's diversity and complexity. In many respects, this entire book could be taken as a definition, specifying what clinical psychologists do, how they think, and what the field encompasses. This chapter, like the brief definition above, will set the stage for later material. As a first step, let us analyze the above definition.

Clinical psychology is, first of all, a branch of psychology. As will be discussed below, clinical psychologists share much of their training with general (i.e., experimental) psychologists and employ much basic psychological knowledge in their work. Principles of learning, perception, physiology, group process and social interaction, cognition, and child development all play a central role in the clinical psychologist's methods and in the conceptualization of human problems. Consider a clinical child psychologist working with a youngster who is having academic problems. In evaluating the problems, the psychologist might consider and assess the child's perceptual ability (can he see properly?), neurophysiological functioning (can he comprehend the material?), and social-emotional development (do the problems result from psychological difficulties, such as anxiety?). A remediation program might well be based on operant conditioning procedures (shaping new skills by systematic reinforcement).

As the reader is well aware, psychology is a scientific discipline. Clinical psychology, too, has a strong scientific basis. Not only is the clinician's knowledge based on scientific research, but (traditionally) he or she is trained as a scientist. The preeminent model used in training clinical psychologists is the scientist-professional model. This scientific training serves clinical psychologists in three ways: (1) they are prepared to conduct research to add to our basic knowledge about human behavior, as well as how to assess it and change it in a therapeutic direction; (2) they are trained to evaluate systematically their own (or their colleagues') clinical services; and (3) they are sophisticated consumers of new research, so that skills are continually upgraded along with advances in knowledge. These three advantages are sometimes more apparent in theory than in practice, and some clinical psychologists have questioned the wisdom of scientific training. We will consider these arguments, pro and con, in a later section. The types of research conducted by clinical psychologists will be described in Chapter 10.

According to our definition, clinical psychology strives to "understand and help alleviate human problems." An applied discipline, it is allied with other human service and mental health professions in an effort to eliminate distress and improve the quality of life for all people. As scientists, clinical psychologists work to increase our understanding of psychopathology and psychological distress, as well as to develop effective treatment methods, educational programs, and prevention programs. As practitioners, they implement these various services and programs. Besides conducting psychotherapy and psychological assessments, they develop and implement educational and remedial programs for children, the mentally retarded, and severely disturbed psychiatric patients. They develop social service programs for communities and special groups such as the aged, juvenile delinquents, alcoholics, and drug addicts. They also do extensive consultation and teaching. This vast range of clinical and service activities will be considered in Chapters 3-9.

Clinical psychology has been described (with some fondness) as a "schizophrenic" occupation, with a dual emphasis on science and human service. On the one hand, the clinical psychologist is a scientist, with an unyielding curiosity and a need to know. Inquisitiveness about human behavior is one of the primary motives of prospective clinical psychology students and helps to shape their activities and approach after graduation. Why do people become anxious? Why does the schizophrenic have hallucinations? What causes depression? Why does this person not get along with anyone? Why is that person so painfully shy? This side of the profession involves an objective, dispassionate, and often skeptical approach to the world.

On the other hand, clinical psychologists are concerned about other people. They see distress and suffering and have a desire to help. They are interested in people and are motivated to listen, to be sympathetic, to do something for others. The vast majority of students who seek to become clinical psychologists do so precisely for this reason. Thus, most clinical psychologists spend much of their time directly serving people. They are humanists and generally politically and socially liberal. They are concerned with injustice, prejudice, poverty, and other aspects of human welfare, as well as with psychological difficulty. This side of the profession is more aligned with the humanities than with science. It involves introspection, philosophy, values, and subjectivity. Clinical psychologists are (and need to be) concerned, sensitive, feeling people.

These two seemingly incompatible orientations, scientist and humanist, have created much controversy in the field. It has been argued that the disparity is basic and will ultimately lead to a split between scientists and practitioners. However, thus far they have been successfully combined to produce a unique, dynamic, and vital profession. The combination of research and clinical skill is a hallmark of clinical psychology, and is probably responsible for the profession's rapid and extensive development. It is also important in the tremendous diversity of roles clinical psychologists fill (see Chapter 2). If the field is "schizophrenic," it appears to be coping with its difficulties extremely well.

Psychology as a Profession

So far, we have referred to clinical psychology as a *profession*. This term raises clinical psychology above the level of an *art* or a *trade* and equates it with medicine and law (Peterson, 1976). A profession is defined by the following: (1) a set of techniques which evolve from a science or theory, which require considerable intellectual activity to employ, and which must be applied differently for different problems; (2) a professional society in which membership is based at least partially on competence; and (3) a code of ethics and a commitment to work (at least in part) for the benefit of society (Peterson, 1976).

Referring to clinical psychology as a profession has more than semantic importance. It reflects status, influence, income, and the freedom to function in an independent and responsible manner (rather than under the direction of some other profession). The medical profession, arguing that clinical psychology is not a qualified mental health profession, has attempted to limit the right of psychologists to practice psychotherapy independently. However, the professional status and competence of clinical psychologists are now widely recognized by both the law (e.g., see Chapter 2 on the licensing of psychologists) and the public. Clinical psychologists have been elevated from a limited role—primarily under the direct supervision of psychiatrists—to positions of responsibility, authority, and self-determination.

The American Psychological Association, the professional organization of psychologists, has identified twelve criteria which psychologists meet as professionals. These criteria clarify the principles which guide the profession. Psychologists:

1. Guide their practice and policies by a sense of social responsibility.
2. Devote more of their energies to serving the public interest than to "guild" functions and to building ingroup strength.
3. Represent accurately to the public their demonstrable competence.
4. Develop and enforce a code of ethics primarily to protect the client and only secondarily to protect themselves.
5. Identify their unique skills and focus on carrying out those functions for which they are best equipped.
6. Cooperate with other professions having related or overlapping skills and common purposes.
7. Balance the efforts devoted to research, teaching, and application.
8. Further communication among "discoverers," teachers, and appliers of knowledge.
9. Avoid nonfunctional entrance requirements into the profession, such as those based on race, nationality, creed, or arbitrary personality considerations.
10. Insure that their training is meaningful in terms of their later functions.
11. Guard against prematurely adopting any technique or theory as a final solution to problems.
12. Strive to make their services available to all who need help, regardless of social and financial considerations (APA, 1968, pp. 199–200).

Clinical Psychology Versus Other Mental Health Professions

In addition to clinical psychology, there are many professional and subprofessional groups which provide mental health services to the public. In some cases their roles, activities, and responsibilities vary with their training and skills. Frequently activities overlap, causing confusion about the differences between groups and their areas of competence.

Clinical psychologists earn the Ph.D. or Psy.D. degree after four or more years of graduate school training beyond the bachelors degree (see below). They also have a full-time, one-year internship (or two years half-time) to refine their clinical skills. They are trained to do research and to conduct psychological assessment (see Chapters 4, 5, and 10) and treatment (see Chapters 6, 7, 8, and 9). Some clinical psychologists seek postdoctoral training to become proficient in a specialized area (e.g., neuropsychological assessment). When clinical psychologists work with other professionals on an interdisciplinary "team," they typically are uniquely qualified to perform psychological assessments and to plan and conduct research (e.g., to evaluate the quality of services or determine the types of patients who profit from specific services).

Psychiatrists are physicians who specialize in psychiatry. They receive M.D. degrees after attending medical school to receive a general medical education. Following a one-year internship, they take a three-year psychiatric residency, during which they learn the skills of the field of psychiatry. Since they are physicians, psychiatrists are legally permitted to prescribe medication. They are also specially skilled in diagnosing medically related psychiatric difficulties and in treating severe psychopathology. Some psychiatrists receive training in verbal psychotherapy (especially psychoanalysis), and some are trained to conduct research. However, they are uniquely qualified to use biological treatments (i.e., drug therapy).

Psychiatric social workers generally earn the Master of Social Work (M.S.W.) degree after two years of graduate training. While some are trained in a variety of psychological treatments, most concentrate on family case work. They conduct extensive family interviews, visit clients in their homes, and attempt to help by using relevant community resources (e.g., finding jobs for ex-patients). *Psychiatric nurses* also perform psychotherapeutic interventions. More often, they provide general nursing care and supplemental treatment services for psychiatric inpatients (e.g., helping to foster social interaction).

Development of the Profession

The field of clinical psychology has no clear trail of milestones or discoveries which mark its early development. Rather, it evolved slowly out of other disciplines and bodies of knowledge in an almost random and coincidental fashion. Interest in human behavior, especially maladaptive or pathological behavior, can be traced back through history. For example, William Shakespeare was a brilliant observer of human nature and motivation; many of his character sketches are valid today. Philosophical analyses and arguments about human nature, such as those of Hobbes and Locke, are also part of the background of clinical psychology. Similarly, Darwin exerted an important influence by bringing the study of humanity into the arena of science. In fact, the somewhat conflicting values of science and philosophy are a continuing major source of controversy for clinical psychology.

More direct lines for the development of the field are usually traced back to the later nineteenth century (Watson, 1953). After Wundt's development of the first psychology laboratory in 1879, the systematic, scientific study of human behavior became more important. This importance was shown by the so-called "psychometric tradition"—the emphasis on careful and specific measurement. In 1890, James McKeen Cattell coined the term "mental tests" to refer to the procedures for measuring psychological processes such as sensation and perception. This was the unofficial beginning of the *testing movement*. Mental testing became not only the backbone of the field but also the major source of activity and professional identity for clinical psychologists for the next sixty years. One milestone was the first useful intelligence test, published by Alfred Binet in 1905. Developed for use in the Paris school system, this test (by Binet and his colleague, Simon) showed that children could be compared and classified according to intellectual level. Previously they were had been categorized as only normal or retarded. As a result of this refined measurement, Binet's work also led to new training programs for the more educable mentally retarded. This gave impetus to applied psychology in general.

The second major source in shaping the field was the "dynamic tradition"—the interest in human motivation, needs, drives, and psychological processes. This emphasis was stressed by William James and G. Stanley Hall—two of the important academic psychologists of their time. However, the most significant influence was the work of Sigmund Freud. Freud's work, of course, had a tremendous impact on the entire mental health field. His emphasis on intrapsychic processes and psychodynamics was revolutionary at the time. Curiously, his initial impact was much greater on psychology than on psychiatry (Garfield, 1965). His writings created much interest in the psychological basis of behavior, as well as in the possibilities of using psychological approaches to change behavior.

The term *clinical psychology* apparently was first used by Lightner Witmer, who in 1896 established the first psychological clinic at the

University of Pennsylvania (Garfield, 1965; Watson, 1953). Psychologists at that clinic, and in general over the next twenty years, worked primarily in the area of testing and educational or rehabilitative programing for children. It was not until World War I that clinical psychologists really began to work with adults. The United States armed forces, faced with a sudden dramatic expansion, needed some way to sort and classify recruits. Given their expertise in the area of psychometrics and test construction, psychologists were enlisted to develop classification procedures. Two group intelligence tests (Army Alpha and Beta), along with a personality test (the Woodworth Personal Data Sheet), were created to meet this need. The success of these devices led to a rapid increase in the use of testing and the development of numerous other tests over the next several years. The profession during the period was further enhanced by the development of projective tests, including the Rorschach and Thematic Apperception Test (see Chapter 4). With their special expertise in this area, clinical psychologists became increasingly identified and valued as psychodiagnosticians.

While the field was gradually growing, clinical psychology was not a recognized profession prior to World War II. Few psychologists identified themselves as clinicians, and their training had no systematized or accepted form. Furthermore, clinical psychologists were primarily limited to testing and educational work with children. Psychotherapy (primarily psychoanalysis) was considered a medical activity and (with few exceptions) was limited to physicians. Many clinical psychologists served on psychiatric teams, conducting psychological assessments to guide the treatment plan carried out by a psychiatrist.

World War II brought about a dramatic change. Many academically oriented psychologists were drafted into the armed forces and thrust into clinical roles, often to help provide therapeutic services. By the time they were discharged, many of them had become interested in clinical work; the number of clinical psychologists mushroomed. But more important were the needs of the thousands of psychological casualties of the war. Available mental health personnel resources were totally inadequate. In response, the federal government began hiring more personnel and provided funding so that more people could be trained. Not only were clinical psychologists included, but the restrictions against their practice of psychotherapy began to disappear.

However, since there was no systematic training plan for clinical psychologists at that time, the government found it difficult to identify qualified persons and the training programs needed. For this reason, the

Veterans Administration and the U.S. Public Health Service asked the American Psychological Association (APA) to develop and publicize a training plan. In response, the APA convened a committee of leading figures, led by David Shakow. The resulting plan, referred to as the Shakow Report (APA, 1947), was published in 1947 and has served as a blueprint for the field ever since. The few training programs in existence at the time quickly adopted the plan in order to qualify for federal funding, as well as because of its inherent good sense. In 1949 a national conference on training in Boulder, Colorado, reaffirmed the Shakow recommendations, which then became known as the *Boulder Model* (Raimy, 1950). This model (see below), which underscores the scientist-professional concept, is still the basic approach for training clinical psychologists. In the thirty years since the Boulder Conference, the number of clinical psychologists has grown dramatically. Their numbers, their occupational roles, and their influence in society as well as in their job settings have increased geometrically. This growth is greatest in the United States. While clinical psychology exists in other countries, it is primarily an American profession. First, the U.S. government has the money to underwrite the cost of training by providing fellowships and traineeships to students. Both the Veterans Administration and the Public Health Service have continued their funding since the end of World War II. This support has promoted the development of new graduate training programs, as well as permitting graduate study for many students who could not otherwise afford it. Second, national, state, and local governments are major employers of clinical psychologists. Third, the country as a whole demands and supports social services, not the least of which is mental health care. While many clinical psychologists are in private practice or work in the private sector (e.g., industry), the majority owe their training and employment to the public.

Training of Clinical Psychologists

The Boulder Model, which called for the training of clinical psychologists as scientist-professionals, was almost universally adopted after the conference report was published. It remains the dominant approach to training today. However, it has come under increasing fire in recent years, and new models have been offered. The basic question is, is it feasible to train people to be both scientists *and* professionals? Given the growing doubts, many strictly professional programs have been proposed. In fact, the most recent national training conference, held at Vail, Colorado, in 1973 (Korman, 1976), advocated that practitioners and researchers be trained independently. In this section, we will describe and compare these alternative models and provide examples of the types of graduate programs they produce.

The Boulder Model

As stated above, the Boulder Conference adopted the Shakow Report almost completely. That report provided certain general principles which were to guide the nature of training, as well as specific recommendations for actual programs. First, the clinical psychologist was to be trained as a psychologist, sharing a common core of knowledge with other psychologists. The training program was to be as rigorous as that of the traditional doctorate. This recommendation has placed an added burden on clinical students, who must learn clinical skills as well as the various academic and research skills mastered by their nonclinical colleagues. Also, the clinical psychologist was to earn a doctoral degree; bachelors and masters level training were presumed to be inadequate.

The Shakow Report emphasized that clinical psychologists should *not* be trained as technicians, who would only be capable of performing a limited number of tasks (e.g., giving intelligence tests). Rather, they were to be trained as scientist-professionals, capable of conducting research as well as being sophisticated consumers of the research literature. This dual role was considered especially important since the field was just beginning to develop. Little was known about the nature or causes of psychopathology, and the effectiveness of available treatment techniques was uncertain. Thus, the report recommended a training strategy which would both advance the state of knowledge and allow clinical psychologists to continually update their skills as the field developed.

One implication of this recommendation was that courses should focus on theory and principles rather than only teach specific technical skills. The clinician would then have a solid basis on which to generate and integrate new ideas. Second, students should take courses in research methods (e.g., statistics) and conduct at least one independent research project (i.e., the dissertation). In practice, most programs require students to conduct a master's thesis, which is a small-scale research project, as well as a dissertation. Third, students should be imbued with a sense of scientific skepticism. Rather than accepting ideas and procedures on faith, they should have a questioning attitude, asking "why" and "how" and looking for evidence.

The training program must also develop clinical skills. It was recommended that clinical, academic, and research activities be integrated throughout the program. The hope was that these potentially contrasting activities would complement one another, rather than being discrete or incompatible. Clinical training would take three forms. First, research activities and courses would refer to clinical material and issues. Essentially the entire program was to be relevant to clinical training. Second, students would participate in clinical practicum from their first year. For beginning students this might entail interviewing and testing, observing advanced students, and participating in clinic conferences. Later, students would learn to perform psychotherapeutic interventions and conduct extensive assessment procedures. Many graduate programs operate their own mental health clinics in order to provide practicum training. Faculty members supervise and serve as role models. Other programs rely on community agencies to provide training opportunities. The third form of clinical training is the *internship*. This is a concentrated period of clinical work, either for one year full time or two successive years half time, generally in the third or fourth year of graduate school. The student spends the year immersed in clinical work in the field (e.g., at a psychiatric hospital), often geographically removed from the university. Practicum training is viewed as preparation for the internship, during which clinical skills are refined and the student encounters more seriously disturbed persons.

Two other recommendations in the Shakow Report also warrant comment. The training program was to encourage intensive "self-evaluation." Students were expected to become aware of their own motives, values, anxieties, and biases so that these factors would not interfere with clinical work or appraisal of the literature. One way to do this is through intensive, one-on-one therapy supervision, in which the student's clinical activity is carefully examined and discussed. In this manner, the student might be made aware of a consistent blind spot, anger, anxiety, or other problem. Another way for the student to gain self-knowledge is through personal psychotherapy. Some programs encourage all students to undergo therapy, but in most cases this is left to the student's discretion. It was also recommended that the program foster a sense of social responsibility. The clinical psychologist was expected to have a commitment to society, as well as to him or herself and any particular client. This is consistent with the APA guidelines for the profession.

The Scholar-Professional Model

The Boulder Conference model for training has promoted the tremendous growth of clinical psychology. Its value is reflected in the increased number and success of programs based on the model. Most such programs have thirty to fifty student applicants for each opening. The job market for clinical psychologists remains solid, in contrast to the decreasing demand for nonclinical psychologists and many other professionals. The blend of research and clinical training is unique among the mental health professions and gives clinical psychologists a special identity and repertoire of skills. Nevertheless, the scientist-professional aspect of the model has recently come under increasing fire, and its utility has been severely challanged (cf. Coffey, 1970; Derner, 1975; Korman, 1974; Peterson, 1976).

The basic criticism is that training students as scientists *and* professionals may be desirable in theory but is impossible in practice. Several factors have led to this conclusion. Most people who wish to become clinical psychologists have primarily applied interests. They want to become *clinicians*; their attitudes toward research activities and statistics often range from disinterest to hostility, and they attend research classes quite unwillingly. Conversely, graduate programs are controlled and conducted by academic (i.e., research oriented) faculty members. They are neither skilled clinicians (since they do not do much clinical work) nor committed clinical supervisors. Finally, it is argued that there is simply not enough time to train people to be competent scientists *and* competent clinicians. Too often, the graduates of Boulder Model programs are mediocre in both spheres rather than experts in either or both.

Several noted figures in the field have advocated separate training for students interested in professional as opposed to research careers (Derner, 1975, 1976; Peterson, 1976). The 1973 Vail conference on training reached the same conclusion (Korman, 1974). In addition to the arguments presented above, it was felt that clinical knowledge and techniques are now so well grounded that the major justification for the

Boulder Model is no longer valid. While further research and the training of scientists were certainly to be encouraged, the training of practitioners was now seen as justifiable and necessary.

Gordon Derner (1975, 1976) has used the term *scholar-professional* to describe the new model for training. This term stresses that clinical practitioners should not be technicians, but should receive rigorous training which emphasizes a scholarly, creative, and sophisticated approach to the clinical enterprise.

> In a clinical psychology program that strives for excellence in preparation for clinical practice, the core of substantive courses and seminars will offer depth in scholarship but clearly relevance will serve as a crucial criteria [sic] for inclusion of such course or seminar. The program will be marked by extensive and intensive clinical practice from the first year under qualified clinical practitioners and the program will have available and encourage students to have a personal therapy experience. The scholarship will be encouraged through continuing reference to the literature of the field and the culminating scholarly production, the dissertation, will be relevant to the person's career goal of clinical service (Derner, 1975, p. 3).

Several strategies have been proposed for scholar-professional programs. Derner advocates the Doctor of Philosophy (Ph.D.) as the professional degree, regarding it as the pinnacle of academic achievement. Others (cf. Peterson, 1968) have suggested that the professional status and competence of clinical psychologists would best be represented by a new degree: the Doctor of Psychology, or Psy.D. According to this view, the Ph.D. is a research degree which does not differentiate degree holders by discipline (i.e., physicists, sociologists, psychologists, and others all earn the Ph.D.). In contrast, the Psy.D. is unique to psychology and would be viewed publicly as comparable to the degree of Doctor of Medicine (M.D.) or Doctor of Dental Surgery (D.D.S.). Also, the requirements for the degree would be less restricted. Today, opinion on this issue is clearly divided; which degree will ultimately prevail is uncertain.

Another basic problem is, what is the best setting for professional training? Boulder Model programs are usually found in university psychology departments. Many (most?) advocates of professional training argue that such programs need a less restrictive setting. Two different strategies have been offered. One suggests that the programs remain within university settings but function as separate schools, like schools of law, medicine, and dentistry (Derner, 1976; Peterson, 1976). This would allow for close ties with academic psychology departments, including joint course offerings and an interactive faculty. The other model calls for independent professional schools which function autonomously. The California School of Professional Psychology, which has several branch campuses throughout the state, is a prime example of this approach. In addition to the Ph.D., it offers several lower-level degrees for psychological aides and technicians. The independent school lacks the prestige and support provided by a major university, but it has greater freedom to develop its own programs.

Boulder Versus Vail

How will future clinical psychologists be trained? Professional programs are now well established, and more will probably be developed in the future. While the number of independent schools may increase, the university-based programs seem to have more promise because of their greater prestige, the availability of other resources (e.g., academic psychology faculty), and the university's economic base. However, it seems unlikely that professional training programs will become the norm. Unlike the Boulder Report, the Vail Report has not been widely accepted by the field. Most traditional programs still prosper, and the Boulder Model is still widely accepted. Furthermore, graduates of these programs are still highly regarded by the public and other mental health disciplines.

Our feeling is that the Boulder Model still represents the most reasonable way to train clinical psychologists. As Leitenberg (1974) notes, the scientist-professional approach is not designed to train laboratory researchers and practicing psychoanalysts. It is most suited for training applied researchers—people who can do clinical work, evaluate it, and develop empirically based clinical procedures or programs. Effective therapeutic techniques cannot be developed solely in the laboratory, without clinical sophistication and clinical trials. The researcher must know what depressives or phobics are like and what it means to work with them in order to devise reasonable interventions. Conversely, we do not know enough to justify the uniform adoption of today's technology. As Chapters 3 to 10 will show, every clinical technique used today is under continuing evaluation. We also believe that doctoral-level training is unnecessary for most clinical techniques. Technicians can be trained to conduct assessments and treatments. The doctoral-level professional can thus train and supervise, develop programs, and evaluate programs and procedures. Boulder Model clinical psychologists are those best qualified to conduct such critical applied research. High-quality professional programs may be appropriate for those who have no desire or ability for research. However, we believe they cannot totally substitute for Boulder-type programs.

What Is Graduate School Like?

The Boulder and Vail training conferences provided general guidelines but did not specify the form and content of graduate programs. Based on these conferences, the APA has developed a set of standards for evaluating programs and provides *accredidation* for those which meet the criteria. But, like the conference recommendations, these criteria simply provide a framework and set acceptable limits. Ultimately, each graduate program determines its own curriculum, requirements, and method of operation. No two graduate programs are exactly alike. In fact, no two students in any particular program have exactly the same course of study and activity. Almost all programs have some required courses and activities, but beyond these, students tailor their graduate career to their own needs, interests, and career goals.

Most programs are geared for three years of full-time study on campus followed by one year of internship. It is not unusual for a student to extend the time on campus. Some students devote a fourth year to dissertation research, either before or after the internship. In most programs, the first-year curriculum consists mainly of required courses. Students also become involved in research (in Boulder Model programs) and practicum activities. Many programs have some required courses in the second and third years, but most work beyond the first year is elective. Much time is also devoted to research and practicum. Most Boulder Model programs require the student to complete two independent research projects: the masters thesis and the doctoral dissertation. The thesis is generally completed during the second year.[1] The

---

1. Most programs which offer doctoral degrees only accept students who plan to work toward that degree. However, many of these programs award the masters degree when the student finishes a thesis project. Since students continue their studies without interruption, the masters degree has little significance. On the other hand, there are numerous programs which offer the masters as the terminal degree. Students in these programs either seek employment or later apply to doctoral programs.

majority of programs also require students to take a comprehensive examination at the end of the first or second year. Its format varies considerably, but generally covers a broad range of material and demonstrates the student's potential as a scholar.

Tables 1.1 and 1.2 present recent curricula from the University of Pittsburgh and Syracuse University, respectively. We emphasize the word "recent" since most programs gradually and continually change. This is because of changes in the field and in faculty and students. Both of these programs are designed to train scientist-professionals. Table 1.3 consists of a recent curriculum from the Psy.D. program at Baylor University. This program, designed to train professionals; includes training in "research utilization." No dissertation is required.

Strupp (1974) emphasizes that graduate training in clinical psychology is an individual, personal experience. Most programs attempt to

Table 1.1.   Ph.D. Program at the University of Pittsburgh (1978)

FIRST YEAR

Fall

Statistics
Clinical-Research Clerkship
Clinical Assessment
Psychopathology

Winter

Statistics
Field Placement
First Year Research
Clinical Psychology I
Developmental or Learning Course

Spring

Statistics
Field Placement
First Year Research
Clinical Psychology II

SECOND YEAR

Fall

Practicum
Psychometrics
Clinical Psychology III
Elective

limit the number of admissions each year to the number of full-time clinical faculty (e.g., a one-to-one ratio). Students not only get individual attention and guidance but often form a close relationship with an advisor or mentor. The mentor generally helps the student plan his or her education and formulate career goals. The mentor is also usually the research supervisor; student and mentor spend many hours discussing research ideas and procedures. Clinical training also typically involves a close, individual faculty-student interaction. It is not uncommon for a student to receive one hour of supervision for each hour of clinical work. Extensive interaction between students is also an important part of the training program. Students provide informal research and clinical supervision for one another, as well as conducting such activities jointly. They discuss complex material and vigorously debate issues. Thus, much of what the student receives from the program comes outside of

Table 1.1. (Continued)

Winter
Practicum
Learning or Developmental Course
Elective
Masters Thesis

Spring
Practicum
Elective
Masters Thesis

THIRD YEAR

Fall
Electives
Dissertation

Winter
History and Systems
Electives
Dissertation

Spring
Electives
Dissertation

FOURTH YEAR

Internship (12 months, full time)

Table 1.2.   Ph.D. Program at Syracuse University (1977)

First Year

Fall

Clinical Assessment I
Statistical Methods in Education and Psychology II
Advanced Personality
Family Evaluation Practicum
Research in Psychology: Thesis
(Ten hours per week are required in research activity under the direction of a clinical faculty member.)

Spring

Family Evaluation Practicum
Clinical Assessment II
Statistical Methods in Education and Psychology III
Seminar in Psychopathology
Research in Psychology: Thesis
(Ten hours per week are required in research activity under the direction of a clinical faculty member.)

SECOND YEAR

Fall

Introduction to Psychotherapy
Advanced Practicum in Clinical Psychology
Experimental Design and Statistical Tests
Research Apprenticeship (20 hours per week)
Research Group

Spring

Principles of Behavior Modification
Survey of Psychotherapy Research
Advanced Practicum in Clinical Psychology
Research Apprenticeship (20 hours per week)
Research Group

THIRD YEAR

Fall

Electives
Clinical Traineeship (20 hours per week)
Research Group
Elective Practica offered are:
    Family Intervention Practicum
    Clinical Behavior Therapy

Table 1.2. (Continued)

Spring
Electives
Clinical Traineeship (20 hours per week)
Research Group

Summer
Electives

FOURTH YEAR

Fall
Research in Psychology: Dissertation
Electives
Research, Teaching, or Clinical Traineeship (20 hours per week)
Research Group

Spring
Supervision Practicum
Research in Psychology: Dissertation
Research, Teaching, or Clinical Traineeship (20 hours per week)
Research Group

FIFTH YEAR
Internship (Full time, 12 months)

---

classes. Faculty and fellow students serve as role models, sources of feedback, and stimuli for ideas and activities. A quality graduate education requires and results from a full-time involvement in the program, not simply from attending classes and reading required textbooks.

Internships

Internships vary as much as graduate programs do, and also are individually tailored by each student. Because internship training is provided by independent clinical agencies, students must apply for admission in much the same way that they apply to graduate school. Most programs provide a stipend or pay the student a salary during the internship year. The APA provides accreditation for quality internships

Table 1.3. Psy.D. Program at Baylor University (1978)

FIRST YEAR

    Clinical Practicum
    Clinical Psychology
    Learning
    Psychological Assessment I
    Counseling Psychology
    Community Mental Health
    Advanced Psychopathology
    Developmental Psychology
    Individualized Professional Development
    Human Information Processing

SECOND YEAR

    Clinical Practicum
    Behavior Therapy
    Psychological Assessment II
    Social Psychology and Group Dynamics
    Theories of Psychotherapy
    Group Psychotherapy
    Personality
    Clinical Procedures with Children

THIRD YEAR

    Clinical Practicum
    Experimental Design
    Community Psychology
    Neurophysiology and Neuropharmacology
    Medical Psychology
    Psychophysiology and Biofeedback
    Case Studies in Clinical Psychology
    Individual Project in Clinical Psychology

FOURTH YEAR

    Internship (12 months, full time)

in the same way that it accredits graduate schools. According to the APA:

> Internships should provide the trainee with the opportunity to take substantial responsibility for carrying out major professional functions in the context of appropriate supervisory support, professional role modeling,

and awareness of administrative structures. The internship is taken after completion of relevant didactic and practicum work and precedes the granting of the doctoral degree.

The internship experience is crucial preparation for the ultimate function as an independent professional. It should be an intensive and extensive experience related to the graduate program's training objective (Education and Training Board, 1978, pp. 24–25).

Internships generally give students a variety of treatment and assessment experiences with different types of patients. Frequently, there is also an opportunity to engage in research, consultation, and community mental health activities (see Chapter 9) if the student desires. Internship facilities also offer seminars and lectures, often of a multidisciplinary nature (i.e., they are attended by professionals and students from other disciplines). The typical pattern of training involves a series of *rotations* across various clinical units. For example, an intern may spend three months in an inpatient unit, three months in an outpatient clinic, three months in a pediatric unit, and three months in an emergency service. Each of these rotations may be full time, or the intern may spend several hours each day or week on a secondary rotation. In addition to direct clinical experience, the intern is closely supervised by psychologists on each service. By the end of the internship year, students are usually prepared and qualified to begin their career as clinical psychologists.

Advanced Training

Education and training for any profession is a lifelong process. The lawyer must keep abreast of new statutes and court decisions, the physician must be aware of new medications and procedures, and the clinical psychologist must be familiar with research findings and new developments in the field. Various steps are involved. For one thing, professionals must continually read journals or significant new books throughout their career. Failure to keep up with the literature results in quick outdating of knowledge and potential incompetence. Another practice is attendance at regional or national meetings of professional associations, such as the APA, the Association for Advancement of Behavior Therapy, and the Eastern, Southeastern, Midwestern, and Western Psychological Associations. These organizations each hold national conventions with various training opportunities: symposia, workshops, seminars, demonstrations, and others. For example, an expert on a new therapeutic technique may lead a workshop and demonstrate its application.

The clinical psychologist may wish to learn a new skill or develop a new area of specialization which requires extensive training. For example, interns often develop new interests and sometimes cannot receive enough training in the new area during the internship year. For this reason, some psychologists pursue one or two years of *postdoctoral training*. The "post-doc," as it is called, is typically a full-time program which pays a stipend or salary. The training may be offered by a skilled researcher or clinician or by an agency. For example, the person who seeks training to conduct behavior therapy or work with learning-disabled children spends a year at an agency specializing in that area. Most clinical psychologists do not take post-docs. Most of those who do, take them immediately after their internship year, before they have begun their careers.

Summary

This chapter has presented an introduction to the field of clinical psychology. We first provided a definition of the field and emphasized its dual nature: a cross between science and the humanities. We next described clinical psychology as a profession, together with the criteria which govern the psychologist's attitudes and activities. Then we examined the differences between clinical psychology and the other mental health professions. We next looked at the brief history of the field, including the work of Freud, the testing movement, and the impact of the two world wars. World War II and its aftermath was especially critical in two ways: it promoted psychologists as psychotherapists and stimulated federal funding of training programs.

The training of clinical psychologists was then examined. First, we discussed the Shakow Report and the resulting Boulder Model of the scientist-professional. Recent criticisms of this model then were mentioned, and the scholar-professional model was described. Our own views, favoring the continuation of scientist-professional training, were then offered. Graduate school and internship programs, including representative curricula, were provided. Finally, we described continuing education for clinical psychologists.

CHAPTER TWO

Role of the Clinical Psychologist

In Chapter 1, we traced the development of clinical psychology. From a historical perspective, it is clear that major changes have occurred during the profession's brief lifetime. Not only has clinical psychology gained in popularity—as shown by the geometric increase in the number of professionals—but the scope of its activities has grown dramatically. As a result, the role of clinical psychologists has become more varied and flexible, while their prestige in many institutional settings has been enhanced. Of course, with an expanding role, clinical psychology has sometimes encountered difficulties and resistance from other professional groups (e.g., psychiatry) (see Kiesler, 1977; Matarazzo, Lubin, & Nathan, 1978). However, this is only natural when one expanding professional group is perceived as encroaching on the territorial rights of another.

In this chapter, we will examine the role of the clinical psychologist today in a variety of educational, research, clinical, and community settings. First, let us consider what the term *role* means. Like McGinnies (1970), we believe that "The concept of role is a convenient shorthand for designating certain well practiced behaviors that are specific to situations in which particular individuals are involved. To 'play a role' is simply to perform in a manner that has been reinforced in certain classes, or categories, or situations" (p. 228). Also, as Blanchard and Barlow state, (1976) "*role* refers to the expectations persons hold in common toward any person occupying a slot or position in a system. It is impossible to view a role apart from its relationship to other roles because the expectations of one role specify behaviors toward other role incumbents . . ." (p. 334). These definitions should be kept in mind when the relationship of clinical psychology to other professions or other areas within psychology is discussed.

We will first look at three traditional areas within clinical psychology: teaching, research, and clinical practice. We will consider job satisfaction and the typical work week of several clinical psychologists in each area. In addition, we will deal with new areas in clinical psychology in the 1970s and 1980s.

Next, we will consider the clinical psychologist's professional identity, discussing the psychologist's relationship to the APA and other professional groups (e.g., Association for Advancement of Behavior Therapy [AABT]; Society of Behavioral Medicine). We will also be concerned with publications specifically designed for clinical psychologists.

Then we will look at the ethical considerations of the clinical psychologist. Some of the principles of the APA Code of Ethics will be summarized and reported violations described. Finally, we will turn to the relationship between clinical psychology and psychology in general, and finally to other professional groups. Some of the problems inherent in these relationships will be outlined and discussed. Issues of certification, licensing, and other relevant legislative action regarding accreditation will be examined.

Before describing the variety of roles carried out by clinical psychologists, we might point out that most of us in this field find the profession to be rewarding, exciting, and stimulating. Many doors are opened with the Ph.D. in clinical psychology. Consider the clinical psychologist working in a pediatric setting who helps parents adjust to their child's chronic illness; doing psychotherapy with dying patients; or working in industry to select managerial personnel and setting up institutes to improve staff relations. These, of course, are some of the more unusual activities carried out by clinical psychologists. But they all are possible!

Variety of Roles

Because of their comprehensive training, clinical psychologists today have many employment opportunities after obtaining the doctoral degree (cf. American Psychological Association, 1975; Woods, 1976). Final job selection often means pursuing a major area of interest during graduate training (e.g., teaching, clinical practice, research, consultation, or some combination of the four). A position that combines teaching, research, and clinical practice approaches the goals of the Boulder Model. However, the ideal equal split among the three areas of endeavor is rarely achieved. Most often, individual career choice, luck, and financial considerations ultimately determine the balance. In some instances, the financial lure of clinical practice may overshadow the desire to do research. In others, the dedicated teacher may achieve greater job satisfaction by teaching than by doing research. In still other cases, the pursuit of new knowledge will supersede all else. Also, in any given employment setting, teaching, research, or direct clinical service will be given highest priority. Thus, how a clinical psychologist pursues a career obviously involves many issues.

In their 1973 survey, Garfield and Kurtz (1976) assessed the current activities, theoretical views, and career choice satisfaction of clinical psychologists. A twenty-two-item questionnaire was mailed to one-third of the members of Division 12 (the Division of Clinical Psychology) of the APA. Within one month, 69 percent had responded; data from 855 members and fellows of Division 12 were the basis for the final report.

Table 2.1 shows the primary affiliations of today's clinical psychologists. About 33 percent are employed in clinical settings such as hospitals (general and psychiatric), outpatient clinics, and medical schools. About 30 percent are employed in university settings. Next, 23 percent have private practice as their main source of income. Then 11.5 percent are affiliated with public schools, the federal government, rehabilitation centers, corporations, juvenile correctional facilities, and state departments of mental health. No significant differences in institutional affiliation are found between men and women. About 47 percent are involved in part-time private practice work.

The breakdown of positions held by clinical psychologists in this survey is very similar to that reported by Kelly (1961) some fifteen years earlier. However, these data do not reflect the qualitative differences in roles in such settings. The changing role of the clinical psychologist in these settings will be discussed later.

Table 2.2 shows how respondents to this questionnaire view themselves as professionals. The vast majority describe themselves as clinical practitioners, whereas only 20 percent and 4.68 percent, respectively, label themselves academicians and researchers.

Table 2.1.   Primary Institutional Affiliations

Primary affiliation	N	%
None	10	1.17
Mental hospital	72	8.42
General hospital	51	5.97
Outpatient clinic	44	5.15
Community mental health center	64	7.48
Medical school	68	7.95
Private practice	199	23.27
University psychology department	188	21.99
University, other	60	7.02
Other	99	11.58
Total	855	100.00

From: Garfield & Kurtz (1976), Table 2.

Table 2.3 presents the percentage of time devoted to designated activities by this sample of 855 clinical psychologists. As noted by Garfield and Kurtz (1976), 41 percent of professional time is used to provide clinical services (i.e., individual psychotherapy, group psychotherapy, behavior modification, diagnosis and assessment), whereas 35 percent is engaged in training and research (i.e., teaching, clinical supervision, research, research supervision). The relatively small amount of time devoted to research is not at all consistent with the goals of the Boulder Model. However, the small proportion of time spent diagnosing and assessing clients and patients reflects the changing role of the

Table 2.2.   Primary Professional Self-Concept

Primary view	N	%
Clinical practitioner	502	58.71
Academician	171	20.00
Researcher	40	4.68
Consultant	41	4.80
Supervisor	20	2.34
Administrator	69	8.07
Other	12	1.40
Total	855	100.00

From: Garfield & Kurtz (1976), Table 3.

Table 2.3. Percentage of Time Devoted to
Designated Activities

Activity	%
Individual psychotherapy	25.07
Group psychotherapy	4.35
Behavior modification	2.00
Diagnosis and assessment	9.79
Community consultation	5.23
Teaching	13.82
Clinical supervision	7.78
Research	7.04
Research supervision	2.71
Sensitivity group	.40
Scholarly writing	3.77
Administration	13.21
Other	4.82
Total	99.99

From: Garfield & Kurtz (1976), Table 4.

clinical psychologist (see Chapters 4, 5, and 6). It may also indicate the increased use of paraprofessionals and M.A.-level psychologists, who are serving as assessors under the direct supervision of doctoral-level clinical psychologists (cf. Cohen, 1974; Hersen & Bellack, 1976a, 1978a).

Most clinical psychologists (54.97 percent) view themselves as eclectic. A relatively equal proportion are divided between psychoanalytic (10.76 percent) and behavioral (i.e., learning theory) (9.94 percent) orientations. Compared to Kelly's 1961 survey, fewer clinical psychologists today are psychoanalytic, while a much greater proportion are eclectic (see Table 7.2 for a complete breakdown).

Finally, in terms of career satisfaction, 71.11 percent indicate that if they had to do it again, they would still be clinical psychologists. Of those who said they would select a different profession, 14.74 percent chose medicine. In discussing this survey, Garfield and Kurtz (1976) conclude that ". . . one cannot ascribe any particular view or orientation to clinical psychologists in general—except that the overwhelming majority are happy with their choice of career and that the views of the majority of clinical psychologists lie between those at either end of the continuum" (p. 9).

The Clinical Psychologist as Educator and Researcher

As Table 2.1 shows, many clinical psychologists work in settings where education is a primary responsibility. Of course, the type and amount of teaching required will vary both within and across settings. For example, in university psychology departments, teaching is often formal, with the clinical psychologist preparing and delivering lectures to large undergraduate classes several times a week (e.g., abnormal psychology, introduction to clinical psychology, tests and measurement). Generally, at the undergraduate level (particularly in the more basic courses), there is less interchange between professor and students than in graduate seminars. This, unfortunately (for both), is often the result of large class size.

At the graduate level, teaching is often less formal, with both students and professor presenting material to the seminar group. This format creates considerable interest, interchange, and lively discussion. Also at the graduate level, the apprenticeship model is often followed, with the professor providing direct research and clinical supervision (on a one-to-one basis) in specially designed tutorials. However, in other topic areas (notably statistics), the lecture method usually prevails.

The clinical psychologist's teaching load in the university psychology department varies with the size of the school and the professor's rank. In smaller, poorly funded departments, the load is heavier than in larger, well-endowed departments. Also, the higher the academic rank (instructor, assistant professor, associate professor, professor), the lighter the teaching load. Generally, those with higher ranks (associate professor and professor) are assigned (by clinical directors and chairpeople) fewer courses so that they may pursue other professional interests (e.g., research, consultation, and direct clinical service to clients).

To give a clearer idea of what the academic clinical psychologist does day to day, we include an actual schedule of an associate professor from a large, well-established psychology department. This individual is also director of the psychology clinic in his department. He has a light teaching load, which permits him to pursue his research interests. Primary teaching duties consist of clinical practicum supervision, one graduate behavior therapy seminar that meets twice weekly, and research supervision of graduate students. In addition to research-related activities, he spends time in meetings and clinical consultation at a local Veterans Administration hospital.

Had this person been associated with a junior college rather than a large university, the course load would have been larger, would have consisted of teaching undergraduate students, and of course would have left much less opportunity for doing research. Also, the schedule presented in Table 2.4 does not reflect the many additional hours worked evenings and weekends writing up the results of research endeavors for scientific publication in journals and books.[1]

Clinical psychologists associated with medical schools, VA hospitals, general hospitals, community mental health centers, and institutes for retarded persons also teach. However, teaching, by its very nature, tends to be very different in such settings. The focus is on providing direct services. Hence, with some exceptions (i.e., medical schools and hospitals affiliated with medical schools), teaching is less academic and theoretical, more pragmatic and applied. Although some formal lectures (to medical students and nurses) and seminars (to psychology interns and psychiatric and medical residents) are offered, most of the teaching consists of one-to-one supervision of diagnostic and therapeutic activities. Moreover, in such institutional settings, the clinical psychologist spends a fair amount of time training paraprofessionals (see Hersen & Bellack, 1978b). Indeed, as their prestige in medical settings has increased, clinical psychologists have offered fewer direct services to clients and patients and have become more active in training nondegreed and B.A.-level mental health workers (Cohen, 1974).

Let us now consider the schedule of a young clinical psychologist employed in a research-oriented psychiatry department in a large medical school. As Table 2.5 shows, this clinical psychologist (an assistant professor), working on an inpatient service for highly disturbed children, is almost totally devoted to research. From this schedule, it appears that no direct service is being offered. Rather, the clinical psychologist is serving as a consultant to staff (nurses, nursing assistants, special education teachers, research assistants), to enable them to carry out intervention programs.

In settings that emphasize clinical service, a junior clinical psychologist undoubtedly would spend a lot of time assessing and treating clients (in individual, family, and group psychotherapy). This certainly would be true of the clinical psychologist employed in a community mental health center (cf. Hollingsworth & Hendrix, 1977).

1. Educational and research activities are discribed in one section since most research is done by clinical psychologists employed in university psychology departments and medical schools. However, clinical psychologists in other settings (e.g., VA hospitals) also engage in research.

Table 2.4. Weekly Schedule of Associate Professor in a Psychology Department

Time	Monday	Tuesday	Wednesday	Thursday	Friday
8.30					
9:00	Clinical practicum supervision	Spend morning writing a manuscript	No appointments: spend day writing a manuscript		Appointments with graduate students
9:30					
10:00				Research meeting	
10:30					Read journals
11:00					
11:30		Lunch	Lunch	Lunch	
12:00	Lunch				Lunch
12:30				Faculty meeting	
1:00	Appointments with individual graduate students	Research meeting			
1:30					Correspondence
2:00					
2:30		Graduate behavior therapy seminar		Graduate behavior therapy seminar	
3:00					Consulting at V.A. Hospital
3:30	Read journals				
4:00					
4:30					
5:00					

32

Table 2.5. Weekly Schedule of Assistant Professor in a Psychiatry Department

Time	Monday	Tuesday	Wednesday	Thursday	Friday
7–8	Read	Read	Read	Read	Read
8–9	Meet with research assistants	Meet with research assistants	Meet with research assistants	Meet with research assistants	Meet with research assistants
9–10	Case conference	Admin. paperwork	Admin. paperwork	Case conference	Write
10–11		Write			Admin. meeting
11–12	Admin. meeting	Lunch	Lunch	Lunch	Lunch
12–1	Lunch	Write	Discuss clinical issues	Write	Write
1–2	Write		Write		
2–3	Admin. meeting		Inservice	Discuss clinical issues	
3–4	*Discuss clinical*				
4–5	*problems of Unit*		Admin.	Read	

Before describing clinical psychologists as practitioners, let us consider their role as researchers. In later chapters, we will present a more comprehensive analysis of the kinds of research carried out. Here, however, we should note that in most cases, the setting and the availability of subjects will influence the type of research that a given clinical psychologist is able to pursue. For example, the clinical psychologist in a university setting will probably carry out theoretical analogue research with college students. By contrast, the individual in a hospital setting is more likely to do research with seriously disturbed patients that has clinical import (see Leitenberg, 1974). Such research could involve diagnostic comparisons or the effects of specific treatment. Individuals working with retarded subjects may focus on developmental factors, while those working with outpatients in community mental health settings may wish to assess how well the program serves the community at large.

In any event, the possibilities for doing research are limited only by the availability of subjects, research supports, time, and ingenuity. Among the areas in which clinical psychologists have made a major research contribution are epidemiology, personality, psychopathology, assessment and diagnosis, psychotherapy evaluation, and program evaluation. (See Chapter 10 for further details.)

The Clinical Psychologist As Private Practitioner

In the Garfield and Kurtz (1976) survey of clinical psychologists, 23 percent were in full-time private practice. Further, 47 percent had at least part-time private practice. Thus, the private sector of clinical psychology is a sizable proportion.

As a private practitioner, the clinical psychologist offers certain services to the public, much as a dentist or general medical doctor does. Office hours are established, and patients (i.e., clients) are seen for assessment, diagnosis (see Chapters 4 to 6), and psychotherapy (see Chapters 6 to 8). Fees are charged for services rendered. This, of course, is in contrast to the clinical psychologist who is hired by an institution where the same services may be performed for a yearly salary).

There are many myths about the practices of clinical psychologists. In a tongue-in-cheek description entitled "Demythologizing Private Practice," Taylor (1978) accurately points out that "Today, many of the children seen are Medicaid beneficiaries. The fathers are commonly deceased or missing and the mothers frequently migrant. There are middle-class children referred for the treatment of active ulcers resistant to medication. There are the military dependents, predominantly the families of enlisted men living in mobile home parks and often eating with the help of food stamps. I am a consultant to two children's homes, working with staff and residents in a population that has been exposed to both economic and educational deprivation, has been frequently abused sexually and otherwise, has spent portions of its youth on the run, and is emerging from jail or other confinement" (p.68). This can hardly be considered the glorious upper-middle-class practice so often attributed to the private sector. Indeed, this description sounds very much like the kind of private practice one of the authors had when he did this on both a full-time and a part-time basis.

By contrast, Taylor (1978) adds, "Of course we all 'know' of the psychologist working a 35-hour work week at $60 per hour. His clients are movie stars, successful writers, and the wives of corporate executives, with maybe a sprinkling of high-level bureaucrats. They come in three to five times a week for 6 or 7 years, so he only needs about 10 referrals a year. He hasn't learned anything lately and the clients won't either. We know he is out there. Have you met him yet?" (p. 70). The authors of this book have known a very few that might fit this description. However, they are in the minority.

What do clinical psychologists in private practice actually do? Perhaps this can best be answered by looking at the schedule one of the authors followed when he was in full-time private practice in a suburban community in Connecticut. Table 2.6 indicates three basic activities: individual psychotherapy, assessment, and group psychotherapy. In addition, this practicing clinician (like many others in the community) also consulted at a local VA facility, supervising psychology interns in their diagnostic assessments of patients. His schedule often extended through Saturday. In some instances, when married couples were seen together, later evening appointments were required, particularly for working couples.

Let us consider the sources of information that clinicians use in the consulting room. These sources are diverse. Some data may come from an analysis of the case history, with the patient, relative, friend, or employer as the main informant (see Chapter 3). They may be confirmed by psychological testing (see Chapter 4) or by direct observation (see Chapter 5) during the assessment. At times, home visits may be indicated. This is time-consuming (i.e., travel to and from office) and costly, but

Table 2.6. Weekly Schedule of a Practicing Clinician

Time	Monday	Tuesday	Wednesday	Thursday	Friday	Saturday
8:30						
9:00	VA consultation	Case conference	Psychological assessment	Ind. psychotherapy	Ind. psychotherapy	Psychological assessment
9:30						
10:00		Ind. psychotherapy		Ind. Psychotherapy	Ind. psychotherapy	
10:30						
11:00		Ind. psychotherapy		Ind. psychotherapy	Ind. psychotherapy	
11:30						
12:00		Lunch	Lunch	Lunch	Lunch	Lunch
12:30						
1:00	Read journals	Ind. psychotherapy	Ind. psychotherapy	Ind. psychotherapy	Ind. psychotherapy	Ind. psychotherapy
1:30						
2:00		Ind. psychotherapy	Ind. psychotherapy	Ind. psychotherapy	Ind. psychotherapy	Ind. psychotherapy
2:30						
3:00		Ind. psychotherapy	Read journals	Ind. psychotherapy	Ind. psychotherapy	Ind. psychotherapy
3:30			Group psychotherapy			
4:00		Ind. psychotherapy		Ind. psychotherapy	Ind. psychotherapy	Ind. psychotherapy
4:30						
5:00						

may be necessary when dealing with agoraphobics (i.e., patients whose symptoms will not permit them to leave home) (cf. Emmelkamp, 1979). Other sources of data include school and medical records and other psychiatric records on the client.

The clinical psychologist in individual practice should be certain that the psychological complaint does not have a medical basis (see Adebimpe, 1978; Hersen, 1979). This is particularly important since there are some medical disorders that have major effects on psychological functioning (e.g., hypothyroidism or pancreatic cancer masking as depression). In most cases, then, clients should first have a medical evaluation to rule out such possibilities, even though they are rare.[2] Also, severely psychotic and depressed patients are referred to clinical psychologists in private practice. In these cases, biological treatment is indicated (e.g., antipsychotics, antidepressants). The clinical psychologist here would be remiss in not referring the patient to a competent physician (e.g., psychiatrist) for that aspect of the treatment. However, the clinical psychologist can still continue providing psychotherapeutic treatment to the patient together with the biological approach. Of course, for the suicidal or homicidal patient, hospitalization will be required.

The Clinical Psychologist as Consultant

Although almost no clinical psychologists are full-time consultants, many do supplement their income with consultative work. Such services may be offered to VA facilities, state hospitals, state facilities for the retarded, prisons, community agencies (e.g., group homes, halfway houses, juvenile correctional facilities, police departments, courts), and industry. In working for any of these agencies, the clinical psychologist is expected to offer certain expertise that, for many reasons, may not be available. Thus, as consultant, a specific segment of the clinical psychologist's skills is being purchased. For example, a VA hospital psychiatry department may be interested in applying behavior modification techniques to given patients. The clinical psychologist who is an expert in behavior modification may be hired one-half day per week to teach

2. Unfortunately, this argument has sometimes been used by psychiatrists to restrict the practices of clinical psychologists. Obviously, this is untenable given the precautions suggested here, which are undoubtedly used by most responsible clinical practitioners.

behavioral principles to staff, show them how to implement techniques, and teach them how to assess the effects of the new treatments. This may be done through formal lectures, suggested reading lists, direct personal supervision, and actually modeling of the behavioral technique. (See Chapter 9 for further descriptions of the consultant's role.)

Consultative work may be geared to assessment, treatment, research, staff relations, or the design and implementation of entire programs. For example, as consultants, the authors have been asked to lend their expertise to develop and implement behavior modification strategies in several psychiatric settings (see Bellack & Franks, 1975; Hersen & Bellack, 1978b). The authors know one clinical psychologist who does personality evaluations of candidates for positions in a city police department. Research clinical psychologists are frequently asked by the National Institute of Mental Health and the Veterans Administration Research Service to consult and help evaluate grant proposals. Sometimes a hospital department torn by dissension may ask the clinical psychologist to implement a staff relations training program to reduce the discord and promote better role adjustment for both supervisers and supervisees. (See Chapter 8 on sensitivity training.)

Whatever the consultant's assignment, a particular set of skills is needed. First, of course, the consultant should indeed be an expert in the area. Second, the consultant must be political and sensitive to the needs and interests of the consultees. This is critical when the consultant has been hired by an administrator (e.g., a hospital director) of a given setting, institution, or program. Very often, this has not been discussed with the staff. Hence, such consultation, regardless of its value, may be viewed as an imposition and resented. This could lead to subtle noncompliance with the consultant's advice or even open defiance. Such a situation might occur when the goals of the staff (who work directly with patients) and those of the director differ.

For this reason, Bellack and Franks (1975) have argued on behalf of the "soft-sell" approach: The consultant should be pragmatic and specific in making recommendations; should model the behavior desired; and should use a minimum of technical jargon. These suggestions apply most clearly when the consultant is dealing with staff rather than peers (i.e., nondoctoral professionals and paraprofessionals). Of course, when consulting with peers, the consultant might keep these points in mind without insulting the intelligence of colleagues (jargon may be less a problem here).

Obviously, being a consultant is a demanding job. In addition to requiring relevant knowledge, the individual needs political acumen, interpersonal adeptness, and good timing. It is necessary to be quick on one's feet, especially when put to the test. Often the consultant will be asked to solve very difficult problems. This may be done because no one else has succeeded or simply to test the consultant's expertise. Thus, in the role of consultant, the clinical psychologist with less experience will probably be less successful. The seasoned consultant, in contrast, is fully aware of the kinds of "games" consultees play. Indeed, the role of consultant is one of the most difficult that the clinical psychologist will be asked to perform. However, when done well, it can be quite rewarding.

Other Roles and Specialization

As the number of clinical psychologists has increased and the profession has matured, so have its role boundaries. The role of the clinical psychologist today far exceeds that described in Harrower's (1965) excellent summary statement. For example, 19 percent of all community mental health centers now have a clinical psychologist as their executive director (see Fiester, 1978). In the late 1950s and early 1960s, the notion of the clinical psychologist as administrator had little credence. Indeed, most directors of mental health establishments held the M.D. degree. In addition, many clinical psychologists now serve as ward administrators in mental hospitals (cf. Wildman & Wildman, 1976). Others now are working in the emergency rooms of general medical and surgical hospitals (Barlow, 1974). This contrasts sharply with the more subservient role of clinical psychologists after World War II (i.e., psychological assessor in relation to the psychiatrist, who was administrator-therapist).

The role of clinical psychologists has continued to expand. They have begun to work with lawyers in judicial areas of mutual concern (e.g., the use of corporal punishment; patients' rights) (Bersoff & Prasse, 1978; McCreary, 1977). For example, they have collaborated in developing standards for using aversive techniques (see Chapter 7) in institutional settings. More clinical psychologists are employed in pediatric hospitals than in the past (Drotar, 1977), as well as in dental schools (see Melamed, 1979). The advent of behavioral medicine (i.e., the application of psychological-behavioral principles to the treatment of medical disorders) has opened up new areas for clinical psychologists in hospital departments (e.g., medicine, urology, neurology) formerly considered off limits (see Epstein, Katz, & Zlutnick, 1979; Moos, 1977). An example here might be the use of behavioral techniques in treating bedwetting in children. Other innovative career opportunities are outlined in a volume edited by Woods (1976).

In the 1970s and beyond, specialization in all fields has become the norm. This holds true for clinical psychology as well. In addition to acting primarily as an educator, researcher, or provider of direct service, the clinician's roles have become more clearly defined. There are fewer and fewer generalists as time goes on. Even if a clinical psychologist calls himself a behavior therapist, that label will not fully characterize the activities carried out with particular types of clients. Some behavior therapists specialize in the treatment of children. Others are more concerned with adult neurotics. Some work with inpatients, others with psychiatric outpatients or medical patients (e.g., application of biofeedback techniques). Still others specialize in the treatment of geriatric populations. And finally, some clinical psychologists specialize in group or family therapy or in the assessment and treatment of a given disorder (e.g., obesity, alcoholism, drug addiction).

Professional Identity

Psychologists, particularly clinical psychologists, wish to ensure, maintain, and enhance their professional identities. There are many professional and scientific organizations eager to offer membership to qualified clinical psychologists (e.g., American Association for the Advancement of Science; Association for Advancement of Behavior Therapy; Society for Psychotherapy Research). A quick examination of the curriculum vitae of most clinical psychologists indicates that they have joined several of these associations.[3] Almost all clinical psychologists join the American Psychological Association (APA). This is comparable to the physician joining the American Medical Association (AMA).

---

3. The number of associations joined is often limited by the amount of money one chooses to spend on annual dues, assuming the membership requirements are met. With inflation, membership dues have sometimes become prohibitive, decreasing the number of associations one is likely to join.

There are some 47,000 members[4] of the APA, 4,337 of whom have also joined Division 12 (Clinical Psychology); many clinical psychologists are represented by other divisions of the APA. Also, since membership in the various divisions is not mutually exclusive, a clinical psychologist could belong to several divisions at the same time. Table 2.7 presents the thirty-eight current divisions of the APA, with asterisks denoting those that we feel hold the most attraction for clinical psychologists. Each of these divisions represents the special interests of groups of psychologists. Usually a division newsletter informs members of developments in the area, meetings, and other information of mutual concern. Also, there is a definite social as well as professional value in belonging to a division.

Division 12 probably best represents the general interests of all clinical psychologists. As a division, it has its own government and elected officers. Its members are strongly committed to the profession of clinical psychology and do their best to enhance its status. The division is concerned with legislation and with professional, educational, and research issues relating to clinical psychology. It publishes the *Journal of Clinical Child Psychology* (a scientific publication devoted to clinical issues with children) and *The Clinical Psychologist* (primarily concerned with professional issues of interest to clinical psychologists).

The primary goals of the APA are clearly stated in Article I of the Bylaws of the Association:

> The objects of the American Psychological Association shall be to advance psychology as a science and profession and as a means of promoting human welfare by the encouragement of psychology in all its branches in the broadest and most liberal manner, by the promotion of research in psychology and the improvement of research methods and conditions; by the improvement in the qualifications and usefulness of psychologists through high standards of professional ethics, education, and achievement; by the establishment and maintenance of the highest standards of professional ethics and conduct of the members of the Association; by the increase and diffusion of psychological knowledge through meetings, professional contacts, reports, papers, discussions, and publications;

4. Membership falls into three classes: associates, members, fellows. Associate membership requires a master's degree in psychology from a recognized school or two years of graduate study in psychology in a recognized school. Full membership requires a doctoral degree from a recognized program in psychology. Fellows are nominated by one of the divisions and elected by the Council of Representatives. Required are five years of postdoctoral experience, an outstanding contribution to the field, and membership in the nominating division.

Table 2.7.   Divisions of the American Psychological Association

1. General Psychology
2. Teaching of Psychology
3. Experimental Psychology
5. Evaluation and Measurement*
6. Physiological and Comparative Psychology
7. Developmental Psychology
8. Personality and Social Psychology*
9. The Society for the Psychological Study of Social Issues—A Division of the APA
10. Psychology and the Arts
12. Clinical Psychology*
13. Consulting Psychology*
14. Industrial and Organizational Psychology
15. Educational Psychology
16. School Psychology*
17. Counseling Psychology*
18. Psychologists in Public Service*
19. Military Psychology
20. Adult Development and Aging*
21. The Society of Engineering Psychologists—A Division of the APA
22. Rehabilitation Psychology
23. Consumer Psychology
24. Philosophical Psychology
25. Experimental Analysis of Behavior*
26. History of Psychology
27. Community Psychology*
28. Psychopharmacology*
29. Psychotherapy*
30. Psychological Hypnosis*
31. State Psychological Association Affairs
32. Humanistic Psychology*
33. Mental Retardation*
34. Population and Environmental Psychology
35. Psychology of Women*
36. Psychologists Interested in Religious Issues
37. Child and Youth Services*
38. Health Psychology*

*Refers to divisions of special interest to clinical psychologists.

Note: Division 4 (Psychometric Society) decided not to become a chapter member. Division 11 (Abnormal Psychology and Psychotherapy) merged with Division 12.

thereby to advance scientific interests and inquiry, and the application of research findings to the promotion of the public welfare (American Psychological Association, 1978a, p. xxi).

These objectives are carried out through the APA's Board of Directors, the Council of Representatives (members from all the divisions are included), and the membership at large. In addition to a wide variety of public information services, the APA publishes eighteen scientific journals, numerous pamphlets, books, special reports of a variety of task forces, and a monthly newsletter (*APA Monitor*). At the end of each summer the APA holds its annual national convention, which is attended by thousands of members and nonmembers.

Of the eighteen journals published by the APA, several are of some concern to clinical psychologists: *Journal of Abnormal Psychology, Journal of Consulting and Clinical Psychology, Journal of Personality and Social Psychology, Journal of Counseling Psychology,* and *Professional Psychology.* Of the three most relevant to the work of the clinical psychologist, the *Journal of Abnormal Psychology* deals with the study of psychopathological processes; the *Journal of Consulting and Clinical Psychology* with diagnosis, personality assessment, and treatment; and *Professional Psychology* with professional issues faced by the clinical psychologist (e.g., interdisciplinary relations, licensing, training, internship matters, innovative programing). It is very important for all clinical psychologists to read journals in order to keep up with developments in the field. Once the Ph.D. is attained, learning does not stop. The clinical psychologist is (or should be) committed to using effective assessment and treatment strategies in addition to acting in an ethical fashion. As a method of continuing education, reading scientific journals is the mark of the true professional eager to keep abreast of the field.

Up to now, in discussing journals of interest to clinical psychologists, we have listed those published by the APA and Division 12. However, there are many others; some of these are presented in Table 2.8. Several of them are sponsored by associations, whereas others are directed by independent editors and published by large companies.

Regional and Local Associations

In addition to the national APA, there are a number of local, state, and regional associations that may be affiliated. Thus, a clinical psychologist

Table 2.8. Journals of Interest to Clinical Psychologists

Journal	Organizational Support
Addictive Behaviors	None
American Journal of Psychotherapy	Association for the Advancement of Psychotherapy
American Journal of Psychiatry	American Psychiatric Association
Archives of General Psychiatry	American Medical Association
Archives of Sexual Behavior	None
Behavioral Assessment	Association for Advancement of Behavior Therapy
Behavior Modification	None
Behaviour Research and Therapy	None
Behavior Therapy	Association for Advancement of Behavior Therapy
Cognitive Therapy and Research	None
Family Process	None
International Journal of Group Psychotherapy	American Group Psychotherapy Association
Journal of Abnormal Child Psychology	None
Journal of Applied Behavior Analysis	Society for the Experimental Analysis of Behavior
Journal of Behavioral Assessment	None
Journal of Behavioral Medicine	None
Journal of Behavior Therapy and Experimental Psychiatry	None
Journal of Clinical Psychology	None
Journal of Nervous and Mental Disease	None
Journal of Personality Assessment	None
Psychotherapy: Theory, Research and Practice	Division 29, APA
Schizophrenia Bulletin	National Institute of Mental Health
Science	American Association for the Advancement of Science

living in Pittsburgh may simultaneously be a member of the Pittsburgh Psychological Association, the Pennsylvania Psychological Association, the Eastern Psychological Association, and the APA. A clinical psychologist practicing in rural Florida may belong to the Florida Psychological Association, the Southeastern Psychological Association, and the APA. By belonging to a local professional association, the clinical psychologist is able to support clinical psychology in that community, state, or area of the country. Also, by belonging, exchange of information with colleagues is facilitated. Mutual concerns, problems, and issues may be discussed, often leading to enhancement of the profession.

Other Associations

There are many multidisciplinary associations that hold particular interest for clinical psychologists. Although their members include some psychiatric nurses, social workers, and psychiatrists, clinical psychologists are generally in the majority. Let us briefly consider two associations that are well established at the time of this writing and a third that is growing. First, the Association for Advancement of Behavior Therapy (AABT) (about 3,000 members) is, as its title implies, an interest group for those concerned with the application of behavioral principles to treatment, educational, medical, and social problems. The AABT holds a national convention in the late fall and publishes two journals (*Behavioral Assessment; Behavior Therapy*) and a newsletter (*The Behavior Therapist*). Second, the Society for Psychotherapy Research is a somewhat smaller organization that is cross-disciplinary and cross-theoretical in nature. This organization is devoted to the scientific study of the psychotherapeutic process and its outcome. Third is a new organization, The Society of Behavioral Medicine. According to its founding statement, "Behavioral medicine is the *interdisciplinary field* concerned with the development and integration of behavioral and biomedical science, knowledge and techniques relevant to the understanding of health and illness and the application of this knowledge and these techniques to prevention, diagnosis, treatment and rehabilitation. . . . The Society of Behavioral Medicine is an open organization founded to serve the needs of all health professionals interested in the integration of the behavioral and biomedical sciences in clinical areas." The goals of this society are consistent with the expanded role of clinical psychology in dealing with overall health problems. For this reason, it undoubtedly will continue to attract many clinical psychologists as members.

Ethical Standards

A doctoral degree in clinical psychology ensures a certain level of competence in the theoretical, clinical, and experimental understanding of human behavior. The graduate clinical psychologist who successfully completes the internship requirements shows additional evidence of clinical competence. A futher test of competence occurs when certification or licensure is granted by a state board one or two years after internship. But no official recognition or professional competence ensures that the clinical psychologist, in dealing with other colleagues, clients, patients, and the public, will always act in an ethical manner. Of course, throughout one's professional training the importance of adhering to ethical standards has constantly been reinforced. However, a specific code of ethics is the best way of ensuring adherence to a profession's standards of practice. Such a code represents the profession's attempt to police itself.

Over the last four decades, the APA has had many standing committees and task forces on ethics applied to psychology in general and clinical psychology in particular. As the need has arisen, these codes and professional standards have been updated, republished, and recirculated among the APA membership. The most recent task force has dealt with ethical guidelines for conducting psychotherapy with women (American Psychological Association, 1978b).

Before describing these guidelines and a few examples of transgressions, another issue should be mentioned. Psychological assessors, therapists, or consultants will often find themselves in a position of relative power vis-à-vis the client. Very often sensitive and potentially damaging material (to the client) is divulged which, if handled improperly, could be very detrimental to the client. Also, as a result of their disorders, some clients are particularly vulnerable to persuasion and suggestion. Thus, in interacting with the client, certain responsibilities must be assumed (i.e., the relationship is professional, not personal). When a set of guidelines is established, the clinical psychologist, the client, and the public obtain greater protection. In this sense, the clinical psychologist *is* a public servant. Thus, as a public servant he or she must serve the public in a professional, ethical, and humane manner. Taking unfair advantage of the client or the public cannot be tolerated and is definitely inconsistent with the ethics of the profession.

Let us now consider the latest version of the *Ethical Standards of Psychologists* (American Psychological Association, 1977a). This code of ethics, designed for psychologists in general, consists of nine principles dealing with the following areas: (1) Responsibility, (2) Competence, (3) Moral and Legal Standards, (4) Public Statements, (5) Confidentiality, (6) Welfare of the Consumer, (7) Professional Relationships, (8) Utilization of Assessment Techniques, and (9) Pursuit of Research

Activities. Space limitations prohibit a full reproduction of each of them. However, to convey what these principles are like, we will present the Preamble and those principles (5 and 6) concerned with Confidentiality and the Welfare of the Consumer (Table 2.9).

Examples of transgressions of the code of ethics appear in a pamphlet published by the APA entitled: "Casebook on Ethical Standards of Psychologists" (American Psychological Association, 1977b). However, for illustrative purposes, let us consider ethical misconduct in relation to Principles 5 and 6, listed in Table 2.9. For example, discussing the details of a client's private life (e.g., an attractive divorcée's

Table 2.9.   Ethical Standards of Psychologists

PREAMBLE

Psychologists respect the dignity and worth of the individual and honor the preservation and protection of fundamental human rights. They are committed to increasing knowledge of human behavior and of people's understanding of themselves and others and to the utilization of such knowledge for the promotion of human welfare. While pursuing these endeavors, they make every effort to protect the welfare of those who seek their services or of any human being or animal that may be the object of study. They use their skills only for purposes consistent with these values and do not knowingly permit their misuse by others. While demanding for themselves freedom of inquiry and communication, psychologists accept the responsibility this freedom requires: competence, objectivity in the application of skills and concern for the best interests of clients, colleagues, and society in general. . . . (p. 1).

Principle 5.
CONFIDENTIALITY

Safeguarding information about an individual that has been obtained by the psychologist in the course of his teaching, practice, or investigation is a primary obligation of the psychologist. Such information is not communicated to others unless certain important conditions are not met (p. 4).

Principle 6.
WELFARE OF THE CONSUMER

Psychologists respect the integrity and protect the welfare of the people and groups with whom they work. When there is a conflict of interest between the client and the psychologist's employing institution, psychologists clarify the nature and direction of their loyalties and responsibilities and keep all parties informed of their commitments. Psychologists fully inform consumers as to the purpose and nature of an evaluative, treatment, educational or training procedure, and they freely acknowledge that clients, students, or participants in research have freedom of choice with regard to participation (p. 4).

From: American Psychological Association (1977a).

sex life) at a cocktail party, no matter how well disguised, in our opinion constitutes a breach in confidentiality. Similarly, in the case of a married male client, discussing the client's extramarital activities with the client's wife (unless given permission to do so) would also be considered a serious break of confidentiality.

With respect to Principle 6, engaging in a sexual relationship with a client is considered one of the most serious transgressions possible. Unfortunately, such cases are documented in the literature (cf. Holroyd & Brodsky, 1977; Taylor & Wagner, 1976). As noted by Taylor and Wagner (1976), the vast majority of such instances of sexual abuse result in "negative effects." Regardless of the effects, however, this kind of therapist behavior is reprehensible and definitely represents taking unfair advantage of the client (see American Psychological Association, 1978b).

In addition to the possible legal repercussions of violating professional ethics, a clinical psychologist might lose the license or certification in the state where he or she practices, as well as being dropped from the membership of the APA and other prestigious associations. The financial consequences of such censure, to say the least, are staggering.

A more specific code of ethics for applied psychologists has been prepared by the APA (American Psychological Association, 1977b). Essentially this code involves ". . . a uniform set of standards for psychological practice that would serve the respective need of users, providers, and third-party purchasers and sanctioners of psychological services" (p. 1). Specific standards are concerned with: (1) Providers, (2) Programs, (3) Accountability, and (4) the Environment. Finally, most recently (American Psychological Association, 1978b), guidelines for therapy with women, consistent with the changing times, have emphasized the equality of women, particularly in light of the commonly held sex role stereotypes. Thus, the male therapist conducting psychotherapy with women clients is cautioned to respect "the client's assertive behavior" and to avoid treating such assertion in derogatory fashion (e.g., calling it "castrating").

Intraprofessional and Interprofessional Relationships

Clinical psychology may best be described as the "stepchild" of psychology and of the mental health professions. That is, in each instance clinical psychology appeared second and has acted as an interloper.

Thus, it has at times been viewed with considerable suspicion by both academic nonclinical psychologists and practicing psychiatrists.

Let us first consider the relationship between clinical psychology and academic psychology. Hunt (1965) noted that "The basic scholarly and research orientations of psychology as a science make many psychologists suspicious of the service function and reluctant to see the growth of psychology as a profession" (p. 1467). Indeed, there are several renowned universities where psychology departments have never had a clinical division (e.g., Brown University; Princeton University) or where the clinical programs were recently dropped from the curriculum (e.g., Harvard University; Stanford University). The feeling here, again, is that the major mission of an academic department is to pursue knowledge. Application of such knowledge to specific problems is given much less credence.

A second concern of nonclinical psychologists in the early 1950s and 1960s was that clinical psychology was nonscientific. Given the critiques of projective testing and loosely defined psychotherapies, this position was understandable. With the advent of behavioral assessment and therapy and scientific clinical psychology in the 1960s and 1970s (e.g., Bellack & Hersen, 1977b; Eysenck, 1960a; Hersen & Bellack, 1976a, 1978a; Kazdin, 1975), greater rapprochement and improved intradepartmental relationships have ensued (cf. Russell, 1973). However, in the eyes of many purists, clinical psychology is still viewed askance, despite its improved scientific status.

Turning now to interprofessional relationships, we should note that, as professionals, clinical psychologists interact with members of many disciplines (education, nursing, social work, dentistry, medicine, law, and psychiatry). Needless to say, these interactions are sometimes very complex. However, we believe that some general statements are in order. We will present our own interpretation of these relationships, since the data are not always clearly defined for such purposes.

With education, the relationship has been cordial and complementary to some extent. However, at times there has been dissension over the control of training programs at the graduate level (cf. Hunt, 1965). With nursing the relationship, on the whole, has involved clinical psychologists presenting lectures and seminars to nurses and nursing students. Thus, this relationship tends to be one-sided (i.e., nonreciprocal). In some cases, nurses working in psychiatric settings have been caught in the psychology-psychiatry conflict. With social work, the relationship can best be described as cordial but a bit distant. Although clinical psychologists and social workers are part of the so-called "mental health team," there has been little formal interaction between the two disciplines. Most recently, the barrier seems to be breaking down in those graduate schools where teaching of courses may be shared by the two departments (e.g., the behavioral programs at the University of Michigan and the University of Wisconsin).

With dentistry the relationship has been cordial, but until recently little interaction has occurred. Presently, greater interest in joint academic and research endeavors is evident (cf. Melamed, 1979), especially behavioral applications promoting dental hygiene. Similarly, with medicine there now is an upsurge in collaboration, particularly with the advent of biofeedback and behavioral medicine. Undoubtedly these collaborative efforts will yield important results for clients, patients, and society. With law the realtionship has always been good, with joint interest devoted to patients' rights and forensic psychology.

The most complicated interprofessional relationship exists between clinical psychology and psychiatry. This history, dating back to World War II, has often been filled with dissension and animosity. Let us briefly consider these events and the reasons for the problems.

At first the great conflict between clinical psychology and psychiatry was over whether clinical psychologists had the right to conduct psychotherapy independently, without medical supervision. However, before World War II this was not a problem. Clinical psychologists were rarely employed in medical settings; they restricted their activities to teaching, research, testing, and vocational counseling. During and after World War II, clinical psychologists began to assume roles that previously had belonged to psychiatry (diagnosis and psychotherapy). In the late 1940s and early 1950s, despite wide variations in training experiences (i.e., graduate schools for clinical psychologists, medical schools for psychiatrists), clinical psychologists and psychiatrists found themselves in overlapping roles, vying for territorial dominance. Moreover, clinical psychology internships increasingly were begun in medical settings (initially on a very large scale in the VA hospitals).

Most psychiatrists preferred the older model, in which the clinical psychologist was basically an x-ray technician (tester) vis-à-vis the psychiatrist. However, seeing the opportunities (undoubtedly deserved) for an expanded role, more and more clinical psychologists were trained to conduct psychotherapy, not only in medical settings presumably under medical supervision but independently in private practice in direct competition with psychiatrists. (No matter how the arguments are phrased, the competition for private patients and the financial rewards can never be discounted as the real basis for conflict between the disciplines.)

To deal with the growing tension between clinical psychology and psychiatry, joint committees of the APA and the American Psychiatric Association (apa) were formed. These committees have met on and off for the last three decades. Despite these efforts, hostilities broke out. Some of these arguments are documented in Table 2.10.

Table 2.10.   Clinical Psychology–Psychiatry Conflict

Date	Association	Statements
1949	APA	Opposed to practice of psychotherapy not referred by physician
1954	AMA	Psychotherapy is a medical treatment; no basis for the independent practice of clinical psychology
1958	apa	Adopts AMA position
1958	APA	Supports clinical psychology and the right of its members to practice psychotherapy; agrees to provide legal aid for those clinical psychologists sued for practicing medicine by doing psychotherapy

In regard to these arguments, psychiatrists usually state that they alone have the legal right to make medical diagnoses, prescribe drugs, and commit patients to mental institutions. Also, in differentiating a psychiatric from a medical condition, only psychiatrists are legally mandated, given their training, to do so. Hence, clinical psychologists, who are not medically trained, should work under the direction of a psychiatrist. Another argument is that clinical psychologists are not trained well enough to assume responsibility for patients. This can result only from a medical education.

Clinical psychologists, on the other hand, argue that they, because of their training in psychology, are better able to deal with psychological and interpersonal problems. Medical education is definitely not oriented that way. Hence, the psychiatrist is at a distinct disadvantage here. Kiesler (1977) argues that a strong reason for choosing a psychologist ". . . is the more extensive background of the psychologist in the study of human behavior and another is the formal training in science which should lead the psychologist to be up-to-date on scientific findings and produce a healthy skepticism about current fads" (p. 108).

In the 1960s and 1970s some of these arguments died down, clinical psychologists pursued their independent practices, and legislation was enacted to certify and license them. Still, there was considerable opposition from some psychiatrists. For example, Kiesler (1977) points out that quite recently the president of the apa "argued that only psychiatrists should be considered qualified to receive reimbursement under national health insurance" p. 107. So the battle continues, but on different fronts.[5]

Despite the obvious differences between clinical psychology and psychiatry, however, the picture is not totally bleak. There has been much amity and cooperation between the two disciplines. Thus, areas of disagreement may be considered political in nature. At the interpersonal level, cooperation is no different from that between and among clinical psychologists. That is, it is quite variable.

On a day-to-day basis, most clinical psychologists and psychiatrists who are employed in the same settings get along fairly well. For example, in departments of psychiatry, clinical psychologists often find excellent employment opportunities (in terms of professional possibilities and remuneration). In such departments, they teach and supervise medical students and residents. In these same departments, psychiatrists have an important role in teaching psychology students and interns. In dealing with patients, clinical psychologists and psychiatrists work together to ease the problems. Each discipline obviously has unique skills and expertise that may help to eliminate patient psychopathology. Also, a perusal of many psychiatric and some psychological journals shows the results of joint research by clinical psychologists and psychiatrists. Finally, although psychiatry as a whole has resisted the clinical psychologist's assuming the role of mental health administrator both at the ward level and for entire mental health systems (e.g., director of community mental health center; state commissioner of mental health), the more enlightened psychiatrists recognize that possessing an M.D. degree is not synonymous with being an effective administrator.

5. Most recently, there has been considerable controversy over the American Psychiatric Association's new proposed *Diagnostic and Statistical Manual of Mental Disorders* (see Spitzer, Endicott, & Robins, 1975, for a description of *DSM-III*). Aside from its scientific relevance (cf. Zubin, 1977), *DSM-III* has been soundly criticized by Schacht and Nathan (1977) for leading to the ". . . quasi-official recognition of the primacy of physicians in the diagnostic and treatment of the disorders categorized by DSM-III" (p. 1024). The implications for the status of clinical psychology are clear. *DSM-III* represents a definite intent to medicalize all psychological disturbances.

As time goes on, the competent mental health administrator is increasingly recognized, regardless of the degree held. We view this as a healthy trend.

Clinical Psychology, Legislation, and Politics

Over the thirty-five years since World War II, clinical psychologists have realized that certification, licensing, and other forms of accreditation (all of which bring about official recognition) have been necessary not only to uphold the standards of the profession but also to maintain and enhance its status in a sometimes hostile atmosphere. To do this, psychologists have had to influence legislation at the state and federal levels.

To do so, official lobbies have been formed and funded by members of the APA. Notable among these is the Association for the Advancement of Psychology (AAP), which has been very active and effective. For example, at the time of this writing, some twenty-eight states and the District of Columbia provide reimbursement of certified or licensed psychologists by third-party payers (this is known as freedom-of-choice legislation). As noted by Fiester (1978), "Psychology has made considerable progress over the past several years toward the goal of attaining professional parity with psychiatry" (p. 1114). Such parity was granted by federal law in the 1973 Rehabilitation Act, the 1973 Health Maintenance Organization Development Act, and the 1970 regulations concerned with the Civilian Health and Medical Program of the Armed Services (CHAMPUS). In 1978 the State of California supported an act to permit hospital staff rights to psychologists. In 1975 a list of 6,877 psychologists who met specific criteria was published in the National Register of Health Providers in Psychology (Council for the National Register of Health Service Providers in Psychology, 1975). This council was organized in anticipation of a future National Health Insurance plan so as to ensure the inclusion of psychology in its reimbursement policies. This list is updated yearly. Currently more than 11,000 psychologists are listed.

All these legislative actions have increased the prestige of clinical psychology—as reflected in the increasing activities of clinical psychologists. Equally important, many of these laws allow clinical psychologists to be officially paid for their services. Thus, clinical psychologists are gaining greater equality in status when competing with other professionals for clients and patients.

The first law regulating the practice of psychology was passed in Connecticut in 1945. Since then, all fifty states and the District of Columbia have enacted laws that provide either certification or licensure. In addition, in Canada the following seven provinces have certification laws: Alberta, British Columbia, Manitoba, New Brunswick, Ontario, Quebec, and Saskatchewan.

In general, a certification law states who may use the title "psychologist." By contrast, a licensing law defines not only the use of the title but, more specifically, the range of activities performed. These laws restrict the untrained and the "quacks" from offering services to the public. As stated in a 1978 APA news release, "Licensing laws ordinarily exempt from regulation members of recognized professions employing psychological skills, techniques, or knowledge provided those professionals do not hold themselves forth to the public as 'psychologist' or a variation of the term implying training or expertise in psychology." Thus, the licensing law is stronger and supersedes the certification act. Some states that originally enacted certification laws, such as Connecticut, now have passed licensing laws.

Regulations vary from one state to the next. Generally, however, state examining boards require a doctoral degree in psychology or a field primarily psychological in nature (e.g., educational psychology, counseling), an approved internship, and one or two years of postdoctoral supervised field practice. Written and/or oral examinations are mandatory in most states. These are standardized tests prepared by the American Association of State Psychology Boards (AASPB) in conjunction with the Professional Examination Service. Many states offer reciprocity when an individual licensed in one state moves to another. However, some states may require a second written or oral examination.

A higher, and quite prestigious, form of accreditation is the Diplomate, awarded by the American Board of Professional Psychology (ABPP), formerly known as the ABEPP (American Board of Examiners in Professional Psychology). This is an independent incorporated group formed in 1947, with a board of trustees selected by the APA. Diplomates have been awarded by ABPP in clinical, counseling, industrial, and school psychology. Most of the Diplomates are clinical psychologists.

Over the years, the requirements for the ABPP have changed. Initially, both a written and an oral examination were necessary; now the written examination has been dropped. The oral examination may focus on the applicant's theoretical bent (e.g., psychoanalytic, behavioral). To qualify for an examination, the applicant, in addition to paying a rather high application fee, should be a member of the APA or Canadian Psychological Association, and should have a Ph.D. from an APA-approved school and five years of relevant postdoctoral experience. The clinical applicant is asked to submit samples of his or her work, and during the oral examination may be observed (without knowing it) interacting with a client. Basically, the examination covers four areas: (1) assessment, (2) treatment, (3) ethical and professional issues, and (4) application of theoretical principles and research findings to clinical practice.

The real value of the ABPP has long been argued. Many highly qualified and eminent clinical psychologists have refused to subject themselves to yet another evaluation. Others, concerned with legislation and reimbursement policies, think that holding the ABPP will lead to preferred status in the future. Indeed, many state boards of examiners will waive certification or licensing examinations for those who hold the ABPP. Also, in some settings the ABPP may command a higher salary.

Summary

In this chapter, we have described the role of the clinical psychologist. A number of role functions are now available: educator, researcher, practitioner, consultant. The range of possibilities in each area was discussed, and work schedules of actual psychologists were presented. In discussing the professional identity of clinical psychologists, we examined their relationship to the APA and other professional associations. The importance of maintaining high ethical standards was reviewed and underscored, and examples of violations were presented. We then considered the relationship of clinical psychology to psychology in general and to other professional groups. The clinical psychology-psychiatry conflict was documented and discussed. Finally, we looked at legislation and accreditation, both of which maintain and enhance the prestige of the profession.

CHAPTER
THREE

Interviewing

Clinical psychologists, as we have seen, have many different views about human nature. Thus, it is not surprising that the differences have led to equally varied and conflicting strategies of assessment and treatment. One procedure, however, is common to all approaches: the clinical interview. Interviewing typically is the first step in assessment and the cornerstone for all subsequent assessment and treatment. There are, of course, variations in interview style, in what the interviewer attempts to learn, and in the interpretation and weight given to the report. Nevertheless, the various theoretical models probably overlap more in the area of interviewing than in any other activity or viewpoint.

In this chapter, we will first consider the nature of clinical assessment and then the role of the interview in the overall assessment process. Some of the primary functions of the interview are discussed next, including its role as a treatment procedure. The types of information which can be gained from an interview then follow, including the client's self-report and the interviewer's observations of the client's behavior. The next major section of the chapter deals with interview techniques—including general clinical considerations, such as developing rapport, and procedures used in different theoretical approaches. Sample interview transcripts are presented. The final section of the chapter is concerned with the validity of the interview—including interviewer skill and bias, the value of client self-reports, and the communication process.

Clinical Assessment

The stereotyped psychotherapist is a middle-aged, fatherly-looking man with an "all knowing" appearance. His insight is so great that he can instantly figure out the source of the client's difficulty and the treatment needed to resolve it. Like most stereotypes, this one is far from the truth. The experienced clinician can occasionally make an accurate analysis with minimal information. But such successes typically result from educated guesses rather than intuition and are the exception rather than the rule. Initial presumptions based on little knowledge are more often wrong than right, or are so general as to be meaningless.

Textbook examples of clinical problems often give the impression that most clients have discrete, easily diagnosed difficulties with clear-cut causes and treatment needs. Thus, a man might report being afraid of heights. He would immediately be diagnosed as acrophobic—a diagnostic label that would indicate everything important about him and specify how treatment should proceed. This picture is misleading in two critical ways. First, few people who seek help have such single, discrete problems. The real acrophobic would probably also have other fears or anxieties. If his fears were severe enough for him to seek help, he would probably be depressed as well. He may have problems at work and with his family because the fear probably restricts his movements by preventing him from going into tall buildings. Finally, he may have developed excessive self-doubt and guilt due to his inability to control his behavior. While many of these problems may have resulted from the phobia, several have probably become autonomous and would require separate treatment.

Second, since all persons are unique, diagnostic labels provide only a general picture of one aspect of their behavior (cf. Kazdin, 1980). Most psychological disturbances have many different causes. Once symptoms occur, they can be maintained in several different ways. Similarly, there are many treatment strategies which may be used for a specific symptom (such as a phobia). Thus, a diagnostic label provides little understanding of why the individual client behaves the way he or she does, and how the behavior can be changed.

The implication of this complex picture is that to adequately understand the client and his or her problem, extensive and systematic assessment is necessary. While most clinical psychologists would agree with this statement, they would disagree considerably about what such an assessment would entail. For example, what is the purpose of the assessment? We contend that (in clinical service) the only valid purpose of psychological assessment is to plan treatment[1]—that is, to determine what type of treatment is applicable and how it should be conducted. Information that does not pertain to treatment planning is irrelevant. This purpose, we should note, is not consistent with the historical practice of psychological testing (see Chapter 4). Testing has often been used solely to formulate a diagnosis and/or to describe a personality.

With few exceptions, then, diagnostic labels are descriptive over-generalizations. Individuals with the same diagnosis usually vary as much as those with different diagnoses. Although personality descriptions may convey more information, they often do not contain the information needed to determine a treatment strategy. Knowing that a client has "difficulty accepting aggressive urges" or "has ambivalent feelings toward her mother" does not necessarily indicate what must be done for her depression or phobia. The clinician facing a new client always feels uneasy until the client's problem is conceptualized. A diagnosis or personality description may make the clinician feel more comfortable by providing a "handle" on the client. However, it serves little purpose for the client personally.

The various theoretical orientations in clinical psychology lead to very different treatment approaches. Thus, assessment strategies will vary according to the treatment modality in which the psychologist operates. This will be considered more fully in the next two chapters, but a few comments here are in order. Two of the most widely contrasting models are the psychodynamic and the behavioral models. The psychodynamically oriented assessment focuses on personality analysis. This includes both *conscious* attitudes, feelings, desires, and beliefs and *unconscious* processes, such as inner conflicts, unacceptable urges, and feelings, drives, and needs. Psychodynamic assessments often involve various psychological tests, which comprise an assessment *battery*. A typical battery would include self-report inventories (e.g., the Minnesota Multiphasic Personality Inventory), an intelligence test (e.g., the Wechsler Adult Intelligence Scale), and several projective tests (e.g., Rorschach, Thematic Apperception Test) (see Chapter 4). These tests are designed to reveal the different levels and aspects of personality

---

1. We are referring here to the ordinary activity of the clinical psychologist. Under some circumstances, legally a diagnosis *must* be made. An interview might then be conducted primarily for that reason. Other special exceptions include evaluation for educational placement, and for decision making, such as in determining whether a patient is ready for discharge from a hospital.

functioning. All of the findings are integrated to form a comprehensive picture of the client. This detailed personality analysis indicates the critical factors which underlie the client's symptoms. These factors are the focus of therapy, and the client's behavior is understood in relation to them.

The behavioral model is not concerned with underlying personality processes. The client's problem is presumed to result from certain factors in the environment and the client's behavioral skills. Assessment emphasizes direct observation of the client's behavior. The purpose is to ascertain his or her responses and the environmental events which precede and follow the behavior (e.g., reinforcers). For example, a socially anxious person would be observed talking to the therapist's assistant of the opposite sex to see if the client knew how to converse in this situation. Treatment focuses on improving skills and modification of inappropriate environmental control.

Regardless of theoretical orientation, conducting a clinical assessment is very much like doing research. The researcher starts with a question and conducts experiments designed to answer it. Each experiment provides information which helps to shape the next experiment. The clinician begins with a very general picture of the problem based on the client's initial statement. A typical starting point might be, "I don't know what's the matter lately. I seem to have no energy, and I can't get interested in things the way I used to. Sometimes I wonder if it's worth going on." This general complaint must ultimately be converted into a detailed analysis of the client's current state, the source and nature of the distress, and the most likely treatment needs. As information is gathered, the clinician develops hypotheses about what might be going on. Each hypothesis is tested against the amassed information and is either confirmed or discarded. The assessment process continues until the clinician has enough information to confirm one hypothesis and safely rule out others.

The Role of the Interview

The data derived from psychological tests and behavioral observations are like pieces of a puzzle. Alone, they are relatively meaningless; they can be understood only in the context of the whole puzzle. A puzzle can be assembled without reference to its completed picture, but it is a very time-consuming, trial-and-error process. The same is true of a clinical assessment. An accurate appraisal can gradually be developed by assembling the bits of data provided by testing or observation. However, the process can be much faster given a framework in which to place the data. The clinical interview provides such a framework.

The interview is almost invariably the first stage of any assessment. Beginning with a statement of the problem, the client describes its extent, severity, history, and ramifications. Demographic factors such as age, marital status, and educational and work history are reported, along with a general description of current life style, interpersonal relationships, and goals and expectations. This information serves two purposes. First, it suggests to the clinician directions for further assessment. For example, a report of depression would be a cue for questions about suicidal thoughts and impulses, sleep and eating patterns, and social interactions. Second, interview data provide a framework for interpreting material gathered in other ways. Thus, test results which suggest depression would be considered quite differently coming from an individual whose spouse had just died than from someone with no real environmental stress.

In some cases, an interview alone is sufficient. Many clinicians use interviewing as their sole means of assessment. Those who employ psychological testing use interview data to determine which tests to administer and how test responses are to be interpreted. For the behavioral clinician, the interview indicates which behaviors to observe and what environmental events are probably crucial. Often interviews follow as well as precede other assessment procedures. Their purpose is to clarify and expand upon the information gathered. Discovering the client's approach to a behavioral task or a test item, or learning about the client's own interpretation of test behavior, can be more important than the observational or test data. In any case, the interview is the only assessment technique which is never omitted. It is the heart of clinical evaluation.

The Clinical Interview

Having stressed the importance of the interview, let us consider what it actually is. In general terms, an interview is any interaction in which one or a few people attempt to gather information from one or a few other people by conversation. In its most common form, one individual (the interviewer) asks questions of another individual (the interviewee). The interaction may consist of a few questions or require several sessions. It may be highly structured, such as a census interview, or unplanned and free flowing, as on television talk shows. In some instances, the interview is conducted for the benefit of the interviewer, as in job interviews; in others, information is collected to aid the interviewee.

Clinical interviews are often considered unique in two ways. First, the type of information clients report to the clinical interviewer is almost never shared. Self-doubts, anxieties, guilt, sexual difficulties, and the like are rarely confessed to others. In fact, most clients probably have not even acknowledged such concerns to themselves prior to their first clinical interview. Thus, the interview is often a painful experience. Second, the initial interview is often therapeutic for the client. Many individuals approach the interview with great apprehension. Some fear they are "crazy"; others fear that they are beyond help; and still others fear having to admit their need for help. Many people simply need to "get things off their chest" and talk openly about a problem. All of these concerns can be alleviated to some extent by the reassuring response of a warm and understanding interviewer (or increased by one who is callous or unresponsive) (Truax & Mitchell, 1971a). This therapeutic gain is usually temporary, but it can be important in reducing distress until a more comprehensive treatment can begin. Some clinicians do not separate the interview from therapy. Treatment begins from the first moment of contact, and the first session differs little from subsequent sessions. However, if the client has not been previously assessed, we believe that treatment should begin only after a systematic evaluation to determine the treatment.

These two factors place special demands on the clinical interviewer. The ability to ask questions is not enough. The interviewer must also have the clinical skills to draw out a highly distressed individual, while at the same time reducing that distress and leaving the client with some optimism. One skill which is not required is *clinical intuition*: the unspecified ability to "read" the client. Clinical skill consists of a number of learned abilities rather than a sixth sense. Basically it involves knowing a great deal about human behavior and being able to carefully observe the client's behavior. (This will be discussed further below.)

Sources of Interview Data

An interview is largely a question-and-answer procedure; the interviewer tries to collect information by questioning the interviewee. Thus, the client's answers, also called *self-reports,* are a primary source of data.

However, because the interview is a live interaction, the interviewer can *observe* the client and note the *manner* in which answers are given and the way the client *behaves* during the interview. These observations provide a second source of data, which can often be more important than the client's self-report. In this section, we will consider the types of information thus collected and how they can be integrated to produce a comprehensive picture of the client.

Self-report Data. With few exceptions (e.g., children, severely disturbed psychotic individuals), clients are the primary source of information about themselves. Most interviews begin with a discussion of the referral problem: the reason the client seeks help. The interviewer tries to learn exactly what difficulty the client is experiencing, the severity of the distress, and the effect on the client's life. Since few clients have only one problem, other sources of distress and behavioral dysfunctions are explored. The history of the problem is also usually considered: When and how did it begin? Has it become more severe? What was happening in the client's life when it began? Demographic data are collected to flesh out the interviewer's picture of the client; age, marital status, educational background, and occupation are determined during the interview.

Beyond these few basic points, the interview will vary dramatically according to the interviewer's theoretical orientation (cf. Matarazzo, 1965). Psychodynamic interviews stress the client's life history, especially early childhood and family relationships. In contrast, behavioral interviews focus much more on the current life situation: sources of pleasure (reinforcement) and displeasure, interpersonal relationships, behavioral competencies, and so on. Phenomenological interviews emphasize subjective states, such as feelings, hopes, and desires, especially in regard to the client's acceptance of and satisfaction with the self. Of course, there is considerable overlap in coverage, regardless of theoretical emphasis. Most highly competent interviewers are probably more alike than they are different.

Theoretical orientation is also less important when severe psychopathology or the risk of physical harm to oneself or others is involved. Differentiation of psychosis from other disorders usually involves a *mental status* examination, which attempts to discover whether the client is oriented in regard to time, place, and person: Does he know the date (at least the month and year)? Where he is? Who he is? Also, does he hear voices or see things which are not there? The seriously depressed client is *always* questioned about suicide, and the potentially violent client is asked (perhaps indirectly) about self-control and the possibility of harming others.

Observational Data. Communication can be thought of as information transfer across different response channels (cf. Mehrabian, 1972). The most obvious channel—and generally the most informative—is verbal, or speech. However, much information is also contained in the paralinguistic aspects of speech—such as errors, rate, and intonation—and by *nonverbal* behaviors such as posture changes and eye contact. These "noncontent" channels can highlight the content, give meaning to a certain word or phrase, or even contradict the content and reflect deception or discomfort. The interviewer cannot fully evaluate the client's self-report without paying careful attention to these other channels of communication.

The noncontent channels are especially important in expressing emotion. There has been much analysis of how emotional states such as anxiety and tension are communicated. Paralinguistic signs of anxiety include increased speech rate and speech dysfunctions such as errors and blockages (Mahl, 1959; Mehrabian, 1972). On a nonverbal level, anxiety is often shown by a rigid posture (compared to a relatively relaxed and loose manner) and extraneous hand and foot movements (e.g., wringing of hands, self-touching, shuffling of feet) (Mehrabian, 1971). Depression is often associated with decreased speech and muscular tension. Anger and assertion are often shown by a reddening face, a rigid posture or tension, a forward-leaning body, and increased eye contact (e.g., staring) (cf. Bellack & Hersen, 1978). Conversely, submission or passivity is manifested by leaning away and decreased eye contact.

During the interview, most clients' emotions will vary as the nature and focus of the conversation change. These feeling states are often central to behavioral and psychological difficulty. Nevertheless, the client may or may not be aware of these emotional reactions to various topics, and may or may not wish to communicate all of his or her feelings. While speech content may mask the emotions to some extent, strong reactions typically *leak* out into the paralinguistic and nonverbal channels. The interviewer must carefully look for cues to this "emotional leakage" to supplement the client's report, in order to understand the client and his or her problems.

An interview is a unique type of social interaction with special constraints and demands. Nevertheless, some aspects of the client's behavior during the interview will indicate how he or she acts in other settings. The therapist can learn much about the client's *social skills* by observing these interpersonal and communication styles. The first step is usually an appraisal of bodily cleanliness and manner of dress. This reflects knowledge of social norms and the ability to maintain one's personal appearance. Another indicator is the handling of ordinary social amenities, such as reporting on time for the interview, using an ashtray rather than dropping ashes on the rug, and saying "please," "thank you," and "excuse me" in a conventional manner.

Another social skill, the client's ability to carry on a conversation effectively, can also be evaluated to some extent. The interviewer must determine how easy or difficult it is to *establish rapport* with the client— that is, develop a relationship and maintain a free-flowing conversation. More specifically, does the client answer questions coherently, and do the answers match the questions? Does he or she speak freely, with little prompting, or give one-word responses? Does he or she have a sense of social timing, such as by waiting for the interviewer to finish a question before speaking and by slowing down if the interviewer turns to pick something up or make notes? Conversely, does he or she consistently "take over" the interview, interrupting and disagreeing angrily?

Other aspects of social skill, such as appropriate eye contact, use of physical gestures, and response latency to questions, can also be determined during an interview. This picture of the client's skills clarifies and amplifies the self-report data. For example, a report of difficulty with social relationships would be viewed quite differently from an unkempt client with grease-spotted clothing who spoke in one- and two-word sentences than from a stylishly dressed person who continually interrupted the interviewer and rambled on with irrelevant details in response to questions. The first individual would probably require much more comprehensive treatment.

Yet another important aspect of behavior which can be assessed during the interview is *cognitive style*. This refers to such things as the way the individual handles emotions, perceives the world, and solves problems. These become important when they restrict the person's flexibility in adapting to changing situations. The psychoanalytic "defense mechanisms" fall under this category. For example, some individuals fend off unpleasant emotions by dealing with problem areas in a scholarly, super-objective manner, using multisyllabic words where simple ones would be clearer. This pattern is called *intellectualization*. *Rationalization* is another common pattern; here the person uses logic to discount the importance of things and/or explain away events. Some individuals orient the world to themselves. Instead of occasionally taking other people's perspective, they view things totally from their own biased frame of reference. An extreme form of this style is paranoia. Other individuals are prone to rumination, thinking about even simple issues endlessly. Decision making is very difficult for such people, who continuously vacillate between alternatives.

Cognitive styles such as those described above are often part of the problem which bring people for help; however, they are rarely part of the client's self-report. Clients do not complain that they intellectualize too much or that they cannot take other people's points of view. The interviewer identifies these characteristics by listening to the way they describe their experiences, by observing consistencies and inconsistencies in their behavior and reports, and by assessing the way they process information. Notable omissions also can be informative, such as when the client fails to admit or report experiencing any anxiety. Whether or not cognitive styles are directly related to the problem, they often dictate how treatment must be structured.

Integrating the Data. We have already considered three of the interviewer's major responsibilities—therapist, data collector, and observer. One responsibility which requires further comment is conceptualization and analysis. Few clients come for help knowing what their problem really is. They know they are in distress and can sometimes identify a source (e.g., their marriage). The interviewer must determine the actual basis of the distress and what can be done about it. This cannot be done in a vacuum. The interview data cannot be interpreted without reference to normative data. How much ambivalence qualifies as clinically significant rumination? How much eye contact is typical? How long does depression last after the death of a parent? Consequently, the interviewer must be highly conversant with the scientific literature about both normal behavior and psychopathology. Only by comparing the various types of data provided by the client with each other, as well as with the literature, can the interviewer reach a comprehensive and accurate conclusion. Clinical analysis is much more a scientific and scholarly process than a "seat of the pants" intuitive exercise.

Interview Techniques

Organization of the Interview

Interviews can be categorized by their degree of structure. The least structured interview entails little or no interviewer control over the content; whatever the client chooses to talk about is sufficient. A highly structured interview, in contrast, involves a specific set of questions asked in a definite order. Neither of these extremes is suitable for clinical interviewing. On the one hand, too much specific information must be collected to allow for total freedom. On the other, each client is so unique and unpredictable that a highly structured interview would be too restrictive; the interviewer could not follow up on important issues raised.

Most clinical interviews are semistructured. The interviewer has a general plan on how to proceed and some specific questions which must be answered. However, the order of the questions and the organizational plan are quite flexible. As the interview proceeds, the interviewer keeps in mind what topics and descriptive material are relevant for assessment. This naturally varies with the client and the stage to which the interview has progressed. Clients are given considerable freedom to discuss what they like in the manner they prefer, as long as the material is relevant. The interviewer redirects the conversation and/or steers it in certain directions as necessary. For example, having finally found someone who will listen, many clients choose to spend the entire session describing and underscoring their distress. Other clients cannot distinguish relevant from irrelevant detail or simply provide excessive elaboration.

If the interview is to progress, the interviewer must carefully judge when data collection ceases and redundancy begins. Of course, the interviewer steers the client in a clinically responsible manner (see below) so as to balance the client's immediate need to talk with the long-term need to be helped as soon as possible. Thus, a distraught client may need time to cry, while a calmer one may be better off if the conversation is politely redirected.

The interview is often seen to consist of three phases (cf. Benjamin, 1974): (1) the opening phase, (2) development and elaboration, and (3) closing. The *opening phase* consists of two parts. First, interviewer and client must agree on the purpose and goals of the interaction. Most clients have had no experience with therapy and do not know what to expect. The interviewer must orient the client to the situation and indicate how they will proceed. Providing specific instructions not only results in more productive interviews but also improves the interviewer-client relationship (Scheiderer, 1977). Second, once the process is agreed to, the client is asked to describe the problem.

The second stage of the interview involves *development* and *elabor-*

ation. Having stated the problem in general terms, the client is required to provide more specific information about its development and ramifications, personal life situation, and other factors. Overall, the interview proceeds from the general to the specific; the client's report goes from overview to detail, and the interviewer's conceptualization proceeds from rough categorization to unique portrait. The third stage, or *closing,* involves something of a role reversal for the interviewer and client. Almost every client has major concerns about what the problem "really is" and what can be done about it. Consequently, the therapist must share his or her initial ideas with the client, and indicate what types of treatment are applicable and what prognosis the client can expect. Of course, the interviewer will often not know all of the answers after one session and may ask for further information. Nevertheless, at the very least, the client's anxiety and apprehension should be reduced by providing a best guess (or most probable alternatives).

The Clinical Relationship

In preparing a report after an interview, the clinician almost invariably indicates whether or not *rapport* was established. The term "rapport" refers to the quality of the relationship between interviewer and client, or the degree to which they could maintain a positive and communicative interaction. Because the interview is a communication process, rapport is obviously critical for effective interviewing. When rapport cannot be established, the accuracy and sufficiency of the information gathered must be questioned.

When the clinician indicates that rapport was a problem, this usually implies that it was the client's fault: either lack of skill or psychopathology prevented it. However, communication is a two-way process; sometimes the interviewer bears part (or all) of the responsibility. Some persons simply cannot interact effectively with each other; they have styles or attributes which produce conflict. For this reason, some interviewer-client pairings do not work out. One example of this is the *A-B therapist phenomenon* (Betz, 1962). For unknown reasons, some therapists (As) work effectively with psychotic patients but not with neurotic ones. Conversely, B therapists work well with neurotics and poorly with psychotics. There are undoubtedly many other more specific contrasts which prevent every interviewer from working well with some clients.

Also, in some instances, poor rapport is due primarily to the interviewer. Even the most effective clinician has "bad days." Illness, preoccupation with personal problems, or fatigue can all lead to disinterest or lack of responsiveness to client needs. In addition, it has been shown that some certified professionals are poor clinicians, whose clients leave therapy worse than when they began (Bergin, 1971). On the other hand, there are other clinicians who seem to be consistently effective. There is a large body of literature on the clinician characteristics which facilitate interaction and therapy.

Unlike many other interview situations, the clinical interview is conducted for the client's benefit. His or her feelings and needs must guide the clinician's efforts. Recall that most clients approach the interview apprehensively and are apt to experience distress when they discuss their problems. Thus, one of the interviewer's major tasks is to help the client feel at ease. This can be done by creating a positive, helpful atmosphere in which the client feels free to talk without being "put down" or scrutinized like a laboratory specimen.

Three characteristics of the clinician appear to be associated with positive relationships and good therapy outcome (Truax & Mitchell, 1971a): accurate empathy, nonpossessive warmth, and genuineness. *Accurate empathy* involves "the ability to *perceive* and *communicate* accurately and with sensitivity both the feelings and experiences of another person and their meaning and significance" (Truax & Mitchell, 1971a, p. 317). The clinician must do more than log client reports of distress. He or she must develop an understanding of what life is like for the client. Furthermore, the client must be aware of this level of understanding; the clinician must communicate these perceptions to the client.

Nonpossessive warmth involves liking or valuing the client as he or she is. The interviewer must regard the client as a worthwhile person who deserves help and respect, regardless of current problems or incapacity. The interviewer must also be able to value people who are different from himself in education, appearance, cultural background, beliefs, and other factors. That is, the interviewer cannot "look down" at the client for any reason. No interviewer can honestly like all clients; however, he or she cannot be effective with those few who are actively disliked or disparaged. *Genuineness* means that in relating to the client, the interviewer must be "real." That is, he or she must be aware of personal feelings and attitudes and express them honestly. Alternatively, the interviewer must not fake warmth, understanding, expertise, and the like. Of course, no interviewer would bluntly make inconsiderate statements such as, "That's a stupid idea" or "I don't have the slightest idea of what you're talking about." But he or she should not falsely indicate approval or feign understanding. As Truax and Mitchell (1971a) state, the genuine clinician is, above all, not a phoney.

Probably no interviewer can show all three of these characteristics all the time with any one client, let alone with all clients. Nor is it critical that they be present all the time. Generally, however, the more they are exhibited, the more effective the interviewer will be. Certain other interviewer behaviors also enhance effectiveness. For example, the client should be made to feel confident of the interviewer's abilities. Thus, the interviewer must employ a professional manner and appear to be knowledgeable and intelligent. While a casual, friendly relationship is quite positive, it is not suitable for data collection and impartial help giving. The interviewer must also retain some psychological distance and avoid becoming overly involved in the client's life. It is generally felt that clinician and client should not socialize outside of the office. Many other factors might be considered here; basically, however, the relationship hinges on the social skills of the interviewer as well as the client.

Conducting the Interview

Up to now, we have considered the general flavor or tone of the interview. However, the heart of the interview is the verbal interaction between client and interviewer: what they actually say to each other. The interviewer must be able to ask appropriate questions, answer questions, deal with problems such as silences and crying, probe in difficult areas without arousing too much distress, and so on. Regardless of how genuine, empathic, positive, and tactful a clinician is, the interview will not proceed well if he or she does not have a broad range of conversation skills. In this section, we will consider some of the more technical aspects of interviewing. We will first discuss the process of asking questions and then examine some of the problem situations which the interviewer must be able to handle.

Asking Questions. Because the interview is designed to gather information, much of it must involve a question-and-answer process. Asking questions is perhaps the interviewer's most essential tool for maintaining the flow of conversation as well as learning about the client. However, not all questions are alike; they can vary greatly in emphasis and phrasing, as well as in content. Different types of questions have very different effects on the client and can move the interaction in varying directions. The interviewer can facilitate (or impede) the conversation by asking the right (or wrong) type of question.

One major distinction is between so-called *closed-ended* and *open-ended* questions. Closed-ended questions ask for specific information, such as : "What year are you in at college?" "Are your parents living?" "What did you do yesterday after you left work?". Open-ended questions are more general and do not require specific data in response. Examples include, "How are you doing?" "How is school?" "What do you usually do after school?" These two types of questions will produce quite different client behavior. Closed-ended questions will yield specific data but will also result in concrete, terse responses. This is especially true of yes-no questions (e.g., "Did you go to class yesterday?"). Conversely, open-ended questions generally prompt the client to speak more freely and extensively—to talk about the topic—but usually do not produce specific factual information. The interviewer will generally use both types of questions at different points in the interview to serve different purposes.

Benjamin (1974) differentiates between *direct* and *indirect* questions. The former are statements which end in question marks and include terms such as "when," "where," "how," and "why." These types of questions are used extensively, but they can sometimes suppress the flow of conversation. This is especially true when they put the client "on the spot"—for example, when he or she does not know the answer. The interviewer must avoid turning the conversation into an interrogation by bombarding the client with a series of direct, closed-ended questions. Indirect questions provide a valuable alternative; they stimulate the client to talk without the pointed nature of direct questions. Rather, they are nondeclarative statements to which some client response is required, such as, "That must really make you angry," "I wonder how you feel about that," or "Tell me something about your parents." Each of these statements would likely stimulate the client to talk without specifically asking for an opinion or a response. Indirect questions which refer to the client's apparent feelings (e.g., "You must be angry") are known as *reflections* and serve as one of the basic tools of client-centered therapists (see Chapter 8). Most experienced interviewers probably use more indirect questions to focus the discussion than any other type of response.

There are several types of questions which most interviewers try to avoid. One is to ask why a client did or did not do something or felt a certain way (e.g., "Why did you yell at her?"). People rarely know the reasons for their behavior and feelings. Thus, asking "Why?" typically produces discomfort and/or simply wastes time while the client searches for some hypothetical explanation. Indirect questions (e.g., "I wonder why that happens") are usually good alternatives; reasons will often become apparent during the conversation. Another poor form of questioning involves giving the client the answer to the question rather than letting him or her generate a response (e.g., "Did you quit school because you were afraid of failing and having to face your father?"). This type of question often puts words in the client's mouth by suggesting that the interviewer believes the enclosed answer to be true. It also suggests something which the client may never have considered, but which sounds plausible at the moment and is thereby accepted. Similarly, "either-or" questions restrict the client's response and should be avoided (e.g., "Were you anxious or angry?").

Problem Situations. Regardless of how skilled and effective the interviewer is, some interviews do not proceed smoothly. Whether due solely to the client or to the interaction, the interviewer will sometimes be put on the spot. Several types of client responses are difficult for most interviewers. Some clients do not speak freely, and the interview is periodically interrupted by periods of silence. Silences lasting a few seconds are normal and require no special consideration. But when they stretch beyond ten seconds or so, they can become uncomfortable and use up valuable time. Sometimes the interviewer must be silent for several minutes while the client reflects on a problem. At other times, the client is simply reluctant to deal with some issue or is present under duress. This type of silence is a clear form of resistance, which the interviewer must either resolve or temporarily circumvent by changing the subject. In general, the interviewer must become more active, finding other ways to ask questions and stimulating conversation when silences occur.

Similar problems are raised by emotional outbursts. The most common emotional reaction is crying, which can range from a minor sniffle to a complete breakdown in communication. The interviewer must gauge the amount of distress to determine how to act: remain silent until the client regains composure, continue with the interview, or shift gears and provide therapylike support and understanding. A box of tissues is a standard part of interview room decor.

Another common problem occurs when the client asks the interviewer a direct question, such as, "What should I do?" or "Who do you think is right, me or my wife?" Most clinicians prefer to have clients make their own judgments and decisions. The clinician aids the decision-making process by helping the client to view alternatives and think logically. Providing opinions often has an undue influence on clients, since it is difficult for them to go against the clinician's judgment. Thus, the interviewer ordinarily tries to refocus on the client, as by the response, "I really couldn't say, but what do you think you should do?" or "That must really be a hard choice for you to make."

A parallel problem arises when the client asks about the interviewer's personal life: "Have you ever had a problem like mine?" or "What is your religion?". How much should the clinician share about his or her private life? Arguments pro and con range from stylistic preferences to the psychoanalytic belief in the relevance of such questions to the transference relationship. Perhaps the most widely held view is that the clinician should generally avoid personal topics during the interview. The focus is, after all, on the client; the interviewer should not use up time discussing other matters. It is considered preferable to refocus on the reason for the client's question (e.g., "I wonder why that is important to you?").

Regardless of whether or not the clinician does share some personal information, there is general agreement that no attempt should be made to impose his or her values or morals on the client. Professional ethics require the clinician to focus on scientifically determined sources of distress or dysfunction. Morals and values are personal issues, which are not known to be good or bad, healthy or unhealthy. The clinician can help the client to reflect on his or her own beliefs and consider whether to change them, but it is the client's choice. The clinician cannot use professional status to mold the client in any personal image of how people should think and behave. Nor should the clinician express disapproval or criticism of the client. These responses are inappropriate for two reasons. First, the clinician's responsibility is to help the client, not to sit in judgment. Second, the responses can only stimulate negative feelings in the client, such as anger or guilt. Besides being inappropriate, this result also suppresses further conversation. While clinicians cannot avoid all judgments and value comparisons, they must differentiate between subjective and professional opinions and avoid the former in the interview.

Some Examples of Interview Styles

In this section, we will present portions of three actual interviews in the psychodynamic, behavioral, and client-centered modes. The transcripts represent some of the major characteristics of the various interviewing styles. However, these brief segments hardly represent *all* that the different interviewers do. As stated above, good clinicians are probably basically similar. They secure much of the same basic information from their clients, although their emphases and interpretations differ. In fact, if the specific interviewer responses on the three transcripts were compared on a statement-by-statement basis, few actual differences might appear.

A Psychodynamic Interview

The following transcript is part of an initial interview of a thirty-two-year-old single man who was admitted to a hospital for treatment of hypertension, headaches, and palpitations. The letter *D* indicates interviewer comments and *P* the patient responses. Of special interest are the interviewer's thoughts about what was transpiring; these appear in italics following some of the responses. The interviewer presumes that (in general) hypertension is a result of repressed sexual drives. Thus, the interview is directed toward possible sources of repression.

D. Dr. X sent you here?

P. That's right.

D. And asked us whether we can be of any help.

P. I hope so.

D. Can you tell me now—what in your opinion makes it necessary to treat you?

P. As far as he can find—as well as other doctors can find—there's *nothing physically* wrong, yet I seem to have it all the time. I seem to be always *tied up*—always *tied in knots.*

D. You yourself?

P. Yes. I'm in a *nervous sweat* all the time. Perspiration under the arms— I don't know. I can't seem to put my finger on anything definite why I should be that way. Yet everything I do, I *tighten up.* As to why I do, I don't know.

D.   You said *nervous?*
     [*"Nervous" is chosen as the cue word, implying "tied up in knots," and "perspiration"*]

P.   Maybe it is a *nervous* condition. Just what's causing it, I don't know.

D.   What do you mean—nervous?

P.   That's what I don't know. I can't seem to find out just what it is. I've done things over and over again, and I still feel that tightened up feeling all the time, no matter how many times I've done it. Yet I'm not shaky. Outwardly I seem to be all right. Everybody tells me I look good. It's *inside.* It seems to be all *inside.*
     [*The repeated expression "I don't know" is a defense against and a cover for the fear of becoming conscious of the cause of his condition. What are "things?"*]

D.   What do you mean by "inside?"

P.   It seems to be internally. There's nothing I can find to *relax,* so to speak.

D.   You can't relax?

P.   That's about it. The things I like to do that may relax, like *dancing.* I like to dance, but I find the exertion of dancing seems to bring up the pressure. I feel awfully *tired* and *exhausted.* I feel very *warm,* probably because of the pressure. It makes me *perspire.*
     [*"Dancing" is one of the "things" for relaxation, but it makes him hot, sweating and tired, i.e., something about this activity is forbidden.*]

D.   You like to dance?

P.   I do. But I get so *tired* very easily. I like to—but I don't enjoy it. I mean I do *like to dance,* but when I do, I get so tired and so exhausted that I'm almost panting. It's exertion for me. I don't know why I should be *nervous* about dancing. I've done it so many hundreds of times. It's always there. I think of going and I know I'm going to enjoy myself, yet I have that *tightened up* feeling.
     [*Dancing makes him "nervous." What does "dancing" mean?*]

D.   When you're doing *new things,* you get nervous?

P.   If it's something different I were doing and I was in doubt just what it would be, I could see the reason for being *nervous* at something like that. But there are a lot of things I've done time and time again. Yet I still have that tightening up feeling. As Dr. X wrote, when I went up for my Army physical—he said that I don't seem to be fully relaxed. I can see it, but I don't seem to find anything that would be causing it.
     [*Denial as defense against the exposure to the "unknown": I can't find anything that would be causing it."*]

D.   But you said, if you're in doubt whether you can do something, then you get *nervous.* . . .

P. I can see the reason for that.

D. When?

P. Well, I guess the ordinary person—I should think—if you're trying something new and are in doubt about it—I think it would cause it. Maybe I'm different, but I should think if somebody was trying something new, something different—and is in doubt, he'd be *nervous*.

D. For instance?

P. A new job. Different type of work. You might not be able to do it or something like that. Then I can see the reason why a person might be a little nervous about doing it. But doing the same thing, and you know you've done it before—I don't seem to be able to find out just what it is that makes me feel that way. Yet I always have that feeling. Outwardly I probably don't show it. It's inside of me, so to speak. It seems to be internally.
    [*He is trying to ward off his unconscious anxiety by externalizing and rationalizing it.*]

D. You mean you feel it internally?

P. Yes. I try not to show it. That might be causing the tightening up.
    [*The threat comes from within.*]

D. How do you feel internally?

P. In a knot, so to speak.

D. In a knot, as you call it. Is that how you always feel when you're in doubt about doing something new?
    [*Returning to the first cue word to prepare an opening into the past.*]

P. Or even things that I've done before, I find myself that way, too.

D. Do you?

P. Yes. In the case of dancing. Before I even get up to dance, I feel that sort of *tightening up* feeling. I don't know anything it might be. Maybe I've felt that way before and kind of wonder if I'll be feeling that way again.
    [*Fear of failure when "moving toward" the forbidden object.*]

D. Do you mean the first time?

P. When I did go.

D. You felt shaky?

P. That might be it.

D. Do you remember?

P. Maybe there's something in that. The first time I did go, I was a little bit nervous, but still it comes back to the same thing. I don't know why it should be—it *should be* something I like to do. Yet there's no reason I can see why I should be nervous.
    [*This suggests his liking for dancing is somewhat forced. The pressure into the past continues against resistance. When did dancing achieve the meaning of the forbidden activity?*]

(Deutsch & Murphy, 1955, pp. 249–252)

A Behavioral Interview

The patient in the following interview was a young woman who sought treatment for interpersonal anxiety. The interviewer, Joseph Wolpe, is one of the founders of behavior therapy (see Chapter 7). The segment below represents the first effort to specify the nature, extent, and situational factors of the patient's difficulty.

Therapist: So your name is Carol Grant? How old are you?

Miss G: Twenty-one.

Therapist: What is your complaint?

Miss G: I am very very nervous all the time.

Therapist: All the time?

Miss G: Yes, all the time.

Therapist: How long has this been so?

Miss G: Since I was about fourteen.

Therapist: Can you remember what brought it on?

Miss G: No, not really, I wish I could.

Therapist: But, are you not saying that before you were fourteen you were not nervous?

Miss G: Well I was, but not to this extreme. I remember being . . . especially in elementary school when I would have to read something in front of the class, then I would get very nervous about that— giving speeches or anything or answering in class. That would bother me.

Therapist: Well, that is a special situation.

Miss G: Yea, but now all the time. When I go out of the house, or walk out the door.

Therapist: Well, let's try to build up a picture. You say that in elementary school you were only nervous when you had to get up and speak in front of the class. Only then?

Miss G: Yes.

Therapist: And then in high school?

Miss G: It got worse. When we would go out with boys I would be very nervous.

Therapist: Do you mean that you became more nervous in front of the class?

Miss G: I wouldn't sleep for nights worrying about giving a speech in front of class or something like that.

Therapist: And you also said you became nervous about going out with boys?

Miss G: Yes. You know, I was afraid, especially if I would have a blind date I would be scared to death.

Therapist: Well, isn't that to some extent natural?

Miss G: I guess so, but not to the extremes that I would go to.

Therapist: And if you went out with somebody you knew. What about that?

Miss G: Well, after a while I would be a little calmer, but still nervous.

Therapist: And what about if you went out with girl friends?

Miss G: Not as much. I wouldn't be quite as nervous, but still a little bit.

Therapist: Were there any other situations in which you developed nervousness while you were in high school?

Miss G: No others that I can think of, just basically when I would walk out of the house everything would just bother me.

Therapist: Everything? Like what?

Miss G: Well, you know I was afraid to take tests or things like that or make speeches like I said before. Just to be with people would scare me.

Therapist: Just being with any people?

Miss G: Yes, it would bother me more if I was with people I didn't know too well.

Therapist: What about at time of vacation?

Miss G: Vacation? I don't know what you mean.

Therapist: Well, I mean you have to take tests and so on at school, but during vacation there are no tests. So would you still be nervous going out of the house?

Miss G: A little bit. But not quite as much. Because I wouldn't be thinking of that.

Therapist: What year did you graduate from school?

Miss G: 1963.

Therapist: And what did you do then?

Miss G: I went to school and became a technician.

Therapist: What kind of technician?

Miss G: X-ray.

Therapist: Do you like this work?

Miss G: Not really. It's just because I didn't know really what else to do. I thought it would be interesting and the only reason I went into it is because I thought it was interesting, but once I got there, I was very nervous about everything. It would scare me to be with patients.

Therapist: Patients would scare you?

Miss G: Well, especially the sick ones. If something would happen to them.

Therapist: You were scared that something might happen to them?

Miss G: Yes, like they would have an attack or something.

Therapist: Has this ever happened?

Miss G: No, not really.

Therapist: Well, it is now about five years since you became a technician.

Miss G: It is about four.

Therapist: During those four years have you become more nervous or less nervous or stayed the same?

Miss G: Definitely more.

Therapist: You have been getting gradually more nervous?

Miss G: Yes.

Therapist: All the time?

Miss G: Yes. My mouth tightens up all the time.

Therapist: I see. Now, are there any special things that make you nervous nowadays?

Miss G: Special things?

Therapist: Well, let's start off by considering your work situation.

Miss G: Yes?

Therapist: You said that sick persons make you more nervous?

Miss G: And my boss.

Therapist: Yes?

Miss G: He makes me extremely nervous. I am afraid of him.

Therapist: Why, is he very strict?

Miss G: Um, yes, he gives that appearance.

Therapist: Does he carry on? Does he scream and so on?

Miss G: Never at me. But I am always afraid that will happen.

Therapist: And what about nurses?

Miss G: Not really. I am not in much contact with them.

Therapist: And who else scares you?

Miss G: Men.

Therapist: Men?

Miss G: If I go out with them.

Therapist: Yes. What about men who come in where you are working, like medical students?

Miss G: Yes, they scare me too. They do.

(Wolpe, 1969, pp. 42–45)

A Client-Centered Interview

This interview segment comes from the initial interview of an eighteen-year-old man who was referred for therapy for treatment of "many worries and insecurities." The interviewer, William U. Snyder, is a noted client-centered therapist.

A distinguishing feature of this interview is the way the interviewer "follows" the patient by reflecting and clarifying his comments. The interviewer does not ask direct questions or make interpretive comments. The letter *C* refers to the interviewer and *S* to the patient.

C. I believe that Mr. Johnson said you had some things you would like to talk over with me.

S. Yes, I thought maybe I could iron some of the wrinkles out. I'm always worrying about some things—not big things, just little things. I can't get over the feeling that people are watching me. Then I worry about personal things and other things. When I see an ad in the paper I worry about the things discussed in it although I know they aren't true. I always felt that other fellows could always do things, but I could never come up to the other group. No matter how much people said otherwise, I didn't believe them. I'll worry about exams that I've got even though there's no possibility of not making out well on them. Things just cram up inside of my head—little things. They just keep coming back. I keep worrying about them and thinking about them. Like in ads, ads like Lifebuoy ads. When I'm going out on a date I'll take a bath and then maybe I won't feel clean enough so I'll use a cold shower and then after that I'll use a half dozen deodorants. But I still worry about it on the date. And sometimes I worry about—when Jack and I get together—that's my friend. He's a swell guy. It's the same way with him. There's nothing we can do about it. We have just got to let it go on and try to live it out. It just seems like the world is crowding in on us. There's a feeling of frustration and nothing you can do about it.

C. You feel pretty much upset about the thing, and that keeps you worrying about it.

S. Yes, I know I shouldn't worry about it, but I do. Lots of things—money, people, clothes. In classes I feel that everyone's just waiting for a chance to jump on me. It's like they were breathing down my neck waiting for a chance to find something wrong. At school there were fellows like that waiting for me. I can't stand people laughing at me. I can't stand ridicule. That's why I'm afraid of kids. When I meet somebody I wonder what he's actually thinking of me. Then later on I wonder how I match up to what he's come to think of me.

C. You feel that you're pretty responsive to the opinions of other people.

S.   Yes, but it's things that shouldn't worry me.

C.   You feel that it's the sort of thing that shouldn't be upsetting, but they do get you pretty much worried anyway.

S.   Just some of them. Most of those things do worry me because they're true. The ones I told you, that is. But there are lots of little things that aren't true. And time bothers me, too. That is, when I haven't anything to do. Things just seem to be piling up, piling up inside of me. When I haven't anything to do I roam around. I feel like—at home when I was at the theater and nobody would come in, I used to wear it off by socking the doors. It's a feeling that things were crowding up and they were going to burst.

C.   You feel that it's a sort of oppression with some frustration and that things are just unmanageable.

S.   In a way, but some things just seem illogical. I'm afraid I'm not very clear here but that's the way it comes.

C.   That's all right. You say just what you think.

S.   That's another thing. When I speak I know what I want to say but I don't seem to be able to say it. The wrong words come out and I can't express what I want to say even though I have the idea. Sometimes I'll have to go back and recover the thread of it. I'll find I'm not on the subject. Sometimes I can't find words to express what I mean.

C.   It's pretty upsetting when you find you can't express yourself.

S.   Yes, words are just piling up. I've got something to let out but I can't find words to let it out. Sometimes I worry about just where the line between sanity and insanity really is. That's why things I shouldn't worry about worry me. I worry about trivial things that are all illogical.

C.   You worry for fear that these things may be an indication that you are not in control of yourself.

S.   I feel maybe it's not insanity the way most people think of it. I'm not violent but in a certain sense it's unbalanced. Maybe there is a wheel off the track. I had a toy train that if the wheel came off the track, the whole thing slowed down.

C.   You feel you aren't violent like insanity is pictured by most people, but you feel that you're abnormal and it worries you.

S.   Yes, I feel some part may be deranged some place. Some minor part— very small thing, but it upsets everything. Sometimes I want to do something and get the energy out. We used to do things to try to forget. Some things, my parents and my brother didn't know. Sometimes we'd go to Tony's Tavern. Personally I can't stand the stuff. It's just the feeling you forget and everything seems to adjust itself.

C.   You feel a tension which you have to release so sometimes you go away from things and try to get rid of it.

S.   I try to get away from the feeling that things inside of me are going to pull myself apart. I'd do anything to get away from it. We used to go swimming in the quarry when we felt like that. We used to swim and swim until our arms were falling off. That relieved the tension. We used to fight each other just to get rid of the feeling that things were there.

C. You had a sort of inexpressible anxiety about a good many pressures.

S. Yes, internal ones. I can't express it. It's like a balloon swelling up inside and some day it's going to burst. It's like an appendix. It swells up and eventually it bursts and gets rid of infection.

C. You get to the point where you're pretty much worried and you feel you can't do much.

S. Yes, I want—I worry whenever I'm alone. If I'm alone and I think about it, then I know it's going to come. If I keep busy, I don't worry too much.

(Snyder, 1947, pp. 21–24)

Critical Appraisal

The clinical interview is basically an assessment technique. As with any other assessment technique, its reliability and validity cannot be taken for granted; rather, they must be empirically evaluated. However, unlike many other assessment procedures, interviewing is not a discrete, standardized technique with a consistent, specific purpose. It is a complex process with many highly variable factors. Interview format (e.g., the amount of structure) interacts with interviewer style and client type to make each interview unique. Interviews also yield diverse types of data: diagnoses, demographic information, personality profiles, behavioral descriptions, and so on. Thus, any attempt to assess reliability and validity would have to specify at least the type of interview, interviewer, and client, as well as the type of data under study. It would then be rather difficult to generalize the conclusions to other combinations of those variables. Furthermore, lack of reliability or validity can often be ascribed to factors other than the interview. For example, there is generally low reliability in diagnosing patients (cf. Hersen, 1976). Is this because interviews provide faulty information, or because the diagnostic labels are poorly defined, or because the clinicians involved in such research were inefficient, or other reasons? Obviously, it would be difficult to label the interview the source of the problem.

While no general conclusions about interviewing can be drawn, it is possible to examine the assumptions upon which interviewing is based and factors which affect the interview process. In this final section, we will discuss some of the factors which can reduce the interview's reliability and validity. Let us consider difficulties arising from three general sources: the client, the interviewer, and the interaction.

Client Factors

The client is the source of all information in the interview. Basically, then, the validity of the interview hinges on the accuracy of the client's information. Most clients come for treatment voluntarily and are motivated to be truthful and give accurate information. That is *not* the case with people who are being interviewed under duress, such as those sent by the court, children brought in by their parents, and spouses threatened with divorce if they do not seek help. Contrary to popular myth, even skilled interviewers cannot always reliably distinguish truth from lie, accuracy from distortion. For example, research on impression management has demonstrated that even psychotic patients can make themselves appear competent or incompetent, depending upon whether they want to remain in or leave the psychiatric hospital (Braginsky & Braginsky, 1967).

However, even when the client tells the truth, accuracy is not always certain. In fact, outside of factual data such as demographic information, distortion and error seem quite likely (cf. Bellack & Hersen, 1977b). To report a behavior pattern accurately, the client must have observed the behavior, remember it, and be able to reflect back on it without distortion. Most people are rather poor at observing their own behavior and often do not know precisely what they are doing. They are also unaware of the reasons for their behavior, whether environmental (e.g., reinforcers) or internal. Even when they do self-observe, they often have little reason to remember the content. Finally, memories of past behavior are often distorted in one of two ways. First, the clinician is typically interested in anxiety-producing experiences and situations. However, the distress involved in such situations interferes with perception, producing a distorted view of what is happening (cf. Bellack, 1980). For example, a person who is unassertive and afraid of any display of anger may perceive even the slightest expression of annoyance as rage. Consequently, this person could not provide an accurate picture of personal feelings and behavior, or of experience with others.

A second source of distortion affects the recall of material. Most people cannot see themselves with impartiality and objectivity. They form an image of themselves and interpret their behavior so as to be consistent with that image. When they attempt to recall past experience and account for their behavior, bits and pieces of memories are combined, filtered, and interpreted so as to form a coherent and consistent picture. The nature and degree of distortion will vary with the client's dysfunction. For example, depression has been explained as primarily a cognitive disorder (cf. Rush & Beck, 1978). According to this theory, depressed persons have a highly pessimistic view of themselves, their environment, and their future. Hence, current perceptions and memories are painted black by this negative orientation to the world. Anxiety is another factor which can distort both recall and reports (Martin, 1971). Some memories and issues are simply too painful or threatening for the client to face. The so-called defense mechanisms (e.g., denial, repression, rationalization) all serve to reduce anxiety by reshaping experience and memories.

All the factors described above combine to limit the accuracy of self-reports. According to the literature, there is little correspondence between self-report and overt behavior, and between self-report and physiological arousal (Bellack & Hersen, 1977b; Hersen & Bellack, 1977). These limitations of self-report data are the primary reasons for the use of other assessment procedures, such as projective tests and direct observation. We do not mean to suggest that the interview is hopelessly invalid. Quite the contrary. In many cases, client self-report is substantially accurate and no other data are required. However, there is a potential bias in self-reports which occasionally makes them almost useless.

Interviewer Factors

The interviewer must process the client's information, integrating the diverse data and drawing conclusions. Even if the data are accurate, the interview can be invalid if the interviewer introduces some error. We have already considered several possible sources of error: failure to gather enough information to reach valid conclusions, failure to perceive client reports accurately, inability to develop rapport with the client, and simply poor interviewing. The interviewer could also be operating from an inaccurate or inadequate data base. That is, he or she might not be sufficiently aware of the literature on a behavior pattern or the meaning of a particular response to make accurate interpretations.

Consider a situation in which the interviewer is skilled and knowledgeable, and accurately perceives the client's communication. Even under these ideal circumstances, the interview may be invalid. The primary issue here is the adequacy of clinical judgment and subjective inference. Some psychologists argue that such inference is an essential part of clinical evaluation (cf. Holt, 1958; Meehl, 1957). Further, the experienced clinician is said to be in a unique position to integrate the data. After all, he or she is able to creatively and adaptively examine it in the context of the extensive personal norms developed through clinical practice.

Others, however, believe that the clinician is rather poor at processing the data and drawing valid conclusions. Even the full-time private practitioner sees relatively few clients of any specific type in the course of a career; hence, personal norms are not extensive enough to provide a sound basis for judgments. Furthermore, the clinician makes many interpretations and predictions, and reaches many conclusions while interacting with clients. The accuracy of these judgments is rarely checked. For example, the specific basis for a prediction about therapy outcome will rarely be written down (or otherwise recalled) and later examined. Often, associations and assumptions simply become part of the clinician's belief system with no empirical rationale. The tendency of clinicians to persist in drawing invalid conclusions *despite contradictory research data* was shown by Chapman and Chapman (1969). They found that the *appearance* of a relationship or the meaning of a response had more impact on judgments than data—a phenomenon they called "illusory correlation." Finally, there is some question about the clinician's physical ability to integrate all the information involved in clinical decision making. Human information-processing ability is limited; only a certain amount of data can be integrated at any one time. Clinical assessment involves more data than the clinician can effectively process. For this reason, the clinician develops a set of beliefs, pseudo-base rates, and interpretations which are, at best, only partially valid, applies them uncritically, and reaches faulty conclusions. This pattern persists because of occasional chance "hits" (accurate conclusions), overgeneralizations which cover many cases slightly and few specifically, and support from colleagues who are equally in error.

We agree largely with the second position, which questions the validity of clinical judgment. In general, research has not supported the use of clinical inference (Meehl, 1954). However, we do not believe that this difficulty totally invalidates interviewing any more than does the problem with self-report. The more the clinician relies on intuition and the less critical the appraisal, the less valid he or she will be. Conversely, validity and effectiveness can be substantially increased if the clinician systematically refers to the empirical literature and attempts to cross-validate inferences and predictions. In addition, the literature generally suggests that the more objective the evaluation process, the less it is subject to bias and error (e.g., Kent, O'Leary, Diament, & Dietz, 1974). In summary, the good clinician must be aware of his or her own limitations—not the least of which is the data base—as well as the potential inaccuracy of the client's report.

Interaction Factors

The sources of error discussed above are produced by either the client or the clinician alone; for example, the clinician has no role in the client's faulty recollection. Other difficulties, however, are basically joint products. Some of them are created by one person, but some interaction is needed. Perhaps the most obvious potential source of error is the client-interviewer relationship. We have already discussed the importance of a positive relationship in promoting communication. The impact of the client–therapist relationship has been documented in many studies. For example, it has been shown that clients are more communicative and interviews are more productive with warm (as opposed to cold) interviewers (Pope & Siegman, 1972) and with friendly as opposed to reserved interviewers (Heller, 1972). Similarly, high-status interviewers produce greater client productivity than do low-status interviewers (Pope & Siegman, 1972). Both the nature and the extent of the client's communication depend largely on the way he or she perceives the interviewer and the way the two individuals relate to one another. These findings about productivity are important, because the accuracy of the clinician's conclusions depends greatly on the amount of information collected. Conclusions can easily be distorted by omissions as well as by erroneous client reports.

The client's behavior in the interview is very much affected by the interviewer in other ways as well. For example, Matarazzo and his colleagues (cf. Matarazzo & Wiens, 1972) have shown that the duration and latency of client responses vary according to the duration and latency of interviewer comments. Thus, the interviewer can get the client to make longer responses by lengthening his or her own. Siegman and Pope (1972) report that ambiguous (i.e., nonspecific) interviewer questions and comments decreased clients' verbal fluency (making them more hesitant in their replies), but increased the interview's productivity. There is also much evidence that the interviewer can subtly shape the nature of client statements (as well as the direction of the interview) through the use of social reinforcement procedures, such as head nods, "yeh," and "mm hmm" (cf. Murray & Jacobson, 1971). All these forms of influence are potential sources of bias and distortion, especially if the interviewer is unaware of their impact. Of course, the skillful interviewer *may* be able to conduct more effective and valid interviews by systematically promoting appropriate client behavior.

Summary

This chapter has presented an introduction to clinical assessment. We first considered the assessment process, comparing it to a research program in which the clinician formulates and tests certain hypotheses. We then examined the role of the interview as the first stage in the assessment process—providing both a stimulus for further assessment and a context for understanding data secured from other sources.

The remainder of the chapter focused on the interview itself. First, the diverse sources of data in the interview were described, including client self-report and observation of client behavior. The next section focused on interview techniques, including the organization of the interview, the clinical relationship, and some of the specifics of interviewing. Examples of interview styles in the psychodynamic, behavioral, and client-centered modes were then presented.

The final section of the chapter appraised the interview as an assessment device. Three potential sources of invalidity were considered: the client, the interviewer, and the interaction. In general, the interview is critical in clinical assessment regardless of theoretical orientation. When conducted objectively by a skilled interviewer who is familiar with the literature, the interview is likely to be useful and valid. However, the more the clinician relies on intuition and subjective judgment, the greater the likelihood of bias and error.

CHAPTER FOUR

Psychological Testing

The assessment process usually involves psychological testing. A wide variety of tests are available for different client populations. The settings for testing range from clinics to hospitals to schools to industrial concerns. Given the specific referral question, categories have included: intelligence, achievement, aptitude, vocational, objective personality, projective, and neuropsychological tests. Clients include adults, children, and infants, with the whole spectrum of diagnostic possibilities (from normal to pathological) evaluated. Although it is obviously difficult to be precise, several million Americans are tested each year (cf. Cronbach, 1975). Indeed, testing has become a profitable business; many corporations publish and market primarily psychological tests (e.g., The Psychological Corporation; Science Research Associates).

Clinical psychology has been associated with the testing movement throughout the twentieth century. It is little wonder, then, that the media and the public often view psychological testing as the clinician's primary function. Of course, this association has been heavily reinforced by educators and psychiatrists as well as by many clinical psychologists themselves. Despite the stormy history of the testing movement, recent surveys (e.g., Wade & Baker, 1977) suggest that psychological testing (cf. Lewandowski & Saccuzzo, 1976; Tolor, 1973) is thriving. Moreover, scores of books are published regularly on both general and specific aspects of testing (e.g., Andrulis, 1977; Cronbach, 1970; Matarazzo,

1972; Rickers-Ovsiankina, 1977; Russell, Neuringer, & Goldstein, 1970). However, in the last decade, testing has come under heavy attack from the media, the courts (cf. APA Monitor, 1977, 1978), and clinical psychology itself (e.g., McClelland, 1973). (See also the discussion in Chapter 5 of how behavior therapists have substituted direct assessment strategies for traditional psychological testing.)

In this chapter, we survey psychological testing as practiced by the clinical psychologist. In particular, we will examine the use of various psychological tests in light of recent criticisms and controversies. First, we will deal with the tests most often used by clinical psychologists. Second, we will examine the APA recommendations for the development and use of psychological tests, including normative data, reliability, validity, and ethics. Third will be an overview of intelligence testing and the many problems it has created. Fourth will be an assessment of the development and contemporary thinking in the field about the use of projective tests. Fifth, we will describe "objective personality testing," using the Minnesota Multiphasic Personality Inventory (MMPI). Sixth will be a discussion of how neuropsychological tests are being employed. Seventh, we will consider the use of test batteries (i.e., several different tests to identify levels of intellectual and emotional functioning in clients). Eighth, we will evaluate how clinicians use and interpret their test data, including clinical inference, scoring, and use of valid signs. And finally, we will appraise the reliability and validity of tests being used today in terms of experimental, clinical, and societal considerations.

Current Status

The status of psychological testing can best be described as extremely ambiguous. This is true despite the fact that Buros (1974), the editor of *Tests in Print,* listed 2,476 tests that were available in 1974. However, in many respects psychological testing has been on a downhill course in the last two decades. Bersoff (1973) refers to this decline as turning "a silk purse into a sow's ear." He notes:

> For almost 50 years, beginning with World War I, psychological testing was perceived as the vehicle by which major decisions about people's lives could be made in industry, the military, hospitals, mental health clinics, and the schools. Scores derived from psychometric instruments were used to classify, segregate, track, advance, employ, institutionalize, and educate people. Now, IQ testing is outlawed in San Francisco, personnel selection

tests are declared illegal unless directly relevant to employment, group intelligence measures are banned in New York City schools, a whole profession which has distinguished itself from psychiatry primarily because its practitioners can test has been declared moribund, and school psychologists in Boston have been declared incompetent. In the last 10 years, what was once a silk purse has been transformed into a sow's ear.

Who is to be held accountable for this psychological alchemy? The answer is two brands of "psychos": psychoanalysts and psychometricians. Psychoanalysts are to blame because they have perpetrated a fraudulent (Freudulent?) theory of personality and have perpetuated its myth. Psychometrists, the test constructors, are to blame because they have forgotten their historical antecedents and have become overly concerned with psychometric aesthetics to the neglect of validity (p. 892).

The above quotation captures only *some* of the problems in psychological testing and obviously reflects the author's own biases. Although we are generally in sympathy with Bersoff's position, a more objective way to evaluate testing is to look at surveys conducted over the last two decades—surveys on the use of and attitudes toward testing held by clinical psychologists. In addition to determining the popularity of various tests, these surveys have examined the discrepant values ascribed to testing by both academic and clinical psychologists practicing in the community and in institutional settings. The decrease in publishing related to psychological testing has also been documented.

Between 1961 and 1976 three surveys were conducted to determine how psychological tests were used in the United States (Brown & McGuire, 1976; Lubin, Wallis, & Paine, 1971; Sundberg, 1961). The general similarity of these surveys allows us to trace changes in test usage over this fifteen-year period. The questionnaires developed for these surveys listed commonly used psychological tests, allowing the respondent to indicate whether the test was used in the first place, and if so, how frequently (i.e., 0 = never, 1 = occasionally, 2 = frequently, 3 = majority of cases). In each study, an attempt was made to send questionnaires to a cross section of agencies that employ clinical psychologists. For example, Sundberg's (1961) questionnaire was mailed to VA hospitals, state hospitals, institutions for the retarded, outpatient clinics, counseling centers, and university training clinics. The number of questionnaires sent out for the three surveys was 304, 551, and 249, respectively. The return rate for usable completed questionnaires was approximately 50 percent.

Although many data were gathered, we will contrast the top ten tests as indicated in each of the surveys (see Table 4.1). Two types of scores are indicated for each test. TM refers to the total mention of the test. For example, of 251 respondents in the Lubin et al. (1971) survey, how many used a given test (e.g., the Rorschach)? WS refers to the weighted score rank—the percentage of the test's usage from, say, 251 respondents multiplied by the frequency of usage (i.e., 0-3 rating).

The data in Table 4.1 reveal both striking consistencies and impressive changes over the years. Among the top ten tests in Sundberg's (1961) survey were four projectives, four intelligence tests, one objective personality test (MMPI), and one test to evaluate organicity (Bender-Gestalt). Interestingly, the composition of the top ten remained quite consistent in 1971 and 1976: five projectives, three intelligence tests, one objective personality test, and one test for organicity.

However, over the fifteen years some definite changes did take place. The popularity of the Rorschach diminished in each successive survey, while that of the MMPI increased. Also, the Stanford-Binet declined substantially as the WISC (Wechsler Intelligence Scale for Children) and the WPPSI (Wechsler Preschool and Primary Scale of Intelligence) increased. (The TM and WS ranking of 1 for the WISC in the Brown & McGuire study undoubtedly points up sampling error, in that child treatment agencies were overrepresented.)

To summarize the trends, *objective* tests (IQ, personality, organicity) have gained in popularity and usage over the last two decades. However, the use of projective tests, although diminished, is still quite extensive.

Turning now to how testing is viewed in academia, let us consider two surveys designed to ascertain the attitude of academic psychologists toward projective testing. Thelen, Varble, and Johnson (1968) sent their questionnaire to representative faculty from seventy APA-approved clinical training programs and received an 86 percent return. In response to question 1: "Do you feel that knowledge and skill in the use of projectives are as important as they used to be?" 75 percent said yes, 11 percent no, and 13 percent were uncertain. In response to question 5: "Do you think that research generally supports the value of projective techniques?" 62 percent said no, 12 percent yes, and 22 percent were uncertain. And in response to question 9: "Some of the major universities are cutting down on the semester hour time for teaching projective techniques," 51 percent reacted favorably, 22 percent unfavorably, and 25 percent were neutral.

Based on these results, it would indeed appear that academicians have become more negative toward the projectives (cf. Louttit &

Table 4.1.   Test Usage in The United States (1961–1976)

Sundberg (1961)			Lubin et al. (1971)			Brown & McGuire (1976)		
Test	TM	WS	Test	TM	WS	Test	TM	WS
Rorschach	1.0	1	WAIS	1.0	2	WISC	1.0	1
Draw-A-Person (Machover)	2.5	2	Rorschach	2.0	3	Bender-Gestalt	2.5	2
TAT	2.5	4	Bender-Gestalt	3.5	7	WAIS	2.5	3
Bender-Gestalt	4.0	3	TAT	5.0	4	MMPI	4.5	4
Standford-Binet	5.0	6	Draw-A-Person	6.0	5	Rorschach	6.0	5
WAIS	6.0	5	MMPI	7.0	6	TAT	4.5	6
MMPI	7.5	8	WISC	8.0	9	Sentence Completion	7.0	7
Wechsler-Bellevue	7.5	9	Stanford-Binet	8–9	7–8	Draw-A-Person (Goodenough)	8.0	8
Draw-A-Person (Goodenough)	9.0	10	Sentence Completion	9.0	8	House-Tree-Person	11.0	0
WISC	10.0	7	House-Tree-Person	10.0	10	Stanford-Binet	9.0	10

Browne, 1947). In fact, when this survey was further analyzed in terms of the respondents' ages, it became clear that the older professors were the most positive while the younger ones were the most negative. However, in spite of the overall lack of enthusiasm for projective testing (at least in theory), a large majority of those surveyed still wants clinical students to take some course work in projective techniques (see Table 4.2). Although rather contradictory, Thelen et al. (1968) argue that: (1) some respondents may have felt that no viable alternative to projectives was available, (2) others may have been reacting to the demands of the agencies, clinics, and institutions for projectives, and (3) still others may have thought that the clinical student should be exposed to a wide variety of educational experiences, deciding later on the usefulness and validity of projectives.

In a later survey of clinical psychology programs, Shemberg and Keeley (1970) confirmed that in contrast to the prior five years, projectives had definitely decreased as the more objective tests had increased. Of course, the newer clinical programs tended to emphasize objective assessment, whereas the older ones taught projective testing. However, on the whole, there was a deemphasis on diagnostic approaches altogether.

If this picture is confusing, it nevertheless represents the current state of affairs. In fact, as we proceed, the confusion may even increase. We have already noted the academicians' disillusionment with testing in general and projective testing in particular. This is especially true of younger faculty members.

However, it may be a long time before the changes in academia

Table 4.2. Attitudes About Requiring Clinical Students to Take Course Work in Projective Techniques

	% Response		
Technique	Should be required	Should be optional	Should not be offered
Sentence completion	41	51	6
Rorschach	71	24	5
TAT	71	23	4
Figure drawings	36	47	16

From: Thelen et al. (1968), Table 4.

begin to take hold among practicing clinicians. This may cause problems for senior graduate students about to embark on clinical internships (Rice & Gurman, 1973) or when seeking employment (Levy & Fox, 1975). More specifically, Rice and Gurman (1973) point out that internship supervisors ". . . are disappointed in students who arrive for internship with gaps in basic clinical knowledge and are ambivalent about teaching what they consider to be the graduate school's responsibility, that is, familiarity with the basic psychological assessment measures, how to combine a battery of instruments for psychological evaluation. . . . Internship clinicians generally desire to refine and enhance basic skills, not to inculcate them" (p. 405).

Given this discrepancy in training and expectations between the clinical psychology department and the internship facility, the potential for conflict between interns and their supervisors is considerable. Of course, in the last decade, several internship centers have developed specialized programs (i.e., behaviorally oriented) in which behavioral assessment has supplanted traditional psychological testing (see Chapter 5). However, there are too few of these programs to accommodate all of the applicants seeking internship positions.

Similarly, when new clinical psychologists applied for jobs, Levy and Fox (1975) found that for 90 percent of the positions advertised in the *APA Employment Bulletin* in 1971–1972, psychological testing skills were required. Moreover, 84 percent of these positions specified projective techniques. Therefore, Levy and Fox conclude that ". . . testing skills, including those involved in projective testing, are an important part of what clinical psychologists are expected to do" (p. 424).

Another way to gauge the testing movement is to examine the publication rate for the subject. For other aspects of clinical psychology, publication rate in the past has proved a barometer of changes, trends, and fads in the field. Thus, Tolor (1973) looked at the publication rate of articles on diagnosis in five journals (*Journal of Abnormal Psychology, Journal of Clinical Psychology, Journal of Consulting and Clinical Psychology, Journal of Personality Assessment, Psychological Reports*) between 1951 and 1970. With the exception of the *Journal of Clinical Psychology,* articles on the diagnostic process decreased significantly over time. "The evidence based on analysis of the content of articles that appeared in five journals commonly used by clinical psychologists as publication outlets quite convincingly points to the diminished role of diagnostic function on the contemporary American scene" (Tolor, 1973, p. 340).

Psychometric and Ethical Standards

In developing a good psychological test, three basic psychometric qualities must be maintained: norms, reliability, and validity. If they are missing, the extrinsic value of any given test can be seriously questioned (cf. Cronbach, 1970). And once these values for a test are established, the practicing clinician must be fully aware of them. Given the delicate decisions that are often made on the basis of testing, as well as the emotionally charged social climate of testing today, the clinical psychologist would be doubly remiss in giving unreliable or invalid tests whose norms are not clearly defined.

Several booklets outlining technical recommendations for psychological tests have been published by the APA since 1954. The most recent of these, *Standards for Educational & Psychological Tests,* appeared in 1974. "Part of the stimulus for revision is an awakened concern about problems like invasion of privacy or discrimination against members of groups such as minorities or women. Serious misuses of tests include, for example, labeling Spanish-speaking children as mentally retarded on the basis of scores on tests standardized on 'a representative sample of American children,' or using a test with a major loading on verbal comprehension without appropriate validation in an attempt to screen out large numbers of blacks from manipulative jobs requiring minimal communication" (APA, 1974, p. 1). In short, the most recent revision of this manual is designed largely *to avoid the pitfalls of the discriminatory use of tests.*

Let us now examine some of the recommendations in the latest APA manual. In discussing the various tests used by clinical psychologists later on, our appraisals of these tests will be based on how well they conform to the properties defined below.

Norms

Norms refer to the range of scores obtained on a given test by the standardization sample. In practice, the standardization sample is both large and representative. To review, the bell-shaped distribution of scores is arranged so that there are three standard deviations above and three below the mean of all scores. Thus, at times norms may form standard deviation intervals above and below the mean. Sometimes norms are presented as percentile scores (e.g., a score at the mean is equal to the 50th percentile).

The purpose of norms (which are usually presented at the beginning of the test manual) is to allow the tester to compare an individual score with the scores of other similar individuals. For example, how does a particular score on a college entrance examination compare with norms for successful college graduates?

Of course, there is always the danger that norms can be used in a discriminatory manner. Consider the following possibility. Suppose a poor high school student attains a score of 60 on an aptitude test. When comparing this score with norms for high school students of similar status, a score of 60 may fall in the 80th percentile. However, when comparing it with those of wealthy middle-class high school students, the same score of 60 may fall in the 40th percentile.

Clearly, several series of specific as well as general norms must be established for each test developed. Again, this is important not only for the test developer but also for the test user. Without appropriate norms, an individual's test score might be totally misinterpreted. And as a result, the individual could suffer personal harm as a result of mis-classification. This, unfortunately, has often happened when low IQ scores of foreign-speaking persons have been sweepingly interpreted as indicating "mental deficiency"; in fact, there were simply no appropriate norms for such people at the time. As the 1974 APA manual clearly states: "Norms presented in the test manual should refer to defined and clearly described populations. These populations should be the groups with whom users of the test will ordinarily wish to compare the persons tested" (APA, 1974, p. 20).

Reliability

A second important psychometric consideration in test construction is reliability. In general, *reliability* in a scientific sense means that a given observation or event can be reproduced at will under standard conditions. Reliability refers to whether a test score actually reflects the characteristic being measured (e.g., depression) or is simply an indication of chance factors. Such chance factors are often called "measurement error." Thus, if a test is described as reliable, the psychological examiner should be able to accept a given score as being a true indicator of the characteristic being assessed. Also, chance factors of measurement error should be at a minimum.

A test's reliability is expressed as a correlation coefficient ($r = 0.00$ to 1.00). The closer it is to 1.00, the greater the reliability. By convention, however, a test whose reliability is equal to or greater than 0.80 is considered to be sufficiently reliable.

There are several ways to determine reliability. One of the easiest is to give the same test to the same individual (under similar conditions) on two separate occasions (i.e., test-retest). Then the two test scores are correlated. Although this is one of the methods most frequently used, it does have certain limitations. One of the problems is to insure that the test-retest interval is great enough so that practice or familiarity with the items do not affect the retest. On the other hand, if the interval is too long, educational, maturational, and other experiences may influence changed responses on the retest.

An alternative approach is to develop parallel forms of the test. This, then, should mitigate the problems with the test-retest method. However, this is usually a time-consuming and costly procedure. Also, it is difficult to develop test items that have equal value and equal "pull" for a given characteristic. This is especially true in projective testing.

A third method for determining test reliability is the "split-half" reliability approach. Here, instead of developing parallel forms, the existing test is divided into two (odd-numbered versus even-numbered items). The entire test is given as usual, but the total scores obtained on the basis of the odd- and even-numbered items are correlated. The problem here is that odd- and even-numbered items may not be carefully matched in the first place.

Clearly, then, even if a test manual reports respectable reliability levels, the careful examiner should be fully aware of how the reliability figure was determined and calculated. A mere statement that the test is "reliable" is obviously insufficient.

In addition to test reliability, there is the issue of inter-scorer reliability. In tests where scorer judgment may be at issue (e.g., responses to an IQ or projective test), one must be able to demonstrate that independent scorers, given equal training and operational definitions of correct and incorrect responses, are able to arrive at very similar conclusions (i.e., close to identical scores on a particular test). Here too a correlation of $r = 0.80$ would be considered a minimal acceptable criterion for inter-scorer reliability. In the absence of acceptable inter-scorer reliability, the usefulness of the test would indeed be questionable. In demonstrating good inter-scorer reliability, independent scores for both individual items and total test scores would be correlated.

Validity

A high reliability coefficient, unfortunately, does not automatically ensure test validity. On the other hand, if the reliability coefficient is low, it is most unlikely that good validity will be attained. Let us now define validity. According to the APA manual, "Questions of validity are questions of what may be properly inferred from a test score; validity refers to the appropriateness of inferences from test scores or other forms of assessment. The many types of validity questions can, for convenience, be reduced to two: (a) What can be inferred about what is being measured by the test? (b) What can be inferred about other behavior?" (APA, 1974, p. 24). Put more simply, test validity indicates whether the test truly measures what it is supposed to measure. For example, in the case of a depression inventory, is the test really measuring depression? Are scores highly correlated with independent clinicians' ratings of depression? What is the correlation between scores on the depression inventory and other tests of depression? Do scores on the depression inventory relate to observed symptoms of depression (e.g., crying spells, sadness, poor sleep, loss of appetite, loss of energy)?

As with reliability, validity can be determined in many ways. Again, the mere statement that a test is valid or invalid is generally insufficient. The kind of validity that a test possesses is particularly important. Cronbach (1970) contends that "The question to ask is 'How valid is this test for the decision I wish to make' or 'How valid is the interpretation I propose for the test?'" (p. 122).

The first type of validity to be described, *face validity,* is not measured in a numerical or psychometric sense. Instead, it refers more to a global impression that the test appears to be reasonable—that is, it *seems* to be measuring what it says it is measuring. The items appear to be related to the dimension (e.g., anxiety, depression, schizophrenia) in question. However, as astutely pointed out by Cronbach (1970), many tests that appear to have face validity turn out to be very poor predictors of the dimension in question.

A more psychometrically related kind of validity is *content validity.* As the term implies, a test that has sufficient content validity is one in which ". . . the behaviors demonstrated in testing constitute a representative sample of behaviors to be exhibited in a desired performance domain" (APA, 1974, p. 28). For example, does a final examination ask questions about material actually covered in the course? To establish good content validity, the test developer usually takes the primary dimension (e.g., anxiety or depression) and subdivides it into relevant subcategories. In this way, it becomes possible to construct items that are representative of all the subcategories. With this procedure, a truly representative sample of the universe of items emerges.

The next two types of validity—*criterion-related validity*—are extremely important. Here, the test score is correlated with a readily available external criterion. The first validity procedure is called *concurrent validity*. As the term implies, the test score is correlated with an external criterion that is *currently* available at the time of testing. An example of this might be the correlation of achievement test scores with current performance (i.e., grade-point average) in the classroom. By contrast, for *predictive validity,* the test score is correlated with an external criterion that *will* be available in the future. One example is the correlation of college entrance examination scores with subsequent success in college. In either instance (concurrent or predictive validity), the closer the correlation approaches $r = 1.00$, the greater the validity of the test.

Probably the most "amorphous" strategy for determining test validity is *construct validation.*[1] It is amorphous in the sense that *construct validation* is a continuous process "based on an accumulation of research results" rather than being based on any one study. Therefore, construct validity on any given test is always a matter of interpretation. "In obtaining the information needed to establish construct validity, the investigator begins by formulating hypotheses about the characteristics of those who have high scores on the test in contrast to those who have low scores. Taken together, such hypotheses form at least a tentative theory about the nature of the construct the test is believed to be measuring" (APA, 1974, p. 30).

An example of such a construct is anxiety. In researching the construct validity of a test of anxiety, the test developer has certain hypotheses as to how high-anxious and low-anxious people behave (e.g., high-anxious people have increased heart rates when placed in stressful situations). Thus, scores on an anxiety test may be correlated with subjects' heart rates in a behavioral stress situation. Also, the test may be correlated with other tests that presume to measure anxiety. Of course, the test is likely to be more valuable if the correlation with heart rate is higher than with the second test of anxiety. If the reverse were true, needless duplication of measurement would be represented by the

---

1. A *construct* is a hypothesized entity, which therefore can be measured only indirectly.

two tests. Thus, in the ideal situation there should be moderate correlations between and among tests of anxiety and higher correlations with external criteria presumed to differentiate high-anxious and low-anxious individuals.

Ethical Standards

As a professional serving the general public in the role of psychological examiner, the clinician is expected to act in an ethical manner. Although the importance of ethics has been acknowledged (APA, 1974), we contend that this area receives too little attention during the training period. That is not to say that graduate clinical programs avoid the issue. However, certain matters relating to ethical standards need to be underscored more carefully.

Probably the most crucial area is that of test selection. Although perhaps not typically seen in this light, the selection of tests with adequate norms, reliability, and validity for diagnostic purposes *is* the clinician's ethical responsibility. As previously noted, many critical decisions are often made on the basis of test scores and the ensuing psychological test report. In that light, let us consider the following medical analogy. What would happen if a physician made crucial medical judgments on the basis of diagnostic procedures of questionable reliability and validity? It is obvious that the examiner must thoroughly understand the research literature for the tests used. Although this seems so obvious as to be a *given,* a recent survey (Wade & Baker, 1977) suggests that many clinical psychologists pay more attention to their own convictions about a particular test than to the relevant research conclusions. In our judgment, this borders on the unethical.

A second ethical consideration relates to test security. This means that the examiner must safeguard the stimulus materials and the answers (e.g., on IQ and achievement tests) for many tests and inventories. Only those who administer, score, and interpret the tests should have access to such materials. Without test security, the validity of test scores would obviously be greatly reduced. Further, psychological testing is a serious endeavor; it does not and should never fall into the realm of "parlor games."

A third major ethical responsibility relates to how test scores are sent to the referral party and what kind of information is given to the client. For example, if the client scores 119 on the WAIS and the report is being forwarded to another clinical psychologist, one could normally assume that the referral party would know that this score is over one standard deviation above the mean. However, to report the score alone to a referral source who is not knowledgeable is neither sufficient nor appropriate. In this instance, it would be desirable to report that the WAIS IQ score of 119 means that the client is functioning in the upper end of the "bright-normal" range of intelligence and that the score falls in the 90th percentile. Also, it might be useful to explain what the 90th percentile means (i.e., the score is greater than that attained by 90 percent of the population).

Equally important, the psychological examiner and/or the referring source should discuss the test results with the client. Too often the psychological examination has an unnecessary aura of mystery that probably impedes communication between tester and client as well as hindering performance (cf. Towbin, 1961). In the example of our 119 WAIS IQ score, direct feedback as to the actual score is not recommended. However, feedback about the percentile equivalent and what it means and implies is quite consistent with the APA guidelines (APA, 1974). Feedback about performance on "personality" tests should be handled the same way. Again, exact scores are neither recommended nor are they particularly useful to the client. But an overall description in layman's terminology should be given once all materials are scored and interpreted.

We have highlighted only some of the primary ethical responsibilities of the psychological examiner. However, there are many more that become apparent in day-to-day clinical practice. The APA recommendations provide a more comprehensive overview of the issues (APA, 1974).

Intelligence Testing

Early History

The psychological testing movement began with the work of Alfred Binet at the turn of the twentieth century in Paris. Although Galton had measured individual human differences in the late nineteenth century, he never developed a formal and comprehensive examination such as the Binet-Simon Scale. The history of the first intelligence scales makes for fascinating reading and has been beautifully documented in Matarazzo (1972). As is now well known, the original 1905 Binet-Simon Scale grew out of the practical needs of the Paris school system. A diagnostic tool was needed to separate the normal from the retarded, and among the retarded those who were educable, partially educable, and uneducable.

Matarazzo (1972) states that "Recognizing the intense social pressure in Paris for separation of children according to whether they were fully educable, educable with special help in the schools, or retarded to the point of being unable to benefit from public placement, the 16 members of the Society's Commission for Study of the Retarded proposed at the February 1904 meeting that the society insist that (1) a medicopedagogical examination should be authorized by the school authorities before a child was denied public instruction due to mental retardation, (2) those children diagnosed educably retarded be educated in a special class or special establishment, and (3) that, as a demonstration project, a special class be opened in one of the public schools near the Salpétrière" (p. 36). Thus, the first intelligence scale was born in the spirit of humanitarian needs.

After being appointed to the Society's Commission of the Retarded, Binet and his colleagues spent several months developing the Binet-Simon Scale, entitled the "Measuring Scale of Intelligence" in a 1908 report. Here are several items from this scale, consisting of thirty tasks each presumed to be more difficult than the previous one: "1. Following a moving object with one's eyes. 10. Comparing two lines of markedly unequal length. 20. Telling how two objects are alike ('similarities'). 30. Defining abstract terms (e.g., What is the difference between esteem and friendship? . . . boredom and weariness? . . . etc.)" (Matarazzo, 1972, pp. 38–39). Initially the 1905 scale provided a relatively "crude" index of a child's intellectual functioning. No formal method for arriving at a total score was indicated. However, in 1908 the important concept of "mental age" was introduced. Items that *should* be successfully completed by "normal" children of varying age levels (from ages three to thirteen) were now indicated. (The notion of "mental age" will be further explained below.)

Definitions of Intelligence

Throughout the twentieth century, clinical psychologists have sought a comprehensive definition of intelligence. Surprising as it may seem, none of the definitions is fully adequate. Although it is relatively easy to decide whether a given action is intelligent or not, the more global concept of intelligence is more elusive. Indeed, it appears that only situation-specific intelligence can be readily defined. Some clinicians, who despair of finding a suitable definition, have somewhat sardonically decided that "Intelligence is simply what an intelligence test is measuring." Although obviously a circular definition, this underscores the futility of pinpointing the abstraction "intelligence."

In any event, let us look at some of the definitions of intelligence, including the original Binet-Simon notion of mental age. From their 1905 scale, Binet and Simon obviously concluded that judgment, reasoning, and comprehension were three components of intelligent behavior. With the concept of mental age, however, a further idea was introduced. The normal child of a stated age was expected to pass a certain number of items on the scale (as based on the performance of the standardization population). With increasing age, he or she was expected to pass even more of the items. Hence, the idea that intelligence increases with age. If the child exceeded the number of items considered normal for the age group, he or she was above average. By contrast, if fewer items than expected were passed, the child was below average.

Unfortunately, this approach to intelligence testing is limited for an important reason: after a certain age (usually eighteen), intelligence stops increasing steadily. In fact, some data show that the concept of mental age actually begins to break down shortly after age thirteen (cf. Terman & Merrill, 1960). Matarazzo (1972) points out that ". . . although the means of the actual test scores continue to increase with age above that age, they do so by progressively diminishing and ultimately increase by negligible amounts" (p. 95). However, at the lower age levels, conceiving of intelligence as a steadily increasing power certainly does make sense.

The original Binet-Simon Scale has been revised many times (e.g., 1908, 1911, 1916, 1937, 1969, 1973) and is now known as the Stanford-Binet Intelligence Scale.[2] Until recently the concept of mental age was used in calculating the IQ score. Thus, IQ was obtained by using the following formula:

$$IQ = \frac{\text{mental age}}{\text{chronological age}} \times 100$$

2. Beginning with the 1916 revision, the test is known as the Stanford-Binet.

Mental age refers to the basal age (i.e., highest age level at which all six of the tests for a year level are passed) plus scores for each test passed beyond the basal age. Since there are six tests per one year level, each test passed is credited with 2 points. For example, a child of 8 who attains a mental age of 8 (8/8 × 100) would have an IQ of 100. A child of 8 who attains a mental age of 12 (12/8 × 100) would have an IQ of 150. A child of 8 who attains a mental age of 6 (6/8 × 100) would have an IQ of 75.

Between the publication of the Binet-Simon Scale and the development of the Wechsler-Bellevue Scale (WB-I) in the 1930s, many controversies arose on the nature of intelligence. Spearman (1904, 1927) believed intelligence to be a general factor (*g*) underlying all cognitive activities, with some secondary components (S1, S2, S3, etc.) referred to as *specifics*. Thorndike and his colleagues (1927) were most critical of the evidence in favor of *g*. Instead, they interpreted their own test data as reflecting many specific abilities. Still later, Thurstone and Thurstone (1941), as a result of their factor analytic investigations, identified several factors they called *primary mental abilities*. These included such things as work fluency, facility with numbers, memory, verbal meaning, reasoning, perceptual speed, and spatial relations. However, each of these factors also seemed to consist of high levels of Spearman's *g*. Therefore, the work of Thurstone and Thurstone directly supported both Spearman's and Thorndike's positions.

Historically, there were two issues: Did *g* really exist in general intelligence? If so, how important was it? Other issues were also hotly debated: For example, was the IQ score constant? How did environment and heredity influence IQ level? Indeed, these two controversies are still raging some four to five decades later (cf. Cronbach, 1975). It might be noted that the position of a given theorist often was—and still probably is—very much colored by the type of intelligence test used, the population tested, and the statistical manipulations of the data. Thus, many of the controversies were sparked by differences in methodology.

Still more recently, Wechsler (1958) has described intelligence as "the aggregate or global capacity of the individual to act purposely, to think rationally, and to deal effectively with his environment" (p. 7). This definition clearly indicates that Wechsler sees intelligence as consisting of many diverse abilities, including nonintellectual ones (i.e., performance). Also, from Wechsler's perspective, intelligence is not static; it can be affected by motivational and psychopathological factors. Thus, Wechsler theorized, based on his clinical observations, that certain test patterns would emerge in accordance with the client's diagnostic classification. This is known as *pattern analysis*.

In addition to developing a broader definition of intelligence than his predecessors, Wechsler abandoned the notion of mental age. Instead, on the Wechsler scales IQ is calculated with a formula called a *deviation quotient*. The mean score is set at 100, with a standard deviation of 15. Similarly, for each subtest the mean is set at 10, with a standard deviation of 3. Matarazzo (1972) gives the advantages of these categories: "In the first place, they define levels of intelligence strictly in terms of standard deviation units and hence can be interpreted unequivocally. Second, they dispense with the necessity of making any assumptions with regard to the precise relation between mental and chronological rate of growth, and in particular the linearity of the relation. Third, they dispense with the need of committing oneself to a fixed point beyond which scores are assumed to be unaffected by age" (pp. 104–105). In fact, the 1960 revision of the Stanford-Binet has also substituted a deviation quotient for the mental age formula, with a mean of 100 and a standard deviation of 16 for each age level.

The Stanford-Binet Test

Although the Stanford-Binet has declined in use, it still remains one of the major intelligence tests for children (see Table 4.1). It is generally used with children between the ages of two and six, usually administered by a qualified clinical or educational psychologist or possibly a supervised paraprofessional. The test generally takes one hour. Conditions are comfortable, with a well-lit room and table and chairs at an appropriate height for the child.

After establishing rapport with the child, the examiner begins at an age level somewhat lower than the child's chronological age. Thus, for a six-year-old child, the examiner might start at the four-year level. The Stanford-Binet, as noted above, is an age scale, with the tests for each age level ordered with increasing difficulty. For example, one of the six items at the two-year-old level involves the child pointing to various parts of a paper doll's body. At the five-year-old level, one of the items is concerned with definitions of simple vocabulary words. At age ten, one of the items requires definitions of abstract words.

As previously noted, the highest age level at which all tests are *passed* is called the *basal age*. Once the basal age is established, the examiner progresses up the scale until all tests for a given age level are *failed*. This is known as the *ceiling age*. At that point, the testing is complete.

Although the Stanford-Binet is often given to young children, a major disadvantage is that only one IQ score is obtained. In contrast, on the Wechsler scales, total, verbal, and performance IQs are obtained. More recently, Sattler (1974) has developed a scoring system whereby test items on the Stanford-Binet are grouped into seven abilities. Unfortunately, the utility and validity of this system are questionable (cf. Lahey & Johnson, 1978, p. 171).

Various aspects of the Stanford-Binet are reviewed in a large research literature, beginning with the first edition of the test in 1916. Research on each of the revisions has received periodic review. Himelstein (1966) reviewed the first five years of research on the 1960 revision (Form L-M). Some of his conclusions are as follows:

1. Validity is based primarily on correlations with other tests (i.e., concurrent validity). Studies involving predictive validity are definitely lacking.
2. Evidence for reliability (correlations between items and the total score) is relatively poor at the lower ages but much better at the upper ages. One study on test-retest reliability yielded an *r* of 0.88 for young retarded children. The test-retest interval here was one year.
3. Test scores are affected by outside influences (e.g., sex of the examiner).
4. Very few studies dealt with the entire range of intelligence. In summary, the psychometric properties of the 1960 revision are definitely not as good as would be expected for so popular a test.

The Wechsler Scales

We have already pointed out some of the disadvantages of the Stanford-Binet test. David Wechsler's work, spanning several decades, has focused on the development of still better intelligence tests. Thus, Wechsler dropped the notion of mental age in favor of the deviation quotient. Also consistent with his views of intelligence, all of the Wechsler tests have separate verbal, performance, and total IQ scores. However, as with the Stanford-Binet, each test requires about one hour and should be given by a qualified individual.

The Wechsler Adult Intelligence Scale (WAIS), formerly the Wechsler-Bellevue Scale (WB-I), was introduced in 1955. The WB-I had appeared earlier in 1939 and 1944. The Wechsler Intelligence Scale for Children (WISC) is a downward revision of the WAIS and first appeared in 1949. Finally, the Wechsler Preschool and Primary Scales of Intelligence (WPPSI) are a downward revision of the WISC and were first published in 1967. The subtests for the verbal and performance Scales of the three Wechsler tests and the age group for each test are shown in Table 4.3.

Wechsler has also developed a classification scheme based on the percentage of the standardization group obtaining a particular total IQ score. This system, although widely used, is somewhat different than the one adhered to by the American Association of Mental Deficiency. Wechsler's classification of intelligence is presented in Table 4.4.

It should be noted that Wechsler's work arose from his experiences as a clinical psychologist at Bellevue Hospital (associated with the New York University School of Medicine) in New York City. Not surprisingly, Wechsler was interested in a client's qualitative (i.e., clinical) aspects of performance in addition to the objectively obtained IQ. The clinical interpretation of Wechsler's tests has been carefully studied by David Rapaport and his students (e.g., Holt, 1968). Specifically, Wechsler had

Table 4.3. Subtests for WPPSI, WISC, and WAIS

WPPSI (ages 4–6-½)	WISC (ages 7–16)	WAIS (ages 16–75 and over)
Verbal Scales		
Information	Information	Information
Comprehension	Comprehension	Comprehension
Arithmetic	Arithmetic	Arithmetic
Similarities	Similarities	Similarities
Vocabulary	Vocabulary	Vocabulary
Digit span	(Digit span)[a]	(Sentences)[a]
Performance Scales		
Block design	Block design	Block design
Picture completion	Picture completion	Picture completion
Picture arrangement	Picture arrangement	Animal house
Object assembly	Object assembly	Mazes
Digit symbol	Coding (mazes)[a]	Geometric design

[a]Parentheses refer to subtests that may be used as alternates or supplements during the test. However, unless one of the regular subtests is "spoiled," only the standard subtests are given.

Table 4.4. Wechsler's Classification of Intelligence

Total IQ	Classification	Percentage
130 and above	"Very Superior"	2.2
120–129	"Superior"	6.7
110–119	"Bright–Normal"	16.1
90–109	"Average"	50.0
80–89	"Dull–Normal"	16.1
70–79	"Borderline"	6.7
69 and below	"Mental Defective"	2.2

several contentions, based on his clinical observations, as to what the different patterns of scores on each subtest meant clinically (i. e., scatter or pattern analysis). He also assigns diagnostic significance to large verbal-performance and performance-verbal discrepancies on the WB-I and the WAIS. So far, there is no research support for many of these hypotheses (cf. Cronbach, 1970).

Indeed, Cronbach argues that "The simple interpretation of test profiles that Wechsler originally suggested has been replaced by other types of thinking. No rule can transform a Wechsler profile into a psychiatric diagnosis, and such an interpretation would in any event be inappropriate for normal children and adults. But it is highly suggestive to observe that a subject hesitates on an easy item when it follows a previous failure, or that he adequately repeats a string of digits but becomes confused when asked to repeat a somewhat simpler string backward. These observations, combined with the tester's clinical experience and theoretical knowledge, suggest a picture of the individual much richer than the IQ alone provides" (p. 207). Cronbach then points out that scores on Wechsler tests clearly reflect personal and environmental reactions (e.g., "anxiety, self confidence, desire to impress the tester") to the test situation. This being the case, the final IQ number is a composite of many features: "intelligence," experience, possible psychopathology, and others.

The Wechsler scales, like the Stanford-Binet, have been widely researched, and the research reviewed periodically either in journal (e.g., Guertin, Ladd, Frank, Rabin, & Hiester, 1971; Littell, 1960) or book form (e.g., Matarazzo, 1972). While a complete survey is beyond the scope of this chapter, we will present some of the primary conclusions of these reviews.

1. Although the Wechsler scales are generally well standardized, there are not enough separate norms for minority populations.
2. Validity of the scales is based primarily on concurrent and construct validity. Too few studies have been concerned with predictive validity.
3. Because of the only moderate split-half and test-retest reliabilities of the individual performance subtests, the rationale for pattern analysis is questionable.
4. Split-half and test-retest reliabilities for the three tests improve progressively as one goes up the age level for each of the Wechsler tests.
5. The rationale for the WISC and WPPSI is considered less adequate than that for the WAIS. Thus, construct validity is considered superior for the WAIS compared to the other two tests.
6. There is some question as to whether the individual subtests are appropriately categorized in the Verbal and Performance Scales. Some of the performance subtests appear to correlate better with the verbal IQ score than with the performance IQ score.
7. A diagnosis of organicity on the basis of large verbal-performance scale discrepancies (i.e., 15 points or more) is questionable, since such a gross diagnostic label cannot pinpoint cerebral dysfunction. Indeed, anxiety and depression may also sometimes account for a large verbal-performance discrepancy.

Group Testing

The old adage "Necessity is the mother of invention" definitely applies to the situations created by World Wars I and II. In these periods, what was needed was an assessment tool whereby millons of men in the armed forces could be rapidly classified by intellectual level. Prior to the U.S. entry into World War I, this task fell to such luminaries as Yerkes, Terman, Boring, and Otis. They were to develop a test that was at once reliable, valid, and easily and quickly administered. What emerged was the Army Alpha (Yoakum & Yerkes, 1920), a group-administered test of intelligence for literates. The parallel Army Beta (Yerkes, 1921) test was developed for illiterates and non-English-speaking recruits. According to Matarazzo (1972), between September 1917 and January 1919 more than 1,750,000 recruits were given the Army Alpha test.

With the coming of World War II, a new test, the Army General Classification Test (AGCT), was developed. With the millions of military recruits, huge amounts of data were amassed. Thus, it became clear that intelligence really was distributed across the normal curve. Also, with so much data, intellectual level could be correlated with civilian occupation (cf. Harrell & Harrell, 1945). It should be noted that in two studies (Tammimen, 1951; Watson & Klett, 1968) substantial correlations between the AGCT and the WAIS ($r = 0.74$) and the AGCT and WB-I ($r = 0.83$) were reported.

Despite these impressive results, a group test of intelligence is never as precise as the individually administered test. Moreover, qualitative observations made during individual testing are impossible with a group. On the other hand, the group test may be given by a nonprofessional, is easily scored (usually by machine), and takes relatively little time. However, a major problem is that availability and interpretation of scores are often left to unskilled clerks (cf. Cronbach, 1970; Matarazzo, 1972).

Between the world wars and after World War II, many other group intelligence tests were developed and published. All of them, however, suffer from the limitations described above.

Current Issues

Two troublesome issues concerning intelligence have persisted for several decades. The more explosive of these began with an article by Jensen (1969) in the *Harvard Educational Review* entitled "How Much Can We Boost IQ and Scholastic Achievement?" A small part of this article dealt with the relative importance of genetic and environmental factors in determining IQ. The statement which led to public exposure, rebuttal, controversies, and personal harassment was as follows: "The preponderance of the evidence is, in my opinion, less consistent with a strictly environmental hypothesis than with a genetic hypothesis, which, of course, does not exclude the influence of environment . . . (p. 82). This statement was widely interpreted to reflect racial bias, particularly since blacks (primarily because of socioeconomic disadvantages) typically score lower than whites on standardized IQ tests (see Matarazzo, 1972).

This brings us to the second issue, which is closely related to the first: Do IQ tests discriminate against blacks and other disadvantaged minority groups? The answer is obviously yes. WAIS and WISC questions, for example, are clearly directed toward the interests and ideals of the white middle-class majority. The background knowledge needed to answer these questions would be relatively unimportant to black or

Chicano adolescents trying to survive in their ghettoes. In fact, a test known as the BITCH (Black Intelligence Test of Cultural Homogeneity) has been developed (partly in jest and partly as social commentary) which most middle-class whites would probably fail.[3] Correct responses presuppose a knowledge of the black ghetto experience. As might be expected, Blacks do much better than whites on this test.

Questions, then, as to innate black inferiority on intelligence tests are absurd. This is so not only because of their white middle-class bias but for several other reasons as well. First, IQ scores are hardly fixed; they can be influenced by examiner factors and client motivation. Consider, for example, Clingman and Fowler's (1976) finding that primary reinforcement applied contingently led to increased IQ scores in initially low-scoring subjects. Middle- and high-scoring subjects were unaffected by such reinforcement. Second, and probably most important, since there are *no culture-free tests* (this is simply an illusion of test constructors), an IQ test is always biased—especially since the universe of items selected will reflect the test constructor's own background and interests. Third, most IQ tests so far have no outstanding predictive validity.

What is the solution, then? Should IQ tests be discontinued? Some obviously say yes. Others (e.g., McClelland, 1973) talk about testing for "competence" rather than "intelligence." Probably the most reasonable solution is found in the "Guidelines for Testing Minority Group Children," which appeared in the April 1964 supplement to the *Journal of Social Issues:*

> In testing the minority group child it is sometimes appropriate to compare his performance with that of advantaged children to determine the magnitude of deprivation to be overcome. At other times it is appropriate to compare his test performance with that of other disadvantaged children to determine his relative deprivation in comparison with others who have also been denied good homes, good neighborhoods, good diets, good schools, and good teachers. In most instances it is especially appropriate to compare the child's test performance with his previous test performance. Utilizing the individual child as his own control and using the test norms principally as "bench marks" we are best able to gauge the success of our efforts to move the minority group child forward on the long, hard road of overcoming the deficiencies which have been forced upon him.

3. This test is available from Robert L. Williams & Associates, Inc., Educational & Psychological Services, 6374 Delmar Blvd., Suite 204, St. Louis, Missouri 63130.

Many comparisons depend on tests, but they also depend upon *our* intelligence, our good will, and our sense of responsibility to make the proper comparison at the proper time and to undertake proper remedial and compensatory action as a result. The misuse of tests with minority children, or in any situation, is a serious breach of professional ethics. Their proper use is a sign of professional and personal maturity (SPSSI, 1964, p. 144).

Thus, the real issue is not psychometric or genetic in origin. Rather, "The remedy may lie in elimination of unequal learning opportunities, which may remove the bias in the criterion as well as in the test" (SPSSI, 1964, p. 138). This is a laudable social goal which, unfortunately, has not yet been achieved.

Projective Tests

Over the last two decades, one of the most disputed areas in clinical psychology has been the value of projective tests. In spite of the several thousand case reports, research papers, review papers, chapters, and books about projectives (cf. Exner, 1976), responses to the conflicting data are often almost religious in quality. There are the believers and the nonbelievers. The believers are generally untouched by the negative research findings and offer many rationalizations. Similarly, those aspects of projectives that appear to have some reliability and validity (see Goldfried, Stricker, & Weiner, 1971) are dismissed by the nonbelievers. Thus, the response to projective tests seems to be more emotional than rational.

Against this background, we will try to define the projective test, describe its various categories, look at some of the popular tests a bit more closely, and examine some of the problems in doing research with projective tests. (Further discussion of research findings appears in Chapter 5).

Let us first define projective tests. According to Hinsie and Campbell's (1970) *Psychiatric Dictionary,* a projective test is one "in which the test material presented to the subject is such that any response will necessarily be determined by his own prevailing mood or underlying psychopathology" (p. 159). Carr (1964) points out that "an essential characteristic of projective techniques is that they are unstructured in that cues for appropriate action are not clearly specified and the individual must give meaning to [interpret] such stimuli in accordance with his own inner needs, drives, defenses, impulses—in short, according to the dictates of his own personality. Whether the stimuli are inkblots . . . or ambiguous pictures . . . the patient's task is to impose or project his own structure and meaning onto materials which have relatively little meaning or structure and which, in a purely objective sense, are only inkblots or ambiguous pictures" (p. 774).

Many authors (e.g., Goldenberg, 1973) have outlined the unique features of the projective test. First is the unstructured nature of the materials themselves. Thus, the client is usually unable to judge what constitutes a good or poor response. For this reason, projective tests should be most difficult to fake in either direction (i.e., health or psychopathology). Second, projective tests are presumed to tap preconscious or unconscious determinants of the personality. Third, in light of the subjective nature of the responses to these unstructured materials, these responses are often interpreted subjectively—and differ widely from one examiner to the next. These interpretive differences may also result from the various scoring systems used for the same test.

Historical Developments

Prior to the work of Carl Jung (the eminent Swiss psychiatrist, who initially was a disciple of Freud) at the beginning of the twentieth century on his Word Association Test, there had been a few tests with certain features of projective techniques. However, the Word Association Test was the first of the projective techniques as we know them today. A similar Word Association Test was published by Kent and Rosanoff (1910) in the *American Journal of Insanity,* the predecessor of the *American Journal of Psychiatry.*

The next landmark in the field was Hermann Rorschach's (also a Swiss psychiatrist) publication of his *Psychodiagnostik* (Rorschach, 1921), on the diagnostic use of the now famous inkblot test. Although Rorschach died while still in his thirties, several of his students carried on the tradition. The test was brought to the United States in the mid 1920s, with several subsequent doctoral dissertations on the topic (e.g., Beck, Hertz). Bruno Klopfer, a prominent Rorschacher, emigrated to the United States in 1934, promoting the test via his writings and lectures. Klopfer founded the journal the *Rorschach Research Exchange,* later called the *Journal of Projective Techniques* and now entitled the *Journal of Personality Assessment.*

Another significant development was the Thematic Apperception Test (TAT), published in 1935 by Morgan and Murray (1935). Many other projective tests later appeared, including figure drawing tests and the sentence completion approaches. In the 1940s, tests such as the WB-I and the Bender-Gestalt, originally developed to measure intelligence and possible organic impairment, were used as projective techniques as well. The proliferation of projective tests continued through the 1940s and 1950s. Psychoanalytically oriented practitioners, in particular, promoted their use, supposedly to identify certain unconscious dynamics of their clients. Thus, the theoretical basis of the tests dovetailed with the theoretical nature of the treatment technique.

The decline of the projectives (see the prior section) probably began in the 1960s as the psychotherapeutic role of the clinical psychologist grew. We also believe that the move toward greater objectivity in personality measurement, fueled in part by the behavioral movement (see also Chapter 5), contributed to the decline in the routine application of projectives.

Categories

The projective tests developed over the years have been categorized by Lindzey (1961) (see Table 4.5). His classification is based on the response that the test elicits from the client. For example, in the *association techniques* the client is asked to free-associate to stimulus words (Word Association Test) or stimulus blots (Rorschach or Holtzman Inkblot tests).

By contrast, in the *construction techniques,* best exemplified by the TAT, the client is expected to make up a story in response to scenes printed on cards, which often suggest interpersonal conflict or stress. The next category, *completion techniques,* consists of asking the client to *complete* the stems or beginnings of sentences (e.g., I always . . .). Although officially called projective tests, it is unclear whether sentence completion tasks are really projective, since they contain little ambiguity. The task may be clear to the client.

The Szondi Test, developed by a Hungarian psychiatrist, can be called an *ordering technique.*[4] In contrast to most of the projectives, the

---

4. The test is now rarely given, particularly in light of its questionable rationale and its doubtful diagnostic utility.

Table 4.5.   Classification of Projective Tests

Classification	Tests
Association techniques	Word Association Test Rorschach Holtzman Inkblot Test
Construction techniques	Thematic Apperception Test (TAT) Children's Apperception Test (CAT) Blacky Test
Completion techniques	Rotter Incomplete Sentence Blank Sacks Sentence Completion Test Holsopple and Meale Sentence Completion Test
Ordering techniques	Szondi Test
Expressive techniques	Draw-A-Person Test (DAP) House-Tree-Person Test (H–T–P)

range of responses and the amount of spontaneity permitted the client are limited. The client is asked to select, order, and categorize from the stimulus materials, which consist of forty-eight pictures (six sets of eight) of different kinds of mental patients. "The subject is presented with the single series consecutively, with instructions to choose the two pictures from each set that he likes most and the two he dislikes most. Thus, finally, twelve pictures are chosen as liked and twelve described as disliked. These twenty-four choices are recorded graphically in the form of a test profile" (Deri, 1959, p. 300).

Finally, there are the *expressive techniques*. Here the client is given maximum freedom of expression. In the case of the figure drawings, the client is given paper and pencil and asked to draw a person. Then, he or she may be asked to draw a person of the opposite sex. Other than that, the instructions are minimized, giving the client almost no structure but allowing considerable initiative.

Test Descriptions

In this section we will briefly describe the stimulus materials, method of testing, and scoring techniques for some of the more popular projective tests. Let us start with the Rorschach. This test consists of ten cards depicting bilateral symmetrical inkblots which are presented in standard order. Cards, 1, 4, 5, 6, and 7 are gray and black on a white background. Cards 2 and 3 are gray, black, and red on a white background. And cards 8, 9, and 10 are multicolored on a white background.

Instructions given to a client vary somewhat by examiner but generally consist of the following: "I am going to show you some cards that have inkblots on them. I would like you to tell me what you see or what they look like to you." Occasionally a client may refuse to participate or may indicate that he sees nothing but inkblots. However, most will give fifteen to thirty responses; some, of course, see more than one percept per inkblot. As might be expected, both obsessive and more intelligent clients will give more responses. Responses to the first part of the test are known as the *free association.*

The examiner records what the client says in response to each inkblot, as well as latency (using a stopwatch) for the first association to each inkblot. Total time for the complete test is also recorded.

After the ten inkblots are shown, the examiner again presents the cards to determine what aspects of the inkblots contributed to each response. This part of the test, known as the *inquiry,* facilitates scoring of the responses.

An example of a Rorschach test protocol appears in Table 4.6. It was obtained by Hersen in 1969 when he was in private practice and still used projective techniques for evaluating clients. Note the free association and inquiry for each response, as well as the initial response latency for each inkblot.

Although there are some scoring conventions for the Rorschach, several different scoring systems have been promoted by various Rorschach experts (e.g., Klopfer, Beck, Hertz, Piotrowski, Rapaport, Exner). However, despite the differences, there are great similarities. Scores are first determined for the *location* of the blot—the part of the blot used by the client in responding (i.e., whole part, large part, small part, etc.). A second category is the *determinant* of the percept—for example, color, form, shading, or some combination of the three. Third is the *content.* The list of content determinants is extensive and includes people, animals, and inorganic objects. Fourth is whether the percept reported is commonly seen by others. Thus, the response can be scored as a popular (e.g., a bat for Card 1) or an unusual response (e.g., a mountain path leading to a castle for the same card). And fifth is the issue of *form level.* This is determined by judging whether the response

Table 4.6.   Rorschach Protocol for a 16-Year-Old Female Paranoid Schizophrenic

Free Association		Inquiry
I		*2 sec*
1.	looks like a bat	body, wings, getting ready to attack
2.	butterfly	an enlarged butterfly—it's dead, it's mounted in a collection wing, not flying—therefore dead
3.	an x-ray	form, the shape just the way it is just inside of somebody
II		*11 sec*
1.	looks like internal bleeding	the red is blood and hemorrhages
III		*9 sec*
1.	looks like two people thinking about the same things in their mind	hearts going out to each other marks are the same on each side—they're having telepathy—man and a woman
IV		*36 sec*
1.	looks like an animal shedding his skin	prehistoric animal doesn't look like anything else looks like something somebody drew when they were depressed
V		*30 sec*
1.	reincarnated after death as a bat again	faint outline of person inside the outline of it—looking for somebody he knew before he died

appears to fit the stimulus blot. For example, the response to the card I in Table 4.6 (looks like a bat) would be scored an F+ (good form level). On the other hand, the response to Card X (a stomach ache) is a highly personalized percept that has very poor form level (F–).

Thus, a typical Rorschach protocol generates many scores under several categories. Exner (1976) notes that "Once responses are scored, frequency tallies are developed for each kind of score, and numerous ratios and percentages are calculated. These ratios and percentages represent the Structural Summary of the Rorschach and provide a very important interpretation of the test" (p. 84).

Despite its scoring systems, the Rorschach is often interpreted on an impressionistic level. In these more casual interpretations, certain

Table 4.6.   (*Continued*)

Free Association		Inquiry
VI		*11 sec*
1.	cancer under a microscope	because it's ugly— everything
VII		*13 sec*
1.	two angels on a cloud	earth down there wings clouds—they are fluffy
VIII		*20 sec*
1.	two parasites inside of somebody	the organs—liver and the pancreas they're diabolical
IX		*17 sec*
1.	somebody's brain exploding	the tissue it's my imagination that makes it look like brains
X		*18 sec*
1.	a stomach ache	all the things are the bacteria and germs that cause it looks like germs because they're deadly, the esophagus, the stomach

standard symbols are especially important (e.g., caves = womb; elongated objects = phallus). In this connection, Schafer (1948) refers to shading responses in schizophrenics as reflecting chronicity or the potential for "panic attacks with bizarre features" (p. 79).

TAT. Let us now look at the TAT. This test consists of thirty pictures, the majority of which depict people either alone or together. There are enough cards so that the test can be tailored to male or female clients ranging from children to adults. Although Murray (1943) originally suggested that at least twenty of the cards be administered in two one-hour sessions on different days, this requires too much time.[5] Therefore, most practitioners use only eight to ten of the cards and in one sitting.

As with the Rorschach, several types of instructions are given to the client. Again, however, these instructions have a common ground. For

5. One of these cards (No. 16) is blank; here the client is asked to imagine a scenario and then make up a story.

example, Bellak (1959) suggests the following: "I am going to show you some pictures and should like you to tell me stories about what is going on in each picture, what led up to it, and what the outcome will be. I want you to make it lively and full of drama and let yourself go freely" (pp. 188–189). Many examiners often omit the second sentence and ask clients to make up a story containing the past, present, and future.

Table 4.7 contains two stories in response to Card 1. Objectively, this card involves a young boy sitting with a violin and bow in front of him. Before examining the themes in each of the stories, let us consider how the TAT is scored and analyzed.

As noted by Exner (1976), several scoring systems have emerged. Some consist of rating scales to evaluate the stories; others classify the stories; still others relate the stories obtained to those originally noted in the normative sample. Also, many examiners simply evaluate the story content impressionistically (cf. Wade & Baker, 1977). In the TAT manual (Murray, 1943), a form of content analysis is described involving the "hero," motives, trends, and feelings of the "hero," and a variety of "needs and presses" contributing to the outcome of the story. In summary, no single evaluation system is universally accepted or practiced.

Returning now to Table 4.7, note the qualitative differences in the two stories. In the first, there is a question of the "hero" (i.e., little boy) "measuring up" to Father. Here Father appears to be admired. However, meeting his expectations (implicit) seems to be very difficult—indeed, almost futile. In the second story, there seems to be greater conflict between son and father. The son does give in to the father's demands, but in later years pursues his own interests with success. Initial

Table 4.7.   Stories to Card 1 of the TAT

---

1. This is a little boy who is looking at his violin, and he's wondering if he will ever be able to play the violin as well as Daddy. And he's wondering whether or not all the practice he puts in will ever make him as good as Daddy. He's about to start practicing; he's not too pleased with the idea because the task he has set up is to be as good as Daddy. But he has great doubts. He practices and practices, and never becomes as good as Daddy, and he becomes a football player.

2. This little boy is looking at the violin. He would much rather be playing baseball. But his father expects him to practice at least two hours a day. After thinking a while, he forces himself to practice. If he doesn't, he might get punished. He becomes quite good, but after college becomes a very successful lawyer.

---

compliance with Father results from punishment or the perceived threat of punishment.

The casual interpretation mentioned earlier typifies the way the TAT is often analyzed clinically. The clinician looks for themes that occur and recur throughout the various stories that are constructed. He or she looks for both consistencies and inconsistencies, and then "paints" a picture of the personality in the test report.

Rotter Incomplete Sentences Blank (ISB). The Rotter ISB (Rotter & Rafferty, 1950) is one of many sentence-completion tests. The advantage of Rotter's test, however, is that it is short (forty sentence stems), relatively well standardized, and has a nicely defined scoring method. Moreover, there are several forms of the test suitable for different populations (e.g., high school and college forms). Some of the sentence stems and the responses given by a twenty-two-year-old hospitalized male alcoholic appear in Table 4.8.

Since the Rotter test items appear on both sides of a printed sheet, administration is easy and can also be done on a group basis. Written instructions to the client are as follows: "Complete these sentences to express *your real feelings. Try to do every one.* Be sure to make a complete sentence" (Rotter & Rafferty, 1950, p. 5). Generally the test can be completed within fifteen to twenty minutes.

Sentences are scored on a 0 to 6 point basis. Thus, the total score on the Rotter ISB may range from 0 to 240. *Positive* responses to sentence stems are scored as 0–2. *Neutral* responses are scored as a 3. *Conflict* responses indicative of maladjustment, unhappiness, symptomatic distress, hostility, and so on are scored from 4 to 6. Therefore, the higher the total score, the greater the degree of maladjustment. However, in

Table 4.8.   Sentence Stems from Rotter ISB with Responses from an Alcoholic Patient

No.	Stem	Response
5.	*I regret*	"drinking and trouble, I've caused."
13.	*My greatest fear*	"is the love & fear of God."
18.	*My nerves*	"aren't so good since being here."
21.	*I failed*	"to do my duty more than once."
29.	*What pains me*	"is not being free."

From: Rotter & Rafferty (1950), p. 38.

spite of the numerical score, Rotter and Rafferty (1950) acknowledge that "For the clinician working directly with cases, the qualitative interpretation of the records will be of considerably more interest than a numerical score of adjustment. For such purposes no specific method of interpretation is recommended. The clinician's use of the materials will depend on his experience, his level of training, and his theoretical orientation" (p. 30).

Research Problems

The staggering number of research studies on projective techniques show clearly that the results are equivocal at best (see Zubin, Eron, Schumer, 1965). It is equally clear that no broad generalizations and conclusions can be made. As Exner (1976) has correctly argued:

> any attempt to discuss the merits or deficiencies of projective methods *in general* is probably doomed from the onset. The history of some of the methods has been marked by considerable success in both clinical and research endeavors, whereas other methods have been subject to disparate and limited use. In many instances the controversies that have erupted concerning a given instrument have been founded largely on bias rather than on science and, altogether too often, criticisms of a single technique have been naively generalized to encompass all projective methodology. Consequently, it seems important to stress that each method should be evaluated *in and of itself* rather than under some broad umbrella that includes all inkblot methods, all apperception techniques, all sentence completion blanks or all projective techniques (pp. 107–108).

In light of Exner's warning, we certainly will not attempt to review the merits and demerits of projective tests in general. Nor will we review the pluses and minuses of individual projective devices. Rather, we will look at the research problems in this area in light of psychometric considerations.

One of the first research problems with some projectives is that the standard techniques or strategies often do not seem to apply. For example, it would not make sense to attempt a split-half reliability estimate with a test like the Rorschach; the two halves cannot be compared. The Rorschach was not developed with the psychometric tradition in mind. Even with the TAT, such reliability estimates would make little sense either clinically or psychometrically. It would be very difficult to match two sets of TAT cards that would have equal "pull" for a given type of story. On the other hand, a test such as the Rotter ISB, which is amenable to standard psychometric evaluation, does seem to have respectable split-half reliability (see Rotter & Rafferty, 1950).

Returning now to the Rorschach, research here is difficult since the number of responses varies greatly from subject to subject. It is for this reason, and for many other psychometric considerations, that the Holtzman Inkblot Techniques (HIT) was developed (Holtzman, Thorpe, Swartz, & Herron, 1961). The HIT has two well-matched parallel sets of forty-five inkblots (derived from a careful item analysis). Thus, parallel form reliability estimates are possible. Also, only one response per blot is expected. However, despite the greater psychometric sophistication of the HIT, two problems remain (cf. Gamble, 1972). First, the relative merits of the Rorschach and the HIT have not really been evaluated. Second, and perhaps as important, the HIT has not achieved the popularity of the Rorschach, even though it is constructed in the best psychometric tradition.

Still another problem in evaluating projective tests is the sheer amount of instructions given clients for any one test, not to mention the array of scoring systems. Given these inconsistencies, any meaningful inter-study comparisons are difficult to make. This overall lack of standardization is a major stumbling block in this research area.

Finally there is the issue of interpretation. If responses to the Rorschach or TAT are interpreted clinically at a symbolic level, for any one client the unique interpretation may be internally consistent with other data available to the examiner. However, since such symbolism is basically idiosyncratic, when studies are conducted with many subjects (i.e., controlled group comparisons), the importance of the symbolism may be "washed out" in the statistical analysis. As argued by Weiner (1977), "This point is important to keep in mind, because many presumed negative validity studies with the Rorschach have addressed the generality of symbolic interpretations, and critics of the Rorschach have typically focused on symbolic interpretations in arguing that the instrument can neither be validated nor given credence by serious behavioral scientists" (p. 605). This would argue in favor of the single-case approach to specified research problems (cf. Hersen & Barlow, 1976). Nonetheless, proponents of such symbolic interpretations, using single-case analyses, might well document their clinical hypotheses. To date, unfortunately, this has not materialized.

Objective Personality Assessment

In differentiating objective from projective testing, some writers (e.g., Gynther & Gynther, 1976) are fond of quoting Kelly (1958): "When the subject is asked to guess what the examiner is thinking, we call it an objective test; when the examiner tries to guess what the subject is thinking, we call it a projective device" (p. 332). Kelly's amusing definition suggests that some of the "differences" between the two strategies may be more illusory than real. However, objective personality assessment *does* have some unique characteristics. First, all the objective tests are self-report tests filled out by the client, usually with several hundred items per test. Second, items often are presented in a true-false format. Third, the many items are divided into different scales, each presumably measuring separate aspects of the personality. These scales are then graphed to form a clearly delineated personality profile. Fourth, corrective factors are built into the test for ascertaining the client's test-taking attitudes (e.g., faking good or bad). Fifth, many of the objective tests can be machine-scored. Sixth, computer-assisted interpretations of test patterns are available.

Since the first appearance of Woodworth's (1920) *Personal Data Sheet,* many other objective personality tests have been published and marketed in the United States and England. A partial list of these tests appears in Table 4.9. Of the tests listed, the Minnesota Multiphasic Personality Inventory (MMPI) is by far the most popular. Since the original publication of the MMPI, more than 6,000 articles on it have appeared (cf. Gynther & Gynther, 1976), with 100 new ones still being published every year (Cronbach, 1970). Given space limitations, we will therefore focus on the MMPI.

The MMPI

The full-length MMPI contains 566 items, which comprise the various scales of the test (see Table 4.10).[6] Some of the items appear in more than one scale, thus probably accounting for substantial correlations between many of the scales (e.g., Scales 7 and 8). Scales L, F, and K are

6. Several abbreviated forms of the MMPI have been developed that correlate moderately well with the entire test (Hugo, 1971; Kincannon, 1968).

Table 4.9.   Objective Personality Tests

Test	Reference
Minnesota Multiphasic Personality Inventory (MMPI)	Hathaway & McKinley (1942)
Temperament Survey Factor	Guilford & Zimmerman (1949)
Sixteen Personality Factor Questionnaire (16PF)	Cattell (1949)
California Psychology Inventory (CPI)	Gough (1957)
Eysenck Personality Inventory (EPI)	Eysenck & Eysenck (1968)
Edwards Personality Inventory (EPI)	Edwards (1967)

known as the "validity" scales and are indicative of the client's test-taking attitude. The K Scale is a correction factor for the client's defensiveness. Scales 1 to 4 and 6 to 9 are the original clinical scales and the basis of the test. Scales 5 and 0 were developed later, as were many other scales (for both research and clinical purposes) from among the common pool of items. Among the scales that have emerged over the years are those that presume to tap anxiety, "ego-strength," and "repression-sensitization."

In addition to the formal scales indicated in Table 4.10, the number of items (if any) not responded to by the client is presented as a ? score.

Table 4.10.   MMPI Scales

Scale	Scale No.	Abbreviation	Items
Lie		L	15
Frequency		F	64
Correction		K	30
Hypochondriasis	1	Hs	33
Depression	2	D	60
Hysteria	3	Hy	60
Psychopathic deviancy	4	Pd	50
Masculinity-femininity	5	Mf	60
Paranoia	6	Pa	40
Psychasthenia	7	Pt	48
Schizophrenia	8	Sc	78
Hypomania	9	Ma	46
Social introversion-extroversion	0	Si	70

The ? score and the scales listed in Table 4.10 are summarized graphically in a *Profile and Case Summary* (see Figure 4.1). Raw scores are turned into standard scores, with Scales 1, 4, 7, 8, and 9 being K corrected. Any scores above 70 are considered to represent psychopathology. Those between 50 and 70 are in the normal range. In addition, specific *patterns* of scores for various diagnostic groupings have been coded (cf. Marks & Seeman, 1963).[7] These codes have been translated into computerized interpretations (e.g., Kleinmuntz, 1969). For example, the Hoffmann-La Roche Drug Company has an extensive computer facility for scoring and analyzing MMPI protocols. An example of a computerized report for a twenty-nine-year-old woman (WAIS IQ = 115) appears in Table 4.11.

At this point, let us note how the MMPI was constructed. First, 504 items were selected on the basis of psychiatric interviews, clinical papers, and from other personality tests available in the early 1940s. These items were then given to more than 800 psychiatric patients and a "normal" sample of visitors to the University of Minnesota Hospital (N = 724). The patient group fell into eight diagnostic categories that roughly parallel the entities represented by Scales 1 to 4 and 6 to 9. "The typical item selection procedure involved contrasting the responses to the 504 items of the criterion group . . . with the normative sample. Items that had true-false endorsement frequencies that differed at or beyond the .05 level of significance were retained for the final scales. In many cases derivation of the final scale actually progressed through several stages . . ." (Gynther & Gynther, 1976, p. 203).

As noted above, the research on the MMPI is massive. In recent years this research, the original purpose of the MMPI, and its current status have come under considerable attack and criticism (e.g., Norman, 1972; Rodgers, 1972). Some of the problems are as follows (cf. Cronbach, 1970):

1. In the original test, the selection of items involved too few subjects in the clinical and normal groups. Thus, chance factors may have contributed to the inclusion of certain items.
2. Correlation between many of the scales is too high to permit a fine pattern analysis.
3. Many of the test items do not seem to be relevant today.

---

7. Such profiles are often referred to with regard to the two or three highest scale scores (e.g., an 8-7-6 profile).

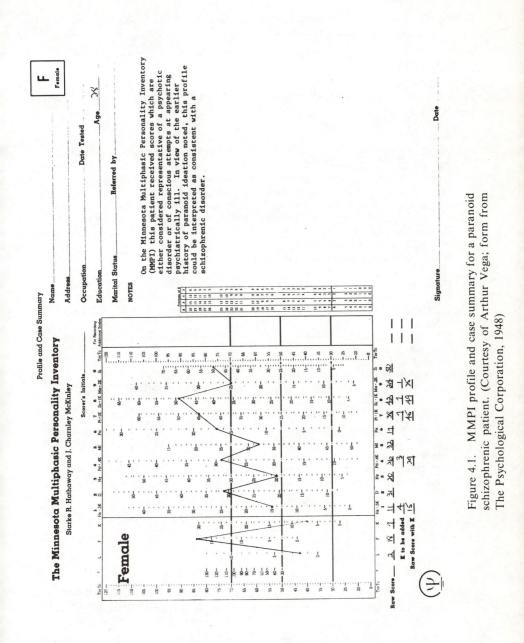

Figure 4.1.   MMPI profile and case summary for a paranoid schizophrenic patient. (Courtesy of Arthur Vega; form from The Psychological Corporation, 1948)

Table 4.11.   Computerized Report of a 29-Year-Old Withdrawn Woman

---

The patient's test-taking attitude suggests the following:
   Help-seeking
   Self-depreciation or confused thinking
The patient's emotional state while taking the test appears to be characterized by the
   following:
   Severe anxiety
   Anger
This evaluation suggests the possibility of the following personality traits, characteristics,
   and diagnostic alternatives:
   Likely to be argumentative, unpredictable, and show delinquent behavior.
   Feelings of being persecuted are easily aroused.
   Has unusual feelings and experiences, also difficulty with thinking.
   Possibly bizarre feelings and thought disorder. May fear losing control of self.
   Rebellious, angry, self-centered, and impulsive with family and social maladjust-
      ments of immature kinds.
   May have psychopathic character traits.
   Can easily become quite anxious.
   Depression, lack of optimism, general dissatisfaction, and self-devaluation.
   Numerous somatic symptoms of a hypochondriacal or psychosomatic type.
   Impulsive behavior. Plans and interest may be constantly changing, maladaptive
      hyperactivity, and grandiose thinking.
   Marked paranoid ideation and paranoid traits such as sensitivity, jealousy, suspi-
      ciousness, and feeling of being treated unfairly.
   Alcoholism in a hostile, oral dependent individual.
   Schizophrenic reaction.
   Emotionally unstable person with characterological problems.
   Impulsive, immature, and emotionally labile individual.
   Chronically depressed and anxious individual.
   This profile is frequent among patients for whom there is chronic severe maladjust-
      ment which may include marked depression, anxiety, social withdrawal, and a
      lack of any feeling of satisfaction or pleasure. Diagnoses usually stress de-
      pression, anxiety, and schizoid elements, but the range of diagnoses is wide and
      may parallel population base rates of schizophrenic and nonschizophrenic diag-
      noses.

Source: Courtesy of Gerald Goldstein.

4. Some of the problems regarding poor diagnostic classification based on
   MMPI categories are directly related to the problems with psychiatric
   diagnosis itself (i.e., unreliability of the current scheme).

5. Age, intelligence, socioeconomic status, and education all affect how a
   client responds to the test. Thus, a "blind" interpretation and some
   computer analyses may be erroneous. In that case, Meehl's (1956) call
   for a good "cookbook" approach has not been fully realized.

6. Black-white differences in responding on the MMPI often lead to misdiagnosis of black patients (Adebimpe, Gigandet, & Harris, in press), especially since blacks typically score higher on Scales F, 8, and 9 than whites (unless matched for socioeconomic factors).

There are further problems with the MMPI. But if this is true, why is this test so popular with clinicians? There are several possible explanations. First, the test has been used for almost four decades. A second reason, related to the first, is the enormous research investment in this test over the years. Third, at times the test has proven quite adaptive in classifying apparent diagnostic problems. And finally, as a gross screening device the MMPI is reasonably good.

Neuropsychological Testing

Neuropsychological testing, in general, is used to detect organic malfunctioning and to specify the relevant site in the brain. In some cases, it can also predict the possibility of functional recovery and general progression of the disorder. However, when it is said that neuropsychological tests identify organicity, much caution is needed. As pointed out by Goldstein (1980), organicity is an inclusive term. It covers many disorders of varied etiology, such as head trauma, brain tumors, brain malfunctions, blood vessel disease, degenerative and demyelinating diseases, alcoholism, toxic and infectious illnesses, and epilepsy. Some organic conditions are reversible (i.e., full functioning returns), while others are irreversible. However, even in the so-called irreversible disorders, there is now evidence that some functions may return, although at lower levels.

Neuropsychological tests generally evaluate perceptual-motor, motor, memory, and other cognitive functions. Many individual tests for these purposes have been developed over the last several decades. For example, the Bender-Gestalt (Bender, 1938) test consists of nine geometric designs that the client is first asked to copy and then reproduce from memory. Although the Bender-Gestalt is often interpreted impressionistically, scoring systems for both children and adults have been devised (Koppitz, 1964; Pascal & Suttell, 1951). A test similar to the Bender-Gestalt is the Benton Visual Retention Test (Benton, 1963). This test is also concerned with visual memory, with the client expected to draw from memory ten geometric designs that were presented one at a time, each for ten seconds. Parallel forms of the test are available. Still another test of memory, developed by Wechsler (1945), has been used extensively for more than thirty years. Although equivalent forms of this test exist, its norms, reliability, and validity are in question.

In the field of neuropsychology, the most sophisticated assessment techniques are not the individual tests. Rather, they are the combinations of many tests—*neuropsychological batteries*. Most of these batteries include tests based on the work of Ward C. Halstead and Ralph M. Reitan (the Halstead-Reitan Neuropsychological Test Battery). Some of the tests in this battery appear in Table 4.12.

Of the current diagnostic tests used by clinical psychologists, the neuropsychological batteries are among the most successful in making correct diagnoses. For example, the Halstead-Reitan battery is able to differentiate brain-damaged from hospitalized controls, with a 73 percent accuracy level for both groups (Vega & Parsons, 1967). The same battery can identify organics versus schizophrenics or medical controls, with correct percentages as follows: organics 78 percent, schizophrenics 67 percent, medical controls 78 percent (Levine & Feirstein, 1972). In a recent study (Goldstein & Halperin, 1977), it was even possible to differentiate among subtypes of schizophrenics using the WAIS and the Halstead-Reitan battery. Greatest predictor accuracy was obtained on short-term versus long-term institutionalization of the patients. Also, as a gross screening device for organicity, the Halstead-Reitan battery proved more effective than all physical measures (e.g., brain scan, EEG, X-ray, angiogram) (Filskov & Goldstein, 1974). Finally, a computer-assisted analysis of Halstead-Reitan data has proven quite effective in locating the site of the organic lesion in many patients (Russell, Neuringer, & Goldstein, 1970).[8]

Test Batteries

Neuropsychological testing, as we have seen, relies greatly on the test battery. However, in day-to-day clinical practice, even more comprehensive batteries are often used. Thus, it is not uncommon for a complete psychological evaluation to require several hours and at least two

---

8. With the development of computerized transaxial tomography (a most sophisticated x-ray procedure), localization of brain damage has been greatly facilitated. However, this procedure will certainly not supplant neuropsychological testing, which determines what a given organic patient is able to perform.

Table 4.12.   Halstead-Reitan Tests

1. Halstead Category Test
2. Halstead Tactual Performance Test
3. Seashore Rhythm Test
4. Halstead Speech Perception Test
5. Halstead Finger Tapping
6. Trail Making
7. Aphana Examination
8. Perceptual Disorders Examination

client visits. Of course, depending on the diagnostic and referral question posed, different tests may be included in a given battery.

Let us consider two possible test batteries in a comprehensive evaluation of an adult client. One battery involves tests that can be scored objectively; the other is the kind a more psychodynamically oriented examiner would use. Here, clear differences in test composition are seen. Both batteries, however, contain the WAIS (intellectual functioning), and both involve assessment of perceptual-motor functioning (Benton, 1963; Bender, 1938). The objective test battery then continues with the MMPI (diagnostically oriented) and the EPI (trait oriented). In contrast, the psychodynamic battery follows with the Rorschach (unconscious dynamics), the TAT (intrapersonal and interpersonal dynamics), and figure drawings (self-concept and sex-role identity). (See Applebaum, 1977, and Holt, 1968, for a detailed discussion of test batteries from the psychodynamic perspective.)

The examiner's theoretical orientation is almost totally responsible for the composition of the test battery. Furthermore, even when the

Table 4.13.   Test Batteries

Objective	Psychodynamic
WAIS	WAIS
Bender-Gestalt	Bender-Gestalt
Benton Visual Retention Test	Benton Visual Retention Test
MMPI	Rorschach
Eysenck Personality Inventory	TAT
	Figure Drawings

same test is used (e.g., the WAIS), the analysis and interpretation of the data will also be a reflection of the examiner's theoretical bias (cf. Waite, 1961).

How Clinicians Use Test Data

Even if a test has clear norms and adequate reliability and validity, the issue of interpretation remains. For those tests with ambiguous psychometric characteristics, do clinicians use parts of the test where adequate validity and reliability coefficients are known? These are important questions since a test is only as good as the examiner behind them.

Unfortunately, these issues are a major problem in our field. Although there are many careful clinicians who use only those tests with established psychometric properties, a very large percentage seem totally unconcerned (cf. Wade & Baker, 1977). As stated by Wade and Baker: "Clinicians' indifference to reliability and validity was patent throughout this study. While poor reliability and validity were recognized as distinct disadvantages of psychological tests, those characteristics were not considered particularly important in test-use decisions" (p. 879).

Some clinicians do not formally score their personality test protocols (i.e., the projectives) but rely on overall impressions based on experience. Others do score them, but if the results are inconsistent with their personal hypotheses, the latter seem to prevail. This, again, is ostensibly based on their own prior "successes" with the test. Still other clinicians score the tests but use invalid signs to reach their diagnostic conclusions (see Chapman & Chapman, 1969). Further, in some cases the test data do not yield greater predictive accuracy than that based on historical data alone (Golden, 1964; Horowitz, 1962).

This situation, unfortunately, can best be described as "Alice in wonderland." We contend that if psychological assessment is to be considered of scientific rather than artistic value, then in testing, scientific practices must be followed. Otherwise, the crystal ball approach (with some very *sporadic* diagnostic successes) will reign supreme.

Critical Appraisal

If any activity is uniquely associated with clinical psychology, it is psychological testing. And paradoxically, psychological testing is now one of the most hotly disputed tools of the profession. The controversy has even become public, which may simply be a sign of the times. More likely, however, it probably reflects the tendency toward increased critical self-evaluation in the field. This we can only applaud.

The problems with the psychometric aspects of today's tests are numerous. The naive critic of psychological testing undoubtedly would focus on the projectives. This, however, would represent needless scapegoating. The so-called "objective" tests (IQ, MMPI, etc.), with the exception of the neuropsychological devices, are filled with psychometric and general construction problems. The intelligence tests, for example, still leave us wondering what they are actually measuring and what their relationship is to future performance. Indeed, the theoretical rationale for tests such as the WISC and WPPSI has been questioned. Also, the rather moderate reliabilities of some of the subtests, as well as their dubious classification into verbal or performance abilities, are undesirable features.

As for the objective personality tests (best represented by the MMPI), their diagnostic success, in spite of the several thousand studies, is not very great. At best, they permit gross categorization; precise or specific classification seems less likely. This, of course, parallels the problems with the current psychiatric diagnostic schemes.

As for the projectives, the psychometric problems are legion (see Zubin et al., 1965). To us, the most distressing aspect of these tests is not the obvious problems of standardization, reliability, and validity. Rather, it is the unfortunate manner in which they are often analyzed and interpreted—namely, the omission of scoring and the tendency to avoid considering those diagnostic signs that *are valid*.

Finally, and of paramount importance today, we must recognize that psychological testing cannot and should not be taken out of its social context. The discriminatory use of intelligence and personality tests is clear. Unfortunately, many of the items on our most cherished tests do not reflect the experiences of the minority groups we are often called upon to evaluate. In that sense, these tests may not be valid (psychometrically or socially) for disadvantaged populations. In any given case, however, the test may be a good barometer as to how that person is doing in reference to white middle-class norms.

In spite of our gloomy assessment of the status of psychological testing, there are some positive things to report. First, the mere fact that the problems have and undoubtedly will continue to be recognized is a necessary first step. In the years to come, both the psychological community and the larger society will be eager to see whether necessary changes will take place. Second, at this point we see psychological testing as a gross screening method. Although we certainly need more refined instruments, gross categorization is useful in day-to-day clinical work. Third, in the neuropsychological batteries a great deal of precision has been attained. Not only are these batteries important for detecting organicity, but there is substantial evidence that the site of the organicity can be located with good predictive accuracy (cf. Russell, Neuringer, & Goldstein, 1970).

Summary

In this chapter, we have examined several general and specific issues related to psychological testing. We first discussed the current status of testing, as indicated in various surveys of practicing and academic clinical psychologists. Then, following our review of the APA guidelines for developing and administering tests, we looked at the various kinds of tests in use today: intelligence, projective, objective personality, and neuropsychological. Next, we considered how tests are combined in batteries to obtain comprehensive client evaluations. This was followed by how clinical psychologists interpret their test data. Finally, we briefly appraised the positive and negative features of psychological testing. Throughout this chapter, we have been concerned not only with the important psychometric issues facing the field but also with the social context in which testing is carried out.

CHAPTER
FIVE

Behavioral
Assessment

In Chapter 4 we examined psychological testing—a major interest of clinical psychologists. As we pointed out, other professionals such as psychiatrists and educators, as well as much of the public, associate clinical psychology with testing. Indeed, Wade and Baker (1977) found that traditional psychological testing occupies much of the clinician's time. However, with the considerable influence of the behavioral movement in the 1960s and 1970s (see Bellack & Hersen, 1977a; Franks, 1969; Gambrill, 1977; Hersen & Bellack, 1978a), many clinical psychologists have altered their assessment approach. In some instances, behavioral procedures have replaced traditional psychological testing.

In behavioral assessment, the behaviors to be treated are directly assessed. For example, if a client experiences fear of heights, his or her behavior in high places will be observed and recorded. This includes not only motor responses but physiological responses (e.g., heart rate) and verbal reports as well. Compare this with, say, the MMPI, which claims to measure personality patterns, or the Rorschach, where the client's projections are presumably obtained.

In turning to behavioral assessment, some clinicians have totally abandoned traditional psychological testing.[1] Others have combined

1. The great majority of behaviorists find objective data obtained from intelligence, neuropsychological, aptitude, and vocational interest tests quite important in assessing their clients (see Rinn, 1978). Most behaviorists, however, give almost no credence to data derived from projective tests such as the Rorschach and TAT, while a few are more positive toward personality pattern analyses derived from tests such as the MMPI or CPI.

objective psychological testing (such as personality, intelligence, and neuropsychological evaluations) with behavioral assessment (Morgenstern, Pearce, & Rees, 1965). Still others combine features of behavioral assessment with those procedures that follow the psychodynamic model (cf. Feather & Rhoads, 1972; Greenspoon & Gersten, 1967).

Regardless of how behavioral assessment is currently viewed and carried out, it has had a strong impact on the field. There are now three major textbooks on the subject (Ciminero, Calhoun, & Adams, 1977; Cone & Hawkins, 1977; Hersen & Bellack, 1976a), with others yet to come. The importance of the *direct* measurement of behavior (see Mischel, 1968) has even affected the psychiatric establishment (cf. Hersen, 1976; Hersen & Bellack, 1978a). Its influence in the field of education is even more striking (e.g., Lahey & Johnson, 1978).

In this chapter, we will first consider behavioral assessment in historical perspective, particularly the factors that have made it so popular. Next, the philosophical basis of behavioral assessment will be reviewed. Several methods of conducting behavioral assessments will then be outlined. The following sections will evaluate how behavioral strategies are typically carried out. That is, we will briefly consider the role of the initial clinical interviews as a first step in identifying the motor, self-report, and physiological measures for each client. Then, we will outline and detail pertinent issues concerned with these three factors. Throughout the chapter, examples from our own clinical research work will be presented, with the rationale for each measure or measurement system used. The interrelationships among the three response systems (motor, self-report, and physiological) evaluated will also be discussed. Then we will examine how behavioral assessment may vary depending on the setting (e.g., consulting room, hospital, classroom) in which it is conducted. Finally, we will present a critical appraisal of behavioral assessment today, stressing certain psychometric considerations often neglected by behaviorists.

Historical Perspectives

It is difficult to determine when the impetus for behavioral assessment really began. Through the 1920s, 1930s, and 1950s, there were sporadic clinical reports of direct measurement used with difficult cases (e.g., Ayllon & Michael, 1959; Jones, 1924; Max, 1935; Watson & Rayner, 1920). Two books in particular (Eysenck, 1960a; Wolpe, 1958) were vital in launching both behavioral assessment and behavioral modification. The first, Wolpe's (1958) *Psychotherapy by Reciprocal Inhibition,* made a comprehensive statement about the theoretical basis for treating neurotic disorders with systematic desensitization therapy. In addition, there were many suggestions for the direct assessment of neurotic symptoms. In the second book, *Behaviour Therapy and the Neuroses,* (1960a), edited by Eysenck, the importance of targeting symptoms and assessing them before, during, and after treatment was stressed.

Another great contribution to behavioral assessment was Lang and Lazovik's (1963) classic paper "Experimental Desensitization of a Phobia." Mention there was made of three assessment strategies now routinely used in behavioral research, especially with phobic subjects. One of the techniques was a fear survey schedule (known as FSS-I), a paper-and-pencil test consisting of fifty common fears rated by the subject on a scale of 1 to 7. The second measure was the Behavioral Avoidance Test (BAT), an objective (i.e., motor) strategy for evaluating a subject's ability to approach a phobic object (in this instance, a harmless, non-poisonous snake securely caged in a glass terrarium). In the BAT the subject is asked to enter a room, marked off in equal intervals, and to approach the snake as closely as possible.[2] The test ends when the subject experiences considerable anxiety. Thus, distance approached can be precisely determined. Those subjects who can move close to the snake are then asked to touch and hold it, if possible. A third measure referred to in this study was the Fear Thermometer, initially described by Walk (1956) in his evaluation of airborne parachute trainees. In the BAT situation the Fear Thermometer is used by asking the subject to evaluate, on a ten-point scale, the degree of discomfort experienced at the closest approach point to the snake. A score of 10 represents maximum discomfort.

Lang and Lazovik's (1963) initial work set the stage for hundreds of later investigations (see Bellack & Hersen, 1977a, Chapters 2 and 3). In these studies, both mild fears in college students and intense fears (i.e., phobias) in severely disturbed clients were assessed. And behind them is the work of Lang and Lazovik (1963), who provided the methodology for making precise assessments possible.

The direct observation of behavior (primarily motoric) has been furthered by the work of operant psychologists with clinical and educa-

---

2. Many other kinds of phobic stimuli, such as laboratory rats, roaches, spiders, dogs, and cats, can be evaluated using BAT procedures.

tional problems. Calling themselves applied behavior analysts, these psychologists have made a great contribution to the methodology of measuring ongoing overt behavior in both naturalistic settings and in settings arranged for the evaluation of motor behavior.[3] This work first appeared in the *Journal of the Experimental Analysis of Behavior* and since 1968 in the *Journal of Applied Behavior Analysis.* (We will present examples of this work in a later section, "Motor Measures.")

In analyzing the strong interest in behavioral assessment in the 1960s and 1970s and the decline in traditional testing, five related factors should be considered. They are: (1) the discontent of clinical psychologists with their professional roles in some settings; (2) the often unclear relationship between psychological testing and treatment; (3) the growing dissatisfaction with projectives tests; (4) the greater predictive value of direct assessment procedures; and (5) the unreliability of standard psychiatric diagnosis. Each of these factors is discussed below.

Professional Role

As indicated in Chapter 1, the profession of clinical psychology became increasingly visible after World War II. Largely because of their unique skills in testing, many clinical psychologists found employment in medical settings, particularly on psychiatric wards in general medical and surgical hospitals and in psychiatric hospitals (VA and large state hospitals). In these settings, clinical psychologists contributed greatly to the diagnostic process. That is, "the clinical psychologist was cast in a role analogous to an x-ray technician whenever a psychiatrist required confirmation of his differential diagnosis based on historical and interview data. Whether the psychologist's report had any impact on the ensuing treatment process seemed immaterial. His role was that of assessor" (Hersen, 1976, p. 8).

Immediately after World War II, many psychiatric settings had restrictive policies concerning the kinds of work that clinical psychologists could perform. In some places, the practice of psychotherapy was forbidden. In others, it was discouraged by allowing it only under close medical scrutiny and supervision. In the last two decades, however, this

---

3. Contrived measurement situations for assessing motor behavior are usually known as "analogue measures." Often such situations are role-played in the attempt to simulate interactions that might take place in the natural setting.

situation has changed markedly. But even today occasional rumblings from the American Psychiatric Association are heard; psychotherapy and biofeedback, it is claimed, are medical procedures and therefore must be carried out by medical doctors or under their close supervision. Indeed, in 1966 when one of us (M.H.) was being interviewed for a clinical psychology position in a large general medical and surgical hospital in Boston affiliated with the Harvard University Medical School, he was informed that 95 percent of his work would involve preparing "psychoanalytically oriented" reports based on projective testing. If time permitted, if there were enough patients "left over" from the psychiatric residents, and if "appropriate" supervision were available, then he could spend the remaining 5 percent doing psychotherapy (i.e., two hours per week). Another such limitation is the statement made in the 1950s by the then chairman of a psychiatry department in a large Northeastern medical school that no clinical psychologist in that city would do psychotherapy during his tenure.

Given this psychiatric attitude in the late 1940s and throughout most of the 1950s, it is hardly surprising that many clinical psychologists developed and expanded their skills as diagnosticians. Their uniqueness in the diagnostic realm was heavily reinforced (by both psychiatrists and educators), with some clinicians establishing lucrative private practices specializing in psychological evaluation. Eventually, many of them began doing psychotherapy in psychiatric settings, often modeling themselves after the psychiatrists (consider, for example, the lay analysts). However, when they emulated psychiatrists (usually psychoanalytic in orientation) in such settings, the uniqueness of the clinician's role was lost. Occasionally clinical psychologists doing psychotherapy were labeled "the poor man's psychiatrist."

However, this pigeonholing of clinical psychologists as assessors did not occur in all settings. In the fields of rehabilitation and mental retardation, for example, clinicians served in important psychotherapeutic and administrative positions. Moreover, the clinical psychologists in academic settings (primarily psychology departments in schools of arts and sciences) rarely became embroiled in the sometimes acrimonious psychology-psychiatry conflicts. Instead, they assessed, counseled, and treated clients in clinics associated with their departments that were not under the jurisdiction of psychiatry. However, most clinical research in that era bore little relation to clinical interests. The majority of such clinicians "conducted research studies of academic import but of remote relevance to pressing clinical issues" (Hersen, 1976, p. 8). (In later sections, we shall see how behavioral assessment not only helped to change the role of clinicians but also enabled them to coordinate their clinical and research activities.)

Relationship of Diagnosis and Treatment

In doing traditional psychological assessments (including the MMPI and projective tests), clinical psychologists often find little or no relationship between test results and later treatment. Part of the reason is the rationale behind traditional personality testing: the assumption that the client's underlying traits will be manifested in test responses. However, consistent with the dynamic approach, overt responses are not taken at face value and targeted for treatment. Thus, the dynamic approach favors a trait interpretation of such data. By contrast, in behavioral assessment the responses (whether motor, verbal, or physiological) are considered in terms of the situation in which they are obtained. This is consistent with the "state" interpretation of data.

Goldfried and Kent (1972) have differentiated the traditional and behavioral approaches to measurement: "Whereas traditional tests of personality involve the assessment of hypothesized personality constructs which, in turn, are used to predict overt behavior, the behavioral approach entails more of a direct sampling of the criterion behaviors themselves. In addition to requiring fewer inferences than traditional tests, behavioral assessment procedures are seen as being based on assumptions more amenable to direct empirical test and more consistent with empirical evidence" (p. 409). Elsewhere, Mischel (1972) has commented on the indirect relationship of TAT and Rorschach responses to overt behavior as the "indirect-sign paradigm."

Given the indirect nature of traditional testing, a precise relationship between diagnosis and treatment is obviously hard to obtain. This is especially so since the behaviors measured (i. e., signs and symptoms found on the Rorschach and TAT) are not the ones actually treated in psychotherapy. To the contrary, the traditional psychotherapist deals with the unconscious conflicts that produce such signs and symptoms. As argued by Hersen (1976), "This being the case, to be consistent with psychodynamic theory, a direct approach linking assessment and treatment would be untenable" (pp. 10–11).

Theoretical bias aside, traditional psychological assessment procedures often involve rather vague, loosely constructed referral questions. In many settings requiring psychological evaluations, the authors often received questions such as "What are the client's personality dynamics?" or "What is the client's personality pattern?". At times, the directives were even less precise. One of us (M.H.) recalls a request to "test for hidden paranoia."

The astute clinician using traditional testing procedures often returns such referrals with a request for clarification and a more specific diagnostic question. However, even if the question is fairly precise, what actually takes place once the client is ready to begin treatment? Usually, with a traditional psychotherapeutic approach, diagnosis and therapy have little to do with each other (cf. Appelbaum, 1977, p. 261). With biological treatment (i. e., drugs), in contrast, the relationship between diagnosis and treatment is closer (e.g., antidepressants for depression, antipsychotics for schizophrenia) (see Detre & Jarecki, 1971).

Still another problem for the traditional psychological assessor is the automatic referral of clients, regardless of whether testing can help. In many institutions clients are tested routinely; hence the question "What are the personality dynamics?" One of us (M.H.) worked in private practice for a psychiatrist who found "psychologicals" profitable. However, the final disposition of psychological test data as related to ongoing treatment or outcome rarely emerged as a focal issue. That is, there was little relationship between the two.

All these problems have led many empirical psychologists to embrace the much more direct behavioral assessment. The attraction lies not only in the direct relationship of behavioral assessment and treatment in the initial stages but also in the ongoing reciprocal relationship between them throughout therapy (see Chapter 7). Assessment becomes more than an isolated exercise taking place before treatment. Indeed, throughout the course of treatment the client is reassessed at stated intervals, thus permitting changes in therapy if needed.

Dissatisfaction with Projectives

From the 1950s through the early 1970s, clinicians became increasingly discontented with the projective tests then in use (e.g., Gross, 1959; Hamilton & Robertson, 1966; Hersen, 1970; Hersen & Greaves, 1971; Marwit, 1969; Zubin, Eron, & Schumer, 1965). The greatest dissatisfaction came not from the clinicians who routinely used these techniques (cf. Wade & Baker, 1977) but from those who wished to establish their psychometric reliability and validity.[4]

The most telling statement about the "state of the art" appeared in the Epilogue to the Zubin et al. (1965) classic text *An Experimental Approach to Projective Techniques:* "Have we established the usefulness of projective techniques? The answer to this question must be qualified. For some limited purposes, perhaps yes. For the general purposes of evaluating personality, the answer must be very tentative and probably negative. Have we made progress in recent years? Here the answer is definitely yes. When we measure our progress against our ultimate aims, the distance we have traveled is infinitesimal" (p. 610). To paraphrase, the effort hardly seemed commensurate with the final results.

The psychometric aspects of projective tests were not the only problem. As the findings accumulated, it became clear that the psychological examiner was hardly a precise, impersonal instrument. To the contrary, the examiner was quite capable of *biasing* clients' responses (e.g., Marwit & Marcia, 1967; Masling & Harris, 1969). This was done by reacting subjectively to clients, thus inadvertently influencing their responses—both quantitatively and qualitatively—to the projective tests.

Let us consider two studies. In one, Hersen and Greaves (1971) gave the Rorschach to four groups of twenty-five college students; all the groups were equated for intelligence. In the first group (continuous reinforcement), after each response made by the subject (regardless of content), the examiner said "Good." In the second group (human reinforcement), each human response was followed by the word "Good." In the third group (animal reinforcement), each animal response was followed by the word "Good." In the fourth group (control), no comment was made, regardless of the number or kind of responses given.

The results of the study indicated that verbal reinforcement (i.e., saying "Good") led to significantly increased total responses, human responses, and animal responses in the three groups compared to the control condition. Hersen and Greaves (1971) state that their study may be viewed as a possible *model* of how tester bias (i.e., reinforcement) may affect the client's responses in projective testing. Naturally, it may

---

4. There is a marked time lag in clinical practices when examined in light of the academic research findings. Although fewer clinical training programs today emphasize projective testing, clinicians who were trained earlier assess clients using their educational experiences of the 1950s and 1960s. Unfortunately, many have not kept up with the latest findings. The newer generation of clinicians is more likely to reflect the current status of projectives in the field.

not exactly duplicate the seasoned assessor's actual response, but it does emphasize that the Rorschach situation *is* amenable to outside influences.

In another study in which the Rorschach was used with psychiatric patients in a large state hospital, it was found (retrospectively) that male psychology interns who tested both males and females obtained a significantly greater number of total Rorschach responses from females (Hersen, 1970). On the other hand, female interns who tested both female and male patients showed no such cross-sex bias. It was concluded "that at least at the intern level, the male psychological examiner can hardly be described as a precise or objective testing instrument" (Hersen, 1970, p. 105). Masling and Harris (1969) also showed cross-sex testing bias for the TAT.

Direct versus Indirect Assessment

Studies on the predictive validity of traditional personality testing are still another source of disenchantment. Usually, when direct (i.e., behavioral) and indirect (i.e., traditional) personality tests are compared the results favor the direct approach (see Goldfried & Kent, 1972; Holmes & Tyler, 1968; Mischel, 1972; Scott & Johnson, 1972). In these studies, the predictive value of data obtained through direct means (e.g., self-reports) and projective tests are compared, using peer ratings, grades, and laboratory tasks.

Two typical studies illustrate this point. In one, Wallace and Sechrest (1963) compared the predictive accuracy of the Rorschach, TAT, and Rotter Incomplete Sentences Blank projective tests and subjects' self-ratings on the following: hostility, somatic concern, religious concern, and assessment of achievement. Peer ratings on these dimensions served as the outside (independent) criterion. The result was a correlation of 0.57 between self-ratings and peer ratings. However, correlations between the Rorschach, TAT, Rotter Incomplete Sentences Blank, and peer ratings, respectively, were only 0.05, 0.08, and 0.14.

More recently, Holmes and Tyler (1968) evaluated the predictive validity of three strategies for measuring need achievement: (1) TAT, (2) self-reports on a rating scale, and (3) a combined self-peer ranking approach (subjects listed ten friends and evaluated themselves in relation to each). The independent criteria were class grades and two laboratory tasks. The results of the study showed significant correlations between the self-peer ranking measure and the outside criteria. No such relationships were found for the TAT or self-reports alone.

In reviewing this literature, Mischel (1972) concludes: "Taken collectively, the studies on the comparative utility of direct and indirect personality assessment are consistent: the predictions possible from S's own simple, direct self-ratings and self-reports generally have not been exceeded by those obtained from more indirect, costly, and sophisticated personality tests, and from expert clinical judges. . . . These conclusions appear to hold for such diverse content areas as college achievement, job and professional success, treatment outcomes in psychotherapy, rehospitalization for psychiatric patients, and parole violations for delinquent children" (p. 322).

Unreliability of Psychiatric Diagnosis

Since many standard personality tests (e.g., the MMPI) are used to determine diagnoses in accordance with the diagnostic scheme of the American Psychiatric Association (the *Diagnostic and Statistical Manual of Mental Disorders-III,* or *DSM-III*), the reliability of psychiatric diagnosis must be considered. Since hundreds of studies have used diagnosis, based on psychiatric appraisal, as either the dependent or independent measure (cf. Frank, 1975), this issue is obviously critical. Moreover, the validity of several personality tests has been established using psychiatric diagnosis as an outside criterion.

Let us examine the concept of reliability of psychiatric diagnosis. Specifically, if a given patient is examined independently by two psychiatrists, what is the likelihood that their diagnoses will agree? The answer, unfortunately, is: very little (see Frank, 1969, 1975, for comprehensive reviews of this literature). In an early study, Ash (1949) had fifty-two male outpatients evaluated by two psychiatrists. In thirty-five of the cases, three psychiatrists were involved. When all three of them assessed the patients, inter-rater agreement was only 20 percent for *very specific* diagnostic categories (i.e., subcategories). However, inter-rater agreement was a bit higher for two psychiatrists (31.4 to 43.5 percent). For *major* diagnostic categories, inter-rater agreement for three psychiatrists was 45.7 percent and 57.9 to 67.4 percent for two. More recently, Sandifer, Pettus, and Quade (1964) evaluated inter-rater agreement for fourteen senior medical doctors (eleven were psychiatrists) assessing ninety-one new admissions to a psychiatric hospital. The likelihood of the second opinion relating to the first averaged only 57 percent.

In a very careful survey of the literature, Frank (1969) concluded that "this research leaves one with the uncomfortable feeling that the results of all the studies that have utilized psychiatric diagnosis as a dependent or independent variable are of questionable validity. The data reviewed herein suggest that an entirely new system of classification is needed, one which can encompass the many variables that define psychological functioning and behavior in the human, including the viewing of these functions from a developmental frame of reference" (p. 67).

The DSM classification system has not been criticized by psychologists alone; psychiatrists themselves (e.g., Hines & Williams, 1975) have proposed new schemes. Indeed, the American Psychiatric Association itself, in response to some of the difficulties in *DSM-II,* is about to publish *DSM-III.* Unfortunately, many problems still remain. Thus, behavioral psychologists such as Cautela and Upper (1973) and Adams, Doster, and Calhoun (1977) have outlined and proposed entirely new classification schemes. These have not had substantial impact on the field. They are rarely followed and have no *official status* (i.e., recognition by a major professional organization or governmental or insurance company approval for statistical purposes). Also, some of the newer schemes are as cumbersome as *DSM-III* and often less comprehensive. On the other hand, *individual* assessment of specified behaviors, independently of the classification used, has gained in popularity among psychologists and, to a lesser extent, psychiatrists.

Philosophical Background

Although we have already alluded to some of the basic features of behavioral assessment, let us consider three philosophical tenets of behavioral practitioners. First and foremost, the behavioral assessor is interested in the direct evaluation of clients. This statement implies many things. The behavioral therapists of the early 1960s, in their reaction to projectives, focused almost exclusively on the observable motor behaviors of their clients. When possible, behavior was observed in a natural setting. If not convenient, either for ethical or practical reasons, analogue or laboratory tasks were devised (see Hersen &

Barlow, 1976, Chapter 4). However, this concentration on motor be-havior led critics of the behavioral approach to label it "simplistic and mechanical."

As behavior therapists began to treat disorders that were much more complex than the simple phobias originally dealt with (e.g., obses-siveness, depression, schizophrenia), it became obvious that thoughts and feelings were just as important as motor behaviors (cf. Begelman & Hersen, 1973; Bellack & Hersen, 1977b; Bellack & Schwartz, 1976; Hersen, 1977; Meichenbaum, 1976). As Goldfried and Pomeranz (1968) state, "Some behavior therapists fail to recognize that the most ap-propriate targets for behavior modification often involve cognitions as well as behavior. Although we could not deny the fact that thoughts and feelings can sometimes be modified by changing the individual's overt behavior, quite often they should be target behaviors for direct modifi-cation themselves" (p. 81).

Also assessed are the client's physiological responses in standard laboratory situations (see Epstein, 1976). With the advent of behavioral medicine and biofeedback, direct psychological intervention for medical disorders (e.g., tension headache, tachycardia) has become possible. Moreover, as behavior therapists evaluated the effects of their treat-ments on the three response systems (motor, cognitive, physiological), it became apparent that treatment was often unsuccessful if one of the three was ignored (cf. Hersen, 1973; Lazarus, 1973).

A second primary feature of behavioral assessment is that it is completely integrated with the therapeutic process. Rather than an empty exercise at the beginning and end of treatment, assessment occurs repeatedly throughout treatment (see Cautela, 1968). Since treatment is directly related to the targets idenitified in the behavioral analysis, new targets sometimes emerge during treatment. This may occur (1) when new problems are identified that require a change in therapeutic direc-tion or (2) when the initial assessment is incomplete or incorrect, thus requiring reassessment to establish different target behaviors and treat-ment strategies (see the illustrative case below).

A third feature of behavioral assessment and treatment is that each case may be conceptualized as an individual experiment (see Lazarus & Davison, 1971). That is, with the integration of assessment and treat-ment, the therapist's hunches about the client can repeatedly be verified or discomfirmed. And in the event of failure, the behavioral approach is flexible enough so the therapy can be changed. Finally, the experimental analysis of individual cases has been formalized in a scientifically rigorous manner and is known as the *single case experimental design* (Hersen & Barlow, 1976). (See Chapters 7 and 10 for a discussion of single case research.)

Let us consider an experimental case report published by Hersen and his research associates (Kallman, Hersen, & O'Toole, 1975) while working in a VA hospital. The case involved a forty-two-year-old white married male who, on admission, was bent forward at the waist at a 45-degree angle; he was seated in a wheelchair, unable to move his legs or to straighten his body. After exhaustive neurological and orthopedic examinations failed to reveal organic causes, a diagnosis of "hysterical leg paralysis" was made.

From the initial assessment based on interviews with the patient, it appeared that his inability to walk (which he called "drawing over") occurred about every four to six weeks for a ten- to fourteen-day period. These episodes resulted in numerous medical treatments and hospitalizations, but none was successful. Also, the patient had retired, received Social Security benefits, and did household chores while his wife worked and supported the family. When "drawing over" occurred, the patient did no work and was served his meals in bed.

From an operant perspective, the case was conceptualized as follows: First, the patient complained about vague back pains. Then he received the family's attention, thus obtaining positive reinforcement for "sick" role behavior. Then his condition worsened, causing him to become bedridden and to receive still further reinforcement (i.e., no household tasks, meals in bed), leading to hospitalization.

Hospital treatment, therefore, had to focus on *reversing* what happened in the patient's evironment. Two targets were selected for initial modification: standing and walking. During the experimental analysis, a young and attractive female research assistant visited the patient for ten minutes three times a day in his hospital room. After a ten-minute conversation unrelated to his symptoms, she asked the patient to stand. If he made any effort to do so, and especially when he was successful, praise and attention were showered on him (e.g., "That's terrific"). Then he was asked to walk; all efforts and successes received the same enthusiastic social reinforcement. Thus, after attention had been paid to all positive behaviors and none to "sick" role behaviors, the patient was discharged eighteen days later.

We had assumed—wrongly—that the patient would be reinforced

for his positive initiatives when he returned home. Unfortunately, his family once again focused on his undesirable behavior; four weeks later, he was returned to the hospital in a wheelchair. This time, normal walking behavior was reinstated in only five days. However, a necessary further assessment was undertaken. The patient and his family were videotaped while interacting during an unstructured conversation. A behavioral analysis revealed that all of the patient's complaints received considerable attention from family members, while his positive statements (i.e., not symptom related) were ignored. Therefore, in subsequent treatment (this time with the patient's family), family members were instructed how and when to respond to the patient's positive and negative initiatives. This procedure, successfully used in the hospital was now extended to the home, thereby ensuring that the gains were generalized to the home environment.

Following the second brief interaction with the family (two sessions), the patient was again discharged from the hospital. At the two year follow-up evaluation (not reported in the original article), he was walking normally but still complaining. Had the authors remained at the VA hospital, a social skills approach might have been instituted to teach this patient a new way of dealing with his environment. In any event, the case shows the experimental nature of the behavioral approach, the initial incomplete behavioral analysis, and the later treatment designed to rectify the initial omission. (See Blanchard & Hersen, 1976, for a comprehensive discussion of the issues involved in the behavioral assessment and treatment of hysterical disorders.) Moreover, this case clearly documents the close relationship between behavioral assessment and treatment.

Behavioral Schemes

The early writings of behavior therapists, such as those in Eysenck (1960a), may have contributed to the notion that behavioral assessment is a straightforward matter requiring little clinical training or experience. This, however, is incorrect. Cautela (1968) contends that this "mistaken notion" may be due to the fact that "Case histories published by behavior therapists . . . do not usually include many important details necessary for full understanding of the diagnosis and treatment procedures" (p. 175). In other words, as a result of space restrictions, only the bare bones of the case appear in print.

In attempts to classify what actually happens during a behavioral assessment, many behavioral schemes have been presented (e.g., Cautela, 1968; Kanfer & Phillips, 1970; Kanfer & Saslow, 1969; Lazarus, 1973). Let us examine three of them in some detail. It might be noted that these three schemes grew out of different theoretical orientations within the behavioral framework.

Cautela (1968) describes behavioral assessment as consisting of three phases. In the first phase, the therapist identifies maladaptive client behaviors. Interviews and the client's responses to structured questionnaires (see Cautela & Upper, 1976, for a description of the questionnaires used) facilitate the process. The second phase involves choosing and implementing treatment strategies. If the maladaptive behavior is anxiety-based, then an anxiety-reduction technique such as systematic desensitization may be used. For maladaptive approach behaviors (e.g., deviant sexual responses), covert sensitization may be applied. If the maladaptive behavior is reinforced by the environment, then an operantly oriented strategy such as differential attention (i.e., attending to positive behaviors and ignoring negative ones) may be considered. In short, the treatment is tailored to the maladaptive response. Also part of this second phase is an ongoing evaluation of the treatment. If it appears to be ineffective, a new strategy may be attempted or the problem may be reassessed, thus leading to a different treatment approach.

The third and final phase consists of a formalized and precise follow-up evaluation of the client. Included is a gradual "phasing out" of therapy for six months, with a more casual follow-up (e.g., writing or calling) over the next one to two years. Throughout the entire process of assessment and therapy, the therapist is cautioned to pay attention to a wide array of the client's behaviors: dreams, imagery, motor and physiological responses, cognitions, and others. (Many of these behaviors, according to nonbehaviorists, are considered to be outside the province of behavior therapy.)

Two other assessment schemes are outlined in Table 5.1. Both are similar in that they tend to reflect the content of the behavioral assessment rather than the phases per se (as was the case with Cautela, 1968). However, it should be noted that in their original descriptions, Kanfer and Saslow (1969) and Lazarus (1973) show that for given clients, the actual content and process of the behavioral assessment may differ considerably. Also, depending on the nature of the problem, some or all of the topic headings may be relevant. These outlines also show that

Table 5.1.   Behavioral Assessment Schemes

Kanfer and Saslow (1969)	Lazarus (1973)
1. Initial evaluation	1. *B* — behavior
2. Clarification of the problem	2. *A* — affect
3. Motivational analysis	3. *S* — sensation
4. Developmental analysis	4. *I* — imagery
5. Analysis of self-control	5. *C* — cognition
6. Analysis of social relationships	6. *I* — interpersonal relationships
7. Analysis of social-cultural-physical environment	7. *D* — drugs (need for medication)

behaviorists are much concerned with how their clients think and feel (cf. motivational analysis, sensation, imagery, cognition) as well as with their motor behavior.

Particularly important is Lazarus' (1973) attention to the sometimes beneficial effects of psychotropic drugs. In many cases (especially those seen in psychiatric hospitals, but also some initially seen in outpatient settings, such as psychological clinics), a psychotherapeutic approach is useless until the client's psychosis is under pharmacological control (cf. Hersen & Bellack, 1976b, 1976c; Liberman & Davis, 1975; Stern, 1978). In other instances, a blend of behavior therapy and drugs may be indicated (cf. Hersen, Turner, Edelstein, & Pinkston, 1975; Rush & Beck, 1978; Turner, Hersen, & Alford, 1974), with the drugs eliminating psychotic and neuro-vegetative depressive symptoms and behavior therapy dealing with the psychosocial aspects of the disorder. In still other clients, drugs are used to enhance or facilitate behavioral strategies (see Stern, 1978).

In this context, we contend that the competent clinical psychologist should not be threatened by the medical-psychiatric approach when warranted. And conversely, it has been our experience that the competent psychiatrist is rarely threatened by the clinician's behavioral therapy. The goal in treatment should be to relieve the client's problem. The client should never become the stimulus for establishing psychological or psychiatric supremacy.

Let us now see how the assessment scheme proposed by Lazarus (1973) works, following one of the cases taken from his files. Note that the problems and the treatments selected for each are indicated for six modalities (behavior, affect, sensation, imagery, cognition, and interpersonal relationships).

Case Illustration

Mary Ann, aged 24, was diagnosed as a chronic undifferentiated schizophrenic. Shortly after her third admission to a mental hospital, her parents referred her to the writer for treatment. According to the hospital reports, her prognosis was poor. She was overweight, apathetic and withdrawn, but against a background of lethargic indifference, one would detect an ephemeral smile, a sparkle of humor, a sudden glow of warmth, a witty remark, an apposite comment, a poignant revelation. She was heavily medicated (Trilafon 8 mg. t.i.d., Vivactil 10 mg. t.i.d., Cogentin 2 mg. b.i.d.), and throughout the course of therapy she continued seeing a psychiatrist once a month who adjusted her intake of drugs.

A life history questionnaire, followed by an initial interview, revealed that well intentioned but misguided parents had created a breeding ground for guilty attitudes, especially in matters pertaining to sex. Moreover, an older sister, 5 years her senior, had aggravated the situation "by tormenting me from the day I was born." Her vulnerability to peer pressure during puberty had rendered her prone to "everything but heroin." Nevertheless, she had excelled at school, and her first noticeable breakdown occurred at age 18, shortly after graduating from high school. "I was on a religious kick and kept hearing voices." Her second hospital admission followed a suicidal gesture at age 21, and her third admission was heralded by her sister's sudden demise soon after the patient turned 24.

Since she was a mine of sexual misinformation, her uncertainties and conflicts with regard to sex became an obvious area for therapeutic intervention. The book *Sex Without Guilt* by Albert Ellis . . . served as a useful springboard toward the correction of more basic areas of sexual uncertainty and anxiety. Meanwhile, careful questioning revealed the following Modality Profile:

Modality	Problem	Proposed Treatment
Behavior	Inappropriate withdrawal reponses	Assertive training
	Frequent crying	Nonreinforcement
	Unkempt appearance	
	Excessive eating	Low calorie regimen
	Negative self-statements	Positive self-talk assignments
	Poor eye contact	Rehearsal techniques
	Mumbling of words with poor voice projection	Verbal projection excercises
	Avoidance of heterosexual situations	Reeducation and desensitization

Modality	Problem	Proposed Treatment
Affect	Unable to express overt anger	Role playing
	Frequent anxiety	Relaxation training and reassurance
	Absence of enthusiasm and spontaneous joy	Positive imagery procedures
	Panic attacks (usually precipitated by criticism from authority figures)	Desensitization and assertive training
	Suicidal feelings	Time projection techniques
	Emptiness and aloneness	General relationship building
Sensation	Stomach spasms	Abdominal breathing and relaxing
	Out of touch with most sensual pleasures	Sensate focus method
	Tension in jaw and neck	Differential relaxation
	Frequent lower back pains	Orthopedic exercises
	Inner tremors	Gendlin's focusing methods . . .
Imagery	Distressing scenes of sister's funeral	Desensitization
	Mother's angry face shouting "You fool!"	Empty chair technique
	Performing fellatio on God	Blow-up technique (implosion)
	Recurring dreams about airplane bombings	Eidetic imagery invoking feelings of being safe
Cognition	Irrational self-talk: "I am evil." "I must suffer." "Sex is dirty." "I am inferior."	Deliberate rational disputation and corrective self-talk
	Syllogistic reasoning, overgeneralization	Parsing of irrational sentences
	Sexual misinformation	Sexual education
Interpersonal relationships	Characterized by childlike dependence	Specific self-sufficiency assignments
	Easily exploited/submissive	Assertive training
	Overly suspicious	Exaggerated role taking
	Secondary gains from parental concern	Explain reinforcement principles to parents and try to enlist their help
	Manipulative tendencies	Training in direct and confrontative behaviors

The Modality Profile may strike the reader as a fragmented or mechanistic barrage of techniques that would call for a disjointed array of therapeutic maneuvers. In actual practice, the procedures follow logically and blend smoothly into meaningful interventions.

During the course of therapy as more data emerged and as a clearer picture of the patient became apparent, the Modality Profile was constantly revised. Therapy was mainly a process of devising ways and means to remedy Mary Ann's shortcomings and problem areas throughout the basic modalities. The concept of "technical eclecticism" came into its own. In other words, a wide array of therapeutic methods drawn from numerous disciplines was applied, but to remain theoretically consistent, the active ingredients of every technique were sought within the province of social learning theory.

In Mary Ann's case, the array of therapeutic methods selected to restructure her life included familiar behavior therapy techniques such as desensitization, assertive training, role playing, and modeling, but many additional procedures were employed, such as time projection, cognitive restructuring, eidetic imagery, and exaggerated role taking as described in some of the writer's recent publications. The empty chair technique and other methods borrowed from Gestalt therapy and encounter group procedures were added to the treatment regimen. Mary Ann was also seen with her parents for eight sessions, and was in group for 30 weeks.

During the course of therapy she became engaged and was seen with her fiance for premarital counseling for several sessions.

The treatment period covered the span of 13 months at the end of which time she was coping admirably without medication and has continued to do so now for more than a year.

From: Lazarus (1973), pp. 408–410.

Interviewing as the First Step

Since we have already explored the role of the interview in clinical psychology in Chapter 3, here we will briefly examine interviewing as a first step in behavioral assessment. Considering how important interviewing is in targeting behaviors for modification, it is surprising how little attention has been given to this issue in both the clinical and research literatures. The notable exceptions are the excellent papers by Morganstern (1976), Kanfer and Grimm (1977), and Matarazzo and Wiens (1977), each of which acknowledges the gaps in the literature.

Morganstern (1976) details, using hypothetical examples, how initial interviews are directed to clarify and redefine the client's problems and to develop an understanding between therapist and client regarding the behavioral approach to be used. It is important to recognize that the typical client does not come to the first few interviews with a clear statement of the problem. Instead, complaints are usually vague and unstructured. Through therapist-client discussion, the problem is narrowed until the specifics needed for a behavioral analysis emerge.

Throughout the initial interviews, a warm and caring therapist attitude is recommended. Such a response is extremely helpful in facilitating therapy. Naturally, this recommendation has been made for years by traditional clinicians, long before the behavioral approach became popular. But Morganstern (1976) does point out that there are few experimental data on how this recommendation affects behavior therapy. Still, since behavioral approaches do require considerable client participation (e.g., relaxation exercises, homework assignments), these interview guidelines certainly make sense—at least at the intuitive level. Of course, there is an extensive literature on interviewing in traditional psychotherapy, nicely summarized by Matarazzo and Wiens (1972).

Following his earlier theoretical work in behavioral assessment (Kanfer & Phillips, 1970; Kanfer & Saslow, 1969), Kanfer more recently has conceptualized how the interview can be used to identify target behaviors for later modification (cf. Kanfer & Grimm, 1977). Client complaints during the interview may be organized into five categories: (1) behavioral deficits, (2) behavioral excesses, (3) problems in environmental stimulus control, (4) inappropriate self-generated stimulus control, and (5) inappropriate contingency arrangements. The factors that contribute to these categories are identified during more detailed interviews. This later permits the therapist to match the problem category with an appropriate form of therapy.

However, despite their focus on information obtained in the interview, Kanfer and Grimm (1977) stress the pitfalls of overreliance on data based solely on self-reports: "The clinician should differentiate the client's verbal reports regarding his problem from his actual performance. Clients will frequently offer appraisals of their difficulties and report the distress they experience. In so doing, they may misrepresent deficiencies or competencies which they fail to demonstrate. While these verbal reports are informative, the behaviorally oriented clinician will need an analysis of actual performances in particular situations before proceeding to a program for change of the categorized target behaviors" (p. 27).

Motoric Measures

The behaviorists' greatest contribution to the field of measurement may be their emphasis on assessing the client's motor responses (cf. Bellack & Hersen, 1978a; Hersen & Bellack, 1976a). There are probably many reasons for this, but two stand out. First, the behavior therapist is reacting to the traditional psychologist's almost exclusive reliance on data from paper-and-pencil tests. Second is the influence of the behavior analysts (operant psychologists), who are generally distrustful of their clients' verbal reports, questioning their reliability and validity (see the section "Self-Report Measures").

As has already been pointed out, many behavioral assessments are done in the client's natural setting. Thus, children have been observed in their classrooms (e.g., Bijou, Peterson, Harris, Allen, & Johnston, 1969) and psychiatric patients on their hospital wards (e.g., Hersen, Eisler, Alford, & Agras, 1973). In making such assessments, the observer remains as inconspicuous as possible. This is done to avoid the client's possible reaction (e.g., change in rate of the behavior being observed) merely as a result of being observed (i.e., reactivity). At other times, however, the surreptitious observation of the client is impossible,[5] and the client's awareness that he or she is being observed remains an artifact of the measurement process. However, it is a consistent factor throughout the baseline and treatment phases.

Since most motor assessments require human observers, the behaviors under study are precisely defined as to time, distance, and motion. Consider the comprehensive response code devised by Bijou et al. (1969) for evaluating children in the classroom (see Table 5.2). Note, for example, the qualifiers listed for the complete definition of an orienting response ("Must be of 4 seconds duration, not rated unless seated; or more than 90° using the desk as a reference"). It is this kind of precision that enables reliable (i.e., reproducible) ratings to be made when two observers are evaluating the same behavior. (See the subsection "Reliability of Ratings" for a more detailed discussion as to how inter-rater reliability is calculated.)

---

5. This may occur because the conditions are not conducive to such observation or because the client has not given prior consent to being observed without his or her knowledge. This latter point is an important ethical consideration, given the current emphasis on patients' legal rights.

Table 5.2.   General Response Code for Studying Children in a Classroom

Symbols	Classes	Class Definitions
X	Gross motor behaviors	Getting out of seat; standing up; running; hopping; skipping; jumping; walking around; rocking in chair; disruptive movement without noise; moves chair to neighbor; knees on chair.
N	Disruptive noise	Tapping pencil or other objects; clapping; tapping feet; rattling or tearing paper; throwing book on desk, slamming desk. (Be conservative, only rate if could hear noise when eyes closed. Do not include accidental dropping of objects or if noise made while performing X above.)
∧	Disturbing others directly	Grabbing objects or work; knocking neighbor's books off desk; destroying another's property; pushing with desk.
→	Aggression (contact)	Hitting, kicking; shoving; pinching; slapping; striking with object; throwing object at another person; poking with object; biting; pulling hair.
⤳|	Orienting responses	Turning head or head and body to look at another person, showing objects to another child, orienting toward another child. (Must be of 4 seconds duration, not rated unless seated; or more than 90° using the desk as a reference.)
V	Verbalizations	Carrying on conversations with other children when it is not permitted. Answers teacher without raising hand or without being called on; making comments or calling out remarks when no question has been asked; calling teacher's name to get her attention; crying; screaming; singing; whistling; laughing loudly; coughing or blowing loudly. (May be directed to teacher or children.)
//	Other tasks	Ignores teacher's question or command; does something different from that directed to do, includes minor motor behavior such as playing with pencil eraser when supposed to be writing; coloring while the record is on; doing spelling during arithmetic lesson; playing with objects; eating; chewing gum. *The child involves himself in a task that is not appropriate.*
———	Relevant behavior	Time on task; e.g., answers question, looking at teacher when she is talking; raises hand; writing assignment. (Must include whole 20-seond interval except for orienting responses of less than 4 seconds duration.)

From: Bijou et al. (1969), Table 4.

Although it is preferable to measure the client's behavior in its natural setting, this approach is sometimes limited. In some instances, there are ethical limitations in observing client activities (e.g., deviant sexuality). In other instances, it would be too costly, time-consuming, and intrusive to follow the client around in order to observe his or her behavior (e.g., a situation that requires an assertive response, such as interaction with an employer). In both of these illustrations, the behavioral assessor often measures the behavior in a laboratory under controlled, contrived, and fully replicable conditions. For example, in the case of male sexual deviation, the client's penile responsivity (i.e., erectile strength) to audiotaped descriptions of deviant behavior (e.g., pedophilia) or pictures of it may be obtained (see Abel, 1976). In the case of an unassertive client, the responses to role-played situations requiring assertiveness may be videotaped and later rated on a number of variables. Table 5.3 presents the kinds of behaviors that are typically assessed when looking at the client's responses to the role-played scenes of the Behavioral Assertiveness Test-Revised (BAT-R) (Eisler, Hersen, Miller, & Blanchard, 1975; Hersen, Bellack, & Turner, 1978).[6]

During the BAT-R, the client is escorted to the videotape studio and sits on a sofa in a comfortable living room setting. Seated next to the client is a *role model* (male or female, depending on the nature of the interaction) who serves as *prompt*. *Narration* of the scene is usually done from an adjoining control room (containing the recording equipment) over the intercom system. Let us look at a typical scene used in the BAT-R. The narrator says: "You have been working very hard while your co-worker has been goofing off on the job. Your boss comes over to complain to you that the job will never be done on time." At this point, the role model seated next to the client enacts the part of the boss and says: "Say, will you stop fooling around and get the job done." Now the client is expected to respond, with the response and the preceding role model prompt being videotaped. Thus, in the case of rating latency (see Table 5.3), time elapsed from the *end* of the role model's prompt to the *beginning* of the client's response is measured in seconds, and so on.

Many behavioral codes have been developed by clinicians to study a variety of motor behaviors in clients. However, there is no viable code for every problem behavior. Thus, during behavioral assessment, a new measurement approach is often necessary.

---

6. Another example of an analogue measure is Lang and Lazovik's (1963) BAT, used to evaluate fear in phobic subjects.

Table 5.3.   Scoring Criteria for the BAT-R

---

1. *Eye contact*—length of time (in seconds) after delivery of prompt that the subject maintains eye contact while responding to the role model.

2. *Response duration*—length of time (in seconds) that the subject responds to the role model. Speech pauses of more than three seconds terminate timing until the subject begins speaking again.

3. *Response latency*—length of time (in seconds) from the delivery of the prompt to the beginning of the subject's response.

4. *Loudness of speech*—voice volume of the subject's speech for each scene, rated on a five-point scale from 1 (very low) to 5 (appropriately loud).

5. *Voice intonation*—rated on a five-point scale from 1 (very flat, unemotional tone of voice) to 5 (full, lively intonation appropriate to each situation).

6. *Smiles*—rated on an occurrence-nonoccurrence basis for each scene after delivery of prompt to termination of response.

7. *Physical gestures*—rated on an occurrence-nonoccurrence basis for each scene after delivery of prompt to termination of response.

8. *Speech disturbances*—frequency categorized by Mahl (1956), including pauses, stutters, and expletives such as "ah," "oh," "um," etc., recorded for each scene.

9. *Compliance*—rated on an occurrence-nonoccurrence basis for each scene. Compliance is scored if the subject does not resist the partner's position (e.g., agrees to stay and work late for the boss or lets a spouse change the television channel).

10. *Request for new behavior from the interpersonal partner*—rated on an occurrence-nonoccurrence basis for each scene. Responses scored in this category require more than mere noncompliance. The subject has to show evidence of wanting the partner to change his or her behavior (e.g., must request the person at the ballgame to remove his coat, or ask the woman who cuts in front at the grocery store to step to the end of the line).

11. *Praise*—indicates that the subject expresses approval, admiration, or was complimentary toward the partner's behavior (e.g., told his wife that she looks very good in a new outfit). Praise is rated on an occurrence-nonoccurrence basis for each scene.

12. *Appreciation*—indicates that the subject expresses gratitude or thankfulness for the partner's behavior (e.g., thanks the boss for a raise). Appreciation is scored on an occurrence-nonoccurrence basis for each scene.

13. *Spontaneous positive behavior*—indicates that the subject volunteers to perform some act for the partner (e.g., offers to buy a beer for a teammate who just bowled three strikes in a row). Positive behavior is scored on an occurrence-nonoccurrence basis for each scene.

14. *Overall assertiveness*—after all previous behaviors are rated, two additional raters who are not familiar with the purposes of the study are asked to rate the subject's behavior on overall assertiveness, using a five-point scale from 1 ("very unassertive") to 5 ("very assertive"). The ratings are done independently after the raters learn Wolpe's (1969) definition of "hostile" and "commendatory" assertiveness.

Hersen and his colleagues (Bernhardt, Hersen, & Barlow, 1972), for example, had to find a measurement strategy for a psychiatric patient with spasmodic torticollis (a disorder in which the neck muscles repeatedly contract, leading to a repetitive jerking of the head from a frontal position to one side). This patient was videotaped two or three times a day for ten-minute sessions while seated with his profile to the camera. In doing this assessment, the investigators wished to determine the percentage of time per session taken up with torticollis movements. Therefore, "A piece of clear plastic containing superimposed black Chart-Pak taped horizontal lines (spaced one-quarter to one-half in. apart) was placed over the monitor. A shielded observer depressed a switch activating the timer whenever the subject's head was positioned at an angle where the nostril was above a horizontal line intersecting the external auditory meatus. This position was operationally defined as an example of torticollis, with percentage of torticollis per session serving as the experimental measure. Conversely, when the horizontal line intersected both the nostril and auditory meatus or when the subject's nostril was below the horizontal line, he was considered to be holding his head in a normal position" (Bernhardt et al., 1972, p. 295). This definition was precise enough for the two independent observers to agree with one another 71.84 to 94.18 percent of the time (mean = 85.41 percent) for the entire study.

Thus, some innovation may be required in developing assessment strategies. However, there are some guidelines for selecting one strategy over another. During the early stages of assessment, the job consists of narrowing the client's complaints and identifying behaviors to be modified. Then one of four basic measurement approaches must be selected: (1) permanent products, (2) event recording, (3) duration recording, and (4) interval recording (cf. Mann, 1976). Let us examine each of these in turn.

Permanent Products

Mann (1976) has defined a permanent product as "any measurable or observable trace, artifact, or change in the environment which is the result of a specifiable behavior. Such a result or product of a behavior may be permanent or short-lived. Nevertheless, when such results or products are observed, it can be inferred reliably that a specifiable behavior has (or has not) occurred" (p. 468). Examples of permanent product measurement include blood alcohol levels as a result of drinking (Miller, Hersen, Eisler, & Watts, 1974), weight loss as a result of dieting (Mann, 1972), and a wet bed as a result of nocturnal enuresis (Miller, 1973).

A permanent products assessment strategy has certain advantages. First, observer time is minimized since only the end product must be noted. The behavior is inferred from the product. Second, extremely high inter-rater agreement is common since the end product is clearly described. In some cases gauges (e.g., a scale for assessing weight) are used for measurement. Also, the permanent product is easily quantifiable (e.g., enuretic episodes per week). Third, this assessment strategy is easy to implement and to teach both to professionals and nonprofessionals (e.g., parents).

Nonetheless, there are a few drawbacks. The most important one is that the behavior is *inferred* rather than directly seen; thus, there is no guarantee that the target behavior was performed appropriately—or at all. A problem with the permanent products measurement approach appeared in a weight loss study reported by Mann (1972). The overweight client was expected (in accordance with a contingency contract signed by therapist and client) to lose two pounds every two weeks. Otherwise, valuables temporarily given to the therapist could be forfeited. After the study, Mann discovered some clients fasted and took laxatives and diuretics a day or two before the next weigh-in so as to lose the weight. So, although the goal was met, the method used was certainly not approved by the therapist (i.e., target behavior not performed appropriately).

Event Recording

Event recording simply involves tallying the rate of the targeted behavior. For example, in Figure 5.1 (Epstein & Hersen, 1974), the rate of gagging in a case of "conversion reaction" was plotted per day during baseline and treatment phases and per week during the follow-up period. On the first day of baseline the rate was eleven gags per day; on the second day of baseline the rate was seventeen gags per day. By contrast, in follow-up during weeks one to eight, the rate was nine gags per week. During week nine the rate was three gags per week.

This example shows that for a low-frequency behavior, a longer time period is required for representative measurement (gags per week in follow-up). However, for a high-frequency behavior, a shorter time

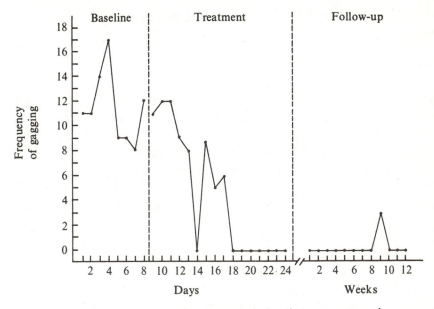

Figure 5.1.   Frequencies of gagging in baseline, treatment, and follow-up periods. (*From:* Epstein & Hersen, 1974, Fig. 1)

period (gags per day in baseline and treatment) is needed (e.g., days rather than weeks; minutes rather than hours).

When several behaviors are targeted for baseline assessment, they can be observed simultaneously if they are precisely defined (e.g., as in the behavioral code devised by Bijou et al., 1969). Note that event recording is appropriate only when the targeted behaviors have clear beginning and end points.

Duration Recording

As with event recording, duration recording requires the targeted behavior to have discrete limits. However, instead of a simple tabulation of the rate of the behavior, its actual duration from onset to termination is determined. For example, in the coding scheme for the BAT-R, duration of speech is measured in seconds from the beginning to the end of the subject's response following the role model's prompt (see Table 5.3). Also, duration recording is more likely to be used than event recording when the targeted behavior is long-lasting (e.g., hours of sleep per night).

Depending on the targeted behaviors and the interests of the clinician or clinical researcher, duration data can be presented in several ways. First, the duration of a high-frequency behavior can be calculated (using a stop watch) each time it occurs. An average of the durations may then be obtained. Second, by adding each duration for each occurrence, a cumulative duration of the behavior is presented. And third, the cumulative duration of the behavior may be presented as a fraction (i.e., percentage of time that the behavior occurred compared to total time measured). Thus, the total time interval is divided by the cumulative number of minutes that the behavior was observed and multiplied by 100.

Figure 5.2 (although actually based on a patient's *self-reports*) shows the use of both frequency and duration measurement (Turner, Hersen, & Bellack, 1977). The bottom part of the graph portrays frequency of hallucinations for probe sessions for a chronic schizophrenic (event recording). The middle part of the graph shows the mean duration of hallucinations per session (duration recording—mean). The top part of the graph gives the percentage of time per session that the patient reported engaging in hallucinatory behavior (duration recording—percent time).

Interval Recording

For certain behaviors, the discrete limits and rate of occurrence are difficult to determine. In such cases, frequency or duration recording methods cannot be used. In such cases, an interval recording strategy (also known as *time sampling)* is more appropriate. With this strategy, the observer chooses a time interval and simply notes whether the targeted behavior *occurs* or fails to occur. Bellack and Hersen (1978a) state the issue as follows:

> Consider rating the hallucinatory behavior of a schizophrenic (i.e., gestures associated with reports of hallucinations). If he gestures constantly for 5 seconds, stops for 2 seconds, then gestures again, should he be scored for two occurrences or one? Any conclusion would be arbitrary, and

Figure 5.2.   Percent time, mean duration, and frequency of hallucinatory behavior during probe sessions and follow-up in a chronic schizophrenic patient. (*From:* Turner, Hersen, & Bellack, 1977, Fig. 1)

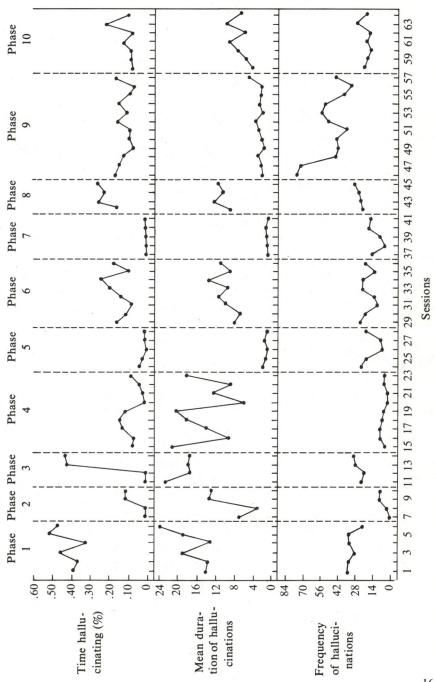

scoring would probably be unreliable. The behavior could be defined such that response breaks of more than x-second would be scored for new occurrences, alleviating some of the ambiguity for the rater. However, each pause would then have to be timed, which is a difficult task; interval recording . . . would probably be a more appropriate alternative (p. 15).

Our hallucinating schizophrenic might be observed for the first ten minutes of each hour between 8 A.M. and 5 P.M. Each ten-minute observation period could then be subdivided into twenty thirty-second intervals. Thus, the patient could be observed for the first fifteen seconds of the thirty-second time interval, with the last fifteen seconds reserved for recording purposes.

A stopwatch is commonly used for interval recording; however, this may prove distracting to the observer. Better yet are prerecorded audiotapes, which delineate the preset time intervals with a beep or buzzer. Figure 5.3 shows the type of data sheet typically used for interval recording. The observer simply puts a check mark or an x in the box (i.e., time interval) if the behavior is noted and then proceeds to observe and record for the following time interval.

Some trial and error may take place while the time interval to be used for observation is chosen. Generally, however, high-frequency and short-duration behaviors will require short observation periods (five to twenty seconds). By contrast, low-frequency and high-duration behaviors require long observation periods twenty-five seconds or more).

Interval recording strategies have several advantages. First, high inter-rater reliabilty is usually obtained. Second, several behaviors (up to five or six may be rated simultaneously, as with the Bijou et al. (1969) behavioral code (see Table 5.2). Third, the strategy is a time saver since only a small portion of the time is spent observing (hence the designation *time sampling*). However, there is one major disadvantage: Interval recording does not allow for differentiation as to frequency versus duration per interval. Thus, if the behavior occurs once in the first interval and three times in the next interval, the rating for each interval is the same (i.e., one check mark to indicate that the behavior occurred). Similarly, whether the behavior lasts five or twenty seconds, this factor does not appear. Once again, the check mark is the only indication.

Reliability (Inter-Rater Agreement)

Except for permanent products measurement, where gauges are sometimes used, most motor indices require human observers. Of course, to

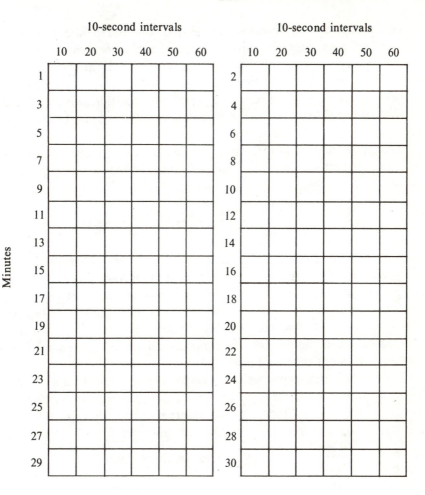

Figure 5.3.   An interval recording data sheet designed for a half-hour observation session. Each minute of the session has been divided into six ten-second intervals. (*From:* Mann, 1976, Fig. 17.1)

minimize the possibility of error, very precise definitions of target behaviors are given and the observers are generally pretrained. However, even with such precautions, error can always occur. Therefore, as a convention, behavioral assessors require two observers. The primary observer makes all the observations needed. The independent observer (the checker) then rates one-third to one-half of the observation periods.

When interval data are obtained (e.g., duration, frequency), the two independent sets of observations are evaluated by a Pearson Product-Moment correlation. If the resulting correlation coefficient is equal to or greater than $r = 0.80$, then an acceptable level of *reliability* between the two observers has been achieved.

Data obtained from interval recording (i.e., occurrence-nonoccurrence) are evaluated differently. The *inter-rater agreement* percentage is calculated as follows:

$$\frac{\text{agreements}}{\text{agreements plus disagreements}} \times 100$$

When agreement occurs, both observers record occurrence of the targeted behavior for the same interval. Although agreements for *nonoccurrence* may be scored when the targeted behavior is infrequent, in most calculations *only* occurrences are scored (see Hersen & Barlow, 1976, Chapter 4). The reason for this is that when agreements for non-occurrences are included, the resulting percentage of agreement is inflated and thus nonrepresentative.

Let us look at a hypothetical example and see how data are evaluated in the above formula. Consider the case where twenty observations are made and the two independent observers agree that the behavior occurred for sixteen intervals but disagree on the other four. Inter-rater agreement $= \dfrac{16}{16 + 4} \times 100 = 80\%$ The resulting inter-rater agreement is 80 percent. Also, by convention, inter-rater agreements of 80 percent or more are considered acceptable.

Finally, even though high inter-rater agreement (or reliability) is attained, the observers may be agreeing on something that is not actually there (cf. Wahler & Leske, 1973). That is, inter-rater agreement does not ensure high *accuracy*. Accuracy can be achieved only by training the observers to a high predetermined criterion and by periodically monitoring their observations.

Presenting Data

Given their empirical orientation, behavioral assessors generally graph the data obtained during baseline, treatment, and follow-up phase.

Further, several data points appear on the graph for each phase. Repeated measures per phase appear in Figures 5.1 and 5.2. Such repeated measurements are made to determine specific trends in the data (e.g., steady and stable, increase, decrease). (See Chapter 10 for a more complete description of baseline and treatment phases as used in single case research designs.) In any event, by analyzing the graphed data, the behavioral clinician can determine whether the targeted behaviors have improved as a result of treatment.

In the graph, the vertical axis (i.e., the ordinate) shows the strength of the targeted behaviors (e.g., rate, duration)—for example, the number of calories consumed by an overweight subject. In Figure 5.1, frequency of gagging is depicted. The horizontal axis (i.e., the abscissa) represents time (e.g., days, weeks, sessions). In Figure 5.1, days 1 to 24 and weeks 1 to 12 appear on the abscissa.

Self-Report Measures

Had this chapter been written in the early to mid-1960s, it would have included only a passing reference to the use of self-reports in behavioral assessment. As has been noted elsewhere (Bellack & Hersen, 1977b; Hersen, 1977), the earlier behaviorists were reluctant to use self-report data. This was based on their reaction against the prevailing "mentalism" of the times. Moreover, it has been argued that "Aside from their concern with objectivity, reliability, and validity, the 'earlier' behaviorists did have the distinct need of being and appearing to be different" (Hersen, 1977, pp. 1–2).

Nonetheless, there were solid reasons for relegating self-reports to the back burner. First was (and is) the issue of reliability. The same questions posed to the same client on two separate occasions (with only a brief time interval between) may elicit totally different responses. For example, if a chronic psychiatric patient intent on remaining in the hospital is interviewed in regard to discharge plans, he might present himself as sick. On the other hand, if the same patient is interviewed for obtaining better hospital privileges, he might present himself as healthy. This has been termed *impression management* (Braginsky & Braginsky, 1967). Under other circumstances, the client's verbal report might be dictated by the perceived "demand characteristics" of the situation (cf. Orne, 1962). That is, if a client perceives that the therapist expects her to get better (a normal expectation), the client may indicate that she is doing better *even though this may not be the truth.*

Second was (and is) the issue of validity. Usually, in assessing the validity of a verbal report, the external criterion against which the report is judged is the client's motor and physiological responses. Of course, in many such attempts at validation, the resulting correlations (self-report and motor; self-report and physiological) have been relatively low (cf. Begelman & Hersen, 1973; Hersen, 1973; Lang, 1968). However, a recent study (Lick, Sushinsky, & Malow, 1977) shows that such low correlations may be due not to invalidity but to the methodological inadequacies in obtaining good self-report data.

Let us examine this issue in greater detail. There are many ways of obtaining self-report data, ranging from open-ended questions, to specific questions, to very specific questions that parallel the motor criteria by which the validity of the self-report will be judged.[7] Unfortunately, many self-report questionnaires (such as the Fear Survey Schedule-II in Table 5.4) include no precise description of what the client or subject may be asked to do motorically in the laboratory or field situation. For example, consider item 39 (snakes). The subject filling out the FSS-II is simply asked to rate his fear of snakes on a scale ranging from 1 (none) to 7 (terror). If greater detail were provided on the specifics of the ensuing laboratory task (to approach, look, touch, and hold a harmless, nonpoisonous snake for thirty seconds), a stronger correlation between self-report and motor indices might be obtained. This is precisely what Lick et al. (1977) demonstrated.

Correlations between self-report and motor indices of fear increase as the FSS-II item (snakes) becomes more detailed as to what the subject is expected to do in the BAT laboratory situation ($r = 0.37, 0.60, 0.68$). These findings have been paralleled in a second study using item 10 (rat). Again, correlations between subjects' self-report and motor indices of fear increased as the FSS-II item became more detailed ($r = 0.53, 0.78, 0.81$).

Although greater precision in questions seems to produce greater concordance between self-report and motor indices, it is equally important for the client to learn how to observe and record his or her own behavior. This is the objective in having a client monitor his or her own behavior (e.g., caloric consumption per meal; number of cigarettes smoked per day; number of deviant sexual urges; number of obsessive thoughts). However, even under this condition, the relationship between self-recorded and observed behavior may vary (cf. Hamilton & Bornstein, 1977).

7. Self-report data may be obtained via the client's oral report or through written responses to questionnaires and test inventories.

Table 5.4.   Fear Survey Schedule II (FSS-II)

		Very Little	A Little	Some	Much	Very Much	Terror
1. Sharp objects	None	Very Little	A Little	Some	Much	Very Much	Terror
2. Being a passenger in a car	None	Very Little	A Little	Some	Much	Very Much	Terror
3. Dead bodies	None	Very Little	A Little	Some	Much	Very Much	Terror
4. Suffocating	None	Very Little	A Little	Some	Much	Very Much	Terror
5. Failing a test	None	Very Little	A Little	Some	Much	Very Much	Terror
6. Looking foolish	None	Very Little	A Little	Some	Much	Very Much	Terror
7. Being a passenger in an airplane	None	Very Little	A Little	Some	Much	Very Much	Terror
8. Worms	None	Very Little	A Little	Some	Much	Very Much	Terror
9. Arguing with parents	None	Very Little	A Little	Some	Much	Very Much	Terror
10. Rats and mice	None	Very Little	A Little	Some	Much	Very Much	Terror
11. Life after death	None	Very Little	A Little	Some	Much	Very Much	Terror
12. Hypodermic needles	None	Very Little	A Little	Some	Much	Very Much	Terror
13. Being criticized	None	Very Little	A Little	Some	Much	Very Much	Terror
14. Meeting someone new for the first time	None	Very Little	A Little	Some	Much	Very Much	Terror
15. Roller coasters	None	Very Little	A Little	Some	Much	Very Much	Terror
16. Being alone	None	Very Little	A Little	Some	Much	Very Much	Terror
17. Making mistakes	None	Very Little	A Little	Some	Much	Very Much	Terror
18. Being misunderstood	None	Very Little	A Little	Some	Much	Very Much	Terror
19. Death	None	Very Little	A Little	Some	Much	Very Much	Terror
20. Being in a fight	None	Very Little	A Little	Some	Much	Very Much	Terror
21. Crowded places	None	Very Little	A Little	Some	Much	Very Much	Terror

Table 5.4.   (*Continued*)

	None	Very Little	A Little	Some	Much	Very Much	Terror
22. Blood	None	Very Little	A Little	Some	Much	Very Much	Terror
23. Heights	None	Very Little	A Little	Some	Much	Very Much	Terror
24. Being a leader	None	Very Little	A Little	Some	Much	Very Much	Terror
25. Swimming alone	None	Very Little	A Little	Some	Much	Very Much	Terror
26. Illness	None	Very Little	A Little	Some	Much	Very Much	Terror
27. Being with drunks	None	Very Little	A Little	Some	Much	Very Much	Terror
28. Illness or injury	None	Very Little	A Little	Some	Much	Very Much	Terror
29. Being self-conscious	None	Very Little	A Little	Some	Much	Very Much	Terror
30. Driving a car	None	Very Little	A Little	Some	Much	Very Much	Terror
31. Meeting authority	None	Very Little	A Little	Some	Much	Very Much	Terror
32. Mental illness	None	Very Little	A Little	Some	Much	Very Much	Terror
33. Closed places	None	Very Little	A Little	Some	Much	Very Much	Terror
34. Boating	None	Very Little	A Little	Some	Much	Very Much	Terror
35. Spiders	None	Very Little	A Little	Some	Much	Very Much	Terror
36. Thunderstorms	None	Very Little	A Little	Some	Much	Very Much	Terror
37. Not being a success	None	Very Little	A Little	Some	Much	Very Much	Terror
38. God	None	Very Little	A Little	Some	Much	Very Much	Terror
39. Snakes	None	Very Little	A Little	Some	Much	Very Much	Terror
40. Cemeteries	None	Very Little	A Little	Some	Much	Very Much	Terror
41. Speaking before a group	None	Very Little	A Little	Some	Much	Very Much	Terror
42. Seeing a fight	None	Very Little	A Little	Some	Much	Very Much	Terror
43. Death of a loved one	None	Very Little	A Little	Some	Much	Very Much	Terror

Table 5.4.   (*Continued*)

		Very Little	A Little	Some	Much	Very Much	Terror
44. Dark places	None	Very Little	A Little	Some	Much	Very Much	Terror
45. Strange dogs	None	Very Little	A Little	Some	Much	Very Much	Terror
46. Deep water	None	Very Little	A Little	Some	Much	Very Much	Terror
47. Being with a member of the opposite sex	None	Very Little	A Little	Some	Much	Very Much	Terror
48. Stinging insects	None	Very Little	A Little	Some	Much	Very Much	Terror
49. Untimely or early death	None	Very Little	A Little	Some	Much	Very Much	Terror
50. Losing a job	None	Very Little	A Little	Some	Much	Very Much	Terror
51. Auto accidents	None	Very Little	A Little	Some	Much	Very Much	Terror

From: Geer (1965), Table 1.

Despite the limitations of the self-monitoring approach, it is a more formalized way of measuring behaviors (e.g., obsessive thoughts) that are not directly observable. In contrast to casually obtained retrospective self-reports, in self-monitoring clients are instructed how and when to observe and record specified behaviors. Thus, for example, instead of relying on retrospective reports as to calories consumed per day, the client is asked to list foods eaten immediately after each meal, with the number of calories equated per food. The time and place of the meal are also to be indicated. The client records these data on lined 3" × 5" cards or in a small notebook, either of which is easily portable. Or, in the case of smoking, a client will be instructed to indicate on a wrist counter each time a cigarette has been lit and smoked.

In spite of the greater precision of self-monitoring strategies, there is evidence that the act of self-monitoring alters the natural rate of the targeted behavior. Sometimes the reactive effects are in the therapeutic direction (cf. Bellack & Schwartz, 1976). Therefore, the behavioral assessor must be cautious in using self-monitoring data as the basis for evaluation.

Another problem in correlating self-reports with motor and physiological measures is that total scores for paper-and-pencil self-reports are used in the statistical computation. As has been pointed out, such correlations are much more likely to be acceptable if individual item scores (cf. Bellack & Hersen, 1977b) or factor scores (cf. Hersen, 1973) are used. Once again, the problem *is methodological*.

Despite the attitude of some behaviorists toward self-report data, and in spite of certain methodological and psychometric problems with current self-report questionnaires, self-report data are used extensively in clinical practice. (A more comprehensive description of such questionnaires is found in Cautela & Upper, 1976). Although many kinds of self-report devices are used in behavioral therapy, most of them fall under four headings: (1) fear, (2) anxiety, (3) depression, and (4) social skill. Several of the more popular self-report measures in these categories are listed in Table 5.5.

In other instances, with more esoteric problems, new self-report inventories are improvised. However, the psychometric properties of these tests are generally not known—nor have they been investigated (see the section "Critical Appraisal" for a more complete discussion of this issue).

Table 5.5.   Self-Report Measures used in Behavioral Assessment

Topic	Scale	Reference
Fear	Fear Survey Schedule I	Lang & Lazovik (1963)
Fear	Fear Survey Schedule II	Geer (1965)
Anxiety	State-Trait Anxiety Inventory	Speilberger, Gorsuch, & Lushene (1970)
Anxiety	S-R Inventory of General Trait Anxiousness	Endler & Okada (1975)
Depression	Beck Depression Inventory	Beck, Ward, Mendelsohn, Mock, & Erbaugh (1961)
Depression	Pleasant Events Schedule	Lewinsohn & Graf (1973)
Depression	Generalized Contentment Scale	Hudson & Proctor (1977)
Social skill	Wolpe-Lazarus Assertiveness Scale	Wolpe & Lazarus (1966)
Social skill	Conflict Resolution Inventory	McFall & Lillesand (1971)
Social skill	College Self-Expression Scale	Galassi, DeLo, Galassi, & Bastien (1974)

Physiological Measures

In the last decade, behavioral assessors have shown an increased concern for their clients' physiological responses—those (e.g., heart rate, blood pressure, pulse rate, galvanic skin response, respiration rate, penile responsivity to sexual stimuli, EMG) directly controlled by the autonomic system. Probably the greatest impetus to measurement of physiological responses is the fact that behaviorists have developed paradigms (i.e., biofeedback) for their *direct modification* (cf. Blanchard & Epstein, 1977). Earlier, the consensus was that physiological responses could not be modified by psychological means.

Another reason for the interest in physiological responses is that they are much less easily distorted by the client. Thus, they are considered to have greater reliability and validity than, say, self-report indices. Nevertheless, physiological responses have their own measurement problems. We will now examine some of them.

Mechanical Problems

With the exception of pulse rate, which can be measured by hand (e.g., Miller, Hersen, Eisler, & Hilsman, 1974), the great majority of physiological responses (e.g., heart rate) require expensive recording equipment, such as polygraphs, in order to obtain good records of repeated assessments. Further, this sensitive equipment involves careful maintenance, delicate calibration, and a thorough knowledge of its operation by the laboratory assistants who usually conduct such assessments. Hersen and Barlow (1976) caution that laboratory assistants "would . . . be well advised to first practice all procedures with non-clinical subjects before actually monitoring physiological reactivity during experimental treatment" (p. 139).

Adaptation Phases

In considering physiological assessment, the behavioral clinician should know that the laboratory situation (with its complicated equipment, gadgetry, and wire leads attached to the client) is itself quite likely to cause extensive physiological arousal and reactivity. Thus, each time a client is evaluated in the laboratory, an appropriate time period (perhaps ranging from five to thirty minutes) is required to obtain an accurate baseline appraisal of the targeted response system. For example, Epstein, Hersen, and Hemphill (1974) used a ten-minute adaptation phase for the frontalis muscle tension evaluation of their headache patient. Similarly, Hersen, Bellack, and Turner (1978) used a fifteen-minute adaptation period in assessing heart rate and finger pulse volume in their female psychiatric patients. In determining the length of the adaptation phase, some trial and error is typical until a stable baseline recording pattern emerges.

Repeated Measurement

Repeated measurements are the mainstay of behavioral assessment. However, in physiological assessments, there are certain disadvantages. For example, some studies show that the magnitude of the galvanic skin response (GSR) decreases upon repeated testing (cf. Montagu & Coles, 1966). Also, in the case of repeated measurements of sexual responsivity to erotic stimuli (i.e., penile responsivity to audiotaped presentations of deviant sexual activity; see Abel, 1976), the fatigue factor later in testing should not be discounted. Thus, when treatment begins after a long series of initial baseline measurements, a decrease in physiological response *may* represent improvements—or simply diminished responsivity due to fatigue.

Individual Response Differences

Changes in physiological response (e.g., elevated heart rate) are often thought to represent increased emotional arousal. For example, in some studies emotional arousal is measured by taking pre- and post-experimental assessments for one or two physiological response systems (e.g., heart rate, pulse rate). However, any resulting statistical differences might be obliterated if all of the subjects in the study are not heart rate and pulse rate responders when stressed. Excellent research evidence shows that individual response patterns to emotional arousal are probably genetically determined (cf. Lacey, 1956). Some persons, when stressed, respond with increased heart rate, others with increased GSR, still others with increased respiration rate, and so on. Of course, in the *individual* assessment of clients, this problem is minimized, particularly if several response systems are measured.

Case Illustration

Let us now examine a physiological assessment strategy used in our clinical work. The client was a fifty-two-year-old man who entered a VA hospital stating that he had had an incestual relationship with his oldest daughter for about five years (Harbert, Barlow, Hersen, & Austin, 1974). Incestual activity consisted of mutual masturbation, kissing, and fondling.

In addition to a standardized self-report test, we wished to obtain physiological measures during baseline, treatment, and follow-up phases that would be less subject to distortion by the client.[8] Therefore, we measured the client's penile reactivity (i.e., penile circumference changes) in reaction to three photographs of his daughter and two audiotaped sequences in which incestual activity with the daughter was narrated.

In this case, a mechanical strain gauge for recording penile circumference changes was used (see Barlow, Becker, Leitenberg, & Agras, 1970). The ring part of the gauge was placed on the mid-shaft of the penis, with the apparatus electronically connected to a Grass preamplifier that recorded circumference changes as erections waxed and waned. In general, this kind of "measurement situation involves the subject being seated in a comfortable chair with the ring placed on the penis. In pre-experimental trials maximum erection diameter is determined. Subsequent responses to . . . deviant sexual stimuli are scored on the basis of percentage of full erection. Response latency to stimuli may vary from 60 to 120 seconds. Inter-trial intervals are determined by the amount of time needed to return to baseline levels of responding. This may require from 30 to 300 seconds. At times initial baseline levels are not retrieved, and new baseline levels are established" (Hersen & Barlow, 1976, p. 156).

Data collected during all phases of this case study are presented in Figure 5.4. The figure shows that mean penile circumference change per probe session was calculated as a percentage of full erection.

---

8. Since penile responsivity is partially under voluntary control, it does have some of the properties of a motor response.

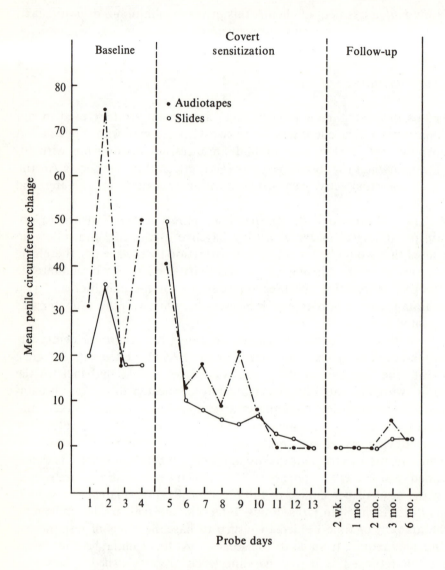

Figure 5.4.　Mean penile circumference change to audiotapes and slides during baseline, covert sensitization, and follow-up. (*From:* Harbert et al., 1974, Fig. 1)

Interrelationship of the Three Response Systems

From our prior discussion of motor, self-report, and physiological measures, it appears that complete concordance among the three response systems is rare (cf. Hersen, 1973; Lang, 1968). Thus, in assessing clients, the behavioral clinician must decide which or how many of the three measurement systems will be used to determine the success or failure of the therapy. In other words, what is the criterion for establishing that improvement has taken place?

As previously indicated, the behaviorists (largely because of their distrust of the verbal report) initially used motor indices almost exclusively. Sometimes they assumed (erroneously) that if the motor behavior was treated and showed improvement, self-reports would follow suit. This has been referred to elsewhere as "attitudinal lag" (Hersen, 1973). Frequently, in fact, indices will improve while self-report and physiological measures remain unaltered.

The more current thinking is that the three response systems, although somewhat correlated at times, may function independently. Thus, a phobic client who learns to approach and confront the phobic object, as a result of treatment focused on motor improvement, may still report feeling uncomfortable as well as show considerable autonomic reactivity in the phobic situation. (Many other combinations are also possible.) Here, direct therapy for the client's cognitions (i.e., self-reports) and physiological system is *definitely* indicated. Certainly, with the advent of biofeedback and the more recent emphasis on cognitive behavior therapy (e.g., Meichenbaum, 1976), these response systems should not only be given equal weight in the behavioral assessment but should also receive equal therapeutic attention. Finally, the client's statement that he or she does not feel well, even though he may appear to be doing well motorically, can *never* be ignored by the competent clinician, behavioral or otherwise (Bellack & Hersen, 1977b).

Range of Settings

Closely related to the previous discussion is the range of settings in which behavioral assessment takes place. The setting has considerable influence on which or how many of the three response systems serve as criteria for determining improvement. Consider private practitioners, for example. Generally, their criteria for improvement are based on clients' self-reports, their own observations of clients' overt behavior, and perhaps the reports of significant others in the clients' lives. It is rare for the private clinician to have the equipment needed for physiological assessments unless biofeedback is used.

On the other hand, the clinical-researcher in the educational or hospital setting may have access to a large staff, including research technicians, who can observe the client's overt behavior in the classroom or on the ward as well as in laboratory situations. Moreover, in both educational and hospital settings, expensive equipment for monitoring physiological responses is more likely to be available.

Another factor in behavioral assessment is whether the evaluation is for clinical or research purposes. Generally, clients assessed for research are examined more precisely than those in the clinical context. However, because of the limited focus of the usual research study (i.e., in large-scale group comparison designs), such an evaluation *may* be less comprehensive (with respect to all possible problem areas) than clinical assessment. But again, the researcher usually has better resources (equipment and staff) for conducting fine-grained analyses of targeted problems.

Probably the most sophisticated assessments are those that occur during single case research (cf. Hersen & Barlow, 1976) in which the client's problems are dealt with sequentially (e.g., Hersen, Turner, Edelstein, & Pinkston, 1975). Here, because of the repeated evaluations in all phases of treatment, the flexibility of the approach, and the equipment and personnel available, behavioral assessment is optimum.

Role of the Paraprofessional

At this point, we feel that the respective roles of the clinical psychologist and the paraprofessional in behavioral assessment should be clarified. Because the target behaviors are specific and the behavioral assessment process is somewhat routine, much of the actual work can be done by paraprofessionals. That is, behavioral technicians with a B.A. or B.S. degree can observe behavior and recording data after the behavioral code system has been established for a given client. Also, as previously noted, in self-monitoring programs, clients themselves observe and record data. However, In either case, supervision by a clinical psychologist with an advanced degree is required. Indeed, without close supervision, the reliability of recordings may actually diminish (cf. Hersen & Barlow, 1976, Chapter 4).

It is the clinical psychologist who usually identifies the target behaviors through both interview and observational procedures. Changes in target measures to be observed are also the primary function of the clinician. Finally, interpretation of resulting data is generally done by the senior clinician. However, it is our experience that with increased practice in a specific area of assessment, the paraprofessional develops the ability to select appropriate targets. By delegating many of the more routine behavioral assessment tasks to technicians, senior clinicians can free their time for professional activities more consistent with their level of education.

Critical Appraisal

Let us now briefly examine how behavioral assessment contributes to overall client evaluation. In so doing, we will identify the positive aspects of this approach as well as some of the current deficiencies and gaps in the measurement devices used.

First, behavioral assessors have shown the importance of measuring motor behavior of clients in both natural and laboratory settings. Many innovative assessment techniques have been developed—often improvised when no strategies were available. Much attention has also been given to obtaining reliable measurements of targeted behaviors. Second, repeated measurements throughout baseline, treatment, and follow-up phases have been the hallmark of behavioral assessment. Third, the importance of looking simultaneously at the client's motor behaviors, physiological responses, and self-reports has repeatedly been stated. Recent emphasis, then, is on the evaluation of the *whole* client. Finally, but probably most important, behavioral assessors have shown how assessment and treatment may be directly related in practice.

However, despite these contributions, behavioral assessment has come under fire in the last few years (e.g., Goldfried & Linehan, 1977; Leitenberg, 1978). In many instances, the criticism is justified.

First, in spite of the innovative measures used to evaluate motor behaviors, particularly those of the analogue variety, the psychometric properties of these strategies are not known. For example, how does role-played behavior relate to actual behaviors in the environment? What is the test-retest reliability of role-played assessment strategies? Although some attempts have been made to look at these issues (e.g., Bellack, Hersen, & Turner, 1978), this is not the norm. And, speaking of norms, where are the normative data for both nonclinical and clinical populations on analogue measures and behavioral codes used in natural settings? Generally, these data have not been reported.

Second, but hardly surprising, the psychometric properties are generally not available for the many self-report inventories developed in clinical work. With some exceptions (e.g., Geer, 1965), issues of item analyses, split-half reliability, test-retest reliability, criterion validity, construct validity, and factorial structure have either been ignored or handled unsatisfactorily. The impression one gets is that in discarding traditional psychological testing, the "baby" may sometimes have been "thrown out with the bath water."

Third is an issue most applicable to behavioral assessors working in psychiatric settings. Often in their zeal to pinpoint appropriate motor targets for behavioral treatment, the more naive of them have ignored or miscast symptoms that have a biological basis. An example of this is the vegetative symptomatology including sleep, appetite, and sexual desire problems associated with unipolar depression. Indeed, some behavioral psychiatrists (e.g., Liberman & Davis, 1975; Stern, 1978) have argued for the much needed collaboration between behaviorally oriented and pharmacologically oriented clinicians.

Summary

This chapter has described the contribution of behavioral assessment to the field of clinical psychology. We first examined the emergence of behavioral assessment. Possible reasons for the recently increased interest in it were provided. Next, the theoretical thinking underlying behavioral assessment was presented, along with several behavioral schemes for assessing clients.

The majority of the chapter dealt with the three response systems (motor, self-report, physiological) evaluated by behavioral assessors, with several illustrative case examples. In addition, we examined the interrelationship of these response systems and considered how certain assessment strategies may be limited by the setting in which they are carried out. Finally, we briefly appraised both the positive contribution of behavioral assessment and the deficiencies in some of the instruments routinely used.

CHAPTER
SIX

Psychoanalytic Psychotherapies

As previously indicated, clinical psychologists fill many roles and work in a great variety of settings. Despite this diversity, the core of the profession remains the treatment of disturbed individuals. Academic psychologists typically teach therapeutic theory and skills to graduate students. Ultimately, clinically oriented research aims at the understanding and relief of disordered behavior. Clinical psychologists in administrative positions usually work in service agencies, and of course, the vast majority of clinical psychologists spend much of their time giving direct service to clients. In essence, clinical psychology is a service-oriented profession. In this section of the book we will describe and analyze the major types of treatment services clinicians provide. We will first consider the psychoanalytic psychotherapies and behavior therapy. Then we will look at the humanistic approach and community psychology. As the student might well imagine, many books have been written about subtopics of each of these chapters. Hence, we will survey a subsample of the most widely used approaches.

This chapter focuses on the most popular orientations: psychoanalytic and psychodynamic psychotherapy. In addition to discussing these strategies, we will consider some general issues in psychotherapy, including what it is, what actually goes on during sessions, what various approaches have in common, and how they (purportedly) differ. As will be seen, most therapists approach their craft as an art rather than a science (or technology), making it difficult to specify what therapy is and how it should be conducted. Furthermore, while the doctrines of the various "schools" or theoretical orientations can be outlined, each therapist really has a personal theory and varies techniques accordingly.

With this general background as perspective, we will next consider classic psychoanalytic therapy, the basis of all contemporary techniques. This will be followed by a discussion of neo-Freudian and psychodynamic therapies. These approaches represent a fairly direct evolutionary chain from early psychoanalytic theory and practice. They attempt to correct some of the major limitations of psychoanalytic theory and technique. The next two sections will deal with extensions of individual adult psychotherapy: group therapy and family therapy. The controversial and confusing status of the voluminous therapy outcome literature will then be discussed, and the problems of therapy outcome research will be highlighted. As will be seen, it is generally presumed that psychotherapy can be effective, but such issues as how it works and for whom remain unanswered. This final section will also consider some of the issues involved in viewing therapy as an art rather than as a scientifically based technology.

What is Psychotherapy?

Psychotherapy is a widely practiced procedure involving thousands of professionals and hundreds of thousands of clients. It is one of the major activities of several professions, including clinical psychology, psychiatry, and psychiatric social work. It has been practiced with little change throughout most of the twentieth century. During this time, it has become an accepted part of our social system, appearing regularly in our humor, literature, television, and in daily conversation. Given its prevasive influence and the prestige of its practitioners, one would expect much agreement about what psychotherapy is, how it should be conducted, who can profit from it, and how it works. Unfortunately, each of these issues is the subject of considerable controversy. Some practitioners and patients swear to its effectiveness, while many critics regard it as no better than quackery. Some regard a medical degree and a personal psychoanalysis as necessary prerequisites for the therapist, while others have argued that, with a little training, housewives, bartenders, and others can perform as effectively as highly educated professionals (cf. Matarazzo, 1971). The effectiveness of therapy has been ascribed to such diverse processes as the helping relationship, nonspecific conditioning effects, and insight. In fact, the only agreed-on point about psychotherapy is that it is mired in confusion and conflict.

One basic source of disagreement pertains to what psychotherapy is. A recent report by the National Institute of Mental Health identified no less than 130 different types of therapy (Brown, 1976). These variants were relatively clearly elaborated. Undoubtedly there are many others which have not been systematically articulated. It has even been argued that every therapist conducts a personal form of psychotherapy (Ford & Urban, 1963). In some cases, two different therapies might differ on some technical point, such as the proper timing and depth of interpretation. In other instances, the differences are quite substantive, extending to the very nature and goals of the entire therapeutic endeavor. It is these major differences which make it impossible to define psychotherapy to everyone's satisfaction. That is, goals, procedures, and the like may vary so greatly that one therapist may simply not regard another therapist's activity as psychotherapy.

This issue has been highlighted by Reisman (1971)—who, in reviewing the literature on psychotherapy, uncovered thirty-one distinct definitions. As with types of therapy, there are undoubtedly many more definitions which have not been clearly specified. According to Reisman, definitions can be classified on the basis of their emphasis on (1) the goals of the interaction, (2) the procedures employed by the therapist, (3) the qualifications of the therapist, or (4) the unique relationship between therapist and client. Definitions emphasizing goals see therapy as a vehicle for such things as personal growth, development of insight, and the elimination of psychological distress. These definitions are problematic since there is little agreement as to what the goals should be. Rather, goals are tied directly to theoretical notions of human behavior and psychological disorder. A comprehensive definition would have to cross such theoretical boundaries. A similar criticism pertains to definitions which emphasize procedures. These definitions also suffer because no adequate data exist to specify which procedures are critical. It seems presumptuous to say that psychotherapy entails doing X, Y, or Z when those procedures might be totally irrelevant to the outcome.

Definitions in the third category usually specify that therapy requires a trained professional. This distinguishes it from other situations in which psychological help is provided, such as confiding in a friend or relative, or a member of the clergy. These definitions do not specify what the professional does or whether or not the professional background is necessary. The final category emphasizes the special relationship between therapist and client. This relationship is generally presumed to play a crucial role in the treatment process, and it will be discussed further below. For the moment, suffice it to say that most of the criticisms of the other definitions also apply here: lack of supportive data, theoretical conflict, and inadequate specification of exactly what the relationship entails and how it operates.

Our own feeling is that any attempt to formulate a comprehensive definition is fruitless for two reasons. First, there is simply too much conflict and diversity in the field to allow for any consensus. Any definition would exclude too many therapists and theorists to be of much use. Second, we do not have enough data about psychotherapy to support any particular definition. One reason why so much theoretical diversity persists is that most conceptualizations cannot be ruled out. One other difficulty with definitions is that they tend to become too concrete, leading to an obsessive analysis of each word. While there is little agreement on any specific definition of psychotherapy, there is much informal agreement. Thus, most mental health professionals who observed a variety of therapy sessions would agree that therapy was going on. They would simply disagree about how appropriate or effective the various interactions were.

Ford and Urban (1963) have identified four widely accepted characteristics of psychotherapy. First, therapy involves two people in an interaction (this refers to *individual* psychotherapy, in contrast to family or group therapy). This interaction is usually face to face (or face to back, as in classic psychoanalysis) and deals with highly personal material. One party (the client) typically divulges material which he or she has never admitted to anyone; often the client has not even admitted some of the material to the self. Because the material is so personal, the interaction is private. Second, the interaction is primarily verbal. Psychotherapy is essentially a special type of conversation; hence the term "verbal psychotherapy." As will be discussed in later chapters, some therapy techniques, such as behavior therapy, do not rely on conversation to produce change. Such nonconversational procedures do not fall under the heading of verbal psychotherapy.

The third commonly agreed upon attribute is that the interaction is prolonged. Change is both difficult and painful. Therapist and client must work hard to explore, evaluate, and alter longstanding feelings, thoughts, and behavioral patterns. Progress ebbs and flows, and is interrupted by many roadblocks. Consequently, the process takes a long time, ranging from months to years. Fourth, the interaction is designed to help one of the participants. One party, the therapist, is there solely to assist the other. While realistically the therapist does seek such things as gratification, money, and prestige, these are secondary. Because of this focus, the patient can forego most ordinary social obligations and restrictions. He or she does not have to worry about burdening the therapist with problems or giving the therapist equal time to talk about personal interests and concerns. Thus, both participants can devote their full attention and efforts to the patient's problems and needs.

In summary, psychotherapy is generally viewed as a special type of verbal interaction; it is prolonged, highly personal, and occurs for the benefit of one of the participants. This picture is broad enough to cover the vast majority of theoretical variations and to exclude most nontherapy relationships, even if they result in some psychological aid. This consensus does not extend to who does the treatment or the precise nature of the conversation. These exclusions are especially important when attempting to evaluate psychotherapy. As we will see later, there is much disagreement about the types of therapists and the procedures which constitute an adequate test of verbal psychotherapy.

Variations of Verbal Psychotherapy

Psychotherapy, in one form or another, has probably been practiced since human languages developed. Sympathetic listening, suggestion, exhortation, and confession have all been used throughout history to reduce depression, fear, anxiety, and ambivalence. However, systematic verbal psychotherapy as we now know it can be traced back to the creative genius of Sigmund Freud in the late nineteenth century. Freud began work with Charcot and then Breur, employing hypnotism to alleviate hysterical symptoms. He soon discovered that hypnotism had two major failings. First, many potential patients could not be hypnotized; second, hypnotic "cures" did not prevent the occurrence of new symptoms. In his search for an alternative, Freud discovered that the illness could also be treated by having patients talk freely and extensively about themselves, their feelings, their lives, and anything else that came to mind (see the discussion of free association below). This procedure developed into the "talking cure": psychoanalysis.

With psychoanalysis as a model and stimulus, many different forms of pscyhotherapy have been developed over the years. Like psychoanalysis, most of them have evolved from theories of personality. Most personality theories have different conceptions of human nature, of pscyhological health, and of pscyhopathology and its development. These conceptions typically dictate specific goals for treatment, as well as the therapeutic process by which change can be achieved and the goals reached. Thus, Freud viewed early childhood experiences as crucial to further development, and psychoanalysis focuses on uncovering repressed memories of those experiences. Alfred Adler considered feelings of inferiority to be a critical factor in neuroses; his therapy, therefore, aims at rectifying those feelings and altering the life style which evolved to compensate for them. These various theories of personality and therapy are usually referred to as "schools," under the name of its creator—e.g., Rogerian, Adlerian, Sullivanian, Freudian.

Unfortunately, these diverse positions are often viewed as religious, each being seen as the only and final answer to all problems. If one attempted to compare these models based on the writing of their most zealous adherents (who are often the most prolific as well), they would each appear to be quite different in many critical ways. However, the differences are more apparent in terminology than in actual therapeutic practice (Weiner, 1976). Furthermore, the adherents of the various schools do not all practice the same way. Wolberg (1967) has suggested that the variations *within* schools are often greater than those *between* schools. Consequently, these self-applied labels do not reflect real differences between approaches.

Wolberg (1967) orders the various forms of therapy into three categories which cut across theoretical lines: supportive, reeducative, and reconstructive. As shown in Table 6.1, this breakdown is primarily based on the major purpose or goals of the treatment. Supportive therapy has the most modest or conservative goals. It is designed more to prevent the patient from getting worse than to produce improvement. It is typically employed either on a short-term basis to assist the patient through a crisis or period of great stress (e.g., depression due to death of a spouse) or to help manage chronic patients (e.g., schizophrenics) over the long term. Supportive therapy does not attempt to produce any fundamental change in the patient's personality or manner of functioning.

Table 6.1.   Varieties of Psychotherapy

Type of treatment	Objectives	Approaches
Supportive Therapy	Strengthening of existing defenses; elaboration of new and better mechanisms of maintaining control; restoration to an adaptive equilibruim	Guidance; environmental manipulation; reassurance; pressure and coercion; persuasion; emotional catharsis and desensitization; prestige suggestion; suggestive hypnosis; inspirational group therapy; supportive adjuncts (somatic therapy, muscular relaxation, hydrotherapy)
Reeducative Therapy	Deliberate efforts at readjustment, goal modification, and the living up to existing creative potentialities, with or without insight into conscious conflicts	Behavior and conditioning therapy; "relationship therapy"; "attitude therapy"; interview psychotherapy; client-centered therapy; directive therapy; distributive analysis and synthesis (psychobiologic therapy); therapeutic counseling; casework therapy; "rational therapy"; reeducative group therapy; family therapy; psychodrama; semantic therapy; philosophic approaches (existential, Zen Buddhist)
Reconstructive Therapy	Insight into unconscious conflicts, with efforts to achieve extensive alterations of character structure; expansion of personality growth, with development of new adaptive potentialities	Freudian psychoanalysis; Kleinian analysis; neo-Freudian psychoanalysis (Adler, Jung, Stekel, Rank, Ferenczi, Reich, Fromm, Sullivan, Horney, Rado); psychoanalytically oriented psychotherapy; transactional approaches; existential analysis; adjunctive therapies (hypnoanalysis, narcotherapy, play therapy, art therapy, analytic group therapy)

Adapted from Wolberg (1967), Chart 1. Reprinted with permission.

Both reeducative and reconstructive therapy do attempt to produce substantial change in the patient. According to Wolberg, these approaches differ in their conceptions of the nature of psychological dysfunction and how it can be rectified. Reeducative approaches focus primarily on overt behavior and conscious processes. They presume that meaningful change can be achieved by focusing on current issues in the patient's life (e.g., ongoing relationships, current attitudes and behavior) and by dealing directly with sources of conflict and distress. In general, adherents of these therapies do *not* believe that extensive alterations in the basic personality must be made to produce meaningful change. These approaches will be considered more extensively in the next two chapters.

Of the three types of approaches, reconstructive therapies aim for the most extensive personality reorganization. In discussing reconstructive procedures, Wolberg (1967) states, "An ultimate goal of psychotherapy is to reduce the force of irrational impulses and strivings and bring them under control, to increase the repertoire of defenses and make them more flexible, and to lessen the severity of the conscience, altering value systems so as to enable the patient to adapt himself to reality and his own inner needs" (p. 173). This approach is based on the notion that psychological distress (or neurosis) is due to some unconscious turmoil. Treatment entails making the patient aware of the inner conflicts and drives: the development of *insight*. Any therapy which attends solely to current issues, such as the reeducative approaches, is presumed to be superficial; any positive results would be short lived and only of partial benefit. Note that reducing distress or eliminating symptoms is *not* stated as part of the goal. It is presumed that such changes will result from alteration of the personality structure.

Wolberg's conception of the goal of psychotherapy is based on a psychoanalytic model. The "irrational impulses" are, essentially, id drives. Psychological defense mechanisms are tools of the ego, and the conscience is part of the superego. Hence, therapy entails curtailing the id and superego while bolstering the ego. Table 6.1 indicates that all the reeducative therapies are variants of psychoanalysis. These related approaches are referred to as psychodynamic, neo-Freudian, or psychoanalytically oriented psychotherapy. They all differ somewhat in their relative emphasis on id, ego, superego, and the environment. However, they all share two common beliefs: (1) the unconscious plays a major role in psychopathology, and (2) the therapist's task is to help the patient become aware of his or her unconscious needs, feelings, and defenses (Singer, 1965). These approaches are, perhaps, the most prevalent forms of psychotherapy (Sloane, Staples, Cristol, Yorkston, & Whipple, 1975a).

Psychoanalysis

Classic psychoanalysis is the model for most current psychotherapies. This approach was developed over many years by Freud as he sought to understand and modify human behavior. The ideas and procedures of psychoanalysis have remained relatively unchanged since his death in 1939. Despite the incursions and modifications made by the neo-Freudian and psychodynamic therapies, classic psychoanalysis retains much influence, prestige, and something of a mystique.

According to Freud, the seeds of neurosis are planted in childhood, when the child fails to pass successfully through the oral, anal, or phallic stages of development. As a result of conflict, trauma, overindulgence, or underindulgence, the child becomes fixated at some level. Unacceptable impulses are repressed, and various defense mechanisms are employed to keep them under control. The defensive network gradually expands and solidifies, and it becomes more and more difficult to deal with new life experiences and normal day-to-day environmental stresses. By the time a full-blown neurosis develops, a substantial part of life experience has been repressed, and the individual is still plagued by anxiety, guilt, and the like. The task of psychoanalysis is to make the person aware of the repressed material, recognize that it is a harmless residue of childhood fears and confusion, and thus accept the feelings and end the defensive process. As a result, the person would then be more open to experience and better able to function, while the major symptoms and distress would be eliminated.

Free Association. The primary tool of psychoanalysis is *free association;* the person is told to talk about whatever comes to mind. He or she can follow any train of thought, discuss any experience, person, or feeling. The stream of association moves from one topic to another, sometimes dealing with important issues, other times not. Periodically the person touches on a focal issue which is close to the defensive structure or the repressed material. Early in therapy, these critical associations are infrequent. Also, they produce great distress and can be considered only briefly. However, over time the person becomes more and more capable of considering such highly sensitive material, and the association stream moves closer and closer to deeply repressed issues.

Interpretation. Of course, if the process were limited to free association, the patient could do this therapy alone. The therapist serves two critical functions, without which the treatment could not work. First, he or she helps the associative process along by making periodic *interpretations.* These are statements which relate various aspects of the person's behavior, explain something, provide new information which helps to clarify the association, or point out something of which the person was unaware. Interpretations can range from simple declarative statements such as, "You're angry about that!" to questions such as, "Is that what you really want to do?" to mini speeches. Regardless of their specific form, they are designed to move the patient in the direction of unconscious material.

The proper use of interpretation is the therapist's greatest and most difficult responsibility. First of all, the interpretation must be *accurate.* The therapist must have tremendous insight into the person's thoughts and feelings, as well as considerable knowledge about behavior and psychopathology, to know what a particular response means. Second, the interpretation must be *timed* properly. Unless the person is ready to hear and consider the material, it can break a train of thought and temporarily disrupt the whole course of therapy. Finally, the interpretation must be of the right level or *depth.* That is, it must present something that is just slightly beyond the person's current level of understanding. If it deals with material which is still too threatening, it will be ignored or perhaps arouse too much distress and interfere with progress. Conversely, it must do more than repeat what the person already knows. The effective interpretation leads but does not push.

The goal of both free association and interpretation is to promote *insight:* understanding and acceptance of unconscious material. The terms "insight" and "interpretation" are deceptively simple. Many nonprofessionals assume that the therapist sits back "analyzing" the patient, and then suddenly makes one brilliant interpretation which gets right to the heart of the problem, such as "Aha, you really hated it when your mother bathed you, and that is why you have a phobia for water!" The patient then has a sudden burst of insight after which all troubles vanish; the so-called "aha" experience makes everything clear. In reality, the process of therapy is exceedingly slow and irregular. It involves many small steps, including frequent dead ends and periods of backsliding, when progress is reversed. A complete analysis can require three to five years of treatment, with five sessions per week.

The session-by-session progress in therapy involves a process known as *working through* (Hartley & Strupp, 1980). The therapist's interpretations are often repeated, rephrased, and directed to different situations, experiences, and associations which have some common element. The person sometimes rejects the interpretation and sometimes accepts part of it; rarely is it totally understood and accepted at any one time. Gradually the person begins to understand, and then to accept what is understood. Even at that point, the process is not complete. At its ultimate, insight involves the ability to generalize and to apply understanding to various new experiences, as well as to be aware of the childhood sources of distress. Thus, by the end of treatment, the person can provide his or her own interpretations, explaining feelings and behavior and identifying the sources of new distress.

Transference. The therapist, we have said, serves two critical functions, the first being interpretation. The second involves facilitating and helping the person work through a *transference neurosis*. The neurotic person employs various defenses to control anxiety, guilt, and id impulses. These defenses result in some distortion of reality. This distortion occurs with the analyst in therapy, in the same manner as with other people in other situations. For example, a person who uses projection might see the analyst—rather than the self—as angry. This process is known as *transference*. Transference is not simply recognized by the analyst but is deliberately fostered. The person lies on a couch while the analyst is seated behind, out of sight. (This position is designed to facilitate the associative process.) The analyst remains almost anonymous, avoiding many of the usual social amenities before and after sessions and remaining relatively silent during sessions. Interpretations are made infrequently. The therapist is relatively passive, providing a blank screen for the person to play against. Faced with this relative vacuum, the person is free to create a picture of what the analyst is like. This picture is distorted by the defensive processes. Furthermore, because the person is steeped in associations to unconscious and emotionally charged material, the analyst becomes involved in these matters. Eventually the entire neurosis is re-created with the analyst as focus: the transference neurosis. For example, the person might begin to see the analyst as a rejecting parent, critical of his or her achievements. Or the analyst might become the focus of sexual urges and a fantasied sexual object. It would be difficult for the analyst to get the person to see how he or she is distorting experience outside of sessions; after all, the analyst is not there and does not know the person's family, friends, and other important objects. However, the transference reaction can be interpreted more easily precisely because the person knows that the analyst is not a parent or lover, and is not critical, seductive, angry, and so on. Thus, the person gains insight into the distortion and its motivation by working through the transference neurosis. This insight is then generalized to behavior and people outside of the analyst's office. This process is the core of psychoanalysis (Wolberg, 1967).

Countertransference. Just as the person brings his or her conflicts, anxieties, and defenses to therapy, so too does the therapist come to the office with family problems, financial concerns, and psychological difficulties. While ideally the therapist's personality and problems should remain apart from the therapy, this is not always the case. In a manner analogous to transference, the therapist sometimes distorts the person's behavior and feelings and responds to things other than the material itself. This process can be a mild interference with misinterpretation of certain communications, such as failure to perceive anger or inability to recognize certain types of conflicts. Or, at the other extreme, the therapist can develop strong emotional reactions to the patient, including hostility and sexual arousal. In either case, this process is called *countertransference* and interferes with treatment. The major strategy for dealing with countertransference is for the therapist to have his or her own psychoanalysis. In fact, a personal analysis is a requirement and one of the major training vehicles for prospective analysts. In this way, the therapist eliminates most of his or her own conflicts and defensive blind spots, and is thus more open to the diverse materials presented. In addition, the therapist can examine his or her own emotional reactions to the person and use them as clues to the effect on others.

Resistance. Psychotherapy, of any form, is a necessarily painful and threatening process. The person must continually deal with highly stressful issues: feelings of inadequacy and guilt, terrifying anxiety, unacceptable urges, and emotional reactions. In addition, change itself is a terrifying prospect. Even though the person's current adjustment is painful and unsatisfactory, it is nevertheless an adjustment. Things might be worse. And so, persons approach each therapy session with ambivalence and trepidation. Sometimes they overcome these feelings and come to grips with the difficult issues, but at other times they avoid them. This avoidance, which is largely an unconscious process, is called *resistance*. Resistance can take many forms. The person might miss a session or come late when therapy is focusing on an especially painful issue. Free association can be stymied as the person reports that nothing comes to mind. Conversely, irrelevant material or issues might be raised, including complaints about the therapist. The therapist's bills may go unpaid, or the accuracy of interpretations may be denied. As with transference, resistance is a potential form of interference which can be turned into a valuable therapeutic tool. The therapist carefully monitors resistive behavior, identifies its source or motivation, and eventually interprets them to the person. Ultimately, the interpretation of resistance and the associated unconscious processes is one of the most important activities of psychoanalysis (Fine, 1973).

Neo-Freudian and Ego Psychology Approaches

Almost from the beginning of the analytic movement, many of Freud's followers began to question his theory and therapeutic strategy. These questions have ranged from rather esoteric points to basic issues, and have led to corresponding changes in theory and technique. In this section, we will consider some of the more important changes which have been adopted by various analytic therapies. Weiner (1976) has distinguished between therapeutic strategies and tactics. *Strategies* are the guiding principles which determine the direction of therapy: its goals and the plans for reaching them (e.g., stimulating a transference neurosis). *Tactics* are the procedures and techniques used to implement the strategy (e.g., making interpretations, asking questions). We will first consider modifications in strategy and then innovations in tactics.

Therapeutic Strategies. Human behavior, according to Freud, is rooted in biological factors, especially instinctual (id) drives. The most important of these is Eros: sexuality. The major "psychological" factor in behavior is the ego, which is more a servant of the id than an independent force. The environment, like the ego, is of secondary importance. Its primary influence is negative or repressive, and is exerted during childhood. Neurosis is considered to be largely a result of society's inhibition of the expression of sexuality. Thus, the primary therapeutic strategies are designed to uncover and free the instinctual drives. Little attention is paid to the person's current environment or to any nondefensive aspects of the ego. Freud's emphasis on sexuality (and biological factors in general), and his relative neglect of the ego and environmental influences on behavior, have been the subject of considerable criticism from within the analytic camp (as well as from other orientations).

Two of Freud's earliest critics were Jung and Adler, both of whom felt that he placed far too much emphasis on sexuality. Jung hypothesized that human beings had a *collective or inherited unconscious* in addition to the personal unconscious emphasized by Freud. One of the major goals of Jungian analysis is to foster insight into both types of unconscious forces and facilitate an accomodation between both of them and the environment (Weiner, 1976). Adler argued that all people are born with feelings of *inferiority* and *helplessness*. In an attempt to compensate for these anxiety-provoking feelings, they strive for superiority and develop unique life styles to deal with environmental demands and pressures (Hall & Lindzey, 1978). Adlerian therapy emphasizes the person's current life situation and the way that situation affects and is affected by the life style (Mosak & Dreikurs, 1973). Interpretations focus on the ongoing interaction between inferiority feelings, life style, and daily events: accomplishments, failures, relationships with others, and so on.

Among those who criticized Freud for his comparative disregard of social and environmental influences on behavior, Harry Stack Sullivan, Karen Horney, and Erich Fromm are the most representative (Hall & Lindzey, 1978). While their particular theories and emphases varied, all three highlighted the central role of *social* factors in shaping adult as well as early childhood behavior. For example, Horney described how the neurotic adapts a defensive posture characterized by moving toward people, away from people, or against people in an effort to curtail and avoid anxiety. Thus, an analysis based on one of these models would emphasize current interpersonal functioning. Interpretations would focus on conflicts between the person, the environment, and defensive interpersonal style, rather than on intrapsychic conflicts and drives.

Probably the most significant modification of Freudian theory has come from the *ego psychologists,* including Erikson, Hartmann, Kris, and Loewenstein (Ford & Urban, 1963; Weiner, 1976; Wolberg, 1967). According to these theorists, the ego is independent of the id rather than its servant. The ego has its own energy and functions, including thinking, remembering, perceiving, and conscious awareness. All behavior is not motivated by drive reduction; instead, the ego has its own sources of gratification and motivation, such as love, creativity, and achievement. The healthy adult is not bound by unconscious instinctual forces but has a good deal of conscious control over behavior and strives to grow and improve. The personality is not solidified by puberty; instead, growth and development continue throughout life. The neurotic individual is characterized by poor ego development. Like children, neurotics are much more under the control of instincts and the environment. Thus, they are less capable of determining the course of their lives and fulfilling their potential.

Treatment based on an ego psychology model strives to strengthen the ego and increase the degree of conscious and adaptive control over behavior. In keeping with the analogy between the neurotic and the child, Hartley and Strupp (1980) have referred to therapy as "reparenting"; the therapist, like the parent, helps the person to become more independent and capable of functioning effectively. Little attention is paid to historical and instinctual influences on development. The emphasis is on current conflicts and anxieties, and the inadequacy of current coping strategies (Weiner, 1976). The ego analysts, like most other neo-Freudians, stress the transference neurosis less than the classic analysts. Transference is either viewed as an impediment to therapy and quickly resolved or it is interpreted as a reflection of current interpersonal style. In neither case is it facilitated by the therapist or viewed as a critical element of therapy.

Therapy Techniques. The theoretical conceptions of the post-Freudian analysts lead to different ways of thinking about behavior and of understanding patient reports. As a result, their therapeutic strategies differ greatly. Their techniques, however, are quite similar (Weiner, 1976). As stated previously, there is greater variation between individual therapists than between schools.

One reason for this peculiar pattern is that research has failed to identify a set of specific techniques to be applied in a particular way at a particular time with a particular client. Therapists are left to their own experience and "best guess" as to what to do. Thus, it would be quite unusual for two therapists to provide the same interpretation at any point. This fact is dramatized at case conferences and supervision sessions, when recordings of therapy sessions are reviewed. While there is often agreement as to very poor and highly effective interpretations, the middle ground is the area where each listener responds differently.

In reviewing the various psychodynamic techniques, it is difficult to even identify their source, let alone tie them to any particular school. The most notable changes from Freudian procedures probably involve the activity and behavior of the therapist. Without the need to develop a transference neurosis, the therapist became free of the classic need for passivity and anonymity. Therapist and client now sit face-to-face in armchairs. Some therapists like to sit behind a desk while others prefer a more casual arrangement, such as around a coffee table. Style of dress also varies with the person, although coat and tie (for men) and dress or skirt and blouse (for women) predominate. The general tone of the therapist-client relationship is often more relaxed and pleasant. While the use of the title "Dr." is most common, some therapists and clients are on a first name basis. While the therapist's personal life is still usually kept out of the relationship, there is less rigidity about this as well. Pre- and post-session conversation takes on a more social atmosphere, with occasional references to vacation plans, family activities, and attitudes about public events. References to personal experiences (e.g., "You know, I felt that way once") are also sometimes used therapeutically by some therapists. A positive relationship is often attempted, and is used to facilitate therapeutic progress.

Therapy sessions are also marked by greater therapist responsiveness. In addition to interpretations, typical responses include questions, clarifications, reflections, exclamations, and confrontations (Weiner, 1976). The various types of questions used by the therapist were described in Chapter 3. Open-ended and indirect questions are most often employed. Clarifications are responses which move the patient in a certain direction while providing no new information. For example, "That seems to be an important issue; I think we should focus on it some more." Clarifications are similar in effect to indirect questions. Reflections summarize and integrate client responses. They usually involve some feelings the patient has directly or indirectly expressed. Examples include, "You seem to be angry," and "I have the feeling you are afraid of what you might learn." Weiner (1976) defines exclamations as noncommittal response facilitators, including "Mm-hmm," "Uh-huh," and "I see." They convey the therapist's interest and reinforce the topic of conversation. Confrontations give the client new information about his or her behavior. They typically involve direct, objective statements about specific responses or issues, rather than the nondefinitive hypotheses offered in interpretations. For example, "You've been late for the last three sessions, and we need to talk about that," or "You say that it's not important, but I find that hard to believe." Confrontations are used sparingly because of their potentially threatening or conflict-producing nature. They are usually reserved for roadblocks or issues left unresolved by more indirect means.

It is clear that free association is no longer the main form of interaction. The process is much more of a two-way conversation, in contrast to the semimonologue format of classic psychoanalysis. The dialogue moves back and forth between the two participants, although the client still does most of the talking. In keeping with the strategies discussed above, the topics covered deal much more with current experiences and interpersonal relationships, and with ego-relevant issues (e.g., feelings of competence, the direction of one's life, sources of pleasure). Some therapists (notably Adlerian) give clients homework assignments—for example, to initiate interpersonal activity (Mosak & Dreikurs, 1973). These assignments are then discussed in later sessions.

The nature of a therapeutic interaction can best be portrayed by an example. The following transcript segments are from Wolberg (1967), a prominent therapist and training analyst. The comments in parentheses indicate the nature and purpose of certain therapist responses. The first segment illustrates transference and its interpretation.

Th. It sounds as if you would like to let loose with me, but you are afraid of what my response would be. (*summarizing and restating*)

Pt. I get so excited by what is happening here. I feel I'm being held back by needing to be nice. I'd like to blast loose sometimes, but I don't dare.

Th. Because you fear my reaction?

Pt. The worst thing would be that you wouldn't like me. You wouldn't speak to me friendly; you wouldn't smile; you'd feel you can't treat me and discharge me from treatment. But I know this isn't so, I know it.

Th. Where do you think these attitudes come from?

Pt.   When I was nine years old, I read a lot about great men in history. I'd quote them and be dramatic. I'd want a sword at my side; I'd dress like an Indian. Mother would scold me. Don't frown, don't talk so much. Sit on your hands, over and over again. I did all kinds of things. I was a naughty child. She told me I'd be hurt. Then at fourteen I fell off a horse and broke my back. I had to be in bed. Mother then told me on the day I went riding not to, that I'd get hurt because the ground was frozen. I was a stubborn, self-willed child. Then I went against her will and suffered an accident that changed my life, a fractured back. Her attitude was, "I told you so." I was put in a cast and kept in bed for months.

Th.   You were punished, so to speak, by this accident.

Pt.   But I gained attention and love from mother for the first time. I felt so good. I'm ashamed to tell you this. Before I healed I opened the cast and tried to walk to make myself sick again so I could stay in bed longer.

Th.   How does that connect up with your impulse to be sick now and stay in bed so much? (*The patient has these tendencies, of which she is ashamed.*)

Pt.   Oh . . . (*pause*)

Th.   What do you think?

Pt.   Oh, my God, how infantile, how ungrown up. (*pause*) It must be so. I want people to love me and be sorry for me. Oh, my God. How completely childish. It is, *is* that. My mother must have ignored me when I was little, and I wanted so to be loved. (*This sounds like insight.*)

Th.   So that it may have been threatening to go back to being self-willed and unloved after you got out of the cast. (*interpretation*)

Pt.   It did. My life changed. I became meek and controlled. I couldn't get angry or stubborn afterward.

Th.   Perhaps if you go back to being stubborn with *me,* you would be returning to how you were before, that is, active, stubborn but unloved.

Pt.   (*excitedly*) And, therefore, losing your love. I need you, but after all you aren't going to reject me. The pattern is so established now that the threat of the loss of love is too overwhelming with everybody, and I've got to keep myself from acting selfish or angry.

(Wolberg, 1967, p. 662)

The patient in the next segment is a woman who began to experience a variety of symptoms after becoming pregnant and quitting her job.

Pt.   And on Wednesday I began thinking. (*laughs*) The funniest thing happened. I was working in the kitchen and suddenly I got that awful feeling. It came on me like a squirmy wave. I got scared and tense and the muscles back here (*strokes the muscles in the back of her neck*) got tight and my head filled up as if I had a tight bandage around, and queasy feelings in the pit of my stomach.

Th. Mm hmm.

Pt. And there was something else that happened. I knew something was bothering me and I just didn't know what.

Th. Mm hmm.

Pt. Something bothering me. It's like something I had to do, supposed to do. It was such a frustrating feeling. (*pause*)

Th. A frustrating feeling, as if you just couldn't grasp what was going on?

Pt. Yes, just like that. So out of desperation, I guess, I turned on the radio. The first thing was one of those breakfast Mr. and Mrs. programs. They were bantering back and forth, and I detected a snide attitude toward the woman. This made me boil. And all of a sudden the thing flashed in mind. It came to me that I promised my husband that I'd buy him several pairs of socks a week ago. I've been putting if off, and putting it off, and not thinking of it. When I'd go out, it wouldn't occur to me to get the socks until I'd remember when I got home. (*laughs*)

Th. (*smiles*) You suspected something was going on inside of you?

Pt. I knew it. As I was listening to the program, it came to me. I suddenly got mad, furious and said, "Darn him, why doesn't he buy socks for himself? Why should I do his dirty work?" (*laughs*)

Th. You resented his making this demand on you?

Pt. (*laughs*) No question about that. My next thought (*laughs*) . . . it was, Damn him, why doesn't he buy socks for *himself.* Why do I have to do *all* the dirty work around here. He wants and expects me to be a slave, just tidy up the place and get nowheres. I thought of him in his nice comfortable office. Then I thought of how wonderful I felt when I was working. At least I felt appreciated and didn't get the constant criticism I get now.

Th. This must really burn you up.

Pt. I suppose marriage is a sacrifice. I do love the children. I don't know what they'd do if I went back to work. But it's the noise, noise, the howling of the kids and the criticism of my husband.

Th. When you were working, you felt you were doing something siginificant that gave you status.

Pt. You know, doctor, I sometimes feel as if I was absolutely crazy to give up my job. I don't know what I imagined marriage was going to be like.

Th. And it turned out to be something where you have to take care of howling kids and buy socks for your husband.

Pt. You know, as soon as I had these thoughts I got very mad. I screamed out loud, "Why doesn't he buy the socks himself." I had a picture of him (*laughs*) this is silly . . . slipping on, (*laughs*) slipping on a banana peel and turning a half somersault in the air, I started laughing. Doctor, do I want him to break his neck? When this all happened I noticed that I felt better. My headache went away and the stiffness in the the neck. (*Ap-

parently, realization and acknowledgment of her hostility removed the
necessity for its repression and its conversion into symptoms.)

(Wolberg, 1967, pp. 670–671)

Before concluding this overview of neo-Freudian technique, one further contrast with classic psychoanalysis must be mentioned. As indicated above, classic analysis typically requires five (fifty-minute) sessions per week for several years. This type of intervention obviously is extremely costly in terms of money as well as in patient and therapist time. Many neu-Freudians have argued that such deep, extensive analysis is of intellectual value rather than a necessity for effective treatment. Many of the modified approaches attempt to speed up the process. Sessions are still often fifty minutes, but longer sessions are not uncommon. Sessions typically are held once or (at most) twice a week, and treatment usually lasts from six months to one or two years. It is presumed that the focus on more current issues and greater therapist activity can produce meaningful change with less intensive and extensive treatment.

A related change involves the timing and nature of termination. Classic analysis continues until all major unconscious conflicts are resolved and the client has relatively complete insight into his or her experience. The briefer neo-Freudian approaches often conclude with less than total personality reorganization. Given the emphasis on current experience, good adjustment with sufficient ego strength to withstand future stress and to grow after treatment are more typical expectations. In any case, termination is always a painful process, much like the adolescent's leaving home for the first time. The client is eager to try to live independently, yet questions his or her ability to function without the therapist. For this reason, termination is usually a gradual weaning process, requiring several sessions and marked by ambivalence and a sense of loss.

Eclecticism

The 1940s and 1950s, which spawned many new theories about behavior and therapy, were the heyday of theoretical "schools." However, as it became apparent that no school had all the answers, therapy procedures became more flexible. This is noted in Garfield and Kurtz's (1976) study of the theoretical orientations of clinical psychologists. The results are summarized in Table 6.2. Note that no specific theoretical view was endorsed by more than 11 percent of the sample. In contrast, almost 55 percent referred to themselves as *eclectic*—that is, borrowing or adopting ideas and procedures from various sources. Eclectic therapists do not adhere to any single theoretical orientation. They either have their own viewpoint, based on bits of several theories, or tailor their concepts and techniques to the individual client (Garfield & Kurtz, 1977).

Perhaps the most noted representative of eclecticism is Frederick Thorne. He advocates that all clinicians be trained in a variety of disciplines (e.g., medicine *and* psychology), be thoroughly versed in the current scientific literature about human behavior, and at the same time be highly experienced so that they can integrate this knowledge with "clinical judgment" (Thorne, 1973). Only this way, he argues, can the most appropriate treatment be selected for each client. However, while this orientation has intuitive appeal, it is uncertain whether either the conceptual eclectism espoused by Thorne or the pragmatic eclecticism usually practiced can be effective.

For eclecticism to work, the clinician would have to operate as a computer. Client responses would automatically be processed and the best possible conceptualization from a variety of possibilities would emerge, as on a computer printout. All the treatment techniques would then be scanned and the correct subset identified and applied. Unfortunately, this is not the case. Therapists are people. Their ability to process

Table 6.2.   Theoretical Orientations

Theoretical orientation	N	%
Other	61	7.14
Psychoanalytic	92	10.76
Neo-Freudian	45	5.26
Sullivanian	26	3.04
Rogerian	12	1.40
Learning theory	85	9.94
Existentialist	24	2.81
Humanistic	25	2.92
Rational-emotive	15	1.75
Eclectic	470	54.97
Total	855	99.99

From: Garfield & Kurtz (1976), Table 5. Reprinted by permission.

information is hampered by bias, such as values and personal problems, by lack of data, and by the urgent need to treat a highly distressed client (Ford & Urban, 1963). Also, the therapist cannot attend to all the material presented by the client; thus, listening is a highly selective process. These limitations can be partly avoided by a consistent theoretical orientation. Theory provides a guide with which to filter information and form hypotheses (Ford & Urban, 1963; Watkins, 1965). The absence of a theoretical orientation leads to a disorganized, inconsistent approach, with various techniques haphazardly applied (Ford & Urban, 1963). Therapy is simply too difficult a process to permit a "seat of the pants" approach with consistent success.

Eclecticism also implies that therapists can master all possible techniques and apply them at will. This is far from the case. Different techniques require different skills, and few if any therapists can apply many with equal success. Therapists probably can be most effective by mastering a few techniques and using them extensively, learning their own strengths and limitations. Furthermore, many techniques are based on incompatible theories, used for inconsistent goals, and require different types of assessment for proper use. Thus, the therapist cannot switch back and forth between models and techiques the way a physician can alternate between two brands of medication.

Of course, not all theories can be correct, and some techniques, no matter how well applied, will not work. We are hardly suggesting that an incorrect theory or an ineffective technique is better than none at all. However, a second advantage to holding a theoretical view and conducting therapy accordingly is that consistency allows for evaluation. A theory generates specific hypotheses and strategies. These can be empirically tested and the theory revised or discarded when necessary. Only in this way can the therapist learn and improve and the field advance. An eclectic approach does not allow for this evaluative process precisely because there are no consistent tenets and principles. The therapist, and the field, have no way of knowing *why* a particular strategy did or did not work. Therefore, systematic change is impossible.

Group Therapy

Since people are social animals, it is not suprising that much human activity has always been done in groups. Education, emotional support, help giving, and other therapylike functions are no exception. Religious organizations provide mutual support and guidance to their members. Funeral rituals serve a therapeutic function for bereaved friends and relatives by preventing isolation, aiding the expression of grief, sharing distress, and so on. It can even be argued that political clubs and organizations are therapeutic in that they channel emotion and provide a forum for complaints and new ideas. These strategies for mutual help are the basis of the more systematic forms known as group therapy.

The first true therapy group was formed in 1905, in Boston, by Joseph Hersey Pratt (Shaffer & Galinsky, 1974). Pratt organized groups of tuberculosis patients in order to give them inspiration, encouragement, and information about their disorder. In time, group members interacted more and more, and Pratt increasingly emphasized mutual support among them. While group treatments continued, this approach received little attention until after World War II. In the early part of the twentieth century, theory and treatment were mainly psychoanalytic. Freud's intrapsychic, biological model focused on the person since pathology was individual, it was only natural that treatment required the privacy, intensity, and concentration of a one-to-one relationship. Group approaches, it was believed, could only dilute treatment.

Several factors interacted to promote group therapy. First was the development of the neo-Freudian and ego psychology orientations. These approaches placed greater emphasis on interpersonal forces and the person's present life. Hence, group interactions are in some ways more relevant to the person's sources of distress than the unique relationship of individual psychotherapy. In addition, transference was deemphasized even in individual treatment, so that dilution of transference in a group is less important. A second factor was the work done by Gestalt and social psychologists, such as Kurt Lewin, which highlighted the unique attributes and functions of groups. It was suggested that groups are more than just a collection of individuals. Just as, in perception, the whole is greater than the sum of its parts, group interactions involve processes which are not apparent in individual or dyadic behavior. The third major stimulus was economic. After World War II, there was a great need for therapy—a need which intensive individual analysis could never handle. Group treatment offered a fine opportunity for the few trained therapists available to increase their caseloads. A group therapist can see more persons in one day than would be possible in a week of individual therapy.

Group therapy has increased dramatically in the past two decades. One of the main reasons is still the economic advantage. Hence, group approaches may well be the most common form of treatment in institutions and community mental health facilities. Group methods are also commonly used to treat individuals with similar, specialized problems, such as parents of children undergoing treatment, recently divorced or widowed adults, alcoholics, and drug addicts. Group therapies generally predominate in day hospital programs for chronic psychiatric patients (Hersen & Luber, 1977). Because members share common problems and experiences, these groups are especially useful for providing support and understanding, communicating information, and teaching members how to solve common problems. Group procedures are usually somewhat limited in their goals and range of application. However, there are now many theories for explaining and conducting intensive group therapy, and many clinicians regard group methods as the best treatment for many neurotic patients (cf. Shaffer & Galinsky, 1974).

Psychodynamic approaches to group therapy usually fall into two or three categories, differing in the relative emphasis on the individual and the group (Spotnitz, 1977). The two primary orientations involve treatment of the individual patient *in* the group and treatment of the individual *by* or *through* the group. These orientations are described in the left and right portions, respectively, of Table 6.3. The third approach (center of Table 6.3) represents a compromise or integration of these two views (Anthony, 1971).

The approaches which emphasize treatment in the group place little emphasis on the group itself. The group setting is viewed simply as a convenient means of treating several patients simultaneously. The focus of treatment throughout is the individual patients' pathology. This orientation is best represented by classic psychoanalytic group therapy, as developed by Slavson (1950) and Wolf and Schwartz (1962). In this approach, the basic psychoanalytic strategy and techniques are translated to the group setting with as little alteration as possible. An attempt is made to individualize the psychoanalysis of each member. Group size is generally held to six to eight members, the preferred size of most group therapies (Spotnitz, 1977). Obviously it is impossible for all group members to free-associate simultaneously. Wolf and Schwartz (1962) have adapted this technique to the group by stimulating a free-flowing, permissive discussion among group members, in which each patient is encouraged to free-associate to the topic discussed. Interruptions, digressions, and reference to fantasies are all encouraged. In addition, groups employ a "go around" procedure in which each member, in turn, reports his or her associations at that moment.

Table 6.3.   The Three Main Approaches to Group Psychotherapy

Individual Oriented Approach (psychoanalytic and analytic group psychotherapy)	Integrative Approach (group analytic psychotherapy)	Transactional Approach (group dynamic psychotherapy)
Classical psychoanalytic orientation and techniques based on psychoanalytic principles; preservation of patient's uniqueness; analysis of individual patient in interaction with others (sibling transference) and of bilateral transference to the therapist, viewed as crucial; concern with making the unconscious conscious	Focus on both individual patient and group; transference recognized and interpreted but emphasis on configurations of interpersonal disturbance and their location within the group rather than on analysis of regressive transference to the therapist; concern with both latent and manifest content	Group as focus of therapy with emphasis on the group-as-a whole, group reactions, group interactions, group roles, group themes, group relationships and communications; concern with manifest content

From: Anthony (1971), Table 1. Reprinted with permission.

One limitation to the group approach is that the therapist-client relationship is less intense than in individual therapy. Hence, transference to the therapist is diluted. However, this limitation is balanced by the fact that clients develop transference reactions to one another. Their distorted responses and perceptions are presumed to represent irrational defensive approaches to peers and siblings—the types of inappropriate responses made in the outside world. As such, they complement the parent-authority oriented transference to the therapist. To facilitate useful interactions (transference or otherwise), clients with many different problems are usually selected (Lubin, 1976). Thus, assertive clients are exposed to unassertive ones, inhibited males are exposed to seductive females, and so on. Homogeneity is usually maintained on demographic variables (e.g., age, socioeconomic status) to insure some common reference point and basis of experience.

As in individual psychoanalysis, the therapist's primary role in group therapy is to interpret transference and resistance. Interpretations are usually directed to individual patients or dyads, rather than the group as a whole. The therapist is aided by group members, who can often identify the interfering resistances of other clients (e.g., changing the topic, avoiding or generating conflict between members) as well as the ways they are misperceived and treated inappropriately (due to transference). Naturally, they react negatively to such behavior and respond accordingly, confronting the resistive client and interpreting inappropriate behavior. These statements are often very powerful precisely because they come from several peers. Because group members serve a major therapeutic role, the therapist can be relatively passive. He or she organizes the group, gets it started, makes occasional interpretations, and sets limits, allowing the clients essentially to act as co-therapists.

Groups therapies which emphasize treatment of the individual by or through the group are characterized by group dynamic approaches, such as those of Foulkes (1965) and Whitaker and Lieberman (1965). These theorists, who are mainly psychoanalytic, view the goal of treatment as individual change. However, they see the group as the mechanism for producing change. As stated above, the group is seen as more than a collection of persons; it has a dynamism of its own. Power struggles between members, rivalries over the attention and affection of the therapist and one another, shifting alliances and subgroups, and mutual resistances all shape the nature and flow of the interaction. These forces, or *dynamics,* can all serve a therapeutic function for individual group members.

The interactive nature of group dynamics is especially clear in Whitaker and Lieberman's (1965) model. Each therapy session is presumed to turn on a *focal conflict* or concern, such as relationships to spouses. The more significant conflicts are periodically repeated as *group themes*. In interactions based on these conflicts and themes, each group member has unique associations to personal conflicts and responds in a characteristic fashion. For example, if the theme is anger, one client could be responding to another as if she were his wife, a second could be responding as he or she does to a parent, and a third could be attempting to defuse the conflict because of an inability to accept angry feelings.

Over time, each group develops a unique *group culture* which establishes rules and sets a pattern for interaction. One function of the culture is to find solutions for the focal conflicts. Early in therapy, these solutions are usually defensive and prevent extensive exploration of underlying motives. For example, the group might agree not to talk about sex. However, as progress is made, these solutions increasingly move the group forward and stimulate exploration. These so-called "enabling" solutions allow the individual members to come to grips with their own particular conflicts. The therapist's task is to help the group reach these facilitating or enabling solutions. Interpretations are directed much more toward the group and what the group is doing than toward individual clients. Therapist responses to individual clients are designed to steer the person in a direction the group should pursue. For example, the therapist might reflect on a patient's anger when he or she believes the group should be confronting anger as a general issue. Eventually all the major conflicts experienced by individual members will be covered, and the group process will facilitate resolution of each of these conflicts.

Family Therapy

Family therapy is a general term encompassing variety of approaches that focus on the family unit. It can entail group sessions for all family members living under one roof, the nuclear family (mother, father, child), the parents alone, or even one family member (cf. Bowen, 1966). Family therapy can also consist of alternating sessions with different subsets of family members. Regardless of who is actually present in the sessions, the various family approaches all see the family as the focus of treatment. Any change in individual members, including any identified patient (I.P.) for whom treatment was initially requested, is presumed to result from change in the family interaction pattern (Beels & Ferber, 1969; Fox, 1976).

Family therapy became a major treatment strategy in the 1950s and 1960s. It grew out of several interrelated sources. First, the 1930s and 1940s saw a dramatic increase in therapeutic services for children—the so-called "child guidance movement." The primary treatment for children was *play therapy*. In this form of psychoanalysis, play is substituted for free association. In keeping with the psychoanalytic orientation, classic play therapy focuses on the child's fantasies and unconscious, and essentially ignores current life experiences. The analyst periodically meets with the parents to keep them informed of their child's progress, but they are not involved in treatment. However, with the increased emphasis on ego psychology and social psychology, as well as observation of the course of treatment, it became apparent that the parents play a central role in the child's current behavior, not just a historical role in its development. Parents could dramatically improve or worsen their child's behavior outside of therapy.

This same observation was made by clinicians working with adult schizophrenics. Their parents, too, seemed to have a tremendous ongoing influence on their behavior and adjustment. Improvement gradually and tediously achieved in the hospital might be undone by a weekend at home. Thus, it became clear that both parents and siblings should be involved in the treatment. Individual treatment of each family member would, of course, be too costly. However, the development of group therapy showed the feasibility of multiple treatment. This possibility was seized upon, and the family therapy movement began.

As with individual and group therapy, numerous theories to explain family interaction patterns and systems for family therapy have been developed. Also, in a parallel manner, the differences are much greater in theory than in practice (Beels & Ferber, 1969; Lecker, 1976). All the therapies consider the family interaction pattern to be at the core of the pathology of any one member. Families develop a variety of rules governing their interactions, many of which are covert. These rules cover such things as the expression of emotion, roles and responsibilities of family members, and communication patterns. All these aspects of family interaction reach a homeostatic level or style, which governs the functioning of all family members. In disturbed families, this homeostasis is pathological and prevents the healthy growth and adaptation of individual members. For example, some families exist by having a "sick child." Parents rationalize or ignore their poor relationship by identifying the child as the source of all family distress. The child, on the other hand, can avoid certain unacceptable feelings or responsibilities by being a "problem." Siblings can discount their own failings by blaming their rotten (or sick) brother or sister. Thus, the disturbed child plays a necessary role in the family's adjustment precisely by being disturbed.

Fox (1976) has identified three broad goals of family therapy, each of which is emphasized differently by various theorists: (1) strengthening the family system, (2) increasing separation—individuation, and (3) strengthening the marriage.

In strengthening the family system, the primary strategy is to improve communication between members and change pathological interaction patterns (e.g., maintaining the sick child). For example, the Palo Alto group of family therapists (Gregory Bateson, Don Jackson, Jay Haley) has emphasized the role of *double bind* communications in disturbed families. Family members (especially the mother) send complex messages to one another in which the overt and covert elements contradict one another. Compliance with one part of the message requires noncompliance with another part. The recipient of the message is punished for noncompliance *in either case,* and is thus in a "double bind." For example, the mother might ask a child to provide affection, yet turn away when the child reaches out and then complain if no further affection is offered. The goal of therapy would be to clarify this process and teach family members to respond consistently in verbal and nonverbal ways and on both overt and covert levels.

Increased separation-individuation refers to the growth and development of individual family members. While the immediate focus of treatment is improved family functioning, this ultimately requires (and facilitates) the individuality and independence of each member. Murray Bowen (1966) views the lack of individuation as a primary factor in disturbed family adjustments. He tries to facilitate personal growth and improve the family system by reducing each member's dependence on the family, and especially, its pathological homeostasis.

The third goal, strengthening the marriage, comes from the observation (and assumption) that a disturbed marital relationship is often the basis of broader family pathology. The classic example here is the couple that remains married "for the children's sake." This naturally produces hidden conflict and distorted interaction patterns. Children's symptoms (e.g., depression, phobias, aggression) often disappear once the parental relationship is improved. Couples therapy is a common variant of family therapy in which the children are not included. Sexual problems, as well as more general family matters and communication patterns, are often part of couples therapy.

Family therapists, as a group, are much more active and demonstrative than most dynamic individual or group therapists. This is partially because the family comes to treatment with an established interaction pattern which the therapist must interfere. Also, there is a greater emphasis on changing ongoing interaction patterns. Awareness, insight, and understanding are generally viewed as less important than directly changing the family's behavior (Beels & Ferber, 1969; Fox, 1976; Lecker, 1976). Therefore, there is less need for the therapist to sit back and allow the family members to cognitively appraise their situation and free-associate. In fact, such a tactic would simply encourage the ingrained pathological interactions.

Beels and Ferber (1969) see family therapists as *conductors* and *reactors*. Conductors, such as Ackerman, Satir, and Bowen, actively direct and structure therapy. All communication flows through them as they challenge, confront, and manipulate family members. Reactors exert control as well, but in more subtle, often covert fashion. Zuk (1967) has coined the term "go-between" to describe this role. The therapist serves as a mediator or negotiator between family members, often stimulating conflict or temporarily taking sides in an effort to modify the interaction pattern. Beels and Ferber divide reactors in two groups: *analysts* and *system purists*. The analysts, including Wynne and Whitaker, are the most traditionally psychoanalytic family therapists. They often work in male-female co-therapy teams so as to facilitate transference reactions and avoid becoming too enmeshed in the family. They place more emphasis on insight and individual anxieties and defenses than do other family therapists. System purists, such as the Palo Alto group, place primary emphasis on current relationships and communication patterns. As stated above, insight is seen as unnecessary; changing interaction patterns is viewed as the sole concern.

The actual process of family therapy includes various techniques. Family members role-play each other or different roles. In order to change communication patterns, they are directed to remain silent, sit on the side, or even observe the interaction from an adjoining room. Dyadic or triadic interactions may occur, or the therapist may talk to or challenge a single family member. Homework assignments, such as to spend time together without talking, are common. With their open, active, and "anything goes" style, family therapists are often called "happy exhibitionists" (Lecker, 1976). Perhaps more than with any other group of practitioners, their work is more an expression of their individual style than of any systematic theoretical perspective (Beels & Ferber, 1969).

Empirical Evaluation

We have described clinical psychology as an applied science and identified psychotherapy as the major area of applied work. Thus, one would expect psychotherapeutic practices to be based on a long history of carefully controlled research. Unfortunately, that is not the case. Despite three decades of research efforts, we still know very little about how therapy works, or for whom, or even if it works. The material presented earlier in this chapter represents the experience and wisdom of many astute clinicians. However, very little of it is based on research or supported by empirical analysis. Instead, the various techniques and theories are based mainly on inference, intuition, and agreement among practitioners.

The reasons for this range from the economic security provided by traditional practices to the need to provide immediate help to troubled persons. The greatest limitation is the complexity of the subject matter and the tremendous difficulty of conducting valid research. This final section of the chapter will focus on research on the outcome of psychotherapy: Does it work? Reflecting the state of the art, we will emphasize the problems rather than answer the question.

At first glance, an outcome study appears to present no problem at all: recruit some persons, test them, give half of them treatment, test them again, and see if those who received treatment fared better than those who did not. In fact, that is the basic outcome design. However, major questions involve the types of persons to recruit, the types of tests (i.e., dependent measures) to administer, the therapists to employ, the form of therapy to use, the types of control groups required, and interpretation of results.

Subjects

Clinicians beginning with Freud have realized that not everyone responds well to psychotherapy. Some persons do not profit from the experience, even after many attempts with various therapists. Others actually seem to be harmed by psychotherapy, leaving with greater distress than when they began (Bergin, 1971). Still others simply dislike therapy and terminate before it has a chance to work. In fact, some data suggest that the majority of patients simply fail to return after five to eight sessions (Garfield, 1971). However, little is known about what kinds of persons benefit most from treatment.

Much research has focused on the characteristics of successful and unsuccessful persons (cf: Garfield, 1971; Luborsky, Auerbach, Chandler, Cohen, & Bachrach, 1971). There appears to be general support for the YAVIS pattern first identified by Schofield (1964). Successful patients tend to be young, attractive, verbal, intelligent, and successful. Psychotherapy appears to work better with middle- and upper-class persons than for those in the lower class. Persons beginning treatment with high motivation and high expectation for change do better than those who do not. Psychotherapy in general is not effective with schizophrenics (Bergin & Suinn, 1975). Finally, persons who are not extremely disturbed yet are experiencing severe anxiety or depression seem to do better than those who are highly disturbed or are not experiencing acute distress.

There are many possible explanations for this pattern. Psychotherapy is a tedious, painful process requiring time, money, verbal skill, and the ability to introspect and integrate information. Thus, to be successful persons may require enough distress to justify the pain of self-exploration, enough "ego strength" to withstand it, and the time, money, and verbal skills to participate. In addition, they must understand what the process involves (Frank, 1978). Those (including many lower socio-economic persons) who expect the "doctor" to do all the work often drop out or do very poorly. On the other hand, the attributes of the successful client might be required more by the therapist than by the nature of psychotherapy. That is, verbal middle- and upper-class therapists might like to work with persons who are like them, who are pleasant and easy to work with, and who are cooperative and motivated to change (Bergin & Suinn, 1975; Sloane et al., 1975a). Positive outcomes for such patients may simply reflect more effective therapist efforts and/or a halo effect in therapist judgments (e.g., therapists see improved persons as more verbal, attractive, and motivated). Further research is needed to identify patient characteristics which predict success with specific types of procedures.

Dependent Measures

The measures to be used in assessing therapeutic change have been a major source of controversy. Kazdin and Wilson (1978a) identify three problems: the manner of assessment, the source of data, and the generality or specificity of the assessment. The *manner* of assessment refers to the type of procedure employed, such as projective tests, interviews, or observation of overt behavior. A major source of disagreement stems from theoretical differences about the nature of pathology and the goals of therapy. Classic psychoanalysts tend to regard changes in overt behavior and self-reports as superficial; hence, assessment must tap psychodynamics. Conversely, many family therapist and ego psychologists target overt behavior and changes (and assessment) at that level are more relevant.

Data about the effects of therapy can come from three sources: the individual, the therapist, and outside observers (e.g., family members, independent judges). The individual is the best judge of his or her own subjective feeling state. But such judgments about improvement are often biased, and self-reports often do not relate to independent judgments of behavior (Bellack & Hersen, 1977b). Because of his or her close involvement with the client, the therapist should be an excellent judge of change, especially at the intrapsychic level. However, therapists are generally as biased as their clients, and therapist ratings have also been shown to differ widely from independent judgments (Garfield, Prager, & Bergin, 1971). While independent ratings thus would seem to be ideal, it has been argued that only the client and therapist know what the critical issues are and whether they have been resolved. Thus, although independent ratings may be objective, they fail to assess the relevant factors (Luborsky, 1971). For example, a wife might think her husband's primary difficulty is alcoholism, yet the husband and therapist might believe that a more basic issue is the feeling of inadequacy which stimulates drinking— something of which the wife is unaware.

The question of generality versus specificity of ratings involves many similar issues. Specific ratings (e.g., work performance, test scores, episodes of drunkenness) can be objective and represent particular aspects of functioning, but they cannot present a broad picture of the client's adjustment and sense of well-being. General measures often take the form "Much improved," "Slightly improved," "Not improved." Such measures can represent feeling states and the overall balance of various aspects of the client's adjustment, but they are highly susceptible to bias and distortion (e.g., halo effects) (Garfield et al., 1971).

These controversies about assessment strategies are critical because they severely confound the interpretation of research results. A particular study can be viewed as supportive, unsupportive, or irrelevant depending on the dependent measures included and the changes in these measures. For example, Paul (1966) found that a behavior therapy group was most effective on the basis of physiological and behavioral measures of change, but that behavior therapy, psychotherapy, and control groups all improved equally on self-report measures. Does this mean that all persons showed meaningful decreases in subjective distress, or that the self-report measures were biased and invalid? Numerous recommendations have been made about how the effects of psychotherapy should be assessed (cf. Kazdin & Wilson, 1978a; Strupp & Bergin, 1969; Strupp & Hadley, 1977). However, the only point of agreement is that a battery of measures is required, covering various aspects of client functioning and sources of information.

Therapists

Psychotherapy is an intense interpersonal activity whose course cannot be planned by a simple, step-by-step blueprint. The moment-to-moment flow of communication depends largely on the particular client and therapist. Obviously, the therapist plays a critical role in the outcome of therapy. Summarizing the literature, Luborsky et al. (1971) conclude that more experienced therapists generally produce better results than less experienced ones, and that therapists judged (by colleagues) to be skillful generally have greater success than those judged less skillful. The interpersonal characteristics that contribute to these findings (empathy, warmth, and genuineness) will be discussed in Chapter 8.

Unfortunately, therapists simply do not vary from good to excellent; they range from harmful to helpful. Bergin (1971) found that up to 10 percent of persons in psychotherapy actually deteriorated during treatment. Some were getting worse before they entered treatment and may have been untreatable. However, Bergin concludes that some were deteriorating but could have been helped if their therapists were not "inept," while others were actually made worse by an inept therapist who disturbed a neurotic equilibrium. These findings have major implications for society given the confidence placed in mental health professionals. They also have more specific implications in regard to our discussion of outcome research. Some critics argue that the effects of therapy should be judged on the basis of the average patient and the average therapist (i.e., what can the average person expect?). Others believe that a fair evaluation requires only good therapists working with appropriate patients (cf. Luborsky, Singer, & Luborsky, 1975) (what is the best that can be achieved?). This disagreement is another factor which confounds interpretation of outcome research. In addition, experienced, highly skilled therapists are often unavailable for participation in research studies. Most outcome research has been conducted with graduate students or relatively inexperienced professionals as therapists.

Type of Therapy

Earlier in this chapter we described many variations of individual therapy, group therapy, and family therapy. Outcome research generally suggests that these variations are roughly equal in effectiveness (Luborsky et al., 1975; Sloane et al., 1975a). However, the literature is flawed by many methodological inadequacies. No series of well-controlled studies has evaluated any particular type of therapy, let alone systematically compared diverse approaches. In addition, it seems likely, on an intuitive basis, that different types of persons would profit from different types of treatment. Specific client-therapist-therapy matches have not yet been adequately identified or tested.

Nonspecific Factors in Therapy

Any treatment procedure, psychological or otherwise, must be evaluated on a relative basis. It makes little sense to say that a certain percentage of persons receiving some treatment improve when we do not know how many would improve with no treatment or with some alternative. Thus, the question becomes, how effective is psychotherapy compared to other treatments or no treatments? This issue is highlighted by the classic papers of Hans J. Eysenck (1952; 1965). Reviewing the outcome literature, he concluded that psychotherapy had an average success rate of 67 percent. This figure has since been verified in several other reviews and is a widely accepted reference point (cf. Luborsky et al., 1975; Malan, 1973). However, Eysenck also attempted to ascertain the amount of recovery which could be expected without treatment—*spontaneous remission*. Again the figure was about 67 percent! Eysenck's data and conclusions have been the subject of intense debate since his first publication appeared.

One of the most notable critics is Bergin (1971), who argues that spontaneous remission rates are really between 30 and 50 percent.

He also indicates that 10 percent of persons deteriorate, reducing the "average" change rate for all treated subjects. Thus, about 80 percent improve with treatment while only 30 to 50 percent improve without it. Bergin also questions the term "spontaneous remission," with its implication that improvement simply occurs with no rhyme or reason. Rather, he suggests, many distressed individuals who are not in therapy receive informal treatment elsewhere. Religious counseling, as well as help from family physicians, friends, and relatives, are all potential sources of therapeutic aid. These sources are also used by persons in the waiting list control groups included in most outcome studies. By implication, subjects in such groups cannot be assumed to be "untreated."

A related issue is the role of specific and nonspecific factors in therapy. It is widely agreed that a significant part of psychotherapy is a group of so-called "nonspecific factors" which relate more to the general nature of the interaction than to anything the therapist does (Hartley & Strupp, 1980; Weiner, 1976; Wolberg, 1967). These include: the act of admitting a problem and seeking help, expectation of change, being understood and accepted, talking about one's problems, and having someone warmly listen. Many of these factors are often called a *placebo* effect. In contrast to the stereotype of the placebo as a useless "sugar pill," Jerome Frank (1978), among others, regards placebo effects as crucial in the effectiveness of psychotherapy. The presence of these factors in all forms of therapy may well explain why their effectiveness is about equal (cf. Luborsky et al., 1975). The placebo effect may also explain why posttreatment differences between treated and untreated subjects seem to disappear over time (Liberman, 1978; Sloane et al., 1978a). Untreated control subjects seem to "catch up" to their treated counterparts. Possibly therapy simply provides a more concentrated dose of the placebo factors than does the environment, rather than providing something unique. If so, therapy may simply speed up change rather than produce more change or a different type of change than would otherwise occur (Bergin & Suinn, 1975; Liberman, 1978).

Interpreting the Literature

We have identified several of the major factors which complicate the course of outcome research. However, there are many others as well. For example, the literature often refers to the proportion of "improved" persons (cf. Luborsky et al., 1975). What does this rating actually mean?

Symptoms entirely eliminated? Decreased distress? Less intrapsychic conflict? When a battery of tests is given, persons rarely show benefits on all of them. How many tests or which tests must change for the treatment to be judged successful? Statistical significance does not require large changes so much as consistent changes. It can be achieved if most subjects change a little bit. Thus, *statistical* significance must be differentiated from *clinical* significance. How much must people change for treatment to be regarded as successful? Another question pertains to the status of dropouts. Eysenck (1952) regards them as failures, while Bergin (1971) does not; this partially explains their dramatically different conclusions about the effectiveness of therapy. The issues relate less to design or even theory than to interpretation. There are no correct answers to these controversies.

Finally, we have the issue of generality of results. Even if we had a "perfect" study and everyone agreed on the interpretation of the data, the effectiveness of psychotherapy would still be an open question. Each study involves a unique set of clients and therapists with an idiosyncratic treatment. Similar results might not be achieved with other clients, therapists, and so on. Hence, each study has only limited generality. A series of good studies is required to reach any conclusion. At this time, it is generally agreed that 67 percent of persons profit from therapy, and that these persons will, at the very least, improve faster than they would without therapy. To these somewhat flimsy conclusions we can only add the ubiquitous statement: Further research is required to resolve this issue.

Summary

This chapter has presented an introduction to psychotherapy and an overview of psychodynamic approaches. We first considered what psychotherapy is and discussed the various definitions of it. The commonalities and differences among the major types of psychotherapy were then presented. The next section described psychoanalysis, including both theory and therapeutic techniques. Ego psychology and other psychodynamic approaches were then presented and compared with the classic analytic procedures from which they evolved. The next two sections covered the major approaches used in treating several clients simultaneously: group therapy and family therapy. Major variants of these forms of treatment were contrasted. The final section of the chapter dealt with the evaluation of the effects of psychotherapy: outcome research. Major problems in conducting and evaluating such research were discussed, including clients, dependent measures, therapists, types of treatment, and nonspecific treatment effects. The lack of definitive information about how therapy works was highlighted.

CHAPTER
SEVEN

Behavior Therapy

Clinical psychologists, it is clear, engage in a wide variety of activities. They have also helped greatly to develop or advance many of the activities they perform (e.g., psychotherapy, research on psychopathology). Two areas however, are generally considered to be almost unique provinces of clinical psychology: psychological testing and behavior therapy. While these areas owe much to other disciplines and professions, they are primarily products of clinical psychology. In fact, it has been argued that both of them were developed, at least in part, because of the desire of clinicians to create a unique professional identity. Of course, their unique training and orientation to the clinical enterprise also stimulated new and creative approaches to clinical problems. In any case, it is interesting that these two special contributions are so highly incompatible with one another. We have already considered several of the reasons; others will become apparent as we consider behavioral treatment techniques. This chapter begins with a brief review of the behavioral model as it applies to treatment and discusses its historical development. Most of the chapter is devoted to the treatment techniques themselves. The diversity of behavioral techniques makes it impossible to cover all of them extensively. Thus, we will discuss a representative sample of the techniques used by clinical psychologists, highlighting those that are most common or are especially creative and exciting.

The Behavioral Model

General Issues

The behavioral model was considered in some detail in Chapter 5. Several aspects of the model deserve reemphasis, however, especially as they pertain to behavioral strategies. Recall that behavior modification involves a scientific orientation to human behavior problems. The primary focus is on the use of empirically grounded techniques. Behavior modifiers assume that maladaptive behavior is learned, and is not fundamentally different from nonmaladaptive behavior. Maladaptive behavior persists because of the individual's learning history and current interactions with the environment. So-called "intrapsychic" processes and motives are presumed to be nonexistent. Thus, both assessment and treatment are relatively direct and focus on specific motor, physiological, and cognitive responses rather than on hypothesized intrapsychic activity.

In addition to these general characteristics of behaviorism, there are other specific factors. First, treatment is generally viewed as an educational process. Just as maladaptive behavior is learned, it can be unlearned and replaced by new adaptive behavior. The client is not manipulated by the therapist but is taught new and more functional ways to behave.

Second, the major focus of treatment is on the measurable change of some specific problem or source of distress. Very often complaints are vague or unclear, such as, "I just can't seem to relax anymore," or "I don't know where I'm going, or why." Before treatment begins, such complaints must be concretized so that both client and therapist know exactly what the goals of therapy are (i.e., what does the client want to do that cannot be done now, or how does the client want to feel about work, school, etc.?). Insight, the major goal of several of the verbal psychotherapies, is not considered a goal for behavioral treatment for two reasons: (1) it is not specific and thus cannot be measured, and (2) intellectual understanding of one's problems has not been shown to improve functioning.

The latter point is of utmost concern and relates to the third characteristic of behavioral treatment: an emphasis on behavior in the client's natural environment. It is much easier to produce improvement in the consulting room (i.e., therapist's office) than in the outside world. It is also much easier to get clients to feel better temporarily. (e.g., be less anxious, more optimistic) than it is to produce enduring change in their manner of functioning. The literature also indicates that client self-reports about feelings do not relate well to what they actually do and how they respond physiologically (cf. Bellack & Hersen, 1977a, Chapter 2; 1977b). Thus, behavior therapists attempt to assess and change the client's functioning in all relevant areas, in and out of the office or hospital.

Fourth, based on intensive assessment, behavioral treatments are tailored to each client. Behavior therapy is more a set of principles and strategies for altering behavior than a group of standard treatments. Therefore, a unique intervention is created for almost every client. As will be discussed below, there are some seemingly standard treatment techniques (e.g., systematic desensitization, social skills training). However, these procedures are not applied in a "cookbook" manner; they are molded to the client's needs. Also, few clients can be treated with only one technique. Most people seeking help either have several problems or sufficiently complex problems so that a variety of procedures is needed. Thus, the behavior therapist typically develops a treatment "package" for each client.

Fifth, and last, treatment is viewed as an experiment. Regardless of how carefully the therapist assesses the client, the resulting treatment plan is always a "best guess." Its adequacy, therefore, must be questioned throughout treatment, just as a scientist tests hypotheses. This is one of the reasons for specifying objective goals and measuring progress during treatment. Too slow an improvement can be quickly discovered and the treatment plan modified or, if necessary, totally revised. When possible, behavioral treatments are conducted according to single-subject research methods (see Chapter 10). The therapist can then be more confident that the treatment is responsible for any improvement in the target behavior.

Ethical Issues

The behavioral approach has been strongly criticized during the past twenty years. One issue is the effectiveness of behavioral techniques—which has now been well documented (cf. Bellack & Hersen, 1977a). As a result, the behavioral approach is now widely acknowledged both by mental health professionals and the public. The second issue is the ethics and values of behavior therapists. While this criticism is also unjustified and invalid, it has been much more difficult to refute.

Behavior therapists are often portrayed as cold, manipulative, and unresponsive to human needs and feelings. Behavioral techniques are widely viewed as robbing the client of freedom and dignity, as well as endangering our democratic society. These criticisms, we must emphasize, are based largely on misconceptions about what behavior therapy is and how it operates, as well as on vast overestimates of the power of conditioning procedures. Many critics equate the entire behavioral spectrum with operant conditioning, which represents only a fraction of behavior therapy. (The reasons for this are clarified in the historical overview.) It is often presumed that operant conditioning is a superpowerful tool which can mold entire societies against the will of the people. In fact, this is far from the truth. Recent research indicates that it is extremely difficult, if not impossible, to alter human behavior without the person's awareness and voluntary cooperation (Bandura, 1974). And even with such cooperation, operant techniques are quite limited.

In discussing the ethics of behavior therapists and behavior therapy, three points must be kept in mind. First, the goal of behavior therapy is to alleviate human suffering in the most effective, economical, rapid, and least aversive manner possible. Second, behavior therapists attempt to enlist the client's cooperation rather than to work against his or her needs or desires. Treatment is usually based on a written contract, in which therapist and client specify both mutually agreed-upon goals and a treatment plan. Third, behavior therapy is designed to teach the client how to control his or her own behavior, rather than to control the client externally. Behavior therapy is specifically defined as fostering self-control.

The ethics of behavior therapy are contained in the Ethical Issues for Human Services, a set of questions developed by the Association for the Advancement of Behavior Therapy (1977). The questions are presented in Table 7.1. Ethical treatment requires an affirmative answer to each question. For example, ethical conduct requires that the client and therapist agree on explicit goals (A1 and 3), that the most appropriate treatment is used (B), and that the effects of the treatment be systematically assessed (E). These standards all emphasize the client's free choice and rights, contrasting strongly to the public image of behavior therapy. The therapists who follow these principles are not cold, heartless, and manipulative. Research has shown that they are as warm and empathic as therapists with other orientations (Sloane, Staples, Cristol, Yorkston, & Whipple, 1975a). Many critics of behaviorism have identified humanistic values with a "mushy," passive approach to other people (especially clients). The straightforward, objective, and educative approach of behavior therapists is quite the opposite, but it is explicitly humanistic in its operation and goals.

Historical Development

Behavioral techniques have probably always been part of human behavior. Wages paid for work or services is a form of positive reinforcement, as are such social amenities as saying "Thank you" or "You look nice today." The Premack Principle (also known as "Grandma's Rule") (Becker, 1971), when applied to children, is a commonsense strategy of letting a child play (or watch television) only after homework or chores are completed. A traditional way of eliminating (or preventing) fears is to reexpose the individual to the feared situation (e.g., put a child back on a horse after a fall, or back in the water after a near-drowning). Exposure is a primary behavioral strategy for fear reduction. Even such complex techniques as token economies have been in use at least since the early 1800s (cf. Kazdin, 1977).

While many behavioral techniques have long been in the public domain, it is only the last twenty years that they have been systematically analyzed and employed in clinical and educational settings. The rapid development of the field during that period is as much a sociocultural phenomenon as a process of scientific growth and discovery. Operant and respondent conditioning, developed and elaborated during the first half of the twentieth century, formed the basis for behavior modification. Examples of conditioning procedures applied to human problems were published throughout that period (e.g., Jones, 1924; Watson & Rayner, 1920). Most of this work, however, involved laboratory animals. It was not until the 1950s that such notable contributors as Bijou, Lindsley, and Skinner began to extend their research on conditioning to human beings (cf. Kazdin, 1977, Chapter 2). Only then were the possible therapeutic and educational uses of these procedures made clear.

In addition to the work on conditioning, two significant works appeared in the 1950s.[1] In 1952, an article by H. J. Eysenck indicated that persons in psychotherapy were no more likely to improve than those who received no treatment. At that time, the most widely available treatment was psychoanalytic psychotherapy provided by a psychi-

1. This account of the development of behavior modification is quite limited. The field could not have evolved without the contributions of many individuals not mentioned here.

Table 7.1. Ethical Issues for Human Services

A. *Have the goals of treatment been adequately considered?*
   1. To insure that the goals are explicit, are they written?
   2. Has the client's understanding of the goals been assured by having the client restate them orally or in writing?
   3. Have the therapist and client agreed on the goals of therapy?
   4. Will serving the client's interests be contrary to the interests of other persons?
   5. Will serving the client's immediate interests be contrary to the client's long term interest?

B. *Has the choice of treatment methods been adequately considered?*
   1. Does the published literature show the procedure to be the best one available for that problem?
   2. If no literature exists regarding the treatment method, is the method consistent with generally accepted practice?
   3. Has the client been told of alternative procedures that might be preferred by the client on the basis of significant differences in discomfort, treatment time, cost, or degree of demonstrated effectiveness?
   4. If a treatment procedure is publicly, legally, or professionally controversial, has formal professional consultation been obtained, has the reaction of the affected segment of the public been adequately considered, and have the alternative treatment methods been more closely reexamined and reconsidered?

C. *Is the client's participation voluntary?*
   1. Have possible sources of coercion on the client's participation been considered?
   2. If treatment is legally mandated, has the available range of treatments and therapists been offered?
   3. Can the client withdraw from treatment without a penalty or financial loss that exceeds actual clinical costs?

D. *When another person or an agency is empowered to arrange for therapy, have the interests of the subordinated client been sufficiently considered?*
   1. Has the subordinated client been informed of the treatment objectives and participated in the choice of treatment procedures?

2. Where the subordinated client's competence to decide is limited, have the client as well as the guardian participated in the treatment discussions to the extent that the client's abilities permit?

3. If the interests of the subordinated person and the superordinate persons or agency conflict, have attempts been made to reduce the conflict by dealing with both interests?

E. *Has the adequacy of treatment been evaluated?*

1. Have quantitative measures of the problem and its progress been obtained?

2. Have the measures of the problem and its progress been made available to the client during treatment?

F. *Has the confidentiality of the treatment relationship been protected?*

1. Has the client been told who has access to the records?

2. Are records available only to authorized persons?

G. *Does the therapist refer the clients to other therapists when necessary?*

1. If treatment is unsuccessful, is the client referred to other therapists?

2. Has the client been told that if dissatisfied with the treatment, referral will be made?

H. *Is the therapist qualified to provide treatment?*

1. Has the therapist had training or experience in treating problems like the client's?

2. If deficits exist in the therapist's qualifications, has the client been informed?

3. If the therapist is not adequately qualified, is the client referred to other therapists, or has supervision by a qualified therapist been provided? Is the client informed of the supervisory relation?

4. If the treatment is administered by mediators, have the mediators been adequately supervised by a qualified therapist?

From: The Association for Advancement of Behavior Therapy, 1977. Reprinted with permission.

atrist. Eysenck's article became a rallying point for those who challenged that treatment and/or who could not use it: notably, clinical psychologists. Then, in 1958, Joseph Wolpe's book *Psychotherapy by Reciprocal Inhibition* presented a conditioning model of neurotic behavior and a new treatment technique: systematic desensitization. Here was a promising alternative to traditional techniques—grounded in laboratory research and conditioning principles, both of which were basic to psychology. (Interestingly, Wolpe is a psychiatrist.)

With this background, the 1960s saw tremendous growth. Many new intervention strategies were developed, tested, and analyzed; behavioral techniques expanded to cover the entire range of psychological-behavioral disorders. As always, however, there were problems. Much of the stimulus for growth was dissatisfaction with traditional models and techniques. In the course of criticizing and rejecting those approaches, some of their positive contributions were also (temporarily) rejected (such as interviewing techniques, cognitive factors in behavior change). Simplistic interventions for complex problems, such as alcoholism and schizophrenia, were greatly overpublicized. These claims helped to produce some of the backlash against behavioral techniques.

The 1970s were a more reflective period. Behavior therapy continued to expand and increasingly influence the mental health and education communities. Whereas all behavioral techniques had once been challenged, many of them are now widely recognized as the intervention of choice. And so, behavior therapy is now less concerned about establishing its identity and is more contemplative. There is an increasing emphasis on improving and refining existing techniques and on developing more comprehensive programs.

Still, behavior therapy is hardly a homogeneous discipline with no theoretical and methodological disagreements. On the contrary, behavior therapists differ greatly. This is especially true of the "radical operant" and "cognitive behavior therapy" perspectives. The former group ignores cognitive processes, focusing solely on observable and measurable phenomena (cognitions cannot be observed). The latter group, in contrast, emphasizes cognition in both the conceptualization of behavior and in treatment. Many of the usual differences between behavioral and nonbehavioral models become hazy when cognitive behavior therapy is considered. The majority of behavior therapists fall somewhere in between, recognizing the importance of cognition but uncertain about how to use it. Research on this and other issues is now underway.

Behavior Therapy Techniques

Behavior therapy, as noted above, contains few standard treatment techniques. It consists primarily of an orientation and a set of principles which are used to create new treatment strategies as needed. Thus, it is impossible to describe the full range of behavioral interventions in a single chapter. Therefore, in the balance of this chapter, the most illustrative strategies will be described to provide an idea of what behavior therapy is like.

Fear Reduction Techniques

Fears and phobias are common forms of psychological distress. From a behavioral perspective, fears are learned, either by aversive experience (e.g., almost drowning) or by observation (e.g., modeling the behaviors of a fearful parent). Fears—even irrational ones—persist, primarily because the individual avoids the feared stimulus and consequently fails to extinguish the fear (i.e., learn that there is no real danger). Many effective strategies have been developed to eliminate fears. All of them expose the individual to the feared stimulus so that the fear can finally be extinguished.

Systematic Desensitization.   The first technique to be developed, and the most influential, is systematic desensitization. This is one of the basic techniques in behavior therapy; its creator, Joseph Wolpe, is a founder of the behavioral movement.

According to Wolpe, desensitization is based on a neurological process called *reciprocal inhibition.* Certain components of the nervous system act mainly to produce incompatible effects (e.g., arousal versus sleep). When one such component is aroused (or dominant), it inhibits the action of any incompatible component (you cannot be awake and asleep at the same time). Two such components are the sympathetic nervous system (SNS) and parasympathetic nervous system (PNS). The SNS is often called the "fight or flight" system, since it gears the organism for action (*increasing* the heart rate, blood pressure, respiration rate, etc.). The PNS is primarily a vegetative or quiescent system, associated with digestion, rest, and other restorative processes (*decreas-*

ing the heart rate, blood pressure, etc.). In preparing the organism for action, the SNS becomes highly aroused in response to fear-producing stimuli. Wolpe (1958), among others, viewed fear basically as an SNS response. If SNS arousal in the presence of fear-producing stimuli could be prevented, he hypothesized, no fear would be experienced. If the person could be repeatedly exposed to such stimuli without SNS arousal, the previously conditioned fear would be counterconditioned (i.e., eliminated). The way to prevent SNS arousal is to produce PNS arousal, which can reciprocally inhibit the SNS.

Desensitization, then, is based on Wolpe's concept of *counterconditioning by reciprocal inhibition*. The technique contains three key elements. First, the individual must be exposed to the phobic stimulus. In most cases, exposure to the actual stimulus is difficult or impossible. Thus, Wolpe employed exposure by imagination: the client simply visualizes him or herself in the feared situation. Such visualization, it has been found, can produce considerable discomfort and SNS arousal (Lang, 1969). Second, the client must generate PNS arousal to inhibit the SNS. To do this, Wolpe used deep muscle relaxation (DMR)—a procedure in which the client is taught to relax all the major voluntary muscle groups (e.g., arms, legs, facial muscles). DMR is learned in a few hours and can produce substantial reductions in SNS activity (Paul, 1969).

The third element concerns the combination of the first two. The phobic individual becomes very upset in response to the feared stimulus (even in imagination). Initially, DMR is not powerful enough to overcome this strong reaction. However, there are usually certain aspects of the feared stimulus which make it more or less fear-provoking. For example, the amount of fear typically decreases as the stimulus is removed in space or time. A dog phobic might be terrified of being right next to a dog, moderately afraid if the dog were twenty feet away, and minimally afraid if it were across the street. Wolpe thus had clients imagine the feared stimuli in a *hierarchical* order, from low fear to high fear. At each stage, DMR is powerful enough to inhibit the fear. As fear is counterconditioned at one level, stimuli at higher levels become less fear-provoking and easier to inhibit.

The first step in desensitization is to develop the hierarchy of feared stimuli. This is usually done by both therapist and client. The hierarchy, carefully tailored to the client's specific fear pattern, consists of fifteen to twenty items, each slightly more fear-provoking than the one before. Representative hierarchies are presented in Table 7.2. DMR training

Table 7.2.   Representative Hierarchies for Systematic Desensitization

Fear of Heights

1. Standing on the first rung of a ladder.
2. Standing on the third rung of a ladder.
3. Standing on the fifth rung of a ladder.
4. Standing on the top rung of a six-foot ladder.
5. Looking out of a third-floor window.
6. Looking out of a sixth-floor window.
7. Looking out of a tenth-floor window.
8. Standing on a balcony on the third floor.
9. Standing on a balcony on the sixth floor.
10. Standing on a balcony on the tenth floor.
11. Standing on the roof of a six-story building.
12. Standing on the roof of a ten-story building.

Fear of Flying

1. Driving past an airport.
2. Driving into the parking lot of an airport.
3. Walking into an airline terminal.
4. Walking to the gate for a flight.
5. Walking up the ramp to an airplane.
6. Entering an airplane.
7. Buckling the seat belt in an airplane.
8. Hearing the airplane's engines start.
9. Feeling the airplane begin to move.
10. Feeling the airplane take off.
11. Feeling the landing gear thump.
12. Coming in for a landing.
13. Seeing the ground "rush up" as the airplane touches down.

typically requires two to three sessions. Training involves alternately tensing and relaxing each of the muscle groups; the client thus becomes more sensitive to feelings of tension and capable of relaxing specific muscle groups at will. Training takes place in a darkened room with the client in a reclining position. The client is usually asked to practice relaxation at home between sessions until he or she can relax completely at will.

Once these two activities are completed, desensitization begins. The client sits in a recliner chair, closes his or her eyes, and is asked to relax. The first item (least fear-provoking) on the hierarchy is then presented in sufficient detail so that the client can actually imagine being in the situation. The client imagines the situation for about twenty to thirty seconds and then focuses solely on relaxation. If any anxiety is experienced prior to that point, the client immediately stops imagining the situation and concentrates on becoming relaxed again. In either case, the item is presented again about sixty seconds later. This sequencing continues until the client can repeatedly imagine the situation with no anxiety. The next item is then presented in the same manner. Treatment continues until the highest item in the hierarchy can be imagined with no distress. In some cases, additional items are added to the hierarchy if the anxiety remains at any one point. If there are several fears, different hierarchies can be employed sequentially. Three to four items can often be completed in each weekly one-hour session; thus, treatment typically requires six to eight weeks.

Desensitization is one of the most carefully examined therapeutic techniques of any theoretical orientation. At this time, it is considered consistently effective. Since 1958 hundreds of studies have documented its effectiveness in eliminating fears (e.g., Lang & Lazovik, 1963; Lang, Lazovik, & Reynolds, 1965; Paul, 1966). However, despite this overwhelming evidence, there is controversy over exactly how it must be applied and how and why it works. Each component of the technique (e.g., DMR, hierarchies) has been shown to be important, yet variations of desensitization excluding the components have also been effective (cf. Bellack & Hersen, 1977a, Chapter 3). Despite Wolpe's contention that the technique must be practiced as he specified, apparently it can be considerably modified and still be effective.

More importantly, Wolpe's conceptions of fear and fear reduction have been shown to be simplistic. The three modalities of the fear response (subjective distress, physiological arousal, and avoidance behavior) appear to be highly independent of one another (Bellack & Hersen, 1977b; Lang, 1969). Thus, fear may be experienced in only one or two of the modalities, and a reduced response in one modality (as in desensitization) may have no effect on the others. Finally, the SNS and PNS interact in a much more complex manner than Wolpe's reciprocal inhibition model would suggest. Therefore, even if SNS arousal were part of the fear response, it might not be inhibited by DMR. Research is still being conducted to resolve these issues. But regardless of the ultimate explanation, desensitization remains one of our most effective therapeutic tools.

Modeling. Albert Bandura has been one of the major figures in psychology for the past 20 years. His research on observational learning has had a profound influence on the field, including the treatment of fears. In general, observational learning, or *modeling,* entails learning by observing the behavior of others, in contrast to the direct experience involved in conditioning. For example, children learn to speak by listening to their parents. Modeling is used in eliminating fears by having a fearful person observe a nonfearful one safely perform the feared activity. There are three aspects of this process which work to reduce the observer's fear and fearful behavior (Bandura & Barab, 1973): (1) The person receives accurate information about the feared situation (e.g., it is not really dangerous or harmful, (2) The individual tends to feel foolish about being unable to do what somewhat else has just done with little difficulty and no harm; thus, there is an increased incentive to approach or interact with the feared stimulus. (3) Most important is *vicarious extinction,* a process analogous to extinction by direct trial and error; this occurs when the individual observes that no harm comes to the person performing the feared response.

The first demonstration of these effects was a study by Bandura, Grusec, and Menlove (1967). Children who were afraid of dogs were exposed to one of four conditions: (1) One group attended a party and observed a fearless peer play with a dog. (2) A second group observed a fearless peer play with a dog in a neutral environment (i.e., no party). (3) A third group was exposed to the dog in the party context of condition 1, but without a fearless model (i.e., the dog was simply placed in the room). (4) A control group attended a party, but no dog or model was involved. Children in both modeling groups were significantly less fearful of dogs after treatment, while exposure alone had little effect. Modeling without the party was just as effective as modeling with the party. These results have been replicated many times with such diverse problems as fear of water (Lewis, 1974), social anxiety and withdrawal (O'Connor, 1969), and fear of impending surgery (Melamed & Siegel, 1975). It has also been shown that filmed modeling displays (i.e., movies of fearless models) can be highly effective (Bandura & Menlove, 1968; Melamed & Siegel, 1975).

With adult clients, the usual form of modeling is called *participant modeling* or *contact desensitization.* Rather than simply observing a model in action, the client "shadows" the model (usually the therapist), performing the modeled activities immediately after the model demonstrates the response. In addition, the therapist-model often guides the client through the response. For example, in treating a height phobic, the therapist may slowly climb a ladder, helping the client up behind.

The therapist may then follow the client up the ladder, holding hands or otherwise maintaining physical contact. Eventually the client would climb up unaided. They may then walk out onto a series of balconies on a tall building: first floor, then third floor, then tenth floor, and so on. In each case, the therapist proceeds first, followed by the client, with therapist support gradually fading out (slowly eliminated). Numerous studies have shown this procedure to be highly effective (Bandura, Blanchard, & Ritter, 1969; Bandura, Jeffery, & Gajdos, 1975; Blanchard, 1970).

Exposure Treatments. Fears persist, we have noted, because people fail to reexpose themselves to the feared stimulus and allow extinction to occur. Thus, it is logical that exposure would be critical to treatment. Systematic desensitization arranges for exposure in imagination; contact desensitization combines exposure with modeling displays and physical support. Several strategies have been developed in which *in vivo* exposure is used alone.

Sherman (1972) studied a procedure called *in vivo desensitization.* The subjects were aquaphobic (afraid of water) college students who were required to pass a swimming test. The procedure involved twenty-six water-related activities, such as sitting at the edge of a pool, standing in knee-deep water, hanging onto the side of the pool in chest-deep water, and so on. The activities were ordered in a hierarchy, and subjects proceeded from one to another at their own pace. Subjects who underwent this procedure improved more than those who received standard systematic desensitization with the same twenty-six items presented in an imagined hierarchy.

A related procedure, called *shaping* or *in vivo exposure,* was examined in a series of studies at the University of Vermont (Agras, Leitenberg, & Barlow, 1968; Barlow, Agras, Leitenberg, & Wincze, 1970; Leitenberg, Agras, Allen, Butz, & Edwards, 1975). In this procedure, clients are directed to expose themselves gradually and systematically to phobic stimuli of increasing intensity. For example, a claustrophobic client might be encouraged to spend as much time as he or she could in a small room, rest, to go back in and try to stay slightly longer, and so on. The therapist may or may not accompany the client during exposure, but ample social reinforcement and encouragement are given. When possible, specific feedback about progress is added (e.g., "You remained in the room for six minutes that time, compared to only two minutes yesterday. That's great; you're really doing well").

A third form of exposure treatment is *flooding*. In contrast to the graduated procedures described above, flooding involves prolonged exposure to the most feared stimuli right from the beginning of treatment. A claustrophobic might be requested to stay in a small room for two hours or until all anxiety dissipated. Several studies have found this procedure to be more effective than systematic desensitization (e.g., Boulougouris, Marks, & Marset, 1971). As might be imagined, this treatment is often quite distressing and is not frequently employed. However, it can be valuable for highly phobic clients who fail to respond to other, milder procedures. Of course, the procedure is explained to the client in detail in advance, and the client is free to withdraw at any time.

Flooding and a related technique called *response prevention* provide the most promising approach for treatment of obsessive-compulsive disorder (cf. Turner, Hersen, Bellack, & Wells, 1979). Severe obsessive-compulsives often require psychiatric hospitalization, since their lives are totally dominated by their repetitive thoughts and rituals. Treatment consists of exposing the client to the stimulus which precipitates the obsessive thought pattern (e.g., dirt) and then preventing the compulsive ritual (e.g., hand washing). This sequence lasts for several hours per day, and the ritual is prohibited throughout the hospital stay. While this treatment is also distressing to the client, it is less aversive and disruptive than the endless ritualizing or such alternative (and less effective) treatments as electronconvulsive therapy (ECT).

General Considerations. How can there be so many treatments, based on different premises, all of which are effective? Several points should be considered here. First, just as there are "many ways to skin a cat," there may also be more than one way to treat any disorder. The procedures described above are all based on the same principle (extinction) and are only slightly different ways of getting to the same point. Second, all clients are quite different, even if they report the same basic disorder. Different clients *prefer* different types of treatment and almost certainly *require* them. Therapists also vary in their preferences and skills with different techniques. Thus, it is not only reasonable but also desirable to have several effective alternatives.

Social Skills Training

Human beings are social organisms, spending much of their lives inter-acting with others. Thus, their interactions have a tremendous influence on the quality of their lives. While satisfactory relationships typically lead to good adjustment, poor ones often provoke anxiety, depression, and psychological disturbance (cf. Bellack & Hersen, 1978). Why do some people have many good relationships while others cannot establish even one? Behavior therapists view social behavior as based on a set of specific *social skills:* learned abilities to make certain responses, avoid others, and accurately perceive the needs and desires of other persons. Those people who perform poorly in interpersonal situations are then viewed as having *social skill deficits.*

The behaviors that comprise social skills vary with the type of skill and the situation involved. By "type of skill" we mean the general purpose or context of the interaction, such as standing up for one's rights (assertion), meeting a prospective date (heterosocial skill), or talking with a stranger (conversational skill). While it is obvious that behavior varies in these different contexts, behavior also varies in different situations *within* contexts—and this is often unclear. For example, Eisler, Hersen, Miller, and Blanchard (1975) show that assertiveness toward women is quite different from assertiveness toward men; with familiar people and strangers, there are still other variations.

Each type of skill consists of several verbal and nonverbal response components, such as maintaining eye contact, smiling at appropriate times, matching the volume and tone of voice to the speech content, and requesting new behavior (rather than complying with an unreasonable situation). Another important group are the "social perception" skills, such as accurately perceiving the emotions of others, timing responses correctly (e.g., not leaving in the middle of someone else's sentence), and the ability to pick up unspoken messages (e.g., a look of boredom). Any and all of these elements can be incorporated in training, depending on the specific pattern of deficits.

The first task in social skills training is to develop a list of situations in which the client experiences difficulty. For example, "You are trying to study when your roommate suddenly turns on the stereo loud." These situations are then arranged in order of increasing difficulty, analogous to a hierarchy in systematic desensitization. The actual training, which focuses on these situations, consists of five components: instructions, role playing, feedback, modeling, and practice (Bellack & Hersen, 1978). *Instructions* entail describing an appropriate response and how it should be made. The client is taught to focus on the deficient verbal and nonverbal elements. Depending on the client's capabilities, these elements may be taught one at a time (as with chronic schizophrenics) or several simultaneously (as with most adult outpatients). A typical instruction is, "It is important to look at the other person when you speak, but not to stare. Try to look at my face for a moment, then look at my head, then my face, then over my shoulder."

Instructions alone may sometimes be sufficient to modify simple behaviors (e.g., eye contact) in well-functioning clients. However, most clients require the more extensive training and rehearsal provided by the following four procedures. *Role playing* consists of enacting a targeted situation as if it were actually occurring. The therapist portrays the partner and the client rehearses the response, just as if he or she were learning a motor skill (e.g., tennis). Afterward the therapist provides *feedback*—an appraisal of the performance. This includes positive reinforcement for improvement or satisfactory aspects of the response, as well as any corrective information needed. Such feedback is highly specific, so that it can be used by the client to alter subsequent attempts. An example might be: "That was pretty good. You maintained good eye contact and spoke clearly. However, your volume was a little low. Try to raise your voice a little this time, especially when you say, 'No!' " The situation would then be role-played again.

In some cases, instructions, feedback, and role playing are sufficient. Often, however, the client cannot master a response without observing a correct performance. In this case, the therapist *models* the response. This process is essentially role playing in reverse, with the therapist enacting what the client should do. The client then tries again. This sequence (instructions, role play, feedback, modeling) is repeated for each behavior and each situation until all are mastered. At the end of each session, the client is given specific homework assignments in which new skills are *practiced.* Practice is just as important for social skills as for motor skills. An assignment for someone who had difficulty meeting people might be: "Each day this week, make at least one comment to someone sitting next to you in a class."

The basic strategy described above has been used successfully with many different populations. For example, Curran and Gilbert (1975) have reduced social isolation and shyness in male college students. Passive and withdrawn psychiatric patients have been taught to be assertive and stand up for their rights (Bellack, Hersen, & Turner, 1976). Assertiveness training has also been used successfully to reduce outbursts of rage and violence in psychiatric patients (Foy, Eisler, & Pinkston,

1975). Finally, social skills training helps to increase the frequency and quality of social interactions of withdrawn elementary school children (Bornstein, Bellack, & Hersen, 1977).

In some cases, social skill deficits are the primary or sole form of distress. In many others, such deficits are either secondary to or associated with other problems. For example, depression has been viewed as resulting, at least in part, from an inability to interact effectively with others and gain social reinforcement (cf. Wells, Hersen, Bellack, & Himmelhoch, 1977). Thus, social skills training has become part of the treatment for such diverse dysfunctions as alcoholism, obesity, sexual deviation, marital conflict, depression, and agoraphobia.

Cognitive Behavior Therapy

Cognition has had an uneasy place in the history of behavior therapy. Initially, hypothesizing about cognitive activity was presumed to be needless and fruitless. Not only could behavior be changed without any reference to cognition, it was thought, but concern for cognitive activity was viewed as a backward step, interfering with the advance of science and behavioral technology. However, while it can be argued that operant conditioning can be applied without attention to cognition, most behavioral interventions do not work this way. Systematic desensitization requires the imagining of hierarchy items, self-appraisal of anxiety and relaxation, and active cooperation—all based on cognition. Observational learning works by cognitive representation of external events (the modeling display) (Bandura, 1977). In general, any voluntary therapeutic intervention relies, to some extent, on the perceptions, beliefs, and desires of the client—all cognitive processes.

For these reasons, cognitive activity has recently received increasing attention from behavior therapists. Not only has the role of cognition been investigated, but various new therapeutic strategies focus on cognitive activity, which is used to change motor or physiological responses. In general, behavior therapists consider cognitive activity as a response, similar to motor and physiological activity. As such, cognitive responses, such as fearful thoughts, are presumed to follow the same rules and operations as other types of responses. Thus, specific thoughts and feelings can be precipitated by certain stimuli, and can be altered by reward or punishment. In addition, certain forms of thinking, such as problem solving, can be seen as learned skills; their absence would therefore be skill deficits.

Self-control. At first glance, the term *self-control* seems antithetical to behavior therapy. Kanfer (1976), however, has developed a model in which self-control is viewed as a series of specific responses rather than as a vague construct. The first response in the series is *self-monitoring* (SM), the observation of one's own behavior. The next response is *self-evaluation* (SE), in which the quality of the response is compared to some criterion. For example, the student can monitor studying: How long and how effectively did he or she study? The results of this observation are then compared with plans for studying, the amount of studying other students have done, the difficulty of the material, and so on. The third stage of self-control is *self-reinforcement* (SR)—reward or punishment. The student (above) could self-reward effective studying by watching television, going to a party, or getting something to eat. Poor studying could be punished by self-criticism or further studying. Each of the self-control responses (SM, SE, and SR) are presumed to operate just like the parallel external events (i.e., SR works in the same manner as reinforcement from others).

Self-control procedures have been used to treat a variety of dysfunctions, including hallucinations, depression, alcoholism, cigarette smoking, and obesity. The treatment of obesity is typical of this approach. Bellack, Glanz, and Simon (1976) gave a two-part treatment to obese clients. First, the clients were given ways to alter their eating behavior so as to lose weight (e.g., avoid high-calorie foods, no eating after 9 P.M.). Second, self-control procedures were used to help the clients follow the instructions. Clients kept a diary in which they wrote down everything they ate (SM). The diary entries were evaluated in regard to daily eating goals, such as number of calories consumed (SE). Clients then self-reinforced in response to the SE. A letter grade was first written next to the diary entry. If the grade was A or B, clients imagined a highly pleasant, diet-relevant situation, such as buying a garment in a smaller size. If the grade was D or F, they imagined an aversive situation, such as bursting a seam when bending over. Individuals who received this treatment lost significantly more weight than others who received instructions alone.

Self-verbalization Techniques. Cognitive behavior therapists have hypothesized that some behavior disturbances result either because people say the wrong things to themselves or fail to say appropriate things (cf. Meichenbaum, 1972; Rush & Beck, 1978). For example, consider a college student who is anxious in social situations. When going to a party, he or she might begin thinking (i.e., self-verbalizing) such things as, "I'm not very attractive" or "I don't know what to say to people" or "I'm not a very good dancer." The party serves as a conditioned stimulus for these self-statements, and they, in turn, are conditioned anxiety-producing responses. Exposure techniques or systematic desensitization may not alter these cognitions and thus may be ineffective for this person. Another strategy is to focus directly on the cognitions: teaching the person to stop making the inappropriate self-statements while simultaneously building in appropriate statements (e.g., "This looks like a great party" or "I wonder if there's anyone here I would like to meet").

This treatment strategy, known as *cognitive restructuring,* is a variant of Rational Emotive Therapy (Ellis, 1958). It can be given in individual or group sessions and typically involves some combination of the following elements: (1) The client is given a rationale for his or her disturbance based on learning theory and the notion that faulty verbalizations are at the root of the distress. (2) The client is taught to analyze the experience and identify the irrational and inappropriate self-verbalizations produced. Training employs instructions, modeling, and practice. (3) The client is taught to produce rational and appropriate verbalizations which are incompatible with the irrational ones. (4) The client rehearses the new pattern of verbalization in the office and practices *in vivo* between sessions. This treatment approach has not yet been systematized or empirically tested to the same extent as the other procedures we have discussed. However, several studies have found it to be highly effective in reducing a variety of fears (e.g., Meichenbaum, Gilmore, & Fedoravicius, 1971; Wein, Nelson, & Odom, 1975).

Cognitive restructuring has been applied in the treatment of fears, and Beck and his colleagues (cf. Rush & Beck, 1978) have developed a related procedure for depression. It is based on a model which considers depression to be a cognitive disorder. The symptoms of depression, such as sadness, crying, sleep, and eating disturbances, are presumed to result from three faulty thinking patterns: the *cognitive triad.* First, depressed persons have a negative self-concept, seeing themselves as unworthy, inadequate, and so on. Second, they view the world (e.g., other people) as making unreasonable demands or presenting insurmountable obstacles. Third, they see the future as being negative or bleak, with no way out of current difficulties and no solutions for present problems. As a result of these three thinking patterns, depressed persons distort experience, being unable to accurately perceive their own abilities or to discriminate real from irrational obstacles. Positive achievements or experiences are denied or explained away.

Cognitive therapy attempts to alter these faulty thinking styles. The client is first taught to identify these irrational beliefs and understand their role. The therapist then begins to explore the client's experience, challenging irrational evaluations and faulty reasoning. The client is given regular homework assignments and required to monitor accomplishments and mood levels. Achievements can thus be pointed out, and the client can be taught to make realistic analyses of his or her experience: i.e., what *really* was the situation and what did the client *really* do. Achievements and changes in mood state are considered in regard to increased hope for the future: e.g., "You really *can* change." In general, the therapist attempts to use logic and evidence from the client's own life and experience to dissuade negative thinking. Simultaneously, the client is taught to think more objectively and positively. Cognitive therapy for depression is a relatively new technique which has not yet been thoroughly investigated. However, in one study it was found to be more effective than antidepressant medication in alleviating depression (Rush, Beck, Kovacs, & Hollon, 1977).

Token Economy

All the techniques discussed so far are designed primarily for outpatients (mostly adults) who are not severely dysfunctional. Such individuals usually come to treatment voluntarily and can help formulate and comply with the treatment plan. Severely dysfunctional patients, such as chronic schizophrenics, the grossly mentally retarded, and some children present a very different picture. Their needs are much more substantial, and they have fewer skills to employ. Treatment is usually requested by another person (e.g., the institutional staff, teachers); therefore, even when treatment is in the client's best interest, cooperation cannot always be expected. With such individuals, the therapist must play a dominant role in planning treatment. Operant conditioning techniques, such as the token economy, were developed primarily for such difficult populations. The token economy, like systematic desensitization, is one of the hallmarks of behavior modification. It is also one of the clearest representatives of the behavioral model—a systematic, objective system which uses learning principles (operant conditioning) to modify discrete behaviors.

The modern token economy was developed by Ayllon and Azrin (1965) at Anna State Hospital in Illinois. Like most state hospitals and institutions for the mentally retarded, Anna State was more of a warehouse than a treatment facility. Patients spent most of their time sleeping, pacing, or watching television. Little socializing, creative activity, or treatment was conducted. This type of nonstimulating and nondemanding environment produces a new disorder, hospitalization syndrome, which often creates permanent vegetating inpatients. The token economy was developed to counter this pattern by motivating patients to become active, sociable, and functional.

The token economy uses the principles of operant conditioning. A behavior followed by a positive consequence tends to occur more often while a behavior followed by no consequence or a negative consequence tends to occur less often. Basically, token economies are miniature economic systems in which individuals are paid (reinforced) for making appropriate responses (e.g., working, socializing), and in which desired commodities (e.g., television, special meals) must be purchased. Without the necessary currency (tokens), the desired goods and services cannot be purchased. This system is the opposite of the typical hospital environment, in which reinforcers are provided noncontingently (i.e., free) or for maladaptive behavior (e.g., the troublesome patient gets attention).

All token programs have four common characteristics.

1. *Pinpointing target behaviors.* All behaviors covered by the system must first be carefully defined so that reinforcement can be consistent. Targets can range from brushing teeth to serving as a librarian; they may be limited to one or two behaviors or govern all aspects of daily life. Table 7.3 presents some of the work and self-care behaviors included in the Anna State system (Ayllon & Azrin, 1968).

2. *Tokens.* Tokens function in the economy as money does in society: as a medium of exchange and a representative of more primary reinforcers (goods and services). Tokens are given when a target response is performed and then traded in for the desired commodity later on. Tokens can be poker chips, metal rings, check marks in a book, holes punched in a ticket, or any other convenient means to bridge the delay between behavior and primary reward. They have the major advantage of permitting immediate reinforcement without disrupting activity by giving the patient the back-up reinforcer on the spot. This

delay also allows a wider variety of reinforcers to be employed (e.g., activities that occur only at specified times).

3. *Back-up reinforcers.* These are the goods and services for which tokens are exchanged. If the system is to work, there must be a wide enough variety of desired back-up reinforcers to motivate behavior over an extended period of time. A heavy emphasis is typically placed on *Premack reinforcers:* desired activities such as television time, movies, and free time. Table 7.4 contains a list of back-up reinforcers employed in the Anna State program. Some of the reinforcers, such as attendance at religious services, can no longer be used. Several recent court decisions have affirmed the inalienable rights of hospital patients, guaranteeing them free access to many things that were previously provided only on a contingent (i.e., earned) basis (cf. Bellack & Hersen, 1977a, Chapter 8). These have reduced the options available for many institutions which lack the resources to provide special reinforcers.

4. *Exchange rate.* The exchange rate specifies the number of tokens provided for each target behavior or job and the cost of each back-up reinforcer. As in real world economies, there is a delicate balance between wages and the cost of goods and services. If back-up reinforcers are too cheap, tokens can be earned easily and performance will fall off. If back-ups are too expensive, performance will also drop off, since too much effort will be required. Tables 7.3 and 7.4 contain exchange rates for listed jobs and reinforcers. Exchange rates can be set for the entire patient group or varied for each patient. For example, a high-level patient might not need tokens for teeth brushing, while a low-level patient might need them simply to hold the brush while an attendant does the actual brushing. In large programs, patients are typically grouped by level of functioning. Each level has its own set of target behaviors, back-up reinforcers, and exchange rates. As patients improve, they are promoted to higher levels, where both privileges and responsibilities are greater (e.g., they can buy passes to go home for weekends, but do not earn tokens for combing their hair).

The discussion thus far has focused on comprehensive programs for institutionalized persons. The same principles have also been applied, in a more limited way, to elementary school classrooms and individual children at home. Ayllon and Roberts (1974) employed a token system to reduce disruptive behavior and increase appropriate behavior in a fifth grade classroom. Tokens were earned for good performance on daily reading tests (the children were deficient in reading skills). The

Table 7.3.   Job Descriptions and Token Rates from the Anna State Hospital Token Economy

Types of jobs	Number of jobs	Duration	Tokens paid
Secretarial assistant			
1. Tooth Brushing Assists with oral hygiene. Writes names of patients brushing teeth.	1	30 min	3
2. Exercises Assists recreational assistant with exercises. Writes names of patients participating in exercises.	2	30 min	3
3. Commissary Assists sales clerk assistant. Writes names of patients at commissary, records number of tokens patient spent. Totals all tokens spent.	3	30 min	5
Assistant janitor			
1. Supplies Places ward supplies in supply cabinets and drawers.	1	10 min	1
2. Trash Carries empty soft drink bottles to storage area, empties waste paper baskets throughout the ward and carries paper to container adjacent to building. Carries mops used during the day outside to dry.	3	5 min	2
3. Porch Sweeps and washes walk adjacent to building. Washes garbage cans with soap and water.	2	10 min	2
4. Washroom Janitor Obtains necessary cleaning supplies and implements from utility room. Cleans four wash basins and four toilet bowls with cleanser and brush. Returns cleaning supplies and implements to utility room.	1	20 min	3
Grooming assistant			
1. Clothing Care Patient sets up ironing board and iron. Irons clothing that belongs to patients other than self. Folds clothing neatly. Returns ironed clothing, iron, and ironing board to nurses' station.	1	15 min	3
2. Personal Hygiene Patient takes basket with grooming aids, gargle, paper cups, lipstick, comb, hairbrush, and powder into patients' washroom. Patient	3	60 min	3

Table 7.3. (*Continued*)

Types of jobs	Number of jobs	Duration	Tokens paid
stays with grooming basket and assists any who need help with their grooming before each meal. Returns grooming basket after the meal has ended.			
3. Oral Hygiene	1	20 min	3
Assembles toothpaste, toothbrushes, gargle solution, and paper cups. Pours gargle into cups and dispenses toothpaste or gargle to all patients.			
Special services			
1. Errands	1	20 min	6
Leaves the ward on official errands through-out the hospital grounds, delivering messages and picking up supplies and records pertaining to the ward.			
2. Tour Guide	1	15 min	10
Gives visitors a 15-min tour of the ward explaining about the activities and token system. Answers visitors' questions about the ward.			
3. Nursing Assistant	1	10 min	10
Assists staff with the preparation of patients to be seen by the medical doctor. Assists staff with the control of undesired interaction between patients.			
Self-care activities			
1. Grooming			1
Combs hair, wears dress, slip, panties, bra, stockings and shoes (three times daily).			
2. Bathing			1
Takes a bath at time designated for bath. (once weekly)			
3. Tooth Brushing			1
Brushes teeth or gargles at the time designated for tooth brushing. (once daily)			
4. Exercises			1
Participates in exercises conducted by the exercise assistant. (twice daily)			
5. Bed Making			1
Makes own bed and cleans area around and under bed.			

Adapted from: Ayllon & Azrin (1968), Table A-6.

Table 7.4.   List of Reinforcers Available for Tokens

		No. of tokens daily
I.	Privacy	
	Selection of room 1	0
	Selection of room 2	4
	Selection of room 3	8
	Selection of room 4	15
	Selection of room 5	30
	Personal chair	1
	Choice of eating group	1
	Screen (room divider)	1
	Choice of bedspreads	1
	Coat rack	1
	Personal cabinet	2
		Tokens
II.	Leave from the ward	
	20-min. walk on hospital grounds (with escort)	2
	30 min. grounds pass (3 tokens for each additional 30 min.)	10
	Trip to town (with escort)	100
III.	Social interaction with staff	
	Private audience with chaplain, nurse	5 min. free
	Private audience with ward staff, ward physician (for additional time—1 token per min.)	5 min. free
	Private audience with ward psychologist	20
	Private audience with social worker	100
IV.	Devotional opportunities	
	Extra religious services on ward	1
	Extra religious services off ward	10
V.	Recreational opportunities	
	Movie on ward	1
	Opportunity to listen to a live band	1
	Exclusive use of radio	1
	Television (choice of program)	3
VI.	Commissary items	
	Consumable items such as candy, milk, cigarettes, coffee, and sandwich	1–5
	Toilet articles such as Kleenex, toothpaste, comb, lipstick, and talcum powder	1–10
	Clothing and accessories such as gloves, head scarf, house slippers, handbag, and skirt	12–400
	Reading and writing materials such as stationery, pen, greeting card, newspaper, and magazine	2–5
	Miscellaneous items such as ashtray, throw rug, potted plant, picture holder, and stuffed animal	1–50

From: Ayllon & Azrin (1968), Table A-1.

back-up reinforcers and exchange rates are presented in Table 7.5. In contrast to many token programs which rely on material reinforcers (e.g., candy, toys, cigarettes), this program used activities which were *natural* to the classroom (i.e., they were present and had been given out noncontingently before). The effectiveness of the system was demonstrated with a single subject research design. Reading accuracy was increased from 40 to 85 percent, and disruptive behavior decreased from 50 percent of the time to 5 percent. Similar programs have been widely used in educational settings, especially in special education classrooms. They are especially valuable in the classroom, since they allow the (typically) overworked teacher to easily control and reinforce the behavior of the entire class, increasing the time available for education.

Token economies have been able to produce dramatic effects, and many consider them to be a "treatment of choice" (Kazdin, 1977; Paul & Lentz, 1977). However, they also have been widely criticized by both behaviorists and others. First, there is little *comparative* research indicating that token economies are better than other systematic treatment programs (in institutions) (cf. Paul & Lentz, 1977); they have generally

Table 7.5.   Points Earning Criteria for Fifth-Grade Reading Class

1. 80% correct on workbook assignments = 2 points	
2. 100% correct on workbook assignments = 5 points	

Back-up Reinforcers

Daily

1. Access to game room (per 15 minutes)	2 points
2. Extra recess time (10 minutes)	2 points
3. Buy a ditto master	2 points
4. Have ditto copies run off (per copy)	1 point
5. Review grades in teacher's book	5 points
6. Reduce detention (per 10 minutes)	10 points
7. Change cafeteria table	15 points
8. Have the lowest test grade removed	20 points
9. Become an assistant teacher	Auction

Weekly

1. See a movie	6 points
2. Have a good work letter sent to parents	15 points
3. Become the classroom helper for one week	Auction
4. Become the ball captain for one week	Auction
5. Do bulletin board (will remain up for three weeks)	Auction

From: Ayllon & Roberts (1974), Table 1.

been compared to "no treatment" conditions (Bellack & Hersen, 1977a, Chapter 8). Second, it has been argued that token systems can alter unimportant behaviors that suit institutional needs but not clinically meaningful behaviors. For example, such targeted behaviors as cleaning hospital grounds and prohibiting children from talking in school hallways help the institution but may have little value for the individual. Third, token programs have been accused of violating individual rights by withholding privileges and materials that are guaranteed by society. This is of special concern in prisons and psychiatric hospitals, where residents are not free to participate in program development. Fourth, there is no consistent evidence that the effects of token programs *generalize* to new environments. That is, once the person leaves the token economy, the new behaviors may or may not persist. Thus, the status of token programs is up in the air. Future research must determine their full and comparative range of effectiveness. Much discussion and thought are needed to resolve the ethical and legal questions about what behaviors can be targeted and what reinforcers can be employed.

Operant Conditioning

Apart from token economies, operant conditioning has been widely used with individuals. In this section, we will highlight some of the strategies used with children and/or adults.

Positive Reinforcement. Positive reinforcement (PR) is one of the most popular behavioral strategies. Not only is it effective in a wide range of situations, but it is socially and humanistically desirable (in contrast to punishment techniques). Positive reinforcement is used to increase the frequency of a certain response, such as speaking to others, doing chores, or reacting quickly to teacher requests. In this strategy, a desirable stimulus (the reinforcer) is given after the target response occurs. At the beginning of the program, the reinforcer is typically given every time and immediately after the response is made. As the response rate increases, the reinforcer can be gradually delayed and presented less often.

There are three types of reinforcers: material, Premack, and social. *Material reinforcers,* such as food, toys, money, and comic books, are generally reserved for use with children and adolescents. A classic example is the work of Lovaas and his colleagues in teaching language to nonverbal autistic children (Lovaas, Freitas, Nelson, & Whalen, 1967). Speech was slowly and systematically shaped by modeling sounds and immediately reinforcing the child's imitation by popping a bit of cereal into his mouth. *Premack* or *activity reinforcers* have been widely used in the classroom and the home. Barrish, Saunders, and Wolf (1969) successfully employed various creative activity reinforcers to reduce inappropriate behavior in a fourth-grade classroom. Each day, children who behaved most appropriately had stars placed next to their name on a chart, were able to line up first for lunch, and received thirty minutes of free time.

Social reinforcement includes all forms of positive interpersonal interactions, including expressions of praise and approval, smiles and head nods, hugs and pats on the back, and conversations or games with special individuals. Social reinforcement is always included as a part of behavioral interventions, even if it is not the primary component. Because social reinforcement is a natural part of human interactions, it is generally used in lieu of other types of reinforcers whenever possible. When other reinforcers are used, an attempt is made to fade them out (i.e., gradually discontinue their use) and substitute social reinforcers.

Social reinforcement from adults is especially effective with young children, but it has also been employed with adults. Hersen and his colleagues (Hersen, Gullick, Matherne, & Harbert, 1972; Kallman, Hersen, & O'Toole, 1975) have successfully used social reinforcement in the treatment of conversion reaction (e.g., a psychosomatic leg paralysis). In each case, hospital staff members systematically praise and encourage the patient's efforts (e.g., leg movements), and favored staff members spend extra time with the patient when the person improves. One case is especially illustrative of the power of social reinforcement. This forty-two-year-old man regained full mobility in the hospital and was discharged. However, not long afterward he was readmitted with full symptom return. Apparently his family failed to respond adequately when he behaved appropriately but gave him ample attention and affection when he was disabled. Thus, they inadvertently reinforced his "sick role" behavior. He subsequently regained mobility in the hospital and maintained his gains after the family was taught to reinforce only his appropriate behavior. We are not suggesting that this patient was purposefully faking illness in order to receive social reinforcement. Rather, the family gradually and inadvertently shaped a real disability by reinforcing nonfunctional behavior.

Feedback. There is much controversy over whether reinforcement can alter behavior automatically without the person's awareness and co-operation (cf. Bandura, 1974). However, there is less disagreement that reinforcement has greater impact when the individual can work actively and purposefully for the reinforcer. In some cases, this cannot occur because the individual has too little information to control the behavior. For example, someone with a tic might not know when it occurs. In such cases, *feedback* about the behavior is useful. Feedback not only provides the information necessary for change but also serves as a reinforcer by signaling improvement (or a punisher by signaling lack of improvement).

One of the most exciting examples of the therapeutic use of feedback is *biofeedback*. This involves giving the client information about some physiological process, such as heart rate, blood pressure, or muscle tension. Once this information is received, the client can begin to use it to modify the physiological function. In the typical procedure, an electrical recording apparatus monitors the relevant response system (e.g., the heart). The client is then instructed to change the response level (e.g., decrease the heart rate). Feedback is provided by a light, tone, click, or other signal. For example, a clicking noise increases as heart rate speeds up and decreases as it slows down. The client can use any means possible (e.g., thinking certain thoughts) to alter the click rate, while never directly "feeling" heart action.

Biofeedback has been used successfully to modify a variety of disorders, including tension headaches, hypertension, epilepsy, ulcers, and impotence (cf. Blanchard & Epstein, 1977). In a recent study, Epstein and Malone (1978) used feedback of muscle activity to return voluntary motor control to two people who had been paralyzed by strokes. Further research must be done to determine the full potential of biofeedback, but initial results are quite promising.

Extinction. One basic principle of operant conditioning is that if a response is not followed by positive reinforcement it will gradually decrease and eventually stop occurring. This phenomenon is called *extinction.* In clinical situations, extinction consists of withholding the reinforcer that has maintained a particular behavior. This procedure is exemplified by a case study reported by Alford, Blanchard, and Buckley (1972). The patient was a seventeen-year-old girl who had a ten-year history of vomiting after every meal. Analysis of her behavior indicated that vomiting was maintained (reinforced) by the attention and concern it produced. Hospital treatment consisted of extinction of this socially reinforced response. The patient was given six small meals per day, during which staff members socialized with her. Whenever she vomited, the staff members left and did not return until the next meal. This simple procedure was highly effective; the patient had vomited only once during the seven months after her release.

While effective, extinction is often difficult to use. It works gradually and often involves a temporary increase in the frequency of the target response. These two factors often rule it out because it is too aversive to the person doing the treatment (e.g., a teacher cannot tolerate an increase in class disruption). Another strategy is *Differential Reinforcement of Other* behavior (DRO). Rather than simply extinguishing a response, the DRO procedure includes positive reinforcement of an incompatible, socially desirable behavior. The individual is thus given another way to produce reinforcement rather than simply being deprived of a previous reinforcer. This procedure was employed by Madsen, Becker, and Thomas (1968) in treating two highly disruptive boys in a classroom. During the intervention, the boys' teacher established rules to govern behavior, tried to ignore (extinguish) all disruption in addition to the rules, and finally praised the boys for appropriate behavior in addition to rules and ignoring. Only the DRO strategy (praise appropriate behavior, ignore inappropriate) was effective. This result has frequently been replicated.

Punishment. It might seem odd that a therapist, in helping a client, would use punishment. However, in some cases positive therapeutic efforts are ineffective, leaving punishment as the only alternative. Ethical guidelines for the use of punishment require that all other measures first be ruled out, and that the target behavior be more harmful or aversive than the treatment. Such is the case with the treatment of self-injurious behavior (SIB). Some severely disturbed patients inflict great injury on themselves by scratching and gouging, punching their heads, or banging their heads against walls. They are typically kept in restraints in order to prevent SIB; however, restraints also prevent any adaptive behavior. The most effective and rapid treatment for SIB is to administer a painful, but harmless, electric shock contingent upon any self-abusive response (Birnbrauer, 1976). For example, Tate and Baroff (1966) used electric shock with a nine-year-old autistic boy who had a cranial blood clot and two detached retinas from head banging. Although it had occurred since the age of four, SIB was essentially eliminated after three days of electric shock, during which only a few shocks were actually needed. The procedure seems justified in such a situation.

Other punishment techniques do not produce the physical or ethical distress of electric shock. In *response cost,* the person forfeits some positive reinforcer if the undesired response occurs (cf. Kazdin, 1972). A common example is a speeding ticket; the person pays a fine and loses money for breaking the law. School teachers employ response cost when they require disruptive students to stay after school; the students then forfeit play time. Response cost is used most frequently in token economies. Specified undesirable behaviors result in fines, for which tokens are forfeited. To avoid taking away too many earned tokens, response cost in token systems is usually limited to behaviors which are otherwise unmodifiable.

Another punishment strategy is *time out* from positive reinforcement (TO). Whenever the target response occurs, the individual is temporarily removed from any source of positive reinforcement. Typically the person is escorted to a special TO area, such as a room containing no reinforcing stimuli. This could be an empty classroom in a school, an empty room on a psychiatric ward, or a specially prepared room devoid of books, television, or other stimuli. TO does not last long; thirty seconds to ten minutes is typical. It is important to differentiate TO from seclusion. The latter is not a behavioral technique, can last for several hours, and can be used either to protect others (as with a violent patient) or for nontherapeutic vindictive purposes by unethical staff members. TO is used briefly, systematically, and objectively to reduce specified behaviors. In addition, TO works by removing positive reinforcement, not because the TO room is aversive. In fact, with younger children, the TO location can be a chair placed in the corner of a room or behind a screen. Barton, Guess, Garcia, and Baer (1970) used TO to teach appropriate self-feeding behavior to retarded children. TO simply entailed removing the food tray for fifteen seconds contingent on inappropriate behavior.

The last punishment procedure we will consider is *overcorrection.* Developed by Foxx and Azrin (1972), this technique is primarily employed with severely disturbed or retarded patients.

The general rationale of the Overcorrection procedure is (1) to overcorrect the environmental effects of an inappropriate act, and (2) to require the disruptor intensively to practice overly correct forms of relevant behavior. The method of achieving the first objective . . . consists of requiring the disruptor to correct the consequences of his misbehavior by having him restore the situation to a vastly improved state from that which existed before the disruption. For example, an individual who overturned a table would be required both to restore the table to its correct position and to dust and wax the table. [For the second objective] the disruptor . . . would also be required to straighten and dust all other tables and furniture in the room. This latter requirement teaches the disruptor the correct manner in which furniture should be treated (Foxx & Azrin, 1973, p. 2).

A few comments are required before closing this section. First, the clinical use of punishment should not be confused with its typical use in society. When parents, teachers, or the courts punish, they generally do it vindictively or in anger; it then benefits them rather than the person being punished. Punishment in treatment is for the patient, and is given in a systematic, controlled manner so as to maximize the effect and minimize the discomfort. Second, punishment is terminated as quickly as possible. This is usually done by building in verbal control over the behavior (e.g., saying "No" before the punishment, making it unnecessary to actually punish). Third, as in DRO procedures, the patient always receives positive reinforcement for another, desirable behavior; he or she is not simply punished.

Family Therapy

Basic to the behavioral model is the idea that behavior is strongly affected by the environment. For most people, the most significant part of the environment is the family. Family members are frequently responsible for maintaining inappropriate behavior and can make it functionally impossible for the person to change. They can also be of great help in developing appropriate behavior and reinforcing the effects of treatment. Thus, it is not unusual for family members to be enlisted to help in the treatment process. In some cases, the client is simply told how to secure family assistance. One of the authors (A.S.B.) had a female client who was afraid of heights. She was asked to enlist her husband's help in an *in vivo* exposure procedure. He escorted her as she systematically ventured higher and higher in office buildings, giving her encouragement and social reinforcement. Family members can also play a more central role in treatment, attending sessions and serving as a therapist-aide. In one recent study, Brownell, Heckerman, and Westlake (1977) examined the role of the spouse in a weight control program. They found that subjects whose spouses attended treatment sessions lost significantly more weight than subjects whose spouses did not attend. The treatment of sexual dysfunctions (e.g., impotence, orgasmic failure) is also greatly aided when the spouse actively participates in treatment (Ascher & Clifford, 1976).

In the above examples, an identified client is the focus of treatment; family members participate in order to help that person. In many other situations, there is no such identified client. Rather, the target problems reside in the family as a unit, and treatment focuses on family interaction. We will consider behavioral treatments for two family problems: marital conflict and parent-child conflict.

Marital Conflict. Behavioral conceptions of marital satisfaction (and conflict) emphasize two factors: reciprocity and communication (Weiss & Birchler, 1978). *Reciprocity* refers to the exchange of benefits or reinforcers between the spouses. Two people who live together must exchange a wide variety of services and interpersonal responses: sex, income, cooking and cleaning, conversation, favors, and others. While some things are mutually enjoyed, much of marriage consists of doing things for one's partner which have no immediate benefit for oneself. If reciprocity is at work, giving and receiving balance in the long run. Marital happiness depends on the balance of the benefits provided and received by each partner.

Unhappy marriages are characterized by negative balances; the partners do not receive sufficient benefits in relation to those they provide. As a result, they resort to *coercion* to secure benefits. For example, the wife nags and nags until the husband agrees to take her to dinner, and the husband verbally harasses the wife until she agrees to engage in sexual activity. Thus, benefits are provided reluctantly to reduce an aversive state, not freely to promote the partner's satisfaction. This coercive pattern typically leads to a breakdown in communication in which the spouses fail to identify their partner's desires or motives and interpret most interchanges as negative or aversive. Discussions quickly become arguments as the spouses seek to win and inflict hurt rather than solve problems.

Treatment attempts to improve communication and alter the exchange balance. Weiss and Birchler (1978) have specified four elements of treatment, which are applied in order. Treatment is usually conducted by male and female co-therapists so as to avoid therapist-client alliances. The first step is to teach the couple to *objectify*. After years of battling, the spouses tend to distort and overgeneralize. In presenting complaints, they use such terms as "You always . . ." or "You never . . .". They must learn to look more openly and accurately at their partner's behavior in order to determine what the spouse really does and doesn't do. Among other things, each spouse is required to keep a daily record of Pleases and Displeases: specific positive and negative behaviors performed by the spouse. The next step is to increase *support and understanding,* which involves teaching the partners how to do and say nice, pleasing things to one another. Tasks range from teaching a partner how to give a compliment to assigning both spouses to do something from the other's list of Pleases each day. *Problem solving* involves teaching the couple how to identify, avoid, and correct problems that lead to conflict. For example, nightly tension might result not from animosity but from the fact that children stay up too late and prevent the couple from conversing in privacy.

Once the couple has these three skills in their repertoire, they are ready for the most critical phase of treatment: *behavior change.* They must now apply the other skills to alter the exchange balance. This is done primarily through a contingency contract, a negotiated agreement in which each partner agrees to perform specified Pleases in exchange for Pleases from the other. For example, the wife agrees to cook dinner each night and engage in sexual activity three nights each week, and the husband agrees to come home one hour after work each day and take her out to dinner or a movie at least once a week. If either partner fails to comply, the other partner may do the same. The contract is written and signed, just like a legal document. New contracts are prepared as the couple experiences success. Under the terms of the contract, each partner is positively reinforced for providing Pleases rather than coerced into doing so. This tends to increase the frequency of spontaneous Please-giving. While initial contracts are somewhat mechanistic, the improved communication skills and increased frequency of spontaneous Pleases improves the relationship and gradually decreases the need for formal agreements.

This strategy for reducing marital conflict is new, and preliminary research results suggest that it can be quite effective (cf. Weiss & Birchler, 1978). However, more definite conclusions wait until more evidence is in.

Parent-Child Conflict. The most critical job in our society is child rearing, yet almost no one receives any training before becoming a parent. Not surprisingly, family conflict is common. When the problem becomes severe, the family may seek treatment. Clinic contact is always begun by the parents, who complain that something is wrong with the child. He or she "is impossible to control," "never listens," "is always in trouble," and so on. However, only rarely does the problem lay with the child. In the vast majority of cases, the undesirable behavior is (1) appropriate for the child's age and/or (2) maintained by parent reinforcement. Thus, the child is rarely the focus of treatment and is often not brought into therapy once assessment is completed. The therapist works instead with the parents, teaching them how to be more effective. The child's behavior changes with more appropriate parental management.

This strategy, often called *child management training,* is an educational approach. For expediency, parents are often seen in groups of four to eight couples. In essence, the parents are taught to be child behavior therapists. Many parental problems can be traced to inadequate information and expectations about what children are like. Often these problems are reduced or eliminated simply by providing information about children and their development. Once this is done, parents are taught how to pinpoint the sources of conflict and identify the problematic child behaviors and the contexts in which they occur. This serves the same purpose as objectification in couples therapy. In becoming specific and objective, much of the parents' overgeneralized dissatisfaction with the child is reduced (e.g., every child listens sometimes).

Training then shifts to techniques for altering the child's behavior. These include any and all of the operant techniques described above, including positive reinforcement, DRO, and token economics. One of us (A.S.B.) worked with a family to develop a token system for a reportedly "lazy, good for nothing" ten-year-old. The system was written as a contingency contract, negotiated by parents and child. A list of reasonable chores and rules were developed for the child, including taking out the garbage, putting his laundry in the hamper each day, and coming to meals within five minutes of being called. Tokens were stars posted on a chart, and back-up reinforcers included staying up at night for an extra half hour, going to a hamburger restaurant for lunch, and playing a game with the father. This system produced a dramatic change in the child's behavior and the parents' feelings about him.

Parent training typically requires six to ten sessions. Training can either focus on relieving one or two specific problems or teach parenting skills in general. The sessions themselves are similar to those in social skills and couples therapy: a stress on role playing and modeling. Many parents must be taught how to express affection or say "No" with conviction. Older children and adolescents generally participate in at least some of the sessions, during which the family might be taught better communication skills and contingency contracting. The parent training approach is one of the best documented behavioral techniques. It has repeatedly been shown to produce rapid, extensive, and durable changes in both child behavior and parental attitudes (O'Dell, 1974). Research is now underway to determine all the problems for which it is effective.

Critical Appraisal

The criticisms of behavior therapy range far beyond the ethical issues discussed at the beginning of this chapter. One consistent complaint is that it focuses on narrow and unimportant problems, missing the critical ones. One supposed consequence of this is *symptom substitution*. According to this argument, the behaviors altered by behavior therapy are symptoms of an inner conflict. This conflict is presumed to produce new symptoms if it is not resolved and removed. No research supports this argument, and follow-up studies on behavioral treatments generally indicate good maintenance and no new disturbances. A related critique is that behavioral treatments fail to deal with the person as a thinking, feeling being who is somehow "more" than the sum of overt behaviors. The subjective nature of this argument is difficult to counter with research data. Behavior therapists clearly consider feelings and thoughts in planning and conducting treatment. The client, too, is involved in the process and thus is free to indicate continued distress or the need for something more. When objective data (which includes self-report) indicate improvement, it seems unreasonable to argue *without* data that something has been missed.

The picture of behavior therapy as simplistic is probably more true of early interventions than of current approaches. Few clients come to treatment with such limited problems as monosymptomatic phobias or limited social skills deficits. Most have either complex problems or several interrelated ones. Current behavioral strategies are much more likely than they were in the 1960s to be comprehensive and deal with all of the client's difficulties. Consider, for example, our psychiatric ward at Western Psychiatric Institute and Clinic. Patients are assigned to either a day hospital or inpatient care according to their level of functioning. They all receive psychotropic medication (e.g., tranquilizers) and attend a variety of behavioral group therapies. The ward is operated as a token economy with three levels. Most patients receive social skills training, and some are also given individual operant interventions to handle specific difficulties (e.g., hallucinations). In many instances, family therapy is also provided. Patients thus receive a multifaceted intervention which deals with all aspects of their functioning.

Another critique pertains to the research support for certain behavioral techniques. Behavior therapists have made extensive use of analogue research to develop and test their techniques. In general, analogue procedures are models of real clinical situations. For example, much of the research on desensitization was conducted with college student subjects who feared small animals (e.g., snakes, spiders). These students were recruited by the researchers, rather than spontaneously requesting treatment. Thus, their fears were often less severe and easier to eliminate than the incapacitating fears of real clients. The implication here is that some behavioral techniques might be less effective in actual clinical practice than the analogue research suggests. A related question concerns the generalization (transfer) of behavioral treatment effects to the environment. Those effects which are limited to the therapy room or hospital have minimal value. The data for behavioral techniques are mixed. In many cases (e.g., child management, fear reduction) the results are quite positive. In other cases, such as token economies, generalization is unsatisfactory. One major concern of current behavioral research is how to foster generalization.

In general, many of the initial claims made by behavior therapists have been overzealous. Many dysfunctions cannot be eliminated so easily and simply. However, evidence still suggests that many behavioral procedures are more effective than nonbehavioral methods. In many instances, such as work with the mentally retarded, behavioral procedures have become the standard approach, rather than one of several alternatives. One advantage of behavioral techniques is that they are *cost-effective*. Not only do they work, but they are inexpensive to administer. These techniques are relatively rapid, and many of them do not require Ph.D. level clinicians. Because most procedures involve teaching and are fairly standardized, they can be given by paraprofessionals: nurses, hospital aides, parents, and bachelor degree level personnel. The Ph.D. trains the paraprofessionals and coordinates and supervises their activities. Often he or she designs the treatment and then has the paraprofessional carry it out. Thus, the Ph.D. can have a much broader impact, helping many more people than would be possible if all of the treatment sessions were conducted personally.

Summary

This chapter has presented an overview of behavioral therapy. The basic assumptions underlying all behavioral techniques were first considered. The ethics of treatment were presented next, followed by a brief history of the behavioral approach. The remainder of the chapter focused on specific treatment techniques, including fear reduction strategies, social skills training, cognitive behavior therapy, token economies, operant conditioning techniques, and family therapy. In each case, the conceptual basis for the procedure was presented, along with a description of its application and an overview of the research support. We then reviewed some of the major critiques. In general, it was suggested that behavior therapy is highly effective for a wide variety of disorders, but is less effective than was previously suggested. Behavior therapists are still investigating such important topics as the range of application, the effectiveness of the techniques with real clinical populations, and the generalizability of the effects of treatment. This research, we believe, will tend to increase support for the behavioral approach.

CHAPTER EIGHT

Humanistic Approach

In the last two chapters, we have considered two of the most prominent forces in contemporary American psychotherapy: psychoanalysis and behavior therapy. The first, psychoanalysis, is rooted in clinical neurology and psychiatry (i.e., by training and initial interest, Freud was a neurologist). The second, behavior therapy, is based on Russian physiology (e.g., Pavlov) and American academic psychology (e.g., Watson, Thorndike, Hull, Guthrie, Skinner). Both of these theoretical approaches have had great impact on clinical psychology. Psychoanalysis legitimized the clinical study of human instincts. That is, it encouraged the examination of sexual and aggressive urges, and showed that much of human action was not based on conscious choice alone.

The behavioral movement, on the other hand, has pointed the way for the objective and scientific study of human action. Although initially tied to a learning theory view of behavior, it has now expanded to encompass all empirical disciplines. A key tenet of behaviorism is that human behavior can be systematically studied, objectively measured, and altered. Thus, the behavioral movement may, in part, be seen as a reaction to the more subjective and less empirical psychoanalytic view of human behavior.[1]

---

1. By scientific we mean the traditional laboratory conception of empiricism that demonstrates cause-and-effect relationships through experimental investigation.

The humanistic approach, often described as the "third force" in psychotherapy, evolved in reaction to both psychoanalysis and behaviorism. The psychoanalytic model views human beings as the passive victims of unconscious sexual and aggressive strivings; humanism is strongly opposed to Freudian determinism. The behavioristic model sees people as the objects of learning and conditioning (classical and operant); humanism is equally opposed to this orientation.[2] Also, in marked contrast to psychoanalysis and behaviorism, the humanistic approach owes its heritage to neither clinical neurology and psychiatry nor academic psychology. Much of its impetus is the writings of the nineteenth and twentieth century philosophers (e.g., Kierkegaard, Buber, Sartre), who underscored free will, the potential for growth, subjectivity, and awareness of one's mortality as uniquely human characteristics.

Just as psychoanalytic and behavioral therapies vary widely, so do those of the humanistic approach. Although technically these therapies are different, they all share common philosophical bases. After examining the humanistic model, we will discuss the Rogerian, existential, and Gestalt approaches to psychotherapy. These are followed by an account of the encounter movement (e.g., T-groups, sensitivity training). Finally, we will present a critical appraisal of humanistic treatments.

Humanistic Model

To understand the humanistic approach to psychological problems, the humanistic view must be clarified. This in itself presents a problem, since there is no one humanistic model. However, certain common themes do emerge. Let us consider a composite picture of humanity based on writings that reflect the humanistic tradition.

To begin with, we will present four statements by humanistic psychotherapists. The first is representative of Rogerian thinking: "The whole trend of current thinking has shifted to the view that human beings are interactional creatures and that the nature of psychological ills is inherently inter-active. It isn't that something is wrong with an individual's psychic machinery; there are no loose screws inside. We don't know how and need not know how to replace worn out units

---

2. These contrasts have been exaggerated so that the student can understand how discontent led to this "third force" in psychotherapy.

inside him. He isn't a machine, a self-contained box, but rather an interaction process" (Gendlin, 1977, p. 40).

The second is an example of existential thought: "Death is something that happens to each one of us. Even before its arrival, it is an absent presence. Some hold that fear of death is a universal reaction and that no one is free from it. . . . When we stop to consider the matter, the notion of the uniqueness and individuality of each one of us gathers full meaning only in realizing that we must die. And it is in this same encounter with death that each of us discovers his hunger for immortality" (Feifel, 1961, p. 62).

The third statement is by Fritz Perls (1970b), the originator and foremost representative of Gestalt therapy: "In my lectures on Gestalt therapy, I have one aim only: to impart a fraction of the word *now*. To me, nothing exists except the now. Now = experience = awareness = reality. The past is no more and the future not yet. Only the *now* exists" (p. 14).

The fourth statement represents the encounter movement: ". . . the encounter group can be an attempt to meet and overcome the isolation and alienation of the individual in contemporary life. The person who has entered into basic encounter with another is no longer completely isolated. It will not necessarily dissolve his loneliness, but at least it proves to him that such loneliness is not an inevitable element in his life. He can come in meaningful touch with another being. Since alienation is one of the most disturbing aspects of modern life, this is an important implication" (Rogers, 1970, p. 176).

Keeping in mind the above quotations, let us now examine the recurrent themes of humanistic writings. Probably one of the most important elements in these writings is a pervasive optimism. Whether the writer is Maslow (1961), May (1961), Havens (1974), Gendlin (1969), Laura Perls (1970), or Rogers (1974), the human potential for growth and new experience is consistently underscored. Even the "well actualized" individual, who can maximize personal experience and communicate honestly and freely, continues to show a futher need for growth. This continued concern with interpersonal growth is reflected in the humanist's interest in encounter groups (which are primarily devoted to improving interpersonal communication among the nonpathological). Thus, the individual is seen in light of the interpersonal relationships in his or her life. However, as stated earlier, the individual is not seen as the hapless victim of biological drives or environmental manipulation. Rather, he or she is perceived as a responsible person capable of making both choices and important personal changes given the right commitment. For those who are unable to maximize their potential and who may suffer anxiety and depression as a result, psychotherapy may prove helpful.

The humanists are especially concerned with the need for close, meaningful, empathic interpersonal relationships. They are keenly aware of the depersonalization, alienation, and loss of personal identity that invariably accompany highly industrialized society. It is little wonder, then, that honesty and closeness (without intrusiveness) in the relationship is highly prized. Attempts are made to cut through duplicity, phoniness, and the gamesmanship that characterize much of one's typical daily interaction. Along with the concern for honest communication is an emphasis on the present—namely, the nature of the current interaction in a given relationship. This is presumed to be critical in the psychotherapeutic relationship—which contrasts sharply to orthodox psychoanalysis, where much attention is paid to historical factors.[3]

The overriding concern with the present (especially for Gestalt theorists) goes beyond the interpersonal relationship. It is, however, largely also a reaction to the mechanized, depersonalized Western world, which stresses the future—future goals and possible future attainments. In the humanistic philosophy, the individual is urged to savor the moment as it occurs, but to refrain from lamenting the past or simply anticipating the future.

Finally, the existentialists, in particular, have shown us that death in Western society has been greatly neglected in understanding human behavior. Indeed, some (e.g., Feifel, 1961) argue that a concern with death is manifested in many psychiatric disorders (e.g., absence of movement in catatonia). The existential position is that without confronting one's own mortality, one cannot lead a truly meaningful life. Indeed, existentialists point out that the one feature that readily distinguishes humanity from other species is the knowledge that life is finite. It is argued that when one comes to terms with death, it is at that moment that life becomes more meaningful.

This healthy concern with death as a psychological factor in life has had considerable influence. Not only has it led to a fuller understanding of the behavior of normal and psychiatric patients, but it has helped us to appreciate the final psychological struggles of patients with terminal

---

3. However, the psychoanalysts' interest in making interpretations as to positive and negative transference does reflect some concern for the therapeutic relationship as it is occurring and being experienced.

illnesses (cf. Kubler-Ross, 1970). These struggles are heightened, of course, when families of dying patients play duplicitous games (i.e., fail to tell the patient about the terminal nature of the illness and their feelings about it), thereby denying themselves and the patient the opportunity to come to terms with death and to maximize honest, meaningful communication in the remaining time.

Rogerian Psychotherapy

For more than forty years, the name Carl Rogers has been associated with the clinical practice and research of psychotherapy in America. Over this long period, "Rogerian" psychotherapy has changed considerably. Initially Rogers (1942) was associated with a therapeutic approach known as "nondirective" therapy or counseling. As the term implies, the therapist followed the client's lead, was not at all directive, but often reflected the client's feeling portion of a communication (e.g., *Client*—"I mean at first, ah, I tried to see if I was just withdrawing from this bunch of kids I'd been spending my time with, and I'm sincere in thinking that, ah, it's not a withdrawal, but it's more of an assertion of my real interests. . . ." Therapist—"In other words, you've tried to be self-critical in order to see if you're just running away from the situation, but you feel really, it's an expression of your positive attitudes" (Rogers, 1951, p. 155). With the publication of his book *Client-Centered Therapy* some nine years later (Rogers, 1951) and, still later (Rogers, 1957), a seminal paper entitled "The Necessary and Sufficient Conditions of Therapeutic Personality Change," it is clear that Rogers' thinking about individual psychotherapy had altered considerably. Whereas the nondirective approach emphasized the therapist's technical skills (e.g., being able to reflect to the client the feeling portion of a communication), the "client-centered" approach stressed the therapist attitudes that would lead to change in the client. Still more recently, Rogers (1970) focused on the elements that contribute to meaningful learning experiences in the encounter group (i.e., sensitivity training and T-groups).

In the remainder of this section, we will look at Rogers' concept of the important therapist attitudes in good psychotherapy. Illustrative therapist-client dialogues that represent both helpful and inappropriate therapy will be presented. Also, we will examine certain innovations developed by Eugene T. Gendlin (1969), one of Rogers' many students. This material is presented in the context of Rogers' conception of personality and general philosophy of humanity.

First, however, let us consider Rogers' impact on research and practice in psychotherapy. In his 1973 address to the American Psychological Association (when he received the Distinguished Professional Contribution Award), Rogers (1974) appeared astonished at his influence on the field. Just to list a few of his contributions:

1. He was the first to record (electronically) therapeutic interactions for research purposes.
2. He and his students were among the first to evaluate (scientifically and empirically) the process of psychotherapy.
3. He and his students were among the first to document that psychotherapy could lead to either positive or negative outcomes, depending on the therapist-client interaction.
4. He battled the psychiatric establishment (and won) concerning the legitimacy of the clinical psychologist as psychotherapist and administrator in the mental health setting.
5. He greatly affected the course of counseling on the college campus.
6. He provided a focal point for the humanistic tradition.

Conditions for Therapeutic Change

In essence, Rogers' approach (Rogers, 1957) consists of six conditions for bringing about personality change in the client. These conditions are as follows:

1. Two persons are in psychological contact.
2. The first, whom we shall term the client, is in a state of incongruence, being vulnerable or anxious.
3. The second person, whom we shall term the therapist, is congruent or integrated in the relationship.
4. The therapist experiences unconditional positive regard for the client.
5. The therapist experiences an empathic understanding of the client's internal frame of reference and endeavors to communicate this experience to the client.
6. The communication to the client of the therapist's empathic understanding and unconditional positive regard is to a minimal degree achieved (Rogers, 1957, p. 96).

In looking at these six conditions, it is obvious that the first, the existence of the therapist-client relationship, is a given for the remaining five to occur. The remaining conditions are the therapeutic task, according to Rogers.

Before going on to a fuller evaluation of conditions 2 to 6, let us consider diagnosis as related to Rogerian treatment. Before psychotherapy begins, clinicians of most orientations obtain a diagnostic assessment. Whether this is done through projective and objective personality tests (as with the analytic clinicians) or via direct behavioral assessment (as with behavior therapists), the consensus is that such assessment will enable the therapist to better understand the client and make therapy more effective. For the behavior therapists, in particular, the behavioral assessment determines the therapeutic strategy to be used. However, Rogers (1951) and his followers dispute this notion.

> In the first place, the very process of psychological diagnosis places the locus of evaluation so definitely in the expert that it may increase any dependent tendencies in the client, and cause him to feel that the responsibility for understanding and improving his situation lies in the hands of another. When the client perceives the locus of judgment and responsibility as clearly resting in the hands of the clinician, he is, in our judgment, further from therapeutic progress than when he came in (p. 223).

In short, diagnostic testing, by its very nature, is a contradiction of Rogerian therapy. Since Rogerian therapy is both nondirective and client-centered (i.e., the client has within himself the potential and capacity for change), it follows that the client-centered therapist will not assume the role of the *expert* by making diagnostic interpretations. Moreover, since therapy is considered appropriate and effective if conditions 2 to 6 are met, *regardless of the diagnostic label,* going through the task of arriving at such a label is seen as superfluous.[4]

Let us now consider condition 2: the client being in a state of incongruence. *Incongruence* is Rogers' term for the discrepancy between a client's feelings at the organismic level and his or her self-concept. Of course, if the organismic level and the self-concept are in line, then no problem exists. To illustrate this concept, Rogers (1957, p. 97) gives the example of the mother who develops "vague illnesses" when her son talks about leaving home. Since the son represents her only source of

---

4. Most of the clients counseled by Rogers and his co-workers have been neurotics or personality disorders seen in the college counseling center. However, in later work, Rogers, Gendlin, Kiesler, and Truax (1967) did client-centered therapy with schizophrenic patients. The therapeutic strategy was modified, but the basic features and tenets remained the same.

gratification, she is eager to restrain him. However, this is not consistent with her self-picture of the "good mother." But on the other hand, illness *does* fit in with her self-concept. The discrepancy here is between her self-concept (mother needing her son's attention because of illness) and her actual experience (the need to keep her son from leaving home).

Rogers points out that there are different levels of incongruence. If the individual is unaware of the incongruence, he or she is then vulnerable to anxiety. If there is a "dim perception" (sub-ception), then a state of tension exists. (These theoretical notions parallel the psychoanalytic discussions of the unconscious and preconscious.) In any event, such incongruence is considered necessary for the client to receive therapy.

By contrast (condition 3), the therapist should enter the therapeutic relationship in a congruent state. This does not mean that each therapist is required to be the paragon of mental health. However, the therapist should be aware of his or her feelings and reactions to the client (here, too, there is a parallel to the psychoanalyst who has undergone an analysis to get rid of personal blind spots). Being congruent, the therapist should be able to communicate freely and directly with the patient. At times, the therapist may even express personal feelings, as long as they are not deceptive or expressed simply for the therapist's benefit. In short, the therapist should be very much in touch with his or her feelings and possible shortcomings and limitations.

Condition 4, unconditional positive regard, should facilitate rapport. Also, when it is strongly displayed by the therapist, a positive outcome should follow. By definition, unconditional positive regard means that the therapist *accepts* the client's positive *and* negative attributes. Thus, the client is freed from the therapist's evaluation: "It means a caring for the client, but not in a possessive way as simply to satisfy the therapist's own needs. It means a caring for the client as a *separate* person, with permission to have his own feelings, his own experience" (Rogers, 1957, p. 98). However, as noted by Truax and Carkhuff (1967), the research literature indicates that unconditional positive regard, as originally defined by Rogers, does not contribute substantially to outcome. Rather, a similar condition, strong *nonpossessive warmth,* seems to have a greater relationship to success. When it is experienced at a high level, "the therapist warmly accepts the patient's experience as part of the person, without imposing conditions. In contrast, at a low level the therapist evaluates a patient or his feelings, expresses dislike or disapproval, or expresses warmth in a selective or evaluative way" (Truax & Carkhuff, 1967, p. 58).

Let us now present two excerpts of therapist (T) and client (C) dialogue, the first marked by low nonpossessive warmth and the second by high nonpossessive warmth.

Low nonpossessive warmth:

T. . . . another part here too, that is, if they haven't got a lot of schooling, there may be a good argument, that, that they—are better judges, you know.

C. Yeah . . .

T. Now, I'm not saying that, that's necessarily true, I'm—just saying that's *reality.*

C. Yeah.

T. And you're in a *position* that you can't argue with them. Why is it that these people burn you up so much?

C. They *get* by *with* too many things . . .

T. Why should that bother you?

C. 'Cause I never got by with anything.

T. They're papa figures, aren't they?

C. (Noise) Yeah—(Pause) I told the aides last night, I said, "You're making me—I *want to forget* the past and—you're making me think of my father again."—They don't *understand.*

T. (Breaking in) But you're bringing it into the present, I don't want to keep dragging up the past; the present seems to me—uh, the same thing you've been going through all your life . . .

C. Mhm.

T. . . . this fighting against this father.

C. (Pause with sigh) So what will it take to straighten it out?

T. You're the only guy that can straighten it out.

C. But, how?

T. You've got to understand—

C. (Breaking in) I mean between me and the aides?

T. How could your dad straighten that out?

C. Tell 'm!

T. *Nah?* (Scornfully)

C. He *would* do it.

T. It is up to you to change.

(Truax & Carkhuff, 1967, p. 61)

High nonpossessive warmth:

T. But you say that, that during that time you, you felt as though no one at all cared, as to what (C: That's right.) . . . what happened to you.

C. And, not only that, but I hated *myself* so that I didn't, I, I felt that I didn't *deserve* to have anyone care for me. I hated myself so that I, I, I not only felt that no one did, but I didn't see any reason why they *should.*

T. I guess that makes some sense to me now. I was wondering why it was that you were shutting other people off. You weren't *letting* anyone else care.

C. I didn't think I was *worth* caring for.

T. So you didn't ev—maybe you not only thought you were—hopeless, but you wouldn't allow people . . . (Therapist statement is drowned out by client)

C. (Interrupting and very loud) I closed the door on everyone. Yah, I closed the door on everyone because I thought I just wasn't worth *bothering* with. I didn't think it was worthwhile for *you* to bother with me. "Just let me alone and—and let me rot that's all I'm worth." I mean, that was my thought. And, I, I, uh, will frankly admit that when the doctors were making the rounds on the ward, I mean the *routine* rounds, I tried to be where they wouldn't see me. The doctor often goes there on the ward and asks how everyone is and when she'd get about to me, I'd move to a spot that she's already covered . . .

T. You really avoided people.

C. So that, so that she wouldn't, uh, *talk* with me. (T: Uh, hm.) and when—the few times that I refused to see you, it was for the same reason. I didn't think I was worth bothering with, so why waste your time—let's just . . .

T. Let me ask you, ask you something about that. Do you think it would have been, uh, better if I had insisted that, uh, uh, you come and talk with me?

C. No I don't believe so, doctor. (They speak simultaneously)

(Truax & Carkhuff, 1967, P. 67)

Condition 5 is the therapist's ability to empathize with the client by entering the client's frame of reference (e.g., understanding and appreciating the client's positive and negative feelings) without losing objectivity (i.e., the "as if" quality of the experience). Moreover, through verbal and nonverbal behavior, the therapist communicates empathic understanding to the client. As Rogers (1957) argues, "When the client's world is this clear to the therapist, and he moves about in it freely, then he can communicate his understanding of what is clearly known to the client, and can also voice meanings in the client's experience of which the client is scarcely aware" (p. 99). This is often done by reflecting the feeling portion of the client's communication.

In discussing accurate empathy, Truax and Carkhuff (1967) separate the high and low levels of empathy into nine stages. In the lowest stage, the therapist "seems completely unaware of even the most conspicuous of the client's feelings; his responses are not appropriate to the mood and context of the client's statements" (p. 47). By contrast, at the highest level of empathy, "The therapist . . . unerringly responds to the client's full range of feelings in their exact intensity. Without hesitation, he recognizes an understanding of every deepest feeling" (p. 56). In short, the therapist is in tune with the felt experience of his client.

Let us now consider examples of extremely low and extremely high levels of accurate empathy taken from actual therapist-client dialogues.

Low accurate empathy:

C. I wonder if it's my educational background or if it's me.

T. Mhm.

C. You know what I mean.

T. Yeah.

C. (Pause) I guess if I could just solve that I'd know just about where to hit, huh?

T. Mhm, Mhm. Now that you know, a way, if you knew for sure, that your, lack, if that's what it is—I can't be sure of that yet.

(C. No)

T. (Continuing) . . . is really so, that it, it might even feel as though it's something that you just couldn't receive, that it, if, that would be it?

C. Well-I—I didn't, uh, I don't quite follow you—clearly.

T. Well (pause), I guess, I was, I was thinking that—that you perhaps thought that, that if you could be sure that, the, uh, that there were tools that, that you didn't have, that, perhaps that could mean that those—uh—tools that you had lacked—way back there in, um, high school

(C. Yah)

T. (Continuing) . . . and perhaps just couldn't perceive how and, ah . . .

C. Eh, yes, or I might put it this way, um (pause). If I knew that it was, um, let's just take it this way. If I knew that it was my educational background, there would be a possibility of going back.

T. Oh, so, I missed that now, I mean now, and uh . . .

(Truax & Carkhuff, 1967, p. 47)

High accurate empathy:

T. . . . I s'pose, one of the things you were saying there was, I may seem pretty hard on the outside to other people but I do have feelings.

C. Yeah, I've got feelings. But most of 'em I don't let 'em off.

T. Mhm. Kinda hide them.

C.   (Faintly) Yeah. (Long pause) I guess the only reason that I try to hide 'em, is, seein' that I'm small, I guess I got to be a tough guy or somethin'.

T.   Mhm.

C.   That's the way I, think people might think about me.

T.   Mm. Little afraid to show my feelings. They might think I was weak, 'n take advantage of me or something. They might hurt me if they—knew I could be hurt.

C.   I think they'd try, anyway.

T.   If they really knew I had feelings, they, they really might try and hurt me. (Long pause)

C.   I guess I don't want 'em to know that I got 'em.

T.   Mhm.

C.   'Cause then they couldn't if they wanted to.

T.   So I'd be safe i I, if I seem like a, as though I was real hard on the outside. If they thought I was real hard, I'd be safe.

(Truax & Carkhuff, 1967, p. 57)

The argument in condition 6 is that unconditional positive regard (or nonpossessive warmth) and accurate empathy must be at least minimal for successful therapy. Thus, it should not be surprising that many process and outcome studies have focused on this point (see Truax & Carkhuff, 1967; Truax & Mitchell, 1971, for reviews). After reviewing the literature, Truax and Carkhuff (1967) concluded that therapists rated high on accurate empathy, nonpossessive warmth, and "genuineness" were truly effective. The higher their ratings on these attributes, the more personality change brought about in their clients and patients. Truax and Carkhuff contend that this is true regardless of therapist training and theoretical orientation and regardless of the population treated (e.g., college students, juvenile delinquents, hospitalized schizophrenics, outpatient neurotics). Moreover, it is claimed that these findings apply equally to individual and group therapy. However, these rather sweeping conclusions have been challenged by Lambert, DeJulio, and Stein (1978) in a recent provocative review paper. We will evaluate Truax and Carkhuff's (1967) conclusions in light of Lambert et al. (1978) in a later section.

New Considerations

In the last few years, certain new strategies have been added to Rogerian psychotherapy. One of these, *experiential focusing* (Gendlin, 1969), is somewhat of a departure in that it involves directing the client. It involves making the client aware of bodily sensations and feelings (at the organismic level). This, of course, *is* consistent with the Rogerian notion that in the *congruent* individual the organismic and experiential levels are consistent with one another.

As Gendlin (1969) cogently argues, "words can come from a feeling." Thus, in experiential focusing, the client is directed to stop talking for about thirty seconds and to concentrate on bodily sensations underlying the problem. "One must wait about 30 seconds without talking at oneself, letting words go by if they come until one fully senses one's bodily feelings of the problem. . . . Words can come from a feeling and such words have a special power, a sensed effect, other words don't have" (Gendlin, 1969, p. 5).

A specific manual for "focusing" has been developed. Further, Gendlin points out that focusing leads to increased "experiential levels," which in turn relates to more successful therapeutic outcome. He presents some data in support of this argument.

A second consideration has been raised by Krebs (1972): When should client-centered therapy end? What signs suggest the possibility of termination, and how, should the therapist handle the termination process? In discussing these issues, Krebs refers to three separate phases: (1) "Things are better," (2) "Should we say goodbye?", and (3) "Saying goodbye." In the first phase, the client reports progress in his or her life experiences. At this point, either client or therapist may raise the possibility of termination. In the second phase, they discuss termination more fully, but invariably some vacillation occurs. Krebs (1972) maintains that "focusing," by both client and therapist, is useful in resolving the ambivalence. "Sooner or later, most clients do get to the point of talking about leaving and the leaving feels right for both of us" (p. 360). In the third phase, the client states that he or she now feels able to "be himself" outside of the therapeutic hour. Consistency between and among systems (i.e., organismic feelings and experiential levels) has been achieved.

Existential Psychotherapy

As noted in the introduction to this chapter, the existential approach to psychotherapy is based on philosophy. This is important since existentialism is not a set of therapeutic strategies but really an *attitude* toward people and, by implication, their psychological treatment. For example, Jean-Paul Sartre's essays on existentialism, presented in his *Existential Psychoanalysis* (1953), can hardly be described as a therapist's manual. Instead, they are a severe critique of the *objective* view of humanity, such as those of the Freudian psychoanalysts and scientific behaviorists. Sartre's dictum, "We are our choices," is obviously in sharp contradiction to Freudian determinism. Sartre's statement points to a view of human behavior that emphasizes the individual's possibility for change, growth, and commitment to change. In existential terms, this active process is often referred to as *becoming*. Thus, not surprisingly, existential psychotherapists are more concerned with *understanding* the client than applying the correct technique. Similarly, May (1958) argues:

> . . . the existential approach holds the exact opposite namely, that *technique follows understanding*. The central task and responsibility of the therapist is to seek to understand the patient as a being and a being-in-his-world. All technical problems are subordinated to this understanding. Without this understanding, technical facility is at best irrelevant, at worst a method of "structuralizing" the neurosis. With it, the groundwork is laid for the therapist's being able to help the patient recognize and experience his own existence, and this is the central process of therapy. This does not derogate disciplined technique; it rather puts it into focus (p. 77).

May's statement makes it difficult to determine what an existential therapist actually does in the therapeutic hour. But then again, this is the criticism that existential therapists level at most other practicing therapists—that they are concerned with technique rather than with understanding where in his life the client is at the time. In practice, however, most existential therapists tend to be psychoanalysts, who do use standard psychoanalytic techniques (e.g., free association) but whose treatment is guided primarily by their understanding of human existence.

To better understand the therapeutic attitude and work of existential psychotherapists, let us clarify the existential view of neurosis.[5] Whereas the psychoanalysts and behaviorists view the symptoms of neurosis as showing maladjustment, the existentialists take a different slant: *"An adjustment is exactly what neurosis is; and that is just its trouble.* It is a necessary adjustment by which centeredness can be preserved; a way of

---

5. This account of existentialism is an attempt to abstract the major issues as clearly as possible. This is difficult given the rather wordy, flowery descriptions and somewhat vague concepts that pervade the writings of existential therapists. Unfortunately, their terminology is not standard among mental health practitioners.

accepting *non-being* . . . in order that some little *being* may be preserved. And in most cases it is a boon when the adjustment breaks down" (May, 1958, p. 77). Put more simply, the neurosis *is* the person's way of dealing (i.e., adjusting) to the threat of non-being (death). It is held that successful adjustment requires a direct, honest confrontation with the eventuality of one's non-being. This, of course, results in existential anxiety, which is central in helping the person to make a commitment that will lead to change.

Existential therapists perceive that everyone functions simultaneously in three distinct, interrelated "modes of world." The first is the *Umwelt*, essentially the biological world of drives, needs, and so on. Existential writers feel that Freud's greatest theoretical contribution was his explication of the *Umwelt*. The second, known as the *Mitwelt*, is the interpersonal world. Here the existentialists pay tribute to the neo-Freudians (especially Sullivan) for their classification of this mode of experience. The third, the *Eigenwelt*, the "own world," is where the existential thinkers feel they have made their greatest contribution—particularly since they contend that depth psychology (i.e., psychoanalysis) has virtually ignored it. May (1961) states, "Eigenwelt presupposes self-awareness, self-relatedness, and is uniquely present in human beings. But it is not merely a subjective, inner experience; it is rather the basis on which we see the real world in its true perspective, the basis on which we relate." May goes on to argue that "the reality of being-in-the-world is lost *if one of the modes is emphasized to the exclusion of the other two*" (p. 63). This latter point is an important guide for the work of existential therapists. They are convinced that there is often a profound gulf in the individual's relationship to the self.

In doing psychotherapy, the existential therapist follows the *phenomenological approach* (cf. Ellenberger, 1958; May, 1958). Phenomenology "is the endeavor to take the phenomena as given. It is the disciplined effort to clear one's mind of presuppositions that so often cause us to see in the patient only our own theories or the dogmas of our systems, the effort to experience instead the phenomena in their full reality as they present themselves. It is the attitude of openness and readiness to hear—aspects of the art of listening in psychotherapy that are generally taken for granted and sound so easy but are exceedingly difficult" (May, 1958, p. 26). May's comment is reminiscent of the empathic listening strategies studied by the Rogerians (cf. Truax & Carkhuff, 1967). Also, as articulated by Havens (1974), an existential psychoanalyst, "The central purpose of phenomenological psychiatry was to see things as the patient saw them" (p. 5). This too sounds much like Rogers' (1951, 1957) comments about the therapist perceiving the world from the client's frame of reference.

Still another existential interest is the concern with time (see Ellenberger, 1958) and its perception by patients bearing different diagnostic labels. Ellenberger (1961), using data taken from patients' subjective experience, notes that in depression time seems to pass slowly: "One of the main symptoms of depression, from the phenomenological point of view, is the subjective experience of time flowing desperately slowly, stagnating, or even being arrested. Certain schizophrenics feel as if time were fixed at the present moment, hence the delusion that they are immortal, an assertion which is incomprehensible from the point of view of the normal mind, but which is quite logical when seen in the perspective of the distortions of the experience of time in the patients" (p. 104). In mania, by contrast, time appears to flow rapidly. Given this concern with time perception as experienced by the patient, it is clear why May (1961) states that one of the effects of therapy is to shake the patient's foundation with regard to time.

Let us now examine specific implications of the existential approach to effective psychotherapy. May (1961), the leading psychological exponent of existentialism, lists six of these. The first concerns *flexibility* of technique. That is, a variety of techniques will be used during therapy. The guiding principle in each case is to "reveal" to the patient his or her "existence" at a given point in life. Second, *psychological processes* (e.g., repression, transference, resistance) derive their meaning from the patient's ongoing existence; they are not mere abstractions. For example, sexual repression is seen as the individual's *holding back of potential.* The third implication is *presence*—the therapist-patient relationship. "By this we mean that the relationship of the therapist and patient is taken as a real one, the therapist being not merely a shadowy reflector but an alive human being who happens, at that hour, to be concerned not with his own problems but with understanding and experiencing so far as possible the being of the patient" (May, 1958, p. 80).

The fourth implication is related to presence. The existential therapist is devoted to "analyzing out" those "ways of behaving" that interfere with presence. Contrary to classic psychoanalysis, the burden is placed not on the patient but on the therapist. It is not that the person is engaging in negative transference. The therapist is responsible for recognizing what *in him is blocking* the relationship (". . . he had obviously best ask himself whether he is not trying to avoid some anxiety and as a result is losing something existentially in the relationship" [May, 1958, p. 85]). The fifth implication is concerned with the aim of therapy— which is "*that the patient experience his existence as real*" (note the similarlity here to Roger's notion of *congruence*). In other words, the person should be aware of his or her capacity and potential, and as a result be able to take advantage of them. The *sixth* implication is concerned with commitment. By commitment, existential therapists do not refer to isolated, sometimes superficial changes (e.g., change in job, even divorce). They mean a fundamental change in attitude—"*a decisive attitude towards existence.*" Such commitment will obviously take place in the three modes of world (Umwelt, Mitwelt, and Eignewelt) and at both the conscious and *unconscious* levels (i.e., commitment will be reflected in the person's dreams).

From a more technical perspective, Havens (1974), in the article "The Existential Use of Self," has attempted to further clarify what existential therapists do during various stages of psychotherapy. He speaks of four issues: (1) "keeping looking," (2) "staying," (3) "the role of feeling," and (4) the phenomenological view of countertransference in the therapist. "Keeping looking" refers to the therapist's attempt to understand the client from his or her frame of reference rather than the objective-descriptive approach that focuses on signs and symptoms. This process continues throughout therapy. In "staying," the therapist maintains a relationship with the client such that new knowledge about the client will not threaten the relationship. "Feeling," according to Havens, is "the distinguishing element of the existential method." It means sharing the client's world, again within his or her frame of reference. Finally, consistent with the existential attitude, it is argued that by the very nature of the therapy, countertransference (i.e., the therapist's negative feelings toward the client) will be minimized. Presumably "the existential method reduces the distance between client and therapist," especially in light of "keeping looking," "staying," and "feeling."

Gestalt Therapy

Just as psychoanalysis is largely the creation of its founder, Sigmund Freud, so is Gestalt therapy the creation of its founder, Frederick Perls. Perls was a physician trained in psychoanalysis. However, like many of those originally trained in classic psychoanalysis, Perls began to challenge many of its theoretical bases. He later became attracted to the existentialists, was keenly aware of the impact of behaviorism, and was particularly interested in the perceptual basis of Gestalt psychology (e.g., the work of Koffka, Kohler, and Wertheimer). Thus, although Gestalt therapy *is* a unique approach, as now practiced it contains elements of existentialism (i.e., the accent on phenomenology), behaviorism (i.e., observation of the patient's motor behavior during therapy sessions), and Gestalt psychology.

Let us first consider the contribution of Gestalt psychology. The Gestalt psychologists were concerned with perception as related to part-whole relationships. They emphasized a wholistic approach in psychology in reaction to the then current (pre-World War I) focus on specific mental processes (i.e., sensations, images, feelings). The Gestalt psychologists coined the familiar saying, that "The whole is different from the sum of its parts." They were especially interested in *perception in the present,* and stressed how the subject was *active* in organizing perceptions. Such organization always took the form of differentiating the figure from the background. In their fascinating perceptual experiments with reversible figures and backgrounds, Gestalt psychologists showed how the perceiver could sometimes focus on one dominant feature in the perceptual field and at other times on a different dominant feature. Hence, the uniqueness of individual perception was established.

Wallen (1970) has outlined the relationship between Gestalt psychology and Gestalt therapy: "The academic Gestalt psychologist dealt largely with external figures, notably visual and auditory. Interestingly enough, the academic Gestalt psychologist never attempted to employ the various principles of Gestalt formation . . . to organic perceptions, to the perception of one's feelings, emotions and bodily sensations. He never really managed to integrate the facts of motivation with the facts of perception" (p. 8). This integration was done by Perls and his colleagues (Perls, Hefferline, & Goodman, 1965).

In looking at the integration of motivation with perception, Wallen (1970) presents a nice example of how needs energize behavior and alter figure-background relationships: consider a person reading a book. The book is the figure; everything else is the background. As the person begins to get thirsty, his mouth becomes the figure and everything else (including the book) the background. As thirst (awareness of this bodily feeling) increases, the relationship to the environment changes. The person drinks a glass of water and returns to his reading. Once more, the book is the figure and everything else the background.

The above process, called "Gestalt formation and destruction," is thought to "provide an autonomous criterion for adjustment." According to Gestalt therapy, this process functions smoothly in the well-integrated personality. In the disordered personality, however, figure-background relationships are fuzzy. Sometimes confusion may cause the process to break down. At other times there may be "poor perceptual contact" with the environment or the patient's own body. Elsewhere the expression of needs may be blocked. Finally, "good Gestalten" (i.e., clear figures) may not be formed or may be inhibited by repression. Repression, for the Gestalt therapists, is a *muscular* reaction. For example, suppressed anger may result in considerable muscle tension in the arms or stomach.

The Gestalt therapist works to reorder good Gestalt formation and destruction. This work is always done *in the present;* it involves helping the patient to re-organize his or her field and "to heighten each emerging figure." Gestalt therapists are very sensitive to the person's body in relation to what he or she is saying. Much feedback about bodily posture that is inconsistent with the verbal comment is given to the client.

We will now examine the Gestalt therapist's view of neurosis.[6] Perls (1970a) describes what he considers to be the five layers of neurosis. The first is termed the *phony layer* and refers to the social games and self-imposed roles of many individuals. "It is always the 'as if' attitudes that require that we live up to a concept, live up to a fantasy that we or others have created whether it comes out as a curse or ideal" (p. 20). This is the antithesis of self-actualization. The second is the *phobic layer,* which means the individual's reluctance to accept what he or she is. Consistent with the label, the individual is afraid to try new modes of functioning. The third layer is the *impasse,* where the individual feels more like an object than an active subject, unsure of his or her own abilities. The fourth or *implosive layer,* occurs when the individual's fears and doubts are about to give way and a major change occur, (note the parallel to the existential notion of commitment). Fifth, "The *explosion* is the final neurotic layer that occurs when we get through the implosive state. As I see it this progression is necessary to become authentic" (Perls, 1970a, p. 22; italics added). According to Perls, there are four ways in which the explosion may be manifested: joy, grief, orgasm, and anger.

Gestalt therapy consists of "peeling away" the five neurotic layers, thus leading the person into the explosive state (analogous to self-

6. Although Gestalt therapists work with some psychotics, (e.g., Dublin, 1973), most of their clinical work involves neurotics.

actualization). However, from session to session there may or may not be continuity. This happens because the Gestalt therapist is concerned with the present (the here-and-now) and how the person impacts upon him or her at the present time. Although the Gestalt therapist does not believe in directing the person's life, specific techniques are used. It is important to have the client take responsibility for his or her own words and deeds. If, for example, during a session the client were to say: "It makes me angry when my mother telephones me twice a day," the therapist might say: "Can you take responsibility for your feelings? Say I." The client then might say: "*I am angry* when my mother telephones me twice a day."

Let us now consider two examples of therapist-client dialogue. The first takes place during individual psychotherapy. The therapist makes the patient aware of autonomic response patterns (i.e., motor behavior) which may or may not be consistent with the verbal message:

P. I don't know what to say now. . . .

T. I notice that you are looking away from me.

P. (Giggle.)

T. And now you cover up your face.

P. You make me feel so awful!

T. And now you cover up your face with both hands.

P. Stop! This is unbearable!

T. What do you feel now?

P. I feel so embarassed! Don't look at me!

T. Please stay with that embarrassment.

P. I have been living with it all my life! I am ashamed of everything I do! It is as if I don't even feel that I have the right to exist!

(Naranjo, 1970, p. 56)

The second example is of a family therapy session (mother, father, Steve) in which mother seems discouraged and ready to abrogate responsibility. The therapist is trying to help her to deal more responsibly with the situation:

M. Our trouble has been mostly with Steve . . .

T. (interrupting) Tell him what you don't like about his behavior.

M. He knows very well what I don't like It doesn't help to tell him.

T. Then I suggest you consult your husband. That's what husbands and wives are for.

M. I know. I've talked to him but he's not interested.

T. Then I suggest you discuss *that* with your husband.

M. I have but when I do he either ignores me or just gets mad at the kids and spanks them. And I don't think that's the way to handle it.

T. Tell him.

M. I do. He won't listen to me.

T. Then discuss that with him.

(Kempler, 1970, pp. 154–155)

Finally, we will look at how Perls (1970b) deals with dream material (taken from a 1966 workshop at the Esalen Institute). In this interaction, J. is asked by Perls to replay various parts of the dream, taking responsibility for her feelings and actions:

Perls: How old are you when you play this part?

J: Well. I'm—in the department store. I'm only—anywhere from six to ten or twelve, or, who knows?

Perls: How old are you, really?

J: Really? Thirty-one.

Perls: Thirty-one.

J: And she's even dead.

Perls: Can you talk as a thirty-one-year-old, to your mother? Can you be your age?

J: Mother, I am thirty-one years old. I am *quite* capable of walking on my own two legs.

Perls: You notice the difference? Much less noise, and much more substance.

J: I can stand on my own legs. I can do anything I want to do. And I can *know* what I want to do. I *don't* need you. In fact, you're not even here when I *did need* you. So, why do you hang around?

Perls: Can you say goodbye to her? Can you bury her?

J: Well, I can now, because I'm at the bottom of the slope, and when I come to the bottom, I stand up. I stand up, and I walk around in this beautiful place.

Perls: Can you say to your mother, "Goodbye, Mother, rest in peace."

J: I think I did that in the dream. Bye, Mother . . . Bye. (*Weeps*)

Perls: Talk, Jean. You're doing great when you talk to your mother.

J: Bye, Mom. You couldn't help what you did. You didn't know any better. It wasn't your fault that you had three boys first, and then you got me. You wanted another boy, and you didn't want me—and you felt so bad after you found out I was a girl. You just tried to make it up to me—that's all. You didn't have to smother me. I forgive you., Mom. Just rest, mama. . . . I can go now. Sure, I can go—

(Perls, 1970b, p. 221)

As our three examples show, Gestalt therapy and theory are highly consistent. The therapist is concerned with wholeness and organization (consistency between motor and verbal behavior). He or she works in the present and always steers the patient back to the present. The therapist also tries to have the patient assume responsibility for feelings and actions (even in reporting dreams), thus helping the patient to confront life situations much more directly.

The Encounter Group Movement

In the more than three decades since the first T-group (T = training) was held in Bethel, Maine, in 1947, hundreds of thousands of individuals have participated in small group encounters. During the 1960s and early 1970s the proliferation of such groups was astounding (cf. Kilmann & Sotile, 1976; Smith, 1975). Although the groups differ in composition and aims, there are some basic similarities. For purposes of identification, all of these small group experiences will be called encounter groups (cf. Rogers, 1970).[7]

Before describing the various groups, let us examine some of the features they have in common. First, these group encounters have been described as "group psychotherapy for the normal." That is, the participants are not considered clients or patients. However, since screening is nonexistent or casual at best, it does appear that some individuals who are psychologically impaired are often attracted to the group experience (e.g., Glass, Kirsch, & Parris, 1977; Yalom & Lieberman, 1971). Second, the groups are generally small, ranging from six to twenty members.

---

7. The work in human relations skills by Kurt Lewin and his students at MIT resulted in the first T-group. Interest continued with the formation of the National Training Laboratories (NTL) at Bethel, Maine, with its national offices in Washington, D.C. NTL has been particularly concerned with providing human relations training for industrial managers and leaders. (See Lubin and Eddy [1970] for a historical account of the laboratory training model.)

Third, members are often strangers to one another, but there are also group encounters consisting of couples and training laboratory experiences for individuals who work together. Fourth, the encounters are not described as "psychotherapy," but obviously the parallel to traditional group psychotherapy exists. Certainly, the aim is to bring about both behavioral and attitudinal change in the participants. The Natural Training Laboratory (NTL), for example, considers the experience educational. Also, some of the groups are formed purely for their entertainment value (see American Psychiatric Association Task Force Report, 1970). Fifth, most of the groups have a leader, facilitator, or trainer, whose style and activity tend to vary. Some of the "leaders" are trained mental health professionals; others are not. Sixth, almost all the groups focus on the present (i.e., the immediate nature of the interaction among the participants). Seventh, the group experience encourages open, nondefensive communication, considerable self-disclosure, emotional outpouring, and general honesty of communication. Confrontation is very common but varies in its intensity across groups.[8] Eighth, depending on the group, the length of time that it meets will vary. Some consist of a continous experience spaced over time, as in standard group psychotherapy. Others may occur during a weekend, with breaks only for sleep, meals, and toileting. Still others are marathon encounters, lasting without a break for hours on end (e.g., fifteen to twenty hours).

Rogers (1970) has described ten different varieties of encounter groups. The *T-group,* working from a social psychological context, focuses on interpersonal relations skills and is construed by the leader as an education experience. The *basic encounter group* emphasizes personal growth and encourages confrontation between and among its members. The *sensitivity group,* according to Rogers, is similar to both T-groups and encounter groups. The *task-oriented* group, as the name implies, focuses on a particular goal (usually interpersonal) in an industrial context. *Sensory awareness groups* emphasize expression through physical means (e.g., dance, movement). *Creativity workshops,* with freedom of expression as the major thrust, emphasize art as the medium. In the *organizational development group,* a primary goal is for the individual to develop leadership skills. This kind of group often consists

8. During an internship, one of us (MH) attended a personal growth group held for one and a half hours twice a week. Many of the sessions were filled with the expression of intense emotions. MH vividly remembers many of the interactions between his graduate student colleagues and himself. The encounter group definitely encourages the types of hostile verbal interchanges that typically do not take place in polite society. With defenses lowered as a result of the group process, many things are expressed that usually would remain unsaid.

of individuals working in industry or other large organizations. Similarly, the *team building group* is based in industry and is devoted to developing an efficient and harmonious team of individuals. The Gestalt group has more of a therapeutic flavor, with the leader focusing on one individual at a time. Gestalt treatment strategies used in individual psychotherapy are applied here as well. Finally, there are the *Synanon games,* developed by the Synanon organization in California for treatment of drug addicts. These games are of a violent verbal nature (e.g., the "haircutting") and attack the "defensive" structure of the participants. When observed by outsiders, Synanon-like games appear to be unorganized "shouting matches."

Two other types of encounter groups have recently attracted attention. One, the *nude marathon* (Bindrim, 1968), takes place in the nude, usually in a swimming pool.[9] Although sexual expression is forbidden, hugging is permitted. The rationale for nudity is that when people are unclothed, their defensive structure is lowered. Thus, nudity is seen as fostering honest and open communication. A second new approach is a "large-group" experience (about 250 trainees at a time) known as the Erhard Seminars Training (est). As described by Glass et al. (1977), "The training is typically conducted in large hotel convention rooms. Trainees sit before a trainer who is located on an elevated central stage equipped with a blackboard. Trainers employ a confrontational, authoritarian model and often respond to disagreement from the participants with intimidation and ridicule. The leader dictates a set of rules that include the following: no watches, no talking, unless recognized by the trainer, no leaving one's seat, and no smoking, eating, or going to the bathroom except during announced breaks. Alcohol, drugs, and unprescribed medication are not permitted. Individuals who break the rules are usually escorted from the room and may be dropped from the program. The usual training day begins in the early morning and continues for about 15 hours with two breaks. Trainees may eat only during the second break" (p. 245).

The Process

Those who have never had an encounter group experience often ask: What is it really like? Adherents of encounter groups undoubtedly would answer: Join one and experience it! It is very difficult to describe

9. Many encounter groups are most popular in the West, particularly in California.

the subtle nuances and range of emotional expression that occur. Although no two encounter group sessions or groups are alike, and most encounter groups have no prescribed direction,[10] some basic patterns of trends may be discerned.

Carl Rogers, one of the first clinical psychologists concerned with the process of individual psychotherapy, has also traced the process of the encounter group (Rogers, 1970), breaking it down into fifteen phases. These phases, although not entirely distinct from one another, appear regardless of how long the encounter takes. They may not follow in sequence from one group to the next, but they can be viewed as an abstraction of the encounter group process.

The *first phase* is called "milling around." This refers to the initial discomfort and indecisiveness experienced by group members after the leader has stated that he or she *will not* take responsibility for directing the group. The group members realize that *they* must create any direction that the group may eventually assume. Thus, during the group's early stages, many suggestions for structure will be proposed; most, if not all, will be rejected by the other participants. In the *second phase,* "resistance to personal expression and exploration," group members present their *public* facade rather than their *private* selves. "It is the public self that members tend to show each other, and only gradually, fearfully, and ambivalently do they take steps to reveal something of the private self" (Rogers, 1970, p. 17).

In the *third phase,* "description of past feelings," the defensiveness of group members begins to break down. Gradually, almost tentatively, they attempt to explore feelings, but usually in the historical vein. In *phase four,* "expression of negative feelings," there is the first attempt to express true feelings related to the here-and-now (i.e., what is occurring in the group at the moment). Usually these feelings are negative; often the leader is attacked for his or her lack of direction. The *fifth phase* indicates the first "expression and exploration of personally meaningful material." Consider Sam's statement following another group member's comment about his strength:

> Perhaps I'm not aware of or experiencing it that way, as strength. (Pause) I think, when I was talking with, I think it was the first day, I was talking to you, Tom, when in the course of that, I expressed the *genuine surprise* I had, the first time I realized that I could *frighten* someone—It really, it was a

10. Exceptions are the est and Gestalt encounter groups.

discovery that I had to just kind of look at and feel and get to know, you know, it was such a *new* experience for me. I was so used to the feeling of being frightened by *others* that it had never occurred to me that anyone could be—I guess it *never had*—that anyone could be frightened of *me*. And I guess maybe it has something to do with how I feel about myself.

(Rogers, 1970, pp. 21–22)

In *phase six* there is "the expression of immediate interpersonal feelings in the group." At this point, members begin to talk about how others affect them. *Phase seven* is "the development of a healing capacity in the group"—the ability of group members to deal empathically with the hurt and pain expressed by various participants. *Phase eight* is characterized by "self-acceptance and the beginning of change." Rogers (1970) presents the following example that was recorded in an encounter group held with adolescents:

Susan: Are you always so closed in when you're in your shell?

Art: No, I'm so darn used to living with the shell, it doesn't even bother me. I don't even know the real me. I think I've, well, I've pushed the shell away more here. When I'm out of my shell—only twice—once just a few minutes ago—I'm really me, I guess. But then I just sort of pull in a cord after me when I'm in my shell, and that's almost all the time. And I leave the front standing outside when I'm back in the shell.

Facil: And nobody's back in there with you?

Art: (Crying) Nobody else is in there with me, just me. I just pull everything into the shell and roll the shell up and shove it in my pocket. I take the shell, and the real me, and put it in my pocket where it's safe. I guess that's really the way I do it—I go into my shell and turn off the real world. And here—that's what I want to do here in this group, y' know—come out of my shell and actually throw it away.

Lois: You're making progress already. At least you can talk about it.

Facil: Yeah. The thing that's going to be hardest is to stay out of the shell.

Art: (Still crying) Well, yeah, if I can keep talking about it I can come out and stay out, but I'm gonna have to, y' know, protect me. It hurts. It's actually hurting to talk about it.

(pp. 27–28)

The next *phase (nine)* is labeled "the cracking of facades." As part of the complex interaction within the group, there is both an implicit and explicit demand that participants reveal their "true" selves. The group begins to punish (verbally) those who continue to play the social games of their everyday lives. When the group attempts to crack facades, "the individual receives feedback" *(phase ten)*. Such feedback can be positive but more often is strongly negative. Mead (1977) presents some guidelines for giving and receiving feedback.[11] Feedback should be given immediately after behavior has been observed, and should refer to specifics, not generalities. The group member should refrain from making moral judgments (i.e., avoid words such as "good," "bad," "immature,"). Feedback is more meaningful if provided by several participants rather than one. As for receiving feedback, the participant should listen attentively; if the receiver can paraphrase it, communication is enhanced. Feedback does not automatically mean that behavior should be changed. But the participant should be able to ascertain whether feedback provided is idiosyncratic or reflects the feelings of other participants. Also, feedback is reciprocal. By giving feedback to others, there is an increased likelihood of having it returned.

Phase eleven is best described as "confrontation." This is an extreme form of negative feedback (usually "hard hitting"). The result of such confrontation is often in that it may lead to closer and more meaningful communication between the antagonists. Consider this illustration of confrontation:

Norma: (Loud sigh) Well, I don't have *any* respect for you, Alice. *None!* (Pause) There's about a hundred things going through my mind I want to say to you, and *by God* I hope I get through 'em all! First of all, if you wanted us to respect you, then why couldn't you respect *John's* feelings last night? *Why have you been on him today?* H'mm? Last night—*couldn't you—couldn't you* accept—*couldn't you* comprehend in any way at all that—that *he felt* his unworthiness in the service of God? *Couldn't you accept this* or did you have to dig into it today to find something *else* there? H'mm? I personally don't think John has any problems that are *any* of *your damn business!* . . . Any real woman that I know wouldn't have acted as you have this week, and particularly what you said this afternoon. That was so *crass!!* It just made me want to puke, right there! ! ! And—I'm just *shaking* I'm so mad at you—I don't think you've been real once this week! . . . I'm so infuriated that *I want to come over and beat the hell out of you!! I want to slap you across the mouth so hard and*—oh, and you're so, you're many years above me—and I respect age, and I respect people who are older than me, *but I don't respect you, Alice. At all!* (A startled pause.)

(Rogers, 1970, pp. 33–34)

11. Openness to feedback, as articulated by Mead (1977), is the ideal, but it can be stimulated by an effective leader or facilitator.

Phase twelve, "the helping relationship outside the group sessions," represents continued interaction between and among individuals in the absence of the leader and many of the other group members. Rogers (1970) views this as a "healthy" (i.e., "healing") extension of the encounter experience. *Phase thirteen* is called "the basic encounter." This refers to the extremely close, honest communication resulting from the group encounter, in contrast to daily life experiences. *Phase fourteen,* "the expression of positive feelings and closeness," seems an inevitable outcome of the group process, where all kinds of feelings are expressed and accepted. Finally, in *phase fifteen,* "behavior changes in the group." According to Rogers, this is manifested both verbally (e.g., tone of voice) and nonverbally (e.g., gestures). Of course, whether such behavioral change generalizes to situations outside of the group is still questionable (cf. Lieberman, Yalom, & Miles, 1973).

Critical Appraisal

In evaluating the humanistic approach, we will consider separately Rogerian psychotherapy, existential psychotherapy, Gestalt therapy, and the encounter group movement. Of the four approaches, only two (Rogerian psychotherapy and encounter groups) have been evaluated in scientific-empirical fashion. Even here, however, the research has been criticized methodologically (cf. Lambert et al., 1978; Smith, 1975).

The reader will recall that Truax and Carkhuff (1967), after reviewing studies on Rogerian psychotherapy, concluded that therapists rated high on accurate empathy, nonpossessive warmth, and genuineness were able to bring about significant clinical change in their clients. It was further argued that these relationships held regardless of the population under treatment. However, a more penetrating analysis of the studies reviewed by Truax and Carkhuff may lead to different conclusions. That is, although accurate empathy, nonpossessive warmth, and genuineness may be necessary for establishing good therapist-client rapport, they *are not* sufficient for bringing about therapeutic change. Indeed, the more recent literature suggests that the correct technique must also be tailored to the client's problem (cf. Hersen & Bellack, 1976a). Thus, there is no universal strategy that works for every client or patient. For example, although client-centered therapy may be valuable for a college student's in-depth exploration of feelings, it should not necessarily be the main approach for, say, juvenile delinquency, schizophrenia, or complex neuroses.

Let us now consider specific research issues concerning client-centered therapy studies. First, data for many of the studies are based on judges' ratings of therapist behavior where inter-rater reliabilities were as low as $r = 0.50$ (see Truax & Carkhuff, 1967, p. 85). That is, independent judges may not be rating the same phenomena. Given the more contemporary standards set in behavioral research (Hersen & Bellack, 1976a), a minimum inter-rater reliability of $r = 0.80$ would be required. Thus, the low inter-rater reliabilities in studies that supposedly substantiate the Rogerian position have often led to *invalid* conclusions. Second, the construct of accurate empathy has been soundly criticized on both logical and empirical grounds (Chinsky & Rappaport, 1970; Rappaport & Chinsky, 1972). Rappaport and Chinsky (1972) argue that it is questionable for judges to rate the therapist's accurate empathy without the client's response. In many instances, only the therapist statement was provided. In addition, the accurate empathy scale used in these studies apparently has poor discriminant validity, again weakening the conclusion.

Third, as we pointed in Chapter 7, scientific evaluation of what Rogers does during therapy indicates that he reinforces certain classes of client verbalizations while concurrently ignoring others (Truax, 1966).

Thus, when doing therapy, Rogers is more of a behaviorist than a Rogerian. Fourth, Lambert et al. (1978) conclude that hypotheses generated from Rogers' theory have received only moderate experimental support. This

> lack of support is due both to the difficulties encountered in sampling and rating therapy sessions and to the failure of client-centered theory to specify more precisely the times when specific conditions (such as empathy) might be most facilitative. It is noted that judges [sic] ratings of audiotape recordings of counseling have not provided better predictions of positive therapeutic outcome than have client perception measures. Also, it is concluded that the efficacy of popular interpersonal skills training models have [sic] not been demonstrated (p. 467).

Despite these problems, Rogers and his adherents have had considerable impact on the field of clinical psychology. The mere fact that psychotherapy (and its process) has been opened up to scientific inquiry can be attributed to Rogers and his students. However, this should not blind us to the methodological and possible conceptual shortcomings of the Rogerian framework.

Let us now consider the impact of existentialism. From an empirical standpoint, this is difficult—particularly as existential psychotherapists *do not* test their theoretical notions in standard statistical fashion. To the best of our knowledge, there are no studies comparing existential psychotherapy with other strategies. Indeed, existential psychotherapists ignore empirical-statistical methods in favor of the phenomenological approach. That is, as we have previously noted, existential therapists are interested in studying (more subjectively) the phenomena of therapy. Arguing against this position is almost like challenging an adherent of a different religious system. The present writers, who adhere to the scientific-empirical method, are unable to present any data in support of or against the existential approach. However, at a more theoretical level (noted earlier in the chapter), there is no doubt that existential therapists have made us aware of the importance of death as a relevant psychological variable in our lives. Further study is needed.

As with existential psychotherapy, Gestalt treatment strategies have not really been empiricially evaluated (cf. Adesso, Euse, Hanson, Hendry, & Choca, 1974; Bornstein, 1974). This is unfortunate, since Gestalt techniques are based on academic Gestalt psychology, tend to be behavioral, and in general are articulated clearly enough to make experimental replication feasible. However, as a group, Gestalt therapists do not seem intent upon empirical validation of their theoretical orientation. In fact, there seems to be a cultist tendency among Gestalt therapists, as exemplified by their idolization of Frederick (Fritz) Perls, the development of their own institutes (e.g., Esalen at Big Sur, California), and an attempt to live by Gestalt rules, even when not engaged in psychotherapy.

The question, Do encounter groups lead to change? is similar to the question first raised almost three decades ago: Does psychotherapy work? Obviously, the later question, like the earlier one, is too broad. There are many kinds of encounter groups, leaders, and participants. Given these three major variables, the questions must reflect the possible interactions among them. Still another issue is: Do changes persist beyond the group? That is, do they generalize? And if they do, how long do they persist? Finally, are the effects of encounter groups always positive?

Smith (1975) reviewed 100 studies on the outcome of sensitivity training that included a control condition and employed a repeated-measures design. In 78 of the studies, significant positive changes were detected. In 31 studies that evaluated changes at least one month after training, significant positive changes were found in 21. However, this means that in only one-third of the studies was any follow-up considered. In general, the changes included reduced prejudice, a more favorable self-concept, and behavioral differences perceived by others who were not involved in the training. However, the studies reviewed have several methodological shortcomings. Two of the most critical problems are: (1) inadequately matched control subjects and (2) biased observers. Biased observation refers to the fact that behavior was rated by individuals who knew subjects had received training. Very few studies involved the perception of trainee behavior by others.

As pointed out by Smith (1975), "The focal research question concerning sensitivity training is no longer whether or not it has effects. A variety of effects have now been documented. The more pressing questions have now become whether the effects persist, whether the effects occur in all types of groups, whether the effects can also be created by other training methods, why the effects are detected by some measures and not others, and why these particular effects occur rather than others" (p. 618).

In a review of forty-five investigations of marathon encounter groups, Kilmann and Sotile (1976) found little evidence that the marathon format was superior to spaced group treatment. Where some superiority was seen, the results appeared to be short-lived. In addition, only 6 of the studies reviewed did not use college men and women as subjects. Thus, the findings cannot be considered widely generalizable.

As with traditional psychotherapy (see Chapter 6), all the effects of encounter groups are *not* positive. Reports in the literature refer to "encounter group casualties" (American Psychiatric Association Task Force Report, 1970; Glass et al., 1977; Kirsch & Glass, 1977; Yalom & Lieberman, 1971). Yalom and Lieberman (1971) define a casualty "as an enduring, significant, negative outcome which was caused by participation in the group" (p. 16). In their study of 209 college students enrolled in 18 encounter groups that met for at least 30 hours, 170 completed the experience. Of those, 16 were described as casualties (i.e., 9.4 percent).[12] These data make it clear that the encounter group is *much more than a mere social game* played out over time. It can result in very

---

12. Casualties include psychotic breakdowns.

serious consequences in the hands of an inept leader.[13] Yalom and Lieberman found that leaders who had the most casualties tended to be aggressive, intrusive, charismatic, and individually as opposed to group-focused. Also, those individuals who became casualties tended to have poor self-concepts and harbored "unrealistically high expectations" for change. Given these data, it is very clear to us that candidates for encounter groups should be carefully screened and that leaders should undergo a carefully supervised period of training. In short, much better *external control* over the encounter group movement is warranted.

Summary

In this chapter, we have presented the treatment approaches of the humanistic movement. We first presented a composite picture of humanity from the humanistic viewpoint. We then looked at the contribution of Carl Rogers and his students, highlighting the client-centered approach to therapy. Therapist variables considered necessary and sufficient for clinical change were examined. This was followed by a description of existential psychotherapy. Next we considered the contribution of Frederick Perls to psychotherapy. The Gestalt view of neurosis was outlined, in addition to the specific techniques routinely used by Gestalt therapists. We then examined the growing influence of encounter groups both inside and outside of the mental health field. The typical process of an encounter group was traced. Finally, we evaluated the contributions of the humanistic orientation. Many of the approaches did not appear to have an empirical basis. Those that did, however, were criticized on methodological grounds.

13. Because of the uncontrolled nature of this area, many individuals without adequate psychological training (no degree in any mental health profession) have become trainers or leaders. Organizations such as the NTL do provide formal training courses for leaders, but unfortunately this is not standard practice.

CHAPTER
NINE

Community
Mental Health

There have been three mental health revolutions. Pinel led the first, bringing humane concern for the mentally ill; Freud led the second, bringing passionate attention to the intrapsychic life of man. The third revolution, now in the making, is appropriately a corporate effort without an eponym as yet. Mental health, always a public health problem, is finally adopting public health strategies, with strong support from some quarters and resistance from others (Hobbs, 1964, p. 822).

This "third revolution" is variously labeled *community psychology, community psychiatry,* and *community mental health.* While definitions of these terms vary, they each reflect a dramatic change in the conceptualization of mental illness and its treatment. The focus of study is no longer the individual patient. Rather, it is society at large. The source of distress is presumed to reside in the community; thus, change entails altering the community. Furthermore, the solution to mental illness and psychological health is not *treatment* of afflicted individuals but *prevention.* The mental health professional attempts to alter society so as to remove sources of psychological stress and disruption, rather than providing therapy. The elimination of poverty and racism, improved nutrition for pregnant women, crisis intervention, and tutoring programs indicate the broad range of programs which fall under the umbrella of "prevention."

In this chapter, we will examine the community mental health revolution: what it is, how it came about, what it encompasses, and how well it has fulfilled its promises. We will first discuss the impetus for change, including the dissatisfaction with traditional forms of service and the sociopolitical climate which made change possible. We will then consider the major ways in which the community approach differs from the traditional orientation: the public health model, with its emphasis on prevention; changes in the role of the mental health professional, including the emphasis on consultation; and the use of nonprofessionals as replacements for and adjuncts to professionals. Next, we will look at some examples of how the community orientation has been put into practice. Topics include community mental health centers, partial hospitalization, crisis intervention, and a prototype school-based prevention program. Finally, we will evaluate the community orientation and its application.

The Community Mental Health Movement

The area of mental health has few definitions which are generally accepted. Most concepts and terms are defined idiosyncratically by subgroups within the field, as well as by many individual practitioners. Community mental health (CMH) is no exception. At the conservative extreme, the term refers to the recognition that factors in the community influence the development and manifestation of psychopathology, and hence warrant attention during treatment. At the opposite (or liberal) extreme, it is argued that social forces are the basis of all psychological distress. Thus, social action, rather than treatment, is the solution. Some view CMH as encompassing both a broad conceptual model of behavior and strategies for improving mental health and reducing distress. Others (cf. Anderson, Cooper, Hassol, Klein, Rosenblum, & Bennett, 1966) argue that CMH is an applied subcategory of *community psychology*. The latter is considered to be a multidisciplinary field which focuses on the "optimal realization of human potential through planned social action. Community psychologists were [sic] characterized as change agents, social systems analysts, consultants in community affairs, and students generally of the whole man in relation to all his environments" (Anderson et al., 1966, p. 26).

Despite this diversity there does appear to be agreement on two principles (Zax & Specter, 1974). First, CMH emphasizes the impact of an adverse environment on the development of distress. The term "environment" can include everything from family interaction, to racism, to welfare laws and the state of the national economy. Second, CMH emphasizes the role of prevention as the primary weapon against distress and psychological disability. While CMH programs may include traditional forms of treatment, the ultimate goal is to modify the social system so as to prevent mental disturbance.

Bloom (1977) has elaborated on this picture by identifying ten practices and beliefs of CMH. These characteristics, outlined below, will be described later on.

1. Practice and activity take place in the community, not in institutions or the therapist's office.

2. Action is focused on the community or population at large, not on a single patient.

3. CMH emphasizes prevention rather than treatment. It operates according to a *public health* model, in contrast to the traditional *clinical* model.

4. The CMH approach emphasizes continuity and comprehensiveness of services. That is, a full range of medical, psychological, and social services should be available, and the movement or transfer from one part of the system to another should be easy (e.g., minimal bureaucratic roadblocks).

5. There is an emphasis on indirect services, such as consultation and education, which can have broad impact on the community. In contrast, the traditional or clinical approach emphasizes direct services, such as psychotherapy.

6. There is an emphasis on innovative clinical strategies (e.g., crisis intervention) which promise to affect more people more rapidly than existing services.

7. CMH emphasizes planning in regard to mental health programing. The goal is to identify community needs and then structure services and apportion resources accordingly, rather than the haphazard application of psychotherapy by individual therapists.

8. The CMH approach advocates expansion of services and the impact of professional mental health workers by tapping new sources of personnel: paraprofessionals, community residents, the police, clergy, teachers, and others.

9. The CMH approach involves a commitment to community control or involvement. Community residents should identify their needs and help determine how they should be met, rather than having these decisions made by mental health professionals in isolation.

10. Sources of stress and distress are viewed as emanating from the community rather than residing in the individual. Hence, there is an emphasis on identifying community-based stressors.

Impetus for the CMH Movement

Revolutions do not occur overnight. Typically, they simmer for many years, based on increasing dissatisfaction with the existing order. The CMH revolution can be traced back at least to the early 1950s and several key factors identified. Let us examine those factors.

Effectiveness of Existing Services. Prior to the 1960s, most persons with psychological disturbance received one of two types of treatment. If the disturbance was mild (e.g., a neurosis) they were given psychodynamic psychotherapy. If it was severe (e.g., a psychosis), they were sent to a state psychiatric hospital for custodial care (unless they could afford private care). Beginning in the 1950s, major questions were raised about the effectiveness of both forms of treatment.

Psychodynamic psychotherapy was evaluated in Chapter 6. Basically, it is uncertain whether that or any other form of psychotherapy can really eliminate psychological distress. While recent research suggests that psychotherapy does have some value, the critiques of the 1950s (cf. Eysenck, 1960b) were quite negative and stimulated much controversy. Clearly psychotherapy was not potent enough to be the primary tool of the mental health professions. The search for alternative strategies began.

The efficacy of the state hospital, also under fire, fared even worse than psychotherapy. The number of state hospitals and the size of their patient populations had grown dramatically during the first half of this century. These hospitals were usually large institutions set in isolated rural areas. While a variety of therapeutic and rehabilitative services were nominally offered, most state hospitals were custodial warehouses for the outcasts of society: the indigent, the bizarre, the belligerent, and those who had neither family nor money to support them in society. In addition, these institutions were always poorly funded, resulting in a small, poorly trained staff. Consequently, few patients received any viable treatment. Those whose illness was acute and could profit from rest and a change of scenery were often discharged quickly with some benefit. However, most such hospitals were filled with chronic patients who spent from five years to a lifetime in "back wards," becoming more and more regressed and dysfunctional—the so called "hospitalization syndrome."

This insidious system became the subject of increasing criticism for humanitarian as well as professional-empirical reasons. Two developments—a new and different form of treatment and a political action—ended in a dramatic change of the state hospital approach. First, the 1950s and 1960s saw the development of the *major tranquilizers,* a variety of drugs which reduced gross psychotic symptomatology (e.g., hallucinations and delusions). With these disturbances under at least partial control, it became possible for the chronic psychotic to return to the community and regain some semblance of a normal life. The political action was the 1961 report of the President's Joint Commission on Mental Illness and Health. Among the recommendations of this official United States Government panel were:

> (1) immediate and intensive care for acutely disturbed mental patients in outpatient community-mental-health clinics created at the rate of one clinic per 50,000 population, inpatient psychiatric units located in every general hospital with 100 or more beds, and intensive-psychiatric-treatment centers of no more than 1000 beds each (to be developed by converting existing state mental hospitals), (2) improved care of chronic mental patients in other converted state mental hospitals, again involving no more than 1000 beds, (3) improved and expanded aftercare, partial hospitalization (hospitalization for less than 24 hours a day), and rehabilitation services (Bloom, 1977, p. 25).

The President's Commission advocated eliminating state hospitals (as they were employed), to be replaced by a variety of services in the patients' *home communities.* Not all of the recommendations were followed, but the report had tremendous impact. It not only supported the CMH approach, but it stimulated the Community Mental Health Centers Act (see below), which provided federal funding for CMH activities.

Distribution of Services. As existing treatment methods came under review, questions were raised about their application as well as their efficacy. It became apparent that there were socioeconomic and racial differences in both the *types* and *quality* of services afforded to different groups (Zax & Cowen, 1976). As mentioned above, referral to state hospitals depended largely on economic status. Lower-class patients were much more likely to be diagnosed as psychotic and hospitalized than were middle- and upper-class patients. Similar biases have been found for racial minorities compared with white patients. There is now much controversy about whether lower-class and minority group members are the victims of diagnostic (and treatment) prejudice, or whether they do, in fact, have a higher rate of psychosis (Dohrenwend & Dohrenwend, 1974). Regardless of the reason, there was, and is, little question that lower-class patients suffered most from the state hospital system.

Conversely, lower-class patients are disproportionately excluded from psychotherapy. On the one hand, they cannot afford to pay for private treatment. On the other hand, even when individual therapy is available through public agencies, compared to middle- and upper-class patients the poor tend to: (1) receive less competent treatment, (2) be seen by less trained personnel, (3) drop out of treatment sooner, and (4) achieve less positive outcomes (Cowen, 1973). It has been hypothesized that this results from a value clash rather than prejudice per se (Reiff, 1966). Most therapists are white, middle class, and have difficulty relating to minority group and poor patients (and vice versa). Similarly, psychotherapy is a slow process, geared to self-exploration and personal growth. In contrast, lower-class patients expect the therapist to resolve concrete problems (e.g., to eliminate wife abuse) quickly. Hence, therapist and patient values, interactive styles, goals, and expectations clash. One solution to this problem is to make lower-class individuals better patients by changing their expectations about therapy (cf. Sue, 1977). However, the CMH perspective assumes that psychotherapy is not, and never will be, an acceptable form of treatment for this population. The solution is not to try to "shoehorn" the poor into a middle-class mold. New and more appropriate methods are needed (e.g., prevention).

The Need for Services. Thus far, we have identified problems in the quality and distribution of services. These problems are magnified by the tremendous *need* for services. Many studies during the past thirty years have examined the prevalence of mental illness. A substantial part of the population, it is believed, suffers from some psychological dysfunction.

Two studies are especially illustrative. Leighton (1956) reported on an extensive study of the population of Stirling County, Canada. The results suggested that about 37 percent were in need of psychiatric treatment—almost eight times the number that were actually being treated. The Midtown-Manhattan study (Srole, Langner, Michael, Opler, & Rennie, 1962) involved a large sample of the residents of Manhattan (in New York City). Srole et al. concluded that 23.4 percent of the population were impaired; obviously, a much smaller percentage were in treatment. While these and other studies have been criticized methodologically (cf. Dohrenwend & Dohrenwend, 1974), it is agreed that they accurately portray a tremendous need for services. In addition, it has been shown that there is far more disturbance among lower-class groups than among the middle and upper classes.

Based on these data, psychological dysfunction has been likened to a national epidemic which primarily ravages the poor. Unfortunately, services available at the time of this conclusion were insufficient to handle this hugh problem. Furthermore, CMH advocates questioned whether those services would *ever* be sufficient for the task. First, there is a limit to the number of people who could or should be hospitalized. Second, individual psychotherapy is too costly and requires too much time to ever have a mass impact. While group therapy is an improvement, it too is inadequate if 20 to 35 percent of the population require services.

Mental Health Personnel. One possible way to provide the needed services is to increase the available personnel. Graduate programs, medical schools, and schools of social work could expand and train more students. While this is an appealing idea, a study by Albee (1959) suggests that it would not be a viable solution even if the various professional schools cooperated. First, professional training is costly and time-consuming. For example, graduate training in psychology requires four to six years and is based on a one-to-one student-faculty ratio in each class. No program could drastically change the number of students without substantially altering the nature of training.

Second, private practice is enticing to mental health professionals. Many people enter training precisely to pursue such a career. Thus, increasing the number of students would probably provide more private services for the middle and upper classes than for the poor. Third, and most important, the demand for services could be expected to increase dramatically, due to population growth and increased public sensitivity to mental health issues. Albee (1959) predicted that increased demand would substantially outpace any efforts to increase the traditional services. The solution to this problem was not "more of the same" but some way to dramatically increase the impact of the mental health professionals available.

The Medical Model. Traditional mental health services have been based on the *"medical model."* This term has taken on a variety of different meanings and is often used imprecisely. There are actually several different medical models, none of which really fit the CMH stereotype. In any case, many of the implications of this model, as well as practices based upon it, have been widely criticized by CMH advocates.

One implication of the medical model is that psychological disturbances are similar to infectious diseases; that is, the external signs are symptoms of an underlying disturbance. As discussed in Chapter 7, this notion is primarily psychoanalytic and has not received empirical support. Research on behavior therapy suggests that this conception is invalid. The infectious disease analogy may not truly represent the beliefs of the majority of traditional mental health professionals. However, the generic concept of disease is widely accepted. That is, psychological dysfunction is viewed as a disability or weakness of the individual. The cause is not some invading organism (as in infectious diseases), but the individual is still considered to be sick. This orientation is reflected in the terminology employed in the field: mental *illness,* patient, diagnosis, treatment, and so on.

If the influence of the medical model were limited to terminology, there would be little dissatisfaction. However, the model has substantial impact on the nature of mental health services. The illness or disease conception suggests that psychological and behavioral dysfunctions are medical problems. Hence, physicians are the logical (necessary) individuals to provide or supervise services. Similarly, afflicted individuals require treatment, which is usually based on a *clinical model* (Hersch, 1972). That is, the therapist (like the physician) waits for the prospective client to recognize the disturbance and request service. Treatment is generally provided in the therapist's office, on a direct, one-to-one basis (or in a small group).

Probably the most serious limitation of the medical model is the stress on illness. Certainly, psychological dysfunction can result from physical disturbance (e.g., organic brain disorders, manic-depressive illness). However, most problems classified as mental illnesses are not like physical medical disorders (cf. Cowen, 1973; Kazdin, 1980; Salzinger, 1980). In most cases, neither the causes of dysfunction nor the maintaining factors are internal. Rather, the critical factors are usually external—that is, environmental (Mischel, 1968; Zax & Cowen, 1976). This concept was discussed in Chapter 7, in regard to the behavioral orientation. However, behavior therapists have a somewhat molecular perspective when they speak of environmental control. Their emphasis is on specific antecedent and consequent stimuli or events which affect specific behaviors (e.g., an anxiety attack).

Advocates of the CMH perspective adopt a more molar view of environmental influence. They emphasize the potentially harmful influence of such things as living conditions, social forces, and economic systems, as well as specific stressors such as marital conflicts and the death of relatives (Cowen, 1973; Zax & Cowen, 1976). For example, extended unemployment can stimulate depression and feelings of hopelessness, marital conflict, excessive drinking, and persistent stress, all of which result in behavioral disorganization and physiological disturbance (e.g., hypertension). Persistent anger, abusive behavior, and aggression might also be expected. A child living in a family "suffering" from unemployment can be physically abused, become fearful and insecure due to parental discord, do poorly in school due to inadequate nutrition, and develop antisocial behaviors as a result of inadequate parental control and supervision.

The above example is hypothetical. Yet, much research has shown that such environmental factors exert a powerful influence on behavior. We have already pointed out the strong relationship between poverty and the incidence of psychopathology. Many situational variables have been shown to affect aggression, including population density (e.g., degree of crowding), temperature, frustration (e.g., blocking of goals or sources of reinforcement), modeling, reinforcement-punishment, organizational structure (e.g., communication channels to leaders), and task demands (Moos, 1973). Similarly, school environments have been shown to affect the behavior, mood, level of curiosity, and educational achievement of children (Zax & Cowen, 1976). Such factors as class size, seating arrangement, time and order in which materials are presented, nature of the curriculum, discipline style of the teacher, and organizational structure imposed by the principal can all have considerable impact.

This brief overview indicates that the illness conception inappropriately locates the source of the difficulty in the individual rather than in the environment. Several interrelated problems follow from this error. The patient-oriented, in-office treatment can have only limited success at best. It either ignores critical environmental circumstances or has minimal impact on them. Even if effective treatments could be devised, the one-to-one format cannot cope with major environmental stressors. For example, one racially prejudiced principal can injure the mental health of all the students in a ghetto school, as well as their parents. This is one of the many environmental stressors impinging on our vast population. It would not be feasible to provide psychotherapy for all affected individuals. (In contrast, consider the potential impact of changing the prinicipal's behavior.)

This example also points up two other problems with the medical model. First, the *passive* nature of traditional services requires the therapist to wait until the person seeks out treatment. But the harmful effects of the environment often take their toll gradually. Psychological disturbances generally develop slowly and subtlely. The individual is often unaware of the problem until it becomes serious. Sometimes this gradual onset can allow the individual to adapt to an unnecessary disability or level of distress. In that case, the problem is viewed as a tolerable but untreatable irritant. Hence, many people seek treatment when the disorder is too severe or too ingrained to be corrected (Cowen, 1973). A more active orientation would permit the professional to seek out and eliminate sources of stress, or to identify persons with new or incipient problems at a stage when intervention is much more likely to be effective.

Second, many people who could profit from treatment never seek it. This is especially true of lower-class people. Rieff (1966) suggests that the traditional medical orientation is not consistent with the view of many working-class and lower-class individuals. For this reason, the illness concept should be limited to severe disturbance (e.g., psychotic behavior):

> To the worker, emotional disability or impairment is either related to a physical illness and should be treated as such by the doctor, or it is the result of undue stresses or strains in the environment; or it is related to a moral weakness and should be treated by a minister or priest or conquered by oneself or accepted and lived with. If one attempts to treat what is considered to be a moral weakness, the worker, with his present view, considers it a tremendous invasion of his privacy (Reiff, 1966, p. 541).

From a CMH perspective, this conflict of values can be solved by developing new interventions for the lower-class population, not by converting them to the traditional view. This too is contrary to medical model practice, which emphasizes physician or therapist control. The professional has generally been regarded as the final authority on what is wrong with the patient and what treatment is needed. CMH advocates give much more responsibility to the consumers, presuming that, with some guidance, they are the best judge of what is wrong and how it should be handled. The emphasis on community control (see below) is based on this viewpoint.

A final criticism of the medical model pertains to its focus on illness rather than health. Mental health is regarded as the absence of dysfunction rather than a clearly defined level of good adjustment. Services are geared to eliminating disturbance rather than promoting good health. In contrast, CMH considers mental health to be an identifiable and desirable condition, involving happiness, life satisfaction, and individual freedom (Hersch, 1972). The goal of CMH services is to facilitate mental health in the community, as well as to eliminate stress and dysfunction.

It would seem that CMH advocates consider the medical model and all that it connotes to be wrong and useless. That is not the case. The model does have positive features, and some individuals can profit from its treatment approaches. However:

> The core of the argument can be summarized as follows: However understandable the evolution and ascendence of the medical model, however necessary that portions of it survive, however much we can improve its efficiency, it fails to deal satisfactorily with today's basic, nonpostponable MH problems, and as such it can no longer stand alone as the guiding frame for long-range planning. Reducing the flow of dysfunction is appealing as a conceptual alternative. If we cannot do this, we risk treading water until we drown! (Cowen, 1973, p. 432).

The CMH revolution was stimulated by a variety of factors which converged in the 1960s. Some of them, such as critical evaluations of existing services and personnel projections, have an empirical basis. However, like any revolution, the CMH movement was stimulated more by emotions, ideology, and values than by any objective appraisal of the traditional approach. It grew out of an awareness of the ravages of poverty and prejudice and the inequities in our society. As stated by Hersch (1972):

> The community mental health movement in the United States reached its fruition during the decade of the 1960's. For the country as a whole, that

decade was characterized by large-scale, general trends of social reform. In such a period of reform, the emphasis is on a revitalized humanistic concern for the disadvantaged, the oppressed, and the powerless. As we shall see, it is not surprising that community mental health developments took place at the same time as the war on poverty, advances in civil rights, the phenomenon of the flower people, the student rebellions, and the various liberation fronts, for, as social-historical movements, they all stand in a kinship relation to one another. (p. 749).

The Public Health Model

The above arguments suggest that the medical model is inadequate because (among other reasons) it is unable to deal with the vast need, offers the wrong type of services for many individuals, and does not distribute services equitably. The CMH movement offers another approach which avoids these limitations (as well as most other problems with the medical model): the *public health model* (Hersch, 1972). Public health has a long history of dealing with mass health problems. In contrast to the one-to-one treatment orientation of clinical procedures, public health concentrates on prevention by *altering environments* as well as *individual action*. Fluoridating community water supplies, bulldozing malarial swamps, and prohibiting the use of lead-based paints are examples of environmental programs to prevent physical illness. Obviously, it is cheaper and more effective to prevent lead poisoning by banning certain paints than it would be to treat poisoning victims. Individual action programs include mandatory vaccinations for smallpox, polio, and rubella. The advantages of prevention over treatment should be apparent.

The public health model has been translated to the mental health arena with little change. Psychological problems are likened to an epidemic; once contracted, they are so widespread and so resistant to treatment that the only solution is prevention. The focus of CMH efforts is the entire community rather than any one patient. Although individuals ultimately benefit, community programs are generally not designed with specific persons in mind. The locus of CMH efforts is also in the community; social reform, education, and institutional change replace individual therapy in an effort to eliminate the sources of distress. In later sections, we will elaborate on this new approach and consider its implications for mental health practices.

Prevention. The most widely accepted model of prevention has been developed by Gerald Caplan (1964), a community psychiatrist. Caplan identified three types of prevention: primary, secondary, and tertiary prevention. *Primary prevention* focuses on reducing the incidence of dysfunction by modifying the environment so as to prevent distur- bance. Primary prevention focuses on groups or the community rather than the individual. *Secondary prevention* aims to eliminate mild dis- turbance before it becomes severe or to reduce the duration of dys- function. In contrast to primary prevention, secondary programs do focus more on individuals or subgroups, who are identified as being "at risk" for specific problems. *Tertiary prevention* entails reducing the negative effects of chronic or well-established dysfunctions. While they are each labeled "prevention," the term "primary," "secondary," and "tertiary prevention" correspond roughly to colloquial definitions of prevention, treatment, and rehabilitation, respectively.

Ideally, primary prevention programs should be geared to the factors which cause or contribute to various dysfunctions. For example, certain preventive programs are aimed at rubella because of its harmful effects on human embryos. Unfortunately, we do not know precisely what factors cause psychological disturbance. We simply know that such environmental factors as family disorganization, marital conflict, poor health, and economic conflict produce stress and are consistently associated with psychological dysfunction (Bloom, 1977). Thus, primary preventive programs often are like shots in the dark, aimed broadly at a host of suspected problem areas. In some cases, this entails facilitating *any* social change which is conducive to a safe, happy, humanitarian, democratic life style (Kessler & Albee, 1975). For example, reducing automobile speed limits and making seat belts mandatory saves lives and reduces serious injury, thus reducing stress and anguish in families where deaths would have occurred. Pollution control reduces physical illness and prolongs life, which similarly prevents family distress and disruption. Government programs which finance low-cost housing im- prove psychological adjustment by eliminating the harmful effect of slums. Citizen control of local school boards allows residents to become more involved in school operations and generate programs they prefer. This reduces community conflict and may improve the educational program, which ultimately has a mental health benefit for the pupils. These examples show that the primary prevention approach has dra- matically altered the role of the mental health professional. To a great extent, *social action* has replaced treatment as a professional role (Hersch, 1972; Zax & Cowen, 1976).

Primary prevention programs are not all so ambitious or abstract. As part of his model, Caplan (1964) proposes a framework for planning preventive programs. The adequacy of adjustment and mental health, he states, depends upon the quantity of certain basic *supplies*. *Physical supplies* include such items as food, shelter, safety, and physical health. *Psychosocial supplies* consist of cognitive and social stimuli from others; they satisfy the need for such things as love, affection, and affiliation. *Sociocultural supplies* are provided by the community and consist of such things as stability, education, and opportunities for personal advancement and improvement. The poorer the quantity and quality of these supplies, the greater the likelihood of dysfunction. Thus, prevention programs should be aimed at maximizing the availability of supplies.

Prevention programs involve two strategies: social action and interpersonal action. *Social action* programs focus on broad social systems, community agencies, and the like. These programs frequently entail legislative changes and other efforts which have mass effects. For example, day care centers make it possible for mothers to find employment, thus improving the family's economic condition and reducing the mother's hostility toward children who had kept her at home. School breakfast programs improve physical health (which affects mental health) and increase the child's ability to concentrate in class (thereby learning more, having a more positive attitude toward school, etc.). Citizen review boards for complaints about the police can improve citizen-police relationships and allow community residents to feel more secure. These examples represent social action programs to increase the various types of supplies.

Interpersonal action programs operate by changing or enlisting individuals who have a significant impact in the community. These programs primarily entail education and consultation (see below). For example, the mental health professional can consult with a police captain or school principal, stimulating a policy change that affects all policemen in the precinct or all teachers in the school. The individual policemen and teachers each have important contact with many community residents. A simple order, such as for police to disperse or ignore groups of adolescents on street corners, can dramatically affect police-community relations, street violence and fear, shopping patterns and the ecomony of the area. Thus, by consulting with a key person, in the community, the mental health worker can reduce conflict or improve conditions for hundreds or thousands of people. One successful intervention can affect more people than a psychotherapist in private practice in an entire career.

Zax and Cowen (1976) describe two types of secondary prevention programs: a longitudinal approach, which concentrates on children who are at risk, and early intervention for adults with incipient or beginning disorders. Child-oriented programs are a hallmark of the CMH approach. There are several reasons for this emphasis. Many adult dysfunctions begin in childhood (Kessler & Albee, 1975). It is almost an axiom in the mental health community that family and school experiences are critical in determining the child's psychological well-being. Children are generally more malleable than adults and their problems are less well-established, making them more responsive to treatment. Because of their dependence on adults, it is easier to control their experience and involve them in programs. Also, schools provide an excellent setting for programs because large groups of children are available. Thus, childhood is the most logical time to intervene.

Bolman (1967) suggests fifteen types of preventive programs for children. His recommendations, which encompass primary, secondary, and tertiary preventive efforts, are presented in Table 9.1. The fourth column of the table, "Approach," refers to three different targets or categories: communitywide, high risk, and milestone. Communitywide programs target all children in a community. High-risk programs are designed for specific children or subgroups of children who are highly likely to develop disturbance. For example, children who lose a parent, whether by death or divorce, generally experience considerable distress and are liable to develop persistent disorders. Children suffering from chronic physical illness and those facing surgery are similarly at risk, as are social isolates and highly aggressive children. Milestones are specific events or developmental stages which are highly stress-producing or difficult to handle, such as beginning school and moving to a new neighborhood.

As stated above, most secondary prevention programs for adults attempt to reduce the disturbance by intervening during the early stages. For example, an individual with a history of recurrent depression or "nervous breakdowns" might receive supportive therapy and be relieved of stress-producing responsiblities at the first signs of a new episode. An important strategy for secondary prevention is *crisis intervention* (see below). Crises are periods of acute distress which can often lead to more chronic disturbance. Several strategies have been devised to minimize that possibility by providing help during the crisis period. One approach is the telephone "hot line," in which someone under acute stress can call and speak with a supportive and understanding person twenty-four hours a day. Many communities have hot lines for suicide prevention, rape victims, abused women, and alcoholics. The term "crisis intervention" also refers to a brief treatment designed to relieve acute problems in a few sessions of psychotherapy.

Secondary prevention programs cover a variety of approaches. At one extreme there is a community focus comparable to primary prevention programs. At the other extreme (e.g., crisis intervention therapy), individual patients are treated; such programs hardly merit the term "prevention." Nevertheless, most secondary programs stress early identification. In contrast to the intensive diagnostic assessments of traditional approaches, secondary prevention requires cost-efficient mass screening procedures which can quickly and easily pick out individuals at risk. As we will note at the conclusion of this chapter, such screening poses major pragmatic and ethical questions (e.g., Can we pry into the lives of people who have not requested any services?).

Tertiary prevention programs are more like rehabilitation than prevention (Cowen, 1973). They are designed primarily to improve the community adjustment of chronic psychiatric patients (e.g., chronic schizophrenics). They are preventive in the sense that they may forestall future acute episodes which require hospitalization. However, targeted individuals have already developed severe disorders and are unlikely to ever make a complete recovery. Tertiary programs include partial hospitalization (see below), in which patients participate in therapeutic activities during the day and return home at night, or work during the day and spend evenings in the hospital. Participants in these programs often live in halfway houses or group homes. These are small, supervised living facilities in the community which supplement the state hospital. Similarly, vocational rehabilitation programs can provide job skills. Whether tertiary approaches are "preventive" or not, they are central to the CMH movement, involving deinstitutionalization, return to the community, and humanistic services for the previously neglected chronic patient.

Epidemiology. One of the major disadvantages of traditional mental health services is that service is not provided on a planned, systematic

Table 9.1. Community-Based Prevention Programs for Children

Population Group	Goals	Type	Approach	Resources Available to Families
1. Prenatal infants	Identification and treatment of maternal diseases, e.g., diabetes, hypertension, kidney disease, anemia, infection, malnutrition, toxemia of pregnancy	Primary	Milestone, high-risk groups	Hospitals, prenatal clinics, traveling clinics Physicians, nurses, social workers, nutritionists, health educators
	Minimizing dangers of irradiation, drugs, german measles, rubella, prematurity, blood incompatibility	Primary	High-risk groups	
	Genetic counseling as a routine part of the premarital examination	Primary	Milestone, high-risk groups	
2. Newborn	Insuring that all children are born with intact faculties	Primary	Communitywide	Hospitals and prenatal clinics
	Reduction in high prenatal and postnatal casualties among deprived groups	Primary	High-risk groups	Physicians, nurses, social workers, nutritionists, health educators
3. Infants and preschool children	Early detection of developmental disturbance from any cause (physical, emotional, and social) and parental counseling on child-rearing concerns	Secondary	Communitywide	Well-Baby-Clinics, hospitals, schools, physicians, nurses, teachers, psychologists, social workers, child development specialists

4. Children born with special problems, e.g., prematurity, blindness, deafness, physical handicaps, mental retardation, brain damage	Recognition of these special hazards to normal development to provide programs which either mitigate the hazards or encourage compensatory skills	Primary, secondary, and tertiary	High-risk groups	Hospitals and clinics, public and private agencies with child welfare functions, parent associations Physicians, nurses, social workers, child development specialists, child psychologists, nursery school educators; rehabilitation specialists; speech and hearing specialists
5. Children exposed to stressful events, e.g., hospitalization, surgery, loss of a parent	Preventing or minimizing damaging responses to these inevitable crises	Primary and secondary	High-risk groups	Hospitals, clinics, schools, and all related personnel e.g., physicians, nurses, teachers, occupational and recreational therapists, ward aides and attendants, social workers, clergy, enforcement personnel
6. Children with chronic illness, e.g., diabetes, heart conditions, orthopedic disabilities, etc.	As above	Primary and secondary	High-risk groups	As above
7. Children exposed to parental deprivation	Preventing or minimizing the physical, intellectual, emotional, and social growth failure often associated with loss of a parent, ex-	Primary, secondary, and tertiary	High-risk groups	Public and private orphanages and child care institutions; adoption and foster placement agencies; hospitals and clinics; schools

Table 9.1. (*Continued*)

Population Group	Goals	Type	Approach	Resources Available to Families
	posure to multiple parents, an inadequate or immature parent, or some institutions			Social workers, child care personnel, physicians, nurses, clinical psychologists, teachers, clergy
8. Children exposed to family disorganization, e.g., separation, divorce, neglect, parental aggression	As in 4 and 5 above	Primary, secondary, and tertiary	High-risk groups	Court, especially family courts; public and private and protective agencies with child welfare and protective functions; hospitals and clinics; schools Judges and lawyers; social workers; marital counselors, clinical psychologists, clergy, especially, pastors, counselors, physicians, nurses, teachers
9. Children in transition between institutional and family settings, e.g., mental institution, training school, foster or group home, etc.	Provision of active support, aftercare, and follow-up during these especially difficult transitions by the institution itself wherever possible	Tertiary	High-risk groups	Child care institutions; residential treatment centers; mental hospitals; training schools and all related personnel, especially social workers, child-care staff, clinical psychologists

306

10. Children exposed to urban or rural poverty which continues from generation to generation	Development of genuine communication and mobility between disadvantaged family groups and the total community to prevent the greatly increased risk of all types of physical, mental, and social disorder	Primary, secondary, and tertiary	High-risk groups	Local, state, and federal government anti-poverty, civil rights, and community action programs; church and church agencies; schools. Citizens, politicians, administrators; urban and regional planners; political scientists, economists, behavioral scientists, clergy; teachers, especially those with knowledge of techniques and programs for reaching culturally deprived children
11. Kindergarten school children	Screening for unrecognized handicaps, developmental disorders, adjustment difficulties upon entrance to school, especially in culturally deprived children	Secondary	Milestone	Schools, greatly expanded "Operation Headstart" type programs Teachers, school psychologists, social workers, nurses; consultative personnel and agencies as needed
12. School children generally	Prompt recognition of children showing maladaptive coping responses to any stress e.g., birth of a sibling, hospitalization, death, etc.	Primary and secondary	High-risk groups	As above

Table 9.1. (*Continued*)

Population Group	Goals	Type	Approach	Resources Available to Families
13. Children failing in school	Prompt recognition, immediate evaluation, and correction	Secondary	High-risk groups	Schools, teachers, counselors, psychologists, social workers
14. School children, especially the 3rd to 12th grade range	Provision of adequate facilities for recreation, group experiences, development of skills, hobbies, interests, values	Primary	Communitywide, high-risk groups	As in 11, above Also, a wide range of private, voluntary and church activities, e.g., Scouts, 4-H groups, special interest clubs, YMCA's, etc.
15. School children	Modification of traditional curricula to include new knowledge or learning, and teaching a causal orientation to human behavior and the social environment	Primary	Communitywide	State and university departments of education; school systems Teachers and consultants as needed

From: Bolman, 1967, pp. 6, 7. Reprinted with permission.

basis. Individual private practitioners are guided by economics rather than need. Thus, the vast majority of professionals are found on the East Coast and in large cities. Similarly, the services offered are selected primarily according to intuition and preference or economics. Thus, vast sections of the country have minimal services available (e.g., rural areas), and other sections have received inappropriate services (e.g., poverty areas). The CMH movement seeks to correct these inequities by determining the nature and extent of mental health needs.

The primary tool for this purpose is *epidemiology*. As discussed further in Chapter 10, epidemiology is the study of the incidence and prevalence of disease (in this case, mental illness or psychological stress). *Incidence* refers to the rate or proportion of occurrence of some dysfunction. A typical incidence question is, "How many lower-class residents of Chicago commit suicide each year?" *Prevalence* is the absolute frequency of a disorder. While incidence refers only to new episodes of a problem, prevalence includes both new episodes and continuing cases. For example, the question "How many schizophrenics live in a ten square block area of downtown Newark?" refers to the prevalence of schizophrenia. "How many people will *develop* schizophrenia in that area this year?" is an incidence question. These two interrelated questions have different implications for CMH programs. For example, prevalence rates can suggest the total need for rehabilitative services, while incidence rates can suggest the need for preventive efforts. Some decayed urban areas contain a high proportion of deinstitutionalized, chronic schizophrenics but a small general population (e.g., families do not live there). These areas may have a high prevalence of schizophrenia but a low incidence, since few new cases develop.

As these examples suggest, epidemiological studies can play an important role in determining the types of disturbances found in a particular area, and thereby indicate how mental health services might best be distributed. The Stirling County and Midtown-Manhattan studies described above are two classic examples of epidemiological research. These studies illustrate the high need for services in the general community and have helped greatly to stimulate the CMH approach.

Epidemiology can also highlight critical factors in the development of disturbance. The extensive literature relating the incidence of mental illness to lower-class environments shows this possiblity. Table 9.2 summarizes various studies on the incidence of mental illness in urban and rural areas and in different socioeconomic groups. As can be seen, lower-class groups show the most dysfunction. However, there appear to

Table 9.2. Comparison of Rates of Different Types of Psychopathology in Lowest and Other than Lowest Social Classes within Rural and Urban Study Sites

| Type of Psychopathology | Study Site | | | | | |
| | Rural | | Urban | | Mixed[a] | |
	Lowest class	Other than lowest class	Lowest class	Other than lowest class	Lowest class	Other than lowest class
	Number of studies in which rate is highest for:					
All	9	4	17	1	2	0
Psychosis	1	5	3	3	2	2
Neurosis	3	3	4	3	0	2
Personality disorder	4	2	5	1	2	0

[a]Data reported for sites that are not predominantly rural or urban with no separation of rural and urban rates.

From: Dohrenwend and Dohrenwend (1974), p. 440. Reprinted with permission.

be greater class differences for personality disorders than for neuroses. More fine-grained analyses may identify more specific factors (e.g., marital conflict, family size, physical illness, level of brutality in the home) associated with various dysfunctions. Preventive and treatment programs could then be instituted. Such empirically based programs tend to be more effective and cost-efficient than programs relying on face validity (i.e., that simply seem to be logical).

Epidemiology holds great promise for improving services, but there are two important limitations. First, epidemiological research places a heavy emphasis on correlational methods. A high correlation does *not* imply or show a causal relationship. Two variables (e.g., poverty and mental illness) might be correlated for several reasons, such as a third common factor. Thus, mental illness may help to produce poverty (rather than vice versa), or both could result from the virulent effects of prejudice. Second, there is little agreement on the classification, diagnosis, or assessment of mental illness. Thus, it is by no means clear who should be classified as disturbed (Kessler & Albee, 1975). It may be that the high prevalence of *diagnosed* dysfunction in lower-class groups reflects the bias and differential values and mores of middle-class diagnosticians rather than poor mental health. Or the symptoms may be temporary responses to environmental stressors, rather than stable disabilities (Bloom, 1977; Dohrenwend & Dohrenwend, 1974). In sum, epidemiology holds great promise, but conclusions must be carefully interpreted.

Consultation. We have indicated that professional mental health personnel could never adequately handle the tremendous need for services using the medical model approach. Also, the shift in emphasis from treatment to prevention requires the professional to engage in very different activities from those in traditional therapy. The CMH movement thus requires a dramatic change in the performance and makeup of mental health workers. In this section, we will discuss a new role for mental health professionals: consultation. In the next section, we will consider new sources of mental health personnel.

Mental health consultation is an educative service in which an expert (the consultant) instructs an individual or agency (the consultee) that provides some mental health related service to the community. The consultee can be another mental health professional, clergy, nurse, police, teacher, community or government leader, industry, and so on. Regardless of the consultee's background or activity, the consultant is enlisted to review the relevant operations and to give information or develop some skill to improve the services provided. In contrast to supervisors (who also provide training), consultants are outsiders who are brought in temporarily and have no authority over consultees. Typically they act as troubleshooters for a limited period of time.

Caplan (1963) defines four types of mental health consultation. *Client-centered case consultation* involves a specific clinical case or set of cases. The consultant may help a clinician formulate a treatment strategy. *Consultee-centered case consultation* is also concerned with particular clinical cases, but the focus is the consultee. An example might be teaching the consultee a clinical skill such as systematic desensitization. *Program-centered administrative consultation* concerns the operation of a program or agency. For example, the staff of a mental health facility may need help in establishing a prevention program for a local school system. *Consultee-centered administrative consultation* focuses on consultee problems in administrative or organizational activity, such as helping an administrator deal with staff more effectively. In each case, the consultant is one step removed from the client or program which ultimately receives service. By improving the performance of front line mental health workers or administrators, the consultant can greatly expand his or her influence, in contrast to the limitations imposed by direct service.

One of the most intriguing and innovative consultation programs was conducted by Bard and Berkowitz (1967) with a group of New York police officers. They determined that police were often called upon in cases of marital conflict. However, the police were ill trained for that task, often aggravated the situation, and often suffered physical injury in the process. To help deal with this problem, Bard and Berkowitz recruited eighteen officers from one precinct and trained them in crisis intervention techniques (especially for marital conflict). They also provided review and consultation after preliminary training was completed. In the next twenty months, not one of the officers sustained an injury, and no complaints were filed against them despite intervention in some 1,400 domestic disputes. In addition, community attitudes toward the police improved. Driscoll, Meyer, and Schanie (1973) later implemented a similar program in Louisville, Kentucky, and also reported quite positive results. Considering the central role police can play in both stimulating and alleviating stress and conflict, such programs provide an excellent example of the use of consultation in CMH efforts.

While consultation has become an important part of CMH programs, the effectiveness of various consultative goals and strategies is uncertain. Reviewing the literature for empirically based consultation programs, Mannino and Shore (1975) found thirty-five studies, of which 69 percent reported some positive effects. However, experimental control and the extent of change varied greatly. It is especially difficult to determine how consultation should be appraised. Its effects can be evaluated in terms of change in the consultee (e.g., increased knowledge) and change in the client or group served (e.g., the consultee now provides better service). Thus far, the only consistent and well- documented effects are improved consultee skills and attitudes (Bloom, 1977).

Nonprofessional Personnel. Consultation can increase the impact of mental health professionals on the community. It also opens up new opportunities in regard to the consultees. One exciting innovation of the CMH movement is the development of new, nonprofessional sources of personnel. To meet the tremendous need for expanded and diversified services, CMH workers have enlisted physicians, clergy, teachers, police, housewives, bartenders, college students, senior citizens, community residents, and even gang leaders. These diverse groups perform a variety of services, including traditional psychotherapy, crisis intervention, tutoring of educationally handicapped children, and organizing community clean-up campaigns.

We have already discussed one example—police training in crisis intervention techniques. Fo and O'Donnell (1974) enlisted community residents to serve as "big brothers and sisters" for adolescents who were having academic and conduct problems in school. These volunteers were trained to provide support, friendship, and positive reinforcement. A variety of programs have been developed to train teachers to manage their classrooms more effectively, thus reducing conflict and improving student education (cf. O'Leary & O'Leary, 1972). Rioch (1967) trained housewives to conduct psychotherapy; they performed about as well as trained professionals. Holzberg, Knapp, and Turner (1967) showed that college students could provide a valuable service as companions to psychiatric patients.

Nonprofessional workers can be divided into four groups. *Caregivers* are individuals such as physicians and clergy who regularly provide mental health related services although they are not really trained for that function. An estimated 80 percent of all people who seek help for psychological problems go to such caregivers rather than mental health professionals. Hence, the value of consulting with them and providing training is obvious. *Urban agents* include the police, teachers, and welfare personnel, the so-called "gatekeepers" and authority figures in our social system. Because of their front line responsibilities for so many important services, these individuals can play a central role in producing or avoiding stress in the community. *Paraprofessionals* are individuals who are trained to provide specific, limited mental health services. Hospital aides, technicians who give tests or conduct structured interviews, tutors, and people trained to provide specialized services (e.g., teach DMR or shopping skills) fall into this category. The fourth group, *indigenous agents,* consists of community residents who perform front line services in the community itself, including organizing citizens councils, following up on the adjustment of ex-patients, identifying problem areas, and facilitating liaison between community groups and government agencies, business groups, and the like.

There are many advantages in using nonprofessionals. Most important, the labor pool is vastly increased. Highly trained professionals have traditionally performed many routine activities for which their extensive backgrounds were unnecessary. In many cases, these functions can be performed by nonprofessionals (e.g., giving tests, gathering family histories), thus freeing the professional's time for more demanding tasks. Nonprofessionals can also perform tasks for which professionals are ill equipped, untrained, or overtrained, such as liaison between community groups and agencies, tutoring and rehabilitative training, and political activity. In many instances, indigenous agents can interact more effectively with their peers than professionals, who are outsiders and often have conflicting values, interpersonal styles, and socioeconomic backgrounds. Also, some programs apparently are therapeutic for the nonprofessional. For example, senior citizen volunteers benefit by being brought out of their homes and given meaningful activities, and children learn more when they tutor their peers or younger students.

These various programs hold great promise, but like all new programs, they are controversial. There are few data on the types of activities nonprofessionals can and cannot perform effectively, the individual characteristics which affect performance, or how training can best be conducted. There is a real danger that these individuals will be recruited simply to perform the menial tasks that professionals prefer to avoid, and that job satisfaction and opportunities for advancement will be severely limited. There is also some question about the adequacy of services provided by minimally trained personnel. In response, Zax and Cowen (1976) argue:

Some are concerned that teachers and physicians, much less police officers and welfare agents, are not well enough trained in mental health to be trusted with fragile human psyches. That argument misses the point. Today's reality is that there are not enough professionals around to meet the need for help. Even if there were, many people still cannot accept the fact that their problems are psychological, or they will not take them to mental health professionals. To say smugly that this state of affairs is "bad" simply denies reality. The mental health professions will use their person-resources best by joining, rather than repressing, reality. That means developing approaches that strengthen the hand of those who inevitably have frontline involvement with emotional distress (p. 500).

Application of CMH

The Community Mental Health Center

In discussing the CMH movement, we pointed out the important role of the Joint Commission on Mental Illness and Health. The Commission was highly critical of existing services and made specific recommendations for drastic changes. Its work culminated in the passage of the Community Mental Health Centers Act on October 31, 1963. Stimulated by President Kennedy, this act supported the recommendations by providing massive federal funding for the development of a new, nation-wide mental health care delivery system. The effects of this act, in terms of both funding and government support of new approaches, are inestimable.

The act specified that a broad range of mental health services be made available to all citizens in the community. The country was divided into *catchment areas,* each of which contained 75,000 to 200,000 persons. Each area was to have one community mental health center. The act provided funds for construction of the centers and for staff salaries. The salary money was to be phased out over four years and replaced by local funding. (Unfortunately, this has been a problem for many centers, especially those in poor communities.)

To qualify for funds, CMH centers had to provide five services: inpatient care, outpatient care, emergency services, partial hospitalization, and consultation and education. The exact nature of these services was not specified; each center was left to determine its own program based on local needs, resources, and prevailing practices. The primary restriction on local control was that no person could be denied services because of inability to pay. Centers were also to involve community residents in planning and review of operations. Finally, the various services were to be integrated, so that no patient was "lost" in moving through the system.

Of the 2,000 community mental health centers projected by the act, about 650 have been developed (of which some 19 percent are directed by psychologists) (Fiester, 1978). Not surprisingly, given community control, no two centers are exactly alike or offer the same form of services. Some catchment areas with previously minimal mental health services constructed new buildings for all five services. Many urban catchment areas already had services and merely expanded their operations. These urban centers are often housed in general medical hospitals or psychiatric institutes. Size and staffing patterns also vary greatly (rural centers still frequently lack sufficient psychiatrists and psychologists). Many centers have a central *base service unit,* which houses administrators and some services, and several *satellite clinics.* The latter are small facilities (often storefronts) located in high-risk areas or areas remote from the base service unit. These mini-clinics typically provide emergency services (e.g., twenty-four-hour walk-in services), referral to other units, and a variety of community-liaison and preventive activities (including providing space for resident groups to meet).

The CMH Centers Act has raised considerable controversy. Undoubtedly it has dramatically expanded the mental health services available throughout the country; 29 percent of mental health contacts occur in CMH centers (Fiester, 1978). This expansion is especially notable in rural and inner-city areas, which previously had been severely neglected. There has also been a substantial shift in the nature of services. The state hospital population declined from nearly 600,000 in 1955 to 216,000 in 1974, despite growth in the general population (Bloom, 1977). Many patients who previously would have been hospitalized are now treated in CMH centers, about 400 of which have partial hospitalization programs (Luber, 1979).

On the other hand, many critics argue that the centers simply provide "old wine in new bottles." Apparently most patients still receive the basic medical model treatments. Inpatient and outpatient services make up the bulk of center activities, and the only change has been in locale, not in format. A recent survey indicated that only about 7 percent of person-hours is spent in community activities (e.g., consultation, prevention) (Bloom, 1977). These findings are not too surprising since most staff members are trained to provide traditional clinical services. Despite these limitations, two services—partial hospitalization and emergency services—do appear to be different and warrant special comment. (These services are not unique to CMH centers, but they are part of their required operations.)

Partial Hospitalization. Partial hospitalization was mandated in the CMH Centers Act in an effort to reduce the need for state hospitalization. Rather than spending twenty-four hours a day in the hosptial, the partial patient lives in the community and reports to the treatment facility for limited periods of time. Comprehensive partial programs include day hospitals, evening hospitals, and weekend hospitals. Patients attend these programs as a function of their treatment needs and living conditions.

Acutely disturbed patients and chronic patients who cannot work or attend school often participate in day programs between 9 A.M. and 4 P.M. They receive a variety of psychotherapeutic services, including individual, group, and family therapies. The authors' program at Western Psychiatric Institute and Clinic emphasizes social skills training in an effort to increase those adaptive interpersonal skills necessary for community living. As in all programs, psychiatric attention (e.g., medication) and medical services are provided as needed. Patients receive up to seven hours of treatment each day and return to family or a community residence in the evening. Thus, they are provided with intensive and extensive treatment without being totally removed from family, friends, and the community. The adverse affects of institutionalization can thus be avoided, and the likelihood of transferring treatment gains to the environment is increased. Inpatient care in the CMH center system is reserved for those patients who cannot care for themselves in the evening or who have no place to live.

Evening and weekend programs are generally for patients who function at a higher level but still need fairly extensive treatment or rehabilitation. Many of these patients work or attend training programs during the day. Often, day hospital patients "graduate" to these programs when their level of functioning improves. Sometimes an inpatient unit and day and evening hospitals operate out of the same facility, sharing staff and providing similar services. Patients shift from one program to another according to their needs at given times.

Partial hospitalization programs have only recently been evaluated. Preliminary results suggest that they are as effective as inpatient programs, with a much lower patient cost per day (Bellack, Turner, &

Hersen, 1977). However, research is needed to determine long-term effects, to identify the most effective program components and format, and to determine the types of patients who can and cannot profit from these partial programs. Some recent data suggest that for many patients, partial hospitalization is simply part of an endless cycle between in-patient care, partial care, no care and degeneration, and reinstitutionalization (Kirk & Therrien, 1975).

Emergency Services. A crisis is a period of acute stress, accompanied by physical disturbance and psychological disorganization and by a decreased ability to cope. Some crises are predictable, such as having a baby, graduating from college, and beginning a new job. Others are unpredictable and often have a more extreme effect, such as death of a parent or spouse, marital disruption, and physical injury. Either type of crisis can have a substantial impact on future adjustment as well as current functioning. Successful resolution can increase the person's ability to cope with stress and resist future crises. Unsuccessful resolution can result in extended dysfunction and decreased future functioning. Most people experience several crises during their lives, making crisis resolution an important public health problem. Caplan (1964) includes crisis avoidance and crisis intervention as a basic part of preventive services.

Crisis intervention encompasses a variety of services designed to minimize disruption and promote adequate resolution. Butcher and Maudal (1976) differentiate between *dispositional* crisis services and *crisis therapy.* The former is primarily a referral service for those who urgently need some community resource, such as health care, legal aid, police protection, or a place to sleep. It is frequently supplied by the storefront and walk-in clinics of CMH centers; the latter are twenty-four-hour services, much like the emergency rooms of general medical hospitals. Quick, appropriate referral in these cases presumably prevents increased distress, illness, and so on.

Crisis therapy involves active treatment for individuals who are unable to cope. It is a form of psychotherapy but differs from traditional approaches in several ways. Crisis therapy is initiated as soon as possible after the request for service, often within twenty-four hours, as it is assumed that the victim is most responsive to help during this acute period. In this regard, treatment lasts for only one to six sessions. The brief nature of the intervention requires different goals and tactics than long-term therapies. Butcher and Koss (1976) have identified three goals of crisis therapy: (1) to remove or relieve the most disabling symptoms as rapidly as possible, (2) to reestablish the precrisis emotional equilibrium as quickly as possible, and (3) to increase the victim's coping ability by increasing his or her understanding of the current disturbance. Crisis therapists are far more active than many traditional therapists. A premium is placed on providing support, empathy, and an opportunity for emotional expression. The therapist also communicates hope and optimism and provides information, advice, and suggestions for resolving the difficulty (Butcher & Maudal, 1976).

Another form of crisis intervention is the telephone hotline (Bloom, 1977). Individuals under acute distress can call well-publicized telephone numbers and talk to someone about their problems. Many hotlines are open twenty-four hours a day. Most are staffed by nonprofessionals who are trained to provide support and encouragement, and to make appropriate referrals to community services and agencies. While some hotlines are open to all callers, others specialize in particular problems, such as suicide, drug abuse, rape, marital conflict and wife abuse, and adolescent concerns about venereal disease or running away from home. Regardless of the problem area, all hotlines strive to provide supportive and accepting help for people experiencing acute distress and with nowhere else to turn.

These various approaches to crisis intervention have been difficult to evaluate. Many clients are seen briefly (or contacted anonymously over the phone) and are unavailable for extended or extensive assessment. Hence, it is difficult to determine the effects of the efforts, let alone compare them with no treatment or other approaches. However, the data now available are generally positive (Bloom, 1977; Butcher & Koss, 1978). Crisis intervention procedures, along with other brief therapies, appear to be as effective as longer-term interventions. They are highly cost-efficient, requiring little professional time and being usable by nonprofessionals. Finally, they are consistent with consumer demands for quick, directive, and pragmatic interventions. They will probably become far more widespread in the future.

A Prototype Prevention Program

During the past twenty years, hundreds of prevention programs have been implemented covering a vast spectrum of services and problems. If one were to include such diverse issues as antipoverty legislation, pollution control, and international arms agreements as preventive mental health, along with all school and educational programs, the list would be endless. Of course, an extensive review of this vast area is impossible. Instead, we will describe one program at length: the Primary Mental Health Project (PMHP) of Rochester, New York. Developed by faculty members at the University of Rochester (primarily Emory L. Cowen and Melvin Zax), the PMHP is especially illustrative, having operated continuously since 1958 and subjected to extensive evaluation.

In developing their program, Cowen and Zax observed that some 30 percent of children have trouble adjusting to school (Zax & Cowen, 1976). Their emotional and educational problems persist, culminating in the transition from elementary to high school. Rather than intervene at that point—when the problems are well established and staff resources insufficient—Cowen and Zax decided to intervene during the early school years.

The first phase of the plan was the early identification of children at risk for later problems. For several years, all children entering first grade in one Rochester public school were evaluated extensively. They were given several tests, observed in school, and evaluated by their teachers. In addition, their parents were interviewed about a variety of topics, ranging from the child's early development to his or her current behavior patterns. Based upon these comprehensive data, each child was classified as *Red-Tag* (i.e., currently having problems or at risk for later disturbance) or *Non-Red-Tag* (i.e., no indication of current problems or potential for future problems). Each child was assessed again in the third and seventh grades. On both occasions (two and six years after the initial "tagging"), Non-Red-Tag children seemed to be performing better in both academic and social-emotional areas (Zax & Cowen, 1976; Zax & Specter, 1974). Thus, the identification process was quite successful.

This initial project also contained a prevention component. Project staff became consultants to school personnel and parents. They provided general information on child development, mental health, and classroom and child management, and specific advice on how to deal with certain problems and troublesome children. An after-school program was also set up to help children with special problems. The effectiveness of this program was assessed by comparing children in the experimental school with children in two control schools with no consultation services. Data collected when the children reached the third grade suggested that those in the experimental school were somewhat better adjusted than children in the control schools. However, when the children were evaluated again in the seventh grade, there were *no* consistent differences favoring the prevention program.

In response to these disappointing results, Zax and Cowen (1967) extended the prevention program, providing many direct services to problem children. To staff this program, they recruited housewifes who had successfully raised their own children. These women received a brief training, with greater emphasis on their "natural reflexes" and desirable personal qualities. Teachers who had problems with specific children alerted the school mental health team. A treatment-educational plan was then developed and implemented by one of the housewife-aides. She would meet with the child up to several times each week, using many tutoring procedures and developing a supportive, therapeutic relationship. Ongoing supervision was provided by the mental health team, and regular feedback was given to (and secured from) the child's teacher.

Evaluations of this program suggest that it was effective. Indeed, several later groups of nonprofessionals were recruited, including college students who staff an after school day-care program (Zax & Specter, 1974). One indication of the program's success has been its widespread acceptance by school personnel, administrators, and community groups. PMHP programs have been established in twenty-five Rochester schools and are now being developed in many other schools around the country (Zax & Cowen, 1976).

In supporting their program, Zax and Cowen (1976) do not suggest that the techniques employed in their project are necessarily the best. Rather, they state:

> PMHP's most important emphases are structural rather than substantive: (1) its focus on young, flexible, modifiable children whose problems are not yet entrenched; (2) its emphasis on systematic *early* detection and screening to locate vulnerable children as soon as possible; (3) its use of nonprofessional help-agents to support early identification with concrete follow-up for large numbers of primary graders who desperately require such help in order to cope with school demands; and (4) changing the role of school mental health professionals in ways that support prompt, geometric expansion of effective help for maladapting primary graders (p. 533).

Critical Evaluation

So far, we have described the CMH movement, emphasizing the thinking of its proponents. In this section, we will evaluate the CMH approach, considering the views of critics within CMH as well as those with other perspectives. The analysis will deal with three questions: (1) Is CMH a mental health activity? (2) Has the CMH approach been effective? and (3) Is the CMH movement really a revolution?

The term *community mental health* contains the words "mental health," but this choice of words is questionable. Traditional approaches to mental health care have attempted to minimize the intrusion of personal values, political philosophy, religious orientation, and the like into treatment. Ethical codes have warned against imposing personal values on patients (cf. Chapter 2). While no treatment can remain totally independent of cultural and moral standards, mental health professionals have attempted to minimize their influence. In contrast, CMH is an explicitly political and value-oriented approach (Hersch, 1972; Paquin, 1977). This is not to say that CMH advocates wish to impose their personal moral codes and religious views on society. But there is a desire to promote a specific life style in which equality and humanitarian values predominate. Few mental health professionals of any orientation would seriously question this value. But most are reluctant to become involved in political and social action to achieve this goal.

In contrast, social action is basic to the CMH approach. Primary prevention, with such goals as eliminating poverty, revising educational practices, and promoting community control, requires social change. The more effective the preventive effort, the greater the change in society. But who asks CMH professionals to work for such changes? Certainly not the social agencies who typically employ them. Ordinarily social change is generated by private citizen groups and elected officials. The dividing line between CMH workers as citizens and mental health professionals is blurred. Should they lead a rent strike or organize a political action group as part of their job, or should it be done after hours in their role as private citizen (Denner & Price, 1973)? Similarly, Hersch (1972) questions whether the CMH worker should run for public office rather than attempt to foster change in the context of mental health. This is not an easy question to answer. No study or logical argument can resolve what is a difference in *belief*, rather than a difference over *fact*.

This issue has important practical implications for the training of mental health professionals. With few exceptions, current training programs do not prepare the professional to engage in politics or to implement social action programs. Many CMH workers have learned this the hard way, when community residents have rejected them and their programs. One of the most classic and tragic examples was a strike and attempted takeover by nonprofessionals at the Lincoln Hospital CMH Center in New York City (Roman, 1973). What had been hailed as a prototype of a CMH center and community control was ultimately shattered by self-interest, jealousy, racial hostility, and naïvté of the professional staff. If mental health professionals are to be prepared for prevention and social action, the training program must be dramatically altered.

The concept of primary prevention has other implications as well. Since everyone is potentially subject to crisis and psychological dysfunction, everyone is a client for the CMH worker. That is, the CMH strategy of mass (social) action is designed to affect all community residents; individual citizens have no choice in the matter (Denner & Price, 1973). This conflicts with most ethical codes, which require clients to provide informed consent prior to treatment. Of course, the government already imposes public health care on all citizens, such as by flouridating community water supplies and requiring certain vaccinations. However, the utility of most mental health prevention programs is entirely uncertain. They have been generated more on the basis of values and face validity than on sound empirical evaluation. In most cases, neither the effects of the programs on the target problems nor the ecological impact is known.

"Effects" refer to changes that the program was designed to produce. For example, deinstitutionalization and partial hospitalization were designed to integrate chronic patients into the community and promote a more normal life adjustment. However, this is rarely the case (Kirk & Therrien, 1975). Most ex-patients are rejected by the community as well as by their families. Many live marginally in rooming houses in rundown urban areas and require periodic rehospitalization. The community mental health center is intended to improve services to the poor and minority group members. However, recent data suggest that these individuals still receive lower-quality services and fare worse than middle-class persons (Sue, 1977). In addition, some programs have potentially harmful effects. Red-tagging children not only intrudes on their privacy but has the danger of stigmatizing them for the remainder of their school careers (Ullmann, 1977). Labeling a child as potentially deviant might create a self-fulfilling prophecy by shaping teachers' expectations and worsening the children's behavior. Furthermore, there is some question about whether or not childhood difficulties do lead to later dysfunction (Clarizio, 1969). While some patterns of early disturbance do seem to be predictive, others are transitory and do not require attention (Zax & Cowen, 1976).

"Ecological" effects refer to the broad impact of an intervention. Consider the liberalization of divorce laws. From a preventive perspective, making divorce easier should have positive effects on both spouses and children, by ending a strained and often hostile relationship. However, critics have questioned the impact of such a change on family structure and the basic fabric of our society. Do liberalized laws stimulate frivolous marriages and frivolous divorces? Do they affect our sense of responsibility and commitment? These questions require empirical analysis, not simply speculation. More importantly, they illustrate the danger of blindly implementing untested prevention programs. The good intentions of CMH advocates notwithstanding, much research is needed before the CMH approach can be safely and confidently applied (Zax & Cowen, 1976).

A final question pertains to the impact of the CMH movement. Has it really been a revolution? Yes and no. It has produced a revolutionary *conception* of mental health, mental health workers, and mental health programs. The movement has also had a decided impact on public policy (e.g., the CMH Centers Act) and views about traditional services and their delivery. On the other hand, the movement has not had a comparable impact on actual mental health practices. Cowen (1973) found that only 2 percent of the literature on CMH actually deals with prevention. Bloom (1977) reported that CMH center staff spend (on the average) no more than seven hours per week in community activities. Most psychiatrists and clinical psychologists still receive little training in the skills required for CMH activities. Finally:

> a continuing deficiency of the community psychology movement has been this [sic] inability to operationalize its rhetoric into specific, programmatic methods for bringing about measurable social change. For the most part, community psychologists are distinguished by the attitudes about how social problems should be conceptualized and not by their development of an effective intervention technology for preventing or treating such problems (Neitzel, Winett, MacDonald, & Davidson, 1977, p. 2).

Only with the development of such technology will the CMH revolution be realized.

Summary

The CMH movement has been described as a "third revolution" in mental health. In this chapter, we have considered what CMH is, how it developed, and typical CMH activities. One of the major factors which stimulated CMH was dissatisfaction with traditional approaches and the medical model on which they were based. Of critical importance was the political climate of the 1960s, which questioned the socioeconomic and racial differences in the nation. Those differences were well represented in mental health service delivery. The CMH movement adopted a public health model in an effort to deal with the tremendous need for services. Primary emphasis was placed on prevention rather than treatment. The major strategy for prevention is social action, broad-based changes in society which facilitate a healthier life. In addition, the CMH approach advocated the use of new sources of personnel and important changes in the activities of mental health professionals (i.e., consultation).

One of the most significant changes of the CMH movement was the passage of the CMH Centers Act, a federal program to develop comprehensive community mental health facilities throughout the country. In addition to making services more available, these centers provide new services, including partial hospitalization and crisis intervention. After these services were described, an example of a comprehensive school-based prevention program was presented.

The final section of the chapter evaluated the CMH movement. One of the major controversies is the intrusion of values into mental health services. This is especially important since little research exists to support the CMH value-oriented changes. Finally, the CMH "revolution" is more of a conceptual change than a change in practice. Traditional forms of service delivery still predominate, and the CMH movement has not developed a techology to challenge them.

CHAPTER TEN

Research Methods and Problems

Modern clinical psychology, an empirical social science, is based firmly on research. Consistent with the Boulder Model of the clinician as a scientist-practitioner, many psychologists today do research that is closely related to their clinical work. This is in sharp contrast to the 1950s and early 1960s, when clinical psychologists divided their practice and research activities, often engaging in research totally unrelated to the needs of their clients and patients.

In the 1970s the number of research areas is impressive. Equally impressive is the range of research possibilities still available. Naturally, the setting in which a clinician is employed often dictates the kind of research that may be done as well as the target population.

In this chapter, we will examine some of the typical research activities of clinical psychologists. Since we are assuming that the student has an understanding of general research principles, we will not discuss basic concepts such as reliability, validity, and independent and dependent variables. (However, less advanced students may wish to refresh their memory; see Hersen, 1980. For more comprehensive analyses of clinical research methodology, the student is referred to Hersen & Barlow [1976] and Kazdin [1980].) Instead, while presenting a cross section of the clinician's research efforts, we will try to highlight the thinking that underlies these endeavors. Research examples will be drawn from the areas of epidemiology, personality, psychopathology, assessment, psychotherapy evaluation, and program evaluation.

Epidemiology

In the epidemiological study, the clinical psychologist attempts to determine the rate of a given disorder (e.g., phobia, depression, obsessive-compulsive disorder, schizophrenia) in a limited population (e.g., town, section of a city, county). In conducting such a study, two types of statistics are important: incidence and prevalence. *Incidence* refers to the rate of *new* cases for a particular disorder at a specific time and place. For example, one might consider the incidence of depression for divorced persons following Christmas and New Year holidays in Chicago. *Prevalence,* on the other hand, refers to the percentage of the population that has the disorder at the time of study. Thus, the prevalence statistic consists of both old and new cases. If, in a population of 1,000, 25 are classified as depressed, then the prevalence of depression for that population is 2.5 percent.

At this point, the student may wonder why epidemiological knowledge is necessary. We feel it is invaluable for determining assessment, patterns of psychopathology, and the response to and need for treatment.

Epidemiological research is expensive, tedious, and time consuming. For these reasons, the results of such studies are generally based on a small segment of the population—a representative sample. However, in selecting a representative sample, which probability method will be used? If the target population is assumed to be relatively homogeneous, then a large enough random sample is appropriate. But if it is not homogeneous (e.g., Hollingshead & Redlich, 1958), then a stratified sample, including a random portion of each social class (or age range, or any other relevant variable), is more appropriate.

Aside from determining the sample, the clinician may find that the persons contacted may not be compliant. In the random selection procedure, individuals or households contacted have no warning that a study is in progress. Thus, depending on a combination of factors (cooperation of the targeted population, understanding of the project), a proportion of the sample will simply not participate. Of course, if this percentage is small, the resulting data will still be representative. But if the percentage is too large, then the resulting data may be misleading. In the epidemiological study by Agras, Sylvester, and Oliveau (1969) on common fears and phobias in Burlington, Vermont, 94 percent of the sample originally contacted (i.e., 1/193 of the total number of households in that city) was successfully interviewed.

To interview members of these households, separate survey schedules, based on existing fear inventories, were developed for adults and children. For the adults, a schedule consisting of "thirty commonly feared situations" was used. In addition, the intensity and duration of the fears were questioned, as well as the respondent's attempts to secure treatment. For children under fourteen years of age, a responsible adult from the household was asked to respond to a twenty-one-item schedule. Responses to the interview schedules were independently coded and rated by two judges. A supervisory interviewer resolved any discrepancies found between the judges.

To differentiate phobia from fear, responses to the interview were

Table 10.1. Prevalence and Standard Errors of Prevalence of Common Fears, Intense Fears, and Phobia: Comparison of Clinical Series of Phobic Patients

Common Fears/1000		Populat'n	SE	Intense Fears/1000		Populat'n	SE
Snakes	390	(M 199	40)	Snakes	253	(M 118	34)
		(F 547	50)			(F 376	48)
Heights	307	(M 278	43)	Heights	120	(M 109	33)
		(F 333	47)			(F 128	36)
Storms	211	(M 95	31)	Flying	109	(M 70	26)
		(F 311	47)			(F 144	38)
Flying	198	(M 105	32)	Enclosures	50	(M 32	18)
		(F 274	42)			(F 63	25)
Dentist	198	(M 174	38)	Illness	33	(M 31	18)
		(F 215	42)			(F 35	19)
Injury	182	(M 185	39)	Death	33	(M 46	21)
		(F 179	38)			(F 21	15)
Illness	165	(M 122	35)	Injury	23	(M 24	15)
		(F 203	40)			(F 22	15)
Death	161	(M 129	36)	Storms	31	(M 9	9)
		(F 184	39)			(F 48	22)
Enclosures	122	(M 99	32)	Dentists	24	(M 22	15)
		(F 140	37)			(F 26	16)
Journeys alone	74	(M 67	26)	Journeys alone	16	(M 0	0)
		(F 101	32)			(F 31	18)
Being alone	44	(M 17	13)	Being alone	10	(M 5	7)
		(F 64	25)			(F 13	11)

From: Agras et al. (1969), Table 1.

evaluated by the study psychiatrists. Subjects designated as phobic were then interviewed by a second psychiatrist. Only those classified as phobic by both psychiatrists were labeled phobic in the final analysis. Diagnoses were based on the severity of the fear and its history and treatment, using criteria stated in the DSM.

Results of the study concerning overall prevalence appear in Table 10.1. They indicate that as the degree of fear changes from mild to intense to phobic reaction, the more common fears (e.g., snakes, height) decrease, whereas fears of injury, illness, and agoraphobia increase substantially. Based on these data, prevalence of phobia was considered to be 76.9 per 1000 (7.69 percent). Of this percentage, 0.22 percent were "severely disabling" and 7.47 percent were only "mildly disabling."

Agras et al. (1969) conclude the following with respect to treatment:

Phobia/1000 Population (Including % of total)					SE	Clinical Phobic Series (% of series; n = 50)			SE
						Agoraphobia	50%	(M	22)
Illness								(F	28)
Injury	42%	31	(M	22	15)	Injury			
			(F	39	20)	Illness	34%	(M	10)
Storms	18%	13	(M	0	0)			(F	24)
			(F	24	15)	Death			
Animal	14%	11	(M	6	8)	Crowds	8%	(M	4)
			(F	18	13)			(F	4)
Agoraphobia	8%	6	(M	7	8)	Animal	4%	(M	0)
			(F	6	8)			(F	4)
Death	7%	5	(M	4	6)	Heights	2%	(M	0)
			(F	6	8)			(F	2)
Crowds	5%	4	(M	2	5)	Darkness	2%	(M	0)
			(F	6	7)			(F	2)
Heights	5%	4	(M	7	9)				
			(F	0	0)				

From the responses to questions concerning treatment, it is estimated that 57/1000 individuals have seen a physician about a severe fear or phobia of a medical procedure such as injection or blood test, so that he could minimize their fearful response in their treatment of them. Less common (9/1000) are those who have received active treatment for a phobia which was severely incapacitating at the time of treatment. Some 6/1000 had received inpatient treatment, about half in a medical ward and half in a psychiatric ward while 3/1000 had received outpatient psychiatric treatment. Finally, a very few persons (1/1000) are estimated to be presently receiving psychiatric treatment for a phobia. . . . (p. 154).

The Agras et al. (1969) study is typical of the epidemiological study on psychiatric disorder. Given the clear definition of fearful behavior as a psychiatric entity, the reliability of the psychiatric judgments in this study is less questionable than it might be for some other psychiatric disablity (e.g., borderline personality, schizo-affective schizophrenia). However, in generalizing the results of one epidemiological study, the question always arises: How well do the data represent the population at large? Although the authors do argue that Burlington, Vermont, provides "a population reasonably representative of the smaller and medium-sized city" (Agras et al., 1969, p. 151), obviously caution is needed in generalizing such results to a city as large as New York. Indeed, prevalence rates for phobia in the Midtown Manhattan Study (Langer & Michael, 1963) were 260/1000. However, prevalence for phobia in Hollingshead and Redlich's (1958) epidemiological study in New Haven (another medium-sized city housing a major university) was only 0.5/1000. Of course, the different criteria used in each of the studies makes it difficult to compare them.

The data for the Agras et al. (1969) study were gathered in 1965. Of some thirty individuals then identified as having phobic fears, twenty-nine were reevaluated in 1966, twenty-nine in 1968, and twenty-seven in 1970 (Agras, Chapin, & Oliveau, 1972). None of the thirty had received treatment during this five-year period, thus permitting Agras et al. (1972) to evaluate the natural progression of the disorder. The results showed that children's phobias improved rapidly, with all children either fully recovered or significantly improved after five years. The results for adults, however, suggested a much slower natural remission rate; 43 percent had fully recovered or were much improved, 20 percent were unchanged, and 30 percent had actually worsened over time. "Severity of the phobia was not predictive of outcome; however degree of generalization of the phobia and fearfulness, were. High generalization and fearfulness were associated with poor outcome" (Agras et al., 1972, p. 315). This study has implications for the treatment of phobic children. Prolonged treatment for such children may not be needed. Brief, target-oriented treatment may be preferable, particularly given the rate of natural improvement seen in the absence of treatment.

Personality

As the above discussion indicates, an epidemiological study, although difficult, is fairly straightforward. However, the clinical psychologist who wishes to study personality is often confused by the many conflicting theories as to how such research should be conducted. These diverse points of view have been clearly articulated in Mischel's (1977) paper "On the Future of Personality Measurement." These issues are largely related to how, and under what conditions, assessment takes place (see discussions in Chapters 4 and 5 of direct and indirect measurement). Thus, it is obvious that the psychologist's theoretical position of human nature will dictate the assessment approach.

Norm-Centered Approach

Let us first consider the traditional approach to the study of personality. Often referred to as a *trait approach,* it has been called by Mischel (1977) "norm centered":

> Traditionally, most attention in personality measurement has been devoted to comparing differences *between* people on some norm or standard or dimension selected by the assessor. Such a norm-centered approach compares people against each other, usually on a trait or attribution continuum—for example, amount of introversion-extroversion. The results can help with gross screening decisions, can permit group comparisons, and can answer many research questions (pp. 247–248).

There are many dimensions (i.e., traits) on which individuals may be contrasted; indeed, the number is limited only by the assessor's imagination. In addition to introversion-extroversion are such traits as assertiveness (Eisler, Miller, & Hersen, 1973), sensation seeking (Zuckerman, Bone, Neary, Mangelsdorff, & Brustman, 1972), social desirability

(Crowne & Marlow, 1964), locus of control (Rotter, 1975), and Type A– Type B behaviors (Glass, 1977). Whatever the trait, individuals high and low on that trait (assessed primarily on the basis of their self-reports) in the typical personality study are contrasted in terms of their overt behavior on a given task (e.g., performance on a test under frustrating and nonfrustrating conditions). To accentuate differences between highs and lows, those in the top and bottom 25 percent of the scale are often selected as contrasting groups.

When doing trait-oriented personality research, the clinical psychologist uses many hypotheses as to how individuals high and low on a given trait will behave. These hypotheses are translated into experimental questions that contrast the highs and lows. When the evidence favors the experimenter's hypotheses, then the construct validity for that trait as a personality factor is enhanced. Of course, as the experiment progresses, the limitations of the trait in predicting behavior will become more apparent.

Let us now consider an experiment on the norm-centered approach to personality. The study was concerned with Type A and Type B behavior patterns. As noted by the investigators (Carver & Glass, 1978), "Pattern A is often characterized in terms of three components: competitive achievement striving, time urgency, and aggressiveness" (p. 361). By contrast, Pattern B behavior is characterized by the relative absence of such strivings. This difference is important since Pattern A individuals appear significantly more prone to coronary heart disease (e.g., Jenkins, Rosenman, & Zyzanski, 1974).

The investigation was designed to evaluate the level of aggression for Type A and Type B individuals under instigation and no-instigation conditions. College undergraduates were selected if they scored in the top or bottom third of the pretest on the Jenkins Activity Survey (Glass, 1977). In the two conditions, subjects (As and Bs) appeared for the study and were informed that they would serve as teachers in a learning experiment. Shortly afterward, a second subject (the experimenter's confederate) appeared. The experimenter then escorted the first subject to a different room and showed him how to present problems and record the responses to a puzzlelike task. The subject was told to flash a light for each correct response and push one of ten buttons (each delivering an increasing electric shock) for each incorrect response made. The amount of shock administered was left to the subject's discretion. Subjects in the no-instigation groups were then returned to the experimental room and the experiment proper began, with electrodes attached to the confederate's finger.

In the instigation condition, the experimenter noted that the purpose of the study was to determine how the subject's learning of a concept (i.e., puzzle task) would influence his ability to teach the second subject (i.e., the confederate). After the experimenter left the room, the confederate made some denigrating remarks about the subject's performance during his demonstration. In fact, the subject was purposely frustrated in that he was unable to complete the task in the three minutes allotted. Subsequently, the experimenter returned and escorted the subject and confederate to the experimental room to begin the experiment proper, with electrodes attached to the confederate's finger. Again, the shock level administered was left to the subject's discretion.

During the experimental task, the confederate's responses had been preprogramed so that subjects in both experimental conditions were expected to deliver shock on thirty-five of the trials. The level of shock administered (the dependent measure in this study) was recorded unobtrusively by the experimenter. To recapitulate, half of the Type As were assigned to no-instigation and instigation groups; the same was true of the Type Bs. This yielded a 2 x 2 analysis of variance design.

As might be expected, the level of shock was higher for instigation than no-instigation conditions when the A–B dimension was collapsed. Also, there were no significant differences in shock levels for Bs between no-instigation and instigation conditions. However, differences approached statistical significance ($p < .08$) between As and Bs in the instigation condition, with As delivering higher shocks. On the basis of these results, Carver and Glass (1978) concluded the following: "These shock-intensity results tend to support our predictions. Type A subjects responded to the threat that was implicit in the instigation procedure with aggression directed toward the instigator. Type B subjects did not react with comparable aggressiveness" (p. 363).

In spite of the nearly significant differences between As and Bs in the instigation condition, a closer examination indicates that there is a confounding factor. Not only was instigation present (the confederate's denigrating remarks) but frustration as well: the subject was not expected to complete the puzzlelike task within the three minute time limit. Therefore, Carver and Glass conducted a partial replication of the study, separating the frustrating element from the instigation procedure. Thus, a 2 x 3 analysis of variance design resulted, with one-third of the As and one-third of the Bs each being exposed to a control, frustration only, and instigation conditions. In this second study, the results indicated that "The simple frustration of being confronted with a task whose challenge could not be met yielded nearly as much aggression among Type A individuals as did the full instigation procedure. In contrast, the frustration manipulation had no effect among Type Bs" (Carver & Glass, 1978, p. 365). In short, this study supports the notion that when striving to achieve, Type As are much more likely than Type Bs to show aggression, particularly when frustrated by the task or criticized for their poor performance. However, even though the data generally support the experimenters' hypotheses concerning A–B differences, the experimental condition is only an analogue to the real world. Whether As and Bs respond similarly in their natural environments is still quite speculative.

Person-Centered Approach

Mischel (1977) has made a distinction between the norm-centered and person-centered approach to personality. The Carver and Glass (1978) study represents the norm-centered variety. By contrast, "With a person-centered focus, one tries to describe the particular individual in relation to the particular psychological conditions of his life . . . some especially interesting recent developments in personality measurement have been of the type arising from clinical work with troubled individuals in the real-life setting in which the behaviors of interest unfold naturally . . ." (Mischel, 1977, p. 248). In this latter approach, the interaction between the person and the environment is of specific interest. Indeed, the setting chosen by the individual and the amount of time spent in it may reflect his or her personality style.

Personality style and environmental choices were evaluated by Eddy and Sinnett (1973) in a very interesting study. Forty-six emotionally disturbed college students (with varying psychiatric diagnoses) were evaluated by senior mental health professionals (one psychiatrist, one clinical psychologist, one counseling psychologist) on an action-oriented scale (action-oriented to inhibited dimensions). Each subject was also given the MMPI. Finally, daily activity records (filled out by subjects) were obtained three times during each semester (beginning, middle, end) for a weekday and weekend day. In total, six activity records per semester were obtained for six semesters for the forty-six subjects. All of these data were then factor analyzed (see Comrey, 1978, for a description of factor analysis).

From the statistical analyses, four major factors emerged. The first factor was labeled "action orientation" and cuts across the three methods of measurement (clinical ratings, MMPI, and activity records). This factor confirms the experimental hypotheses that students rated as action-oriented are expressive rather than introverted and make extensive use of public and social settings. The second factor was called "ego-strength-neuroticism" and appears to reflect the students' general emotional distress. The third factor was labeled "action-oriented out of living setting" and reflects students' unconventional use of the school's dormitory and socialization areas. Given the unusually high proportion of schizophrenic diagnoses in this student sample, this third factor, not suprisingly, represents the students' "suspiciousness" of co-residents and a preference for spending time in dormitory settings other than their own. Finally, the fourth factor, "sex differences," relates to the proportion of time spent in settings as a function of being male or female. "Females spend more time in other people's rooms (weekday and weekend), shopping (weekend), and in the bathroom (weekday and weekend). Males spend more time in the lounge on weekdays" (Eddy & Sinnett, 1973, p. 214).

To summarize, the Eddy and Sinnett study suggests that predictions about personality *may* be derived from how special settings are used. Conversely, use of social settings may have some predictive validity about personality types. However, the level of accuracy in making such predictions still is an open question. Unless measurement procedures are highly refined, such prediction would undoubtedly lead to extensive misclassification (i.e., false positives and false negatives). Thus, to enhance predictive validity, there would have to be much cross-validation in many settings with many different personality types. Nonetheless, despite the relative newness of this approach, the results are encouraging and should stimulate additional research in this direction.

Psychopathology

A prime area of interest for the clinical psychologist is psychopathology. Depending on the definition, psychopathology may include maladaptive behavior ranging from etiology to diagnosis to treatment (cf. Millon, 1969). Moreover, at times, the study of psychopathology also involves the examination of experimentally induced abnormal behavior in animals (cf. Kimmel, 1971). By artifically creating an "experimental neurosis," for example, the psychopathologist develops a possible analogue to human neurosis. Needless to say, such experiments with humans would be impossible for obvious ethical reasons.

In discussing research methods in psychopathology, Millon and Diesenhaus (1972) state:

> The primary objective of research in psychopathology is the discovery of new and verifiable data about maladaptive behavior. No less important is its role in disproving erroneous past findings or refining and elaborating already established relationships. The ease with which so many theoretical ideas in psychopathology have been proved wrong is most disheartening. . . . Although fruitful research depends on the ingenuity of the investigator, his intuition must eventually be tested by rigors of proper scientific methodologies (p. 1).

As one might surmise, the field of psychopathology is vast, the writings are numerous, and the theories and strategies for evaluating human abnormal behavior are diverse and complex. Indeed, the distinction between normal and abnormal behavior, as well as the definitions of abnormality, have been the subject of many scholarly endeavors (e.g., Costello, 1970).

Despite this formidable picture, several experimental designs for assessing abnormal behavior are routinely used by clinical psychologists. In the simplest of these designs, the experimenter compares the behavior (whether written or verbal, motor or physiological) of a clearly designated abnormal group with a "normal" control group (e.g., Saccuzzo & Miller, 1977). However, this strategy has recently been strongly criticized:

> Numerous studies of various psychological functions in schizophrenic subjects have compared the latter mainly with normal controls. Although this may have some value at a certain stage of investigation, it is ultimately of limited value if one is interested in demonstrating particular patterns of responses or thought in a given clinical disorder. What the investigator is actually trying to discover or demonstrate are response patterns that characterize a pathological group. Whether these patterns are distinctive of the particular type of pathology in question can only be demonstrated if the performance of the pathological group is compared with other pathological groups of comparable severity. In this particular instance, other psychotic groups would appear to be the most adequate control groups (Garfield, 1978, p. 600).

A clear example of this latter approach is a study by Oltmanns (1978) comparing selective attention in schizophrenics and manic- depressives. Still another approach is to compare the differences among subtypes of a given diagnostic class (e.g., long-term versus short-term institutionalization; neurologically normal versus neurologically impaired).

In this section, we will examine these three experimental strategies—abnormal versus normal; abnormal versus other abnormal; subtypes within abnormal groups—with illustrations derived from recent papers published in the *Journal of Abnormal Psychology.*[1] We will consider the experimenter's rationale for choice of design and selection of subject population. We will also look at the homogeneity of the population selected for study, the reliability of the diagnostic appraisal, and the appropriateness of the control group used.

Abnormal versus Normal

Hundreds of studies have compared the ability of schizophrenics and normals to perceive and process information. Recently such a study was conducted by Saccuzzo and Miller (1977). They compared ten schizophrenics with delusional symptoms (eight paranoids, two schizo- affectives) who were residing in a halfway house with ten normal college students. Attempts were made to match subjects on WAIS Vocabulary, age, and education. Seven of the ten schizophrenics were receiving phenothiazine medication, while three had ceased taking medication three months before the study. All of the schizophrenics had been hospitalized less than two years before being placed in the halfway facility.

On the experimental task, the letters T and A were presented for six milliseconds on Field 1 of a tachistoscope. A masking stimulus of letters X presented side by side appeared in Field 2 so that, visually, they were superimposed on Field 1; this made indentification of the T or A quite difficult. The masking stimulus was also presented for six milliseconds. The interval between presentations (T or A and the masking stimuli) was gradually increased from zero in two millisecond steps until each subject was able to identify the A or T on six consecutive occasions. This is known as the *critical interstimulus interval*. At that point, the trials were completed. To account for possible daily fluctuations in perceptual ability, the experiment was repeated four times; the mean critical inter-

---

1. This journal specializes in studies that evaluate psychopathological behavior.

stimulus interval for the four presentations formed part of the data analysis.

The analysis indicated a significantly larger critical interstimulus interval for schizophrenics. Saccuzzo and Miller (1977) interpret their findings as follows:

> Results thus demonstrate more visual masking for schizophrenics with delusional symptoms than for a comparable group of nonpatients. This finding . . . adds support to the conclusion . . . that schizophrenics, or at least certain subgroups of schizophrenics, can be characterized by an information-processing deficit prior to the higher cortical processes. Results are also consistent with the hypothesis of slowness of processing in schizophrenics (p. 264).

Given Garfield's (1978) criticism of contrast studies on abnormals and normals, we think Saccuzzo and Miller's conclusions should be tempered. When contrasted to normals on most dimensions, schizophrenics yield significant differences on a greater than chance basis. Moreover, in the study in question, is the increased critical interstimulus interval solely a feature of schizophrenia? Or is it also a feature of other diagnostic groups (e.g., depressives, other subtypes of schizophrenia, manic-depressives)?

In addition, there are certain problems with the diagnosis of the schizophrenic subjects. Although they were so diagnosed, no confirming test data were reported. Given the general unreliability of psychiatric diagnosis, the subject selection procedure may be problematic. Moreover, the schizophrenic group used in the study was not homogeneous, either in terms of receiving medication or with respect to subcategories (both paranoids and schizo-affectives were included). This further limits the confidence one may attribute to the authors' conclusions. Also, comparing schizophrenics with a college sample spuriously heightens the difference between the two groups, certainly with respect to the motivation to perform well. Perhaps a better "normal" control group would be a sample of psychiatric attendants, so that demographic and motivational differences between the two groups presumably would be decreased.[2]

---

2. We acknowledge the difficulties in doing methodologically sound research with difficult clinical populations. However, our criticism of Saccuzzo and Miller (1977) is designed to clarify the issues involved in contrasting clinical and normal control conditions. Again, this is not to say that conclusions based on this study are worthless. We intend only to emphasize the limitations of conclusions that may be reached on the basis on any one investigation.

Abnormal versus Abnormal

Oltmanns (1978) compared two clinical groups of patients—hospital-ized schizophrenics and manic-depressives—with normals recruited from hospital staff and a volunteer fire department. Schizophrenics and manics were selected on the basis of Research Diagnostic Criteria, a structured interview (Schedule for Affective Disorder and Schizophre-nia), and patient responses to an abbreviated form of the MMPI. Attempts were made to match the three groups of subjects on relevant demographic data.

The primary objective of this study was to evaluate the effects of distracting stimuli on the information-processing (i.e., recall) ability of the three groups. A set of *neutral* and *distractor* digit span and word span tests was given. Distraction consisted of a male voice reading irrelevant digits or words in alternation with a female voice reading digits or words that the subject was expected to recall. In addition to neutral (normal presentations without distraction) and distractor pre-sentation of items, speed of presentation varied.

The results indicated that regardless of the speed of presentation, schizophrenics and manics made significantly more errors than normals. However, normals, unlike schizophrenics and manics, improved their performance when rate of presentation was slowed. Generally the schizo-phrenics and manics performed rather similarly. Since both schizophre-nics and manics appeared to exhibit thinking disorders, Oltmanns (1978) concluded: "Problems in retentive attention seem to be more closely related to thought disorder than to diagnostic categories" (p. 212).

The Oltmanns (1978) study clearly reflects the advantage of com-paring two abnormal groups—rather than one—to a normal control. If Oltmanns had only compared schizophrenics to normals, he might have erroneously concluded that differences were due to the schizophrenia per se. However, since schizophrenics and manics performed similarly in this study, such a conclusion is obviously unwarranted.

As for other methodological issues in this study, diagnostic groups were very carefully selected. Also, an appropriate control condition (with matching on relevant variables) was employed.

Subtypes Within Abnormal Groups

An interesting study comparing subtypes within a given abnormal group was conducted by Goldstein and Halperin (1977). The objective was to assess the intellectual (WAIS) and neuropsychological (Halstead-Reitan) test performance of 140 hospitalized schizophrenics. These patients (diagnosed according to Menninger Foundation criteria) were divided on three dimensions: neurologically abnormal versus neurologically normal; short-term versus long-term hospitalization; paranoid versus nonparanoid. The most careful diagnosis concerned the distinction between neurologically abnormal versus neurologically normal (i.e., neurological evaluation, brain scan, skull films, etc.). Long-term hospitalization was defined as more than one year, short-term hospitalization as less than one year. Paranoid–nonparanoid decisions were based on information found in the patients' medical charts. (This was the least stringent methodological aspect of the study; no empirical test data were available to confirm clinical impressions.)

As might be expected, patients with neurological damage did somewhat more poorly than others. Paranoids performed somewhat better than nonparanoids. Most striking, however, were the differences on the hospitalization dimension. Increased hospitalization appears to have considerably worsened the cognitive and perceptual abilities of these schizophrenic patients. However, Goldstein and Halperin do acknowledge that increased hospitalization may simply be a function of greater pathology exhibited in the first place. Thus, no causal relationship between length of hospitalization and poor intellectual and neuropsychological performance on tests is indicated. Also, long-term patients tended to be older. But when these data were reanalyzed with a correction factor to account for age discrepancies between long- and short-term patients, the results were practically identical.

Assessment

As noted in Chapter 5, some of the most exciting and innovative recent developments in assessment have come from the behavioral camp. However, as also pointed out, in their zeal to be innovative, they overlooked many of the traditional psychometric considerations in psychological testing in their new designs. This criticism is certainly true of some behavioral assessment (cf. Bellack & Hersen, 1977b; Hersen, 1979; Hersen & Bellack, 1977). In response, behavioral clinicians have begun to pay greater attention to the important psychometric considerations when evaluating both their self-report (e.g., Curran, Corriveau, Monti, & Hagerman, in press; Hersen, Bellack, Turner, Williams, Harper, &

Watts, 1979) and motor assessment strategies (e.g., Bellack, Hersen, & Turner, 1978).

In this section, we will examine two studies that reflect the behavioral clinician's renewed interest in more adequate evaluation of their assessment devices. The first is concerned with a self-report of assertiveness, the second with a role-play technique to evaluate social skill.

Self-Report

The Wolpe-Lazarus Assertiveness Scale (WLAS) is a thirty-item inventory originally intended by its authors (Wolpe & Lazarus, 1966) as a quick clinical guide to a client's level of assertiveness. But in spite of this, the scale has had considerable exposure in research studies on assertiveness training. However, as pointed out by Hersen et al. (1979), the psychometric properties of this scale were not known. Therefore, Hersen et al. conducted a basic psychometric evaluation to determine in a psychiatric population: (1) the range of scores for males and females; (2) male-female differences, if any; (3) item-total score correlations; (4) split-half reliability; (5) test-retest reliability; (6) factorial structure of the scale; and (7) external validity (see Chapter 4 for definitions of these terms).

In this study the WLAS was given to 100 male and 157 female psychiatric patients. One week later, 46 of the subjects were asked to take the scale again for purposes of test-retest reliability. Also, to determine the scale's external validity, 114 of the subjects were videotaped while responding to the Behavioral Assertiveness Test-Revised (BAT-R), a series of role-played scenarios that requires the expression of positive and negative assertion (Eisler, Hersen, Miller, & Blanchard, 1975; Hersen, Bellack, & Turner, 1978). Bat-R responses are rated on discrete behaviors (e.g., eye contact, latency of response) as well as on overall assertiveness on a five-point scale.

The results of the study were as follows:

1. Scores for males ranged from 4 to 27, with a mean of 15.92; scores for females ranged from 2 to 28, with a mean of 16.09.

2. There were no significant differences between males and females.

3. Item-total correlations (a measure of the scale's internal consistency) indicated that for males, twenty-six of the thirty items were significantly correlated. For the females, twenty-seven of the thirty items were significantly correlated. Thus, in general, the WLAS appears to be internally consistent.

4. Split-half reliability was 0.845 for males, 0.631 for females, and 0.784 for all subjects combined. These correlations also suggest that the WLAS is internally consistent.

5. Test-retest reliability was 0.564 for males, 0.790 for females, and 0.653 for the total sample. These are moderately high correlations since the subjects tested were psychiatric patients.[3]

6. Factor analysis, conducted separately for males and females, yielded four principal factors for each sex. For males they were labeled: *General Expressiveness, Ability to State Views, Behavior with Unfamiliar Persons,* and *Justifiable Complaints.* For females they were labeled: *General Expressiveness, General Passivity, Behavior with Unfamiliar Persons,* and *Response to Being Wronged.* These results show that males and females shared two common factors.

7. To assess external validity, total scores on the WLAS and overall assertiveness on the BAT-R were correlated. This yielded very low correlations: 0.272 for males, 0.111 for females, and 0.284 for the combined group. Given these low correlations, the external validity of the WLAS was not confirmed. However, when high- and low-scoring subjects on the four major factors were compared with BAT-R responses (particularly the discrete behaviors), somewhat better evidence, although quite moderate, for the external validity of the WLAS was obtained.

Role Play

With the increased influence of behavior therapy on clinical psychology, much attention has been paid to the assessment of clients' motor behavior. This is consistent with the behavioral clinician's reluctance to rely too heavily on the client's verbal report. Where possible, attempts have been made to observe clients and patients in the natural environment (Hersen & Bellack, 1976a). However, either for logistical or ethical reasons, this strategy has not always been possible. Therefore, as a substitute, motor behavior (often rated retrospectively using videotape) in role-playing tasks simulating natural events has become very popular. This is especially true for the measurement of assertiveness and social skill. For obvious reasons, it is very difficult to measure assertion and social skill in the natural environment.

Not surprisingly, many role-playing procedures have been devised by clinical psychologists interested in measuring assertiveness. One is

---

3. From one test session to another, particularly as the time interval between them increases, the performance of psychiatric patients tends to vary. This may be dure to intervening treatment, environmental influences, or general intra-organismic variability.

the Behavioral Assertiveness Test (BAT) and its revision, the Behavioral Assertiveness Test-Revised (BAT-R) (Eisler et al., 1975; Eisler, Miller, & Hersen, 1973; Hersen et al., 1978). (A description of the BAT-R appears in Chapter 5.) Researchers using the BAT-R have shown that subjects judged as being high and low in assertiveness tend to differ significantly on the more discrete components of assertiveness (i.e., smiles, compliance, eye contact). Thus, the BAT-R appears to have internal validity. However, a still more important question concerns its external validity. That is, how does performance on the BAT-R relate to performance in an actual situation requiring assertion? This has been the focus of three recent investigations by the present authors (see Bellack, Hersen, & Lamparski, 1978; Bellack, Hersen, & Turner, 1978, 1979). Let us examine the most recent of them.

In the Bellack et al. (1978) study, twenty-eight psychiatric patients were evaluated in a series of staged incidents on a hospital ward to elicit positive and negative assertiveness. In addition, they were asked to role-play twelve situations (six positive, six negative) and were given a structured interview to ascertain what they thought a person "should say or do" in the situations they had to role-play. For example, a staged incident that required a negative assertive response involved a staff person informing the patient that he was using the wrong lounge (whereas in reality he was not). Six of the role-play scenes used were identical to staged items; the remaining six differed in content but were similar in nature.

Within ten days of their agreement to participate in this study, subjects were exposed to the six staged incidents on the ward (three positive, three negative). Responses to these incidents were rated by the experimenters' confederates. One week later, half the subjects first role-played responses and then were given the structured interview; the other half were given the structured interview first. As Table 10.2 shows, several discrete variables and overall assertiveness were rated for the three tasks: role play, structured interview, naturalistic interaction (i.e., staged incidents).

Correlations across the three tasks were computed for similar and dissimilar items. Of the twelve behaviors correlated between role play and naturalistic interaction, five attained statistical significance. However, the only correlation of any magnitude was latency of response ($r = 0.49$). In general, correlations were a bit higher for similar than dissimilar items. In parallel, the extent of correlation between the structured interview and naturalistic interaction was greater for similar than

Table 10.2.   Correlations Across Three Tasks

| | | Naturalistic Interaction | | |
		Similar Items	Dissimilar Items	Structured Interview
Role Play	Latency	.49^c	.33^a	
	Eye contact	.36^a	.38^a	
	Smiles	.09	.10	
	Praise/appreciation	.27	.15	.26
	Requests	.16	.04	.25
	Compliance	.38*	.18	.43^b
	Overall assertiveness/ Overall effectiveness			.67^c
Structured Interview	Praise/appreciation	.51^b	.20	
	Requests	.62^c	.11	
	Compliance	−.03	−.07	

$^a p < .05$
$^b p < .01$
$^c p < .001$
From: Bellack, Hersen, and Turner (1978), Table 2.

dissimilar items. Indeed, two of the correlations were $r = 0.62$ and 0.51. Also, two of the behaviors (compliance, overall assertiveness/overall effectiveness) correlated between role play and structured interview were significant ($r = 0.43$ and 0.67).

Although there appears to be some consistency across the three tasks, the magnitude of the correlations is not overwhelming. These correlations account for a relatively small amount of the actual variance. Moreover, when only similar items are considered, the relationship between the structured interview and naturalistic observations seems to be greater than between role play and naturalistic observations. Thus, on the basis of this study, the external validity of the role-played task did not receive substantial external support. However, that is not to say that some other role-played task evaluated differently might not yield greater external validity. But in the present study, the results were not encouraging.

Despite these results, role-playing techniques are still important from the psychometric viewpoint. That is, additional attempts should be made to document its validity or develop a totally different form of *in vivo* assessment. Thus, negative or nonsignificant findings do have a role in improving the field of clinical psychology.

Psychotherapy Evaluation

As we saw in Chapters 6, 7, and 8, the field of psychotherapy is vast and complicated. There are many systems of psychotherapy, each with its own variations. Given the immense complexity of the issues in psychotherapy, this research area has attracted many clinical psychologists with different theoretical persuasions (cf. Applebaum, 1977; Frank, Hoehn-Saric, Imber, Liberman, & Stone, 1978; Hersen & Barlow, 1976; Kazdin & Wilson, 1978b).

Over the last three decades, psychotherapy research has flourished. However, the questions asked have changed considerably. One is no longer expected to ask: Does psychotherapy work? This is a useless question since *there is no one psychotherapy;* there are many. Thus, more differentiating kinds of questions are being posed today. For example, is one well-defined psychotherapy more effective than another well-defined psychotherapy for a given class of clients? How does medication enhance a particular psychotherapy? Conversely, how does a specific psychotherapy complement the effects of psychotropic medication (e.g., antidepressants)? What are the active ingredients in a given psychotherapeutic strategy (e.g., systematic desensitization)? What kinds of interchanges take place between therapist and client? Are these interchanges different in short-term psychoanalytic therapy and behavior therapy? Can the controlling effects of therapeutic variables be seen in changes in the client's motor, cognitive, and physiological response systems? If so, how durable are these changes? Also, to enhance durability, are booster treatment sessions needed?

These are just a few of the research questions being tackled today. Given this diversity, many different research designs are being used. They range from observation of the natural course of long-term psychoanalytic psychotherapy (Applebaum, 1977), to the group comparison of different therapeutic strategies (Sloane, Staples, Cristol, Yorkston, & Whipple, 1975b), to the analogue design with college subjects (Lang, Lazovik, & Reynolds, 1965), to the single case experimental design, where the subject serves as his or her own control (Hersen & Barlow, 1976). In this section, we will consider four types of psychotherapy evaluations: (1) a group comparison study with a clinical population, (2) process studies evaluating the nature of therapist-client interactions, (3) a group comparison study with an analogue population, and (4) single case research to determine the controlling effects of psychotherapeutic variables. In reviewing these examples, we will consider the rationale for the study, the kinds of clients treated, the experience level of the therapists, the length of and rationale for the treatment, and the methods used to assess change over time. Despite our critical posture toward each study, we should note that no individual study is ever likely to yield the final answer. Quite the opposite; each study often leads to still other questions, which then require investigation. However, it is expected that over time, as the data from many different studies are compared, general conclusions will be reached.

Group Comparison-Clinical

Consistent with the mood of the late 1960s and early 1970s, Sloane et al. (1975b) asked; Is short-term analytic psychotherapy better than behavior therapy? Patients seeking therapy at the Temple University Department of Psychiatry Outpatient Clinic were randomly assigned to three groups: (1) behavior therapy, (2) psychotherapy, and (3) a four-month waiting list control. Of the ninety-four patients in this study, about two-thirds suffered from anxiety neurosis and one-third from personality disorder. These diagnostic categories were selected for treatment in order to avoid using the mono-symptomatic phobics most often employed in studies on this topic. Instead, a broader spectrum of patients was included, more clearly typifying the individual seen in outpatient psychotherapy clinics.

Depending on the patient's problems, behavior therapy consisted of systematic desensitization, assertiveness training, or avoidance conditioning using electric shock. Patients in the behavior therapy condition were seen individually for four months, with an average of 13.2 sessions. Patients in the psychotherapy condition were also seen individually for four months, with an average of 14.2 sessions. Patients in the control group were informed that they would have to wait four months for an opening in the clinic. However, they were telephoned once every few weeks by a research assistant to determine how they were doing. Also, in the event of an emergency or crisis, they were encouraged to contact the psychiatrist who had initially assessed them.

In contrast to many psychotherapy studies, where the therapists are graduate students, Sloane et al. (1975b) had three highly experienced therapists for each treatment condition (five psychiatrists, one clinical psychologist). Of the three psychotherapists, two were full-fledged analysts while the third was undergoing his training analysis. The behavior therapists were eminent contributors to the field (i.e., Joseph Wolpe,

Arnold Lazarus, Michael Serber). Each of the three therapists for the two treatment conditions saw a minimum of ten patients. Also, it should be noted that unbiased posttherapy evaluations of audiotaped sessions indicated that treatment applied *was consistent* with the therapist's theoretical views.

Each patient was evaluated on a pretreatment, posttreatment, and follow-up basis on several dependent measures. Included were three target symptoms rated on a five-point scale, work and social functioning, global ratings of overall improvement, and personality schedules filled out by the patient.

At the end of the four-month treatment period, both active treatment conditions and the waiting list controls showed improvement on their target symptoms. However, significantly greater improvement was shown by the behavior therapy and psychotherapy groups. There were no significant differences between the behavior therapy and psychotherapy patients. On a pre-post basis, behavior therapy patients showed significant improvements on work and social adjustment. Psychotherapy patients showed some improvement on work adjustment. Waiting list patients showed some improvement on social adjustment. However, when the three groups were contrasted, the differences among them were not significant for either work or social adjustment.

In terms of overall improvement, 93 percent of the behavior therapy patients were described as improved or recovered. This compares with 77 percent for the psychotherapy and waiting list patients. Here statistical significance favored the behavior therapy condition.

At the one year follow-up, the three groups of patients all showed improvement. Behavior therapy patients showed significantly greater improvement on target symptoms than the controls. But there was no such differential improvement when the psychotherapy patients were compared to the controls. However, these data are confounded; control patients were offered psychoanalytically oriented psychotherapy by psychiatric residents after the four-month waiting period. Further, both behavior therapy and psychotherapy patients received additional treatment from their original therapists after this period.

Sloane et al. conclude:

There was very little difference between the two active treatment groups in amount of improvement, although it is tempting to argue that behavior therapy was somewhat more effective than psychotherapy. . . . Our data do not support the view that although behavior therapy may have a short-term or limited value in dealing with specific symptoms, only deeper and more analytic treatment can produce general change in the patient by treating the underlying causes of symptoms as well as the symptoms themselves (pp. 376–377).

Although the original question posed by Sloane et al. (Which therapy is superior?) may not have been answered, the data clearly document that behavior therapy has much to offer as a short-term treatment approach with both neurotic disorders and personality disorders. Of course, this study has been criticized on a number of counts (see Kazdin & Wilson, 1978b). First, it is argued (and rightly so) that there is no such thing as behavior therapy; instead, there are many behavior therapies. Thus, from the Sloane et al. study, it is unclear which behavior therapy may have led to the most improvement for which patients. That is, consistent with the experimental design, many different treatment approaches within the behavior therapy condition contributed to overall improvement. Second, pre-post changes were based on patient, therapist, and judges' ratings of interview behavior. Consistent with a behavioral assessment approach, evaluation of actual behavior (whether role-played or natural) would be required. This kind of assessment unfortunately did not take place in Sloane et al.

In spite of these two criticisms, which further limit the generality of findings in Sloane et al., this study definitely merits commendation. The subjects were real (as opposed to volunteer) patients seeking treatment on their own initiative. The therapists were excellent representatives of their respective theoretical camps. Finally, the control condition involved some therapeutic contact, in addition to promoting a positive expectancy in this group. This represents an attempt to equate for expectancy across the three conditions, thus lessening the possibility of spurious differences between the active treatment groups and the controls. In short, many of the features of a good clinical trial were present in the Sloane et al. investigation.

Process Research

In the process study, the clinical psychologist's primary focus is on the therapist-client interchanges that take place during the treatment hour. Although there is interest in identifying those interactions that facilitate therapy, outcome per se *is not* of central concern. Much of this research is rooted in Carl Rogers' efforts to identify therapist activity that would result in effective counseling and psychotherapy (see Truax & Carkhuff, 1967). Research in the 1950s and 1960s on client-centered therapy suggests that certain therapeutic conditions are important in improving client behavior (e.g., a warm and accepting atmosphere, accurate empathy, unconditional positive regard, therapist self-conguence). (See Chapter 8 for a more complete description of these variables.)

In a typical process study, therapist-client interchanges from selected audiotaped sessions are evaluated on both content (e.g., accepting versus nonaccepting therapist comments) and noncontent measures (e.g., speech pauses) as well as overall judgments (e.g., unconditional positive regard). In some studies, differences in the kinds of interactions are traced from early to middle to later sessions during the full course of therapy. In still other studies, therapists with different levels of experience and training are compared.

Although most process studies are Rogerian, a most interesting example appears in a paper by Staples, Sloane, Whipple, Cristol, and Yorkston (1975) evaluating differences between behavior therapists and psychotherapists. The researchers (1975) evaluated process data taken from the Sloane et al. (1975b) study previously described. Tape recordings of the fifth session for both behavior therapists and psychoanalytically oriented psychotherapists were transcribed, coded, and rated. Twenty-eight behavior therapy and twenty-two psychotherapy sessions were evaluated.

Truax therapist variables (i.e., self-congruence, accurate empathy, depth of interpersonal contact, and unconditional positive regard) were examined by rating four-minute samples from the fifth interview. Correlations between two independent raters for these four scales ranged from 0.58 to 0.74.[4] In addition, degree of therapist control over interactions, nonlexical speech patterns, and speech content were rated.

These analyses indicated that the behavior therapists had greater interpersonal contact, accurate empathy, and therapist self-conguence than the psychotherapists. These findings are contrary to the stereotype of the behavior therapist as being cold and mechanistic in regard to patient care. Behavior therapists were more likely to introduce new topics for discussion, wheras psychotherapists tended to limit discussion

---

4. These inter-rater reliabilities are on the low side. Generally, reliabilities much lower than 0.80 are not considered acceptable. Of course, these reliabilities probably reflect the vagueness and overall quality of the concepts being measured. For more precise measures (e.g., length of speech, pauses), much higher reliabilities are usually obtained.

to more general issues. Behavior therapists were more active and directive in sessions, talking twice as much as psychotherapists. Psychotherapy patients talked about twice as much as their behavioral counterparts. With respect to making interpretations to their patients, surprisingly there were no differences between behavior therapists and psychotherapists.

In summary, the study by Staples et al. (1975) clearly documents the differences between behavior therapists and psychotherapists in their interactions with patients:

> Behavior therapy is not psychotherapy with special "scientific techniques" superimposed on the traditional therapeutic paradigm; rather, the two appear to represent quite different styles of treatment although they share some common elements . . . the behavior therapists were more open and natural, answered the patients' questions about themselves and the treatment, and became more personally involved with the patient and his problem. The psychotherapists tended to maintain a greater psychological distance from their patients, reflected direct quesions, and revealed less of themselves during therapy (Staples et al., 1975, p. 1521).

A fascinating process study was reported in a paper by Truax (1966) entitled "Reinforcement and Nonreinforcement in Rogerian Psychotherapy." Truax evaluated excerpts from a long-term successfully treated case by Carl Rogers. According to Rogerian theory, the counselor is expected to provide a therapeutic atmosphere, offering warmth, openness, genuineness, and empathy regardless of the client's behavior. That is, therapist responses are to be *noncontingent*.

To evaluate whether Rogers really practiced what he preached, Truax looked at nine classes of client behavior (e.g., insight, ambiguity, negative feeling expression) and three categories of therapist responses to these behaviors (i.e., empathy, acceptance, and directiveness). Contrary to his own theory, Rogers seemed to respond differently (i.e., reinforcement versus nonreinforcement) to five of the nine client behaviors. Moreover, furthur analyses over time indicated significant increases in four of the five client behaviors apparently verbally reinforced by Rogers.

Truax concludes that these data are more consistent with an operant interpretation (i.e., Skinnerian) of what takes place in psychotherapy than the interpretation offered by Rogers. That is:

> The present data, by demonstrating the role of empathy and warmth as positive reinforcers, suggest that the available evidence relating levels of

those therapeutic conditions to patient outcome in therapy does not argue against a reinforcement interpretation of psychotherapy. On the contrary, the findings that empathy and warmth act as reinforcers suggest that the evidence relating empathy and warmth to patient outcome is open to a behavioristic interpretation, based in part on the therapist's use of differential reinforcement (Truax, 1966, p. 7).

Group Comparison-Analogue

Many clinical psychologists employed in academic settings often have no clinical populations with which to conduct research. Thus, many of them have used college students or volunteers recruited from the community who exhibit subclinical problems (e.g., fear of snakes). In these research efforts, graduate students in clinical psychology often serve as the therapists. Because of the subclinical nature of the "phobias," therapy is generally brief (i.e., two to ten sessions). Hundreds of these investigations have been done by behaviorists, particularly in evaluating various features of systematic desensitization (cf. Marks, 1975).

Although many of these studies have yielded interesting data and conclusions, the relevance of this research for real clinical problems (e.g., full-fledged phobias) has often been questioned (Bernstein & Paul, 1971; Cooper, Furst, & Bridger, 1969; Hersen, 1979). In a recent paper, Kazdin (1978) has countered some of this criticism:

> The value of analogue research is that it allows analytic and well- controlled research to address questions that often are prohibitive or impractical to evaluate in clinical situations. The major source of controversy about the value of analogue studies is their external validity. Much of the controversy stems from conceptualizing therapy investigation directly as either analogue or clinical research. However, all treatment research is an analogue of the situation to which an investigator wishes to generalize. Thus, the main question is the extent to which an investigation is an analogue of the clinical situation (p. 673).

We fully agree with Kazdin's analysis and certainly see the value of analogue research. However, to convince clinical practitioners, when sufficient analogue data are collected, strategies found effective with subclinical populations need to be documented with a clinical population (cf. Hersen, 1979).

In any event, let us consider the analogue snake phobia studies conducted by Lang, Lazovik, and Reynolds (1965). Snake phobic subjects were randomly assigned to a desensitization condition, a pseudotherapy condition, and a no-treatment control. Subjects were under-graduate college students who had rated their fear of nonpoisonous snakes as "intense" on a fear survey schedule, which was later confirmed by a clinical interview. Subjects were also exposed to an avoidance test in which their approach to a tame blacksnake was measured in the labora-tory. They were then asked to provide a self-rating of anxiety on a "fear thermometer." All of these measures were obtained on a pre-post basis.

Subjects in the desensitization and pseudotherapy conditions in-itially had five presessions of hypnosis and deep muscle relaxation (DMR) in addition to constructing a hierarchy of twenty snake phobic situations. Desensitization subjects then had eleven sessions of standard systematic desensitization therapy carried out under DMR conditions. Sessions lasted about forty-five minutes each and occurred at a rate of one to two per week. After the first five sessions (which were identical for the desensitization subjects), subjects in the pseudotherapy condition also had eleven treatment sessions of about the same duration and frequency. However, in this group, items from the anxiety hierarchy were not the basis for desensitization. Instead, they were used as starting points for conversation, with the therapist in each case steering conver-sation away from the phobic elements. Control subjects only received pre- and post-testing.

Since the results of one statistical analysis showed no differences between the pseudotherapy and no-treatment controls, their data were combined and then compared to those of the desensitization subjects. Desensitization subjects showed significantly greater improvement than the combined control group on the snake phobia item of the fear survey schedule, the behavioral avoidance test, and the fear thermometer. In addition, subjects who underwent successful desensitization showed generalized improvement on the entire fear survey schedule. Finally, most of the difference between the desensitization and control subjects was accounted for by those individuals in desensitization who had successfully completed at least fourteen of the twenty items on the anxiety hierarchy.

In interpreting the results, Lang et al. (1965) concluded that the effects of systematic desensitization could not be attributed to sug-gestion, being in therapy, or merely as a result of the therapist-client relationship (i.e., transference). Change was attributed to the systematic desensitization therapy. Given today's greater sophistication about the validity of analogue research data, this study may be criticized in many ways. First, demand characteristics inherent in the snake phobia laboratory assessment were not evaluated (cf. Bernstein & Neitzel, 1977). Second, no measure of client believability of the treatments, particularly pseudotherapy, was reported. However, Lang et al. do note that none of the subjects reported being in a poor treatment. Third, two of the three authors served as therapists for both of the treatment conditions. Thus, the possibility for bias is considerable despite the authors' claim that none was committed to any specific outcome. But in spite of this criticism, the study remains a landmark in helping launch behavior therapy as a respectable co-equal in the field of psychotherapy.

Single Case Research

Single case research is a totally different approach to evaluating psychotherapeutic procedures (cf. Hersen & Barlow, 1976). Instead of comparing different treatments with control conditions using relatively large groups of subjects, in the single case design the client or patient serves as his own control. That is, baseline performance (i.e., the natural frequency of the targeted behavior) is compared with treatment phases, often in alternating fashion (i.e., the A–B–A–B design). In these designs the baseline is labeled A and the treatment intervention B.

Single case research has proven especially important in evaluating the treatment's control of target behaviors. Indeed, when new treatment strategies are being developed, single case methods are both expedient and efficient. Thus, in testing new hypotheses, it is critical to document the causal relationship of treatment over dependent measures before fully evaluating such therapy in a costly and time-consuming group comparison outcome investigation. Also, the single case approach permits considerable flexibility since preliminary treatment strategies may be altered to fit the individual clinical case. Finally, the single case approach allows for the experimental evaluation of treatment strategies for rare disorders, where there are too few subjects for large-scale outcome research.

There are many variations of single case research designs (see Hersen & Barlow, 1976, for a comprehensive discussion). However, two of the most basic designs, to be described here, are the A–B–A–B and multiple baseline strategies. Let us first consider the A–B–A–B design. During baseline (phase A), the targeted behavior is usually measured three or more times until a stable trend emerges. Then, in phase B, treatment is instituted, and the behavior is again measured repeatedly. If the targeted measure has been designated for an increase (e.g., social responses in a chronic schizophrenic patient) and the results in phase B show that trend, this is considered evidence of the treatment's efficacy. However, to show the controlling effects of treatment, baseline conditions (A) are reinstated in the next phase. If data then return to original or near-original baseline levels, the controlling effects of treatment will be documented. (The second A phase is also referred to as a withdrawal or reversal.) Finally, treatment is reinstated (second B phase) to further confirm the strategy's controlling effects. The A–B–A–B design is suitable for assessing only those treatments that can be implemented and withdrawn in succession (e.g., reinforcement or punishment conditions).

An interesting application of the A–B–A–B design appears in a study by Lombardo and Turner (1979) on the effects of thought stopping on obsessive ruminations in a twenty-six-year-old male schizophrenic patient. The patient was attending a day hospital program and complained of obsessive thoughts concerning "imaginal relationships" with patients he had met during previous hospitalizations. Throughout the experiment, the patient was instructed to time the length of each ruminative episode and to record the date on a prepared sheet of paper. Baseline (A) recording lasted six days, with the modal ruminative episode taking forty minutes (see Figure 10.1). In the next phase (B), thought stopping was begun. The therapist shouted "Stop!" whenever the patient signaled that he had visualized his obsessive image. Many such pairings took place, with transfer of shouting "Stop!" from therapist to patient until the patient was able to pair "Stop" and the image at a subvocal level. On days 18 to 27, baseline (A) conditions (recording alone) were reinstated. Finally, on day 28, thought stopping treatment (B) was reinstated. In addition, the patient was followed up six weeks after treatment.

Figure 10.1 indicates the controlling effects of the treatment. When thought stopping first began, a marked decrease in obsessive ruminations was noted. By contrast, when baseline was reinstated in the third phase, ruminations strongly reappeared. Then, when thought stopping was carried out again, rumination dropped to zero, with the gains maintained during the six week follow-up.

Although this study is a nice example of the A–B–A–B design, all the data come from self-reports. Thus, the patient's compliance with therapeutic demand cannot be discounted as the major reason for the pattern of data recorded. However, in cases where obsessiveness is the

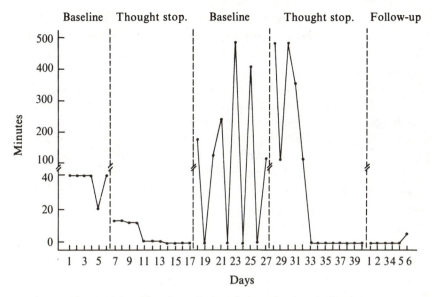

Figure 10.1.   Duration of obsessive rumination during baseline, treatment, and six-week followup. (*From:* Lombardo &
Turner, in press, Fig. 1)

primary symptom, self-reports are mandatory; they are the only record
that can be measured.

Under certain circumstances, the A–B–A–B design is not feasible.
This occurs when there are moral and legal restrictions for removing
treatment in the second A phase. One example of this is a punishment
procedure that helps to reduce self-destructive behavior in retarded
children. Also, if instructions are part of the treatment package, they
cannot be removed, as in the case of reinforcement or punishment. The
multiple baseline design is often used to circumvent these problems. In
this design (across behaviors), three or more independent behaviors are
targeted for treatment.[5] After their initial baseline assessment (A), treatment (B) is applied to the first behavior. If the three targets are truly
independent, treatment should affect only the first behavior. Then, the
same treatment will be applied to the second and third behaviors under
time-lagged conditions. Hersen and Barlow (1976) point out that in the
multiple baseline design across behaviors, "Baseline and subsequent
treatment interventions for each targeted behavior can be conceptual-

5. Multiple baseline strategies can also be conducted across settings and subjects. See Hersen and
Barlow (1976, Chapter 7) for specific examples.

ized as separate A–B designs, with the A phase further extended for each of the succeeding behaviors until the treatment variable is finally applied . . . the effects of the treatment variable are inferred from the untreated behaviors" (pp. 226–227).

Let us now show how the multiple baseline design was used. In this study, social skills treatment was given to an unassertive nineteen-year-old male schizophrenic patient who attended a day hospital treatment program. During baseline, the patient's responses to role-played scenes requiring assertive responses were videotaped. Figure 10.2 shows that eye contact, speech duration, and requests for new behavior were quite low, as were ratings of overall assertiveness. Since requests were low, it follows that compliance was high.

Social skills treatment, consisting of instructions and feedback, was first applied to increase eye contact. Eye contact, as indicated, showed marked improvement when treatment was directly applied. However, no changes in untreated behaviors appeared. Similarly, when treatment was directed to speech duration, improvements were noted but no change in requests was observed. However, when treatment was directed to increasing requests, in addition to improvement in this area, a decrease in compliance was seen. Overall assertiveness, although not treated specifically, tended to increase as each of the specific behaviors came under control. In addition, with the exception of eye contact, where some decrements occurred, behavioral change was maintained at the two, four, six, and eight-week follow-ups.

Thus, improvements occurred only when treatment was directly applied to each of the targets. The exception, was the negative relationship between requests and compliance. As requests increased, compliance decreased. This single case analysis confirms the control of social skills training over targeted behaviors.

Program Evaluation

In the last ten years, more and more clinical psychologists have become involved in what now is termed program evaluation (Perloff, Perloff, & Sussna, 1976; Schulberg & Baker, 1979).[6] This kind of research involves assessing the overall functioning of a given mental health program. However, assessment may vary from an inpatient ward in a mental

6. The first issue of a new journal devoted to program evaluation (*Evaluation and Program Planning*) appeared in January 1978.

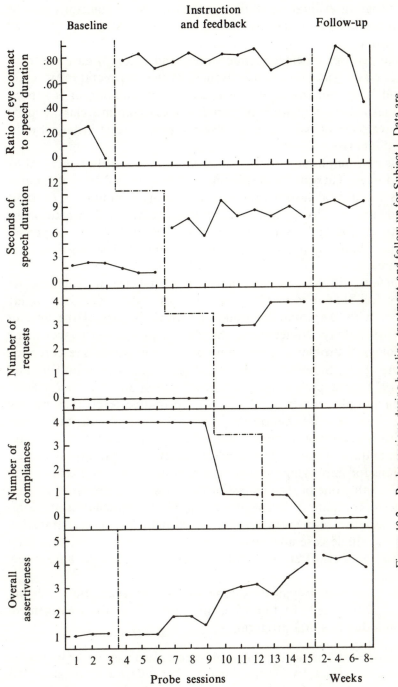

Figure 10.2. Probe sessions during baseline, treatment, and follow-up for Subject 1. Data are presented in blocks of eight scenes. (*From:* Hersen & Bellack, 1976a Fig. 1)

357

health center to the entire center in relation to its catchment area. In the typical program evaluation study, a broad range of questions may be posed, including: (1) type of treatment, number of patients treated, and length of treatment per diagnostic entity; (2) treatment effectiveness as related to age, sex, socioeconomic status, and race; (3) cost per treatment hour and general cost effectiveness of the treatment; (4) whether treatment is offered equally to the catchment population or is applied differentially consistent with the patient's socioeconomic class; and (5) what percentage of patients in a program reach preset criteria by the time of discharge.

This new emphasis on program evaluation is largely motivated by outside forces. There is much pressure from state and federal funding agencies for mental health programs to establish minimal acceptable standards and quality of care. Clearly the mental health practitioners' "claim to infallibility" (Schulberg & Baker, 1979) no longer impresses government bureaucrats, who are much more intent on seeing hard facts and figures.

Whatever the reasons for evaluating mental health programs, we certainly feel that it is in the public interest. Moreover, it is highly consistent with the empirical tradition, which is part of the field of clinical psychology. Nonetheless, the clinical psychologist faces many methodological problems when doing program evaluation research (cf. Schulberg, 1977; Schulberg & Baker, 1979). Indeed, as Schulberg and Baker (1979) note, program evaluation is more of an art than a science. Research in this area is at a somewhat primitive level. It is usually concerned with the evaluation of simultaneous treatments, rarely uses scientifically acceptable experimental designs, and is filled with measurement techniques of unknown reliability and dubious validity. However, suggestions for improving this research have appeared (cf. Perloff et al., 1976). Probably one of the greatest problems is that there are almost no attempts to compare different programs. Thus, the usual group comparison designs are deemed unsuitable. Nonetheless, other strategies, such as the single case and quasi-experimental approaches, have been advocated (cf. Perloff et al., 1976). However, such designs have rarely been used.

Let us consider a typical example of program evaluation research. Bender (1977) raised the following questions about the treatment of clients in a day hospital program:

> How successful are we in helping our clients reach their goals? Is progress related to age, sex, level of education, number of days in the program? It is

difficult to know when a client has gained maximum benefits from day treatment and should be discharged. Are there any trends that could be observed and used as a guide in making this decision? Are there certain problem areas in which our program is less effective than others? What happens to our clients after they leave the program? (p. 2).

To evaluate her program, Bender used an assessment technique known as *goal attainment scaling.* Here the therapist and client identify problems that require modification (e.g., anger, depression, independence, personal appearance, substance abuse, housing). Each problem area is operationally defined and then arranged on a five-point scale "with varying degrees of probable outcome." The most unfavorable outcome is scaled as −2. Zero refers to the *expected* (or desired) level of outcome; the most favorable is scaled as +2. For example, if the problem area is employment, the expected outcome might be part-time employment, the unfavorable outcome unemployment, and the most favorable outcome full-time employment. The raw scores for each scale (ranging from −2 to +2) are then converted to T scores. A T score of 50.00 means that the client reaches his or her expected goal. Scores that exceed 50.00 indicate still further improvement; scores less than 50.00 mean that the expected level was not attained.

Bender reports that mean goal attainment scores at intake (as rated by therapists) for sixty-six day treatment clients was 23.98. At discharge their mean was 47.86, suggesting that expected levels of improvement were almost reached. Progress in the program broken down by age indicated that clients under forty were more successful in achieving goal levels than those over forty. Also, as indicated in Table 10.3, clients with fewer than twenty-three contact days did not do as well as those with twenty-three or more contact days. In addition, Table 10.4 shows that different therapists were not equally successful in helping their clients reach designated goals. Thus, goal attainment scaling may be an interesting method to provide feedback to therapists as to their effects on client functioning (i.e., progress). That is, it indicates how closely goals are approximated and how many of them are actually reached.

Three month follow-up data after discharge from the program for twenty-nine of the sixty-six clients revealed that in fifteen cases goal attainment scores had increased by an average of 11.26 points. By contrast, for fourteen clients such scores decreased by an average of 15.07 points. At the twelve-month follow-up, data on only seven of the original sixty-six clients were obtained. At this point, five had increased scores while two had decreased scores.

Table 10.3.   Contact Days and GAS

Contact Days	Estimated Means
3–12	34.97
13–22	42.40
23–32	49.77
33–42	48.01

From: Bender (1977), Table 3.

Table 10.4.   Therapists as Related to GAS

Therapist	Mean GAS	Number of Clients Terminated
1	54.21	5
2	38.05	9
3	45.96	11
4	43.47	14
5	45.54	15
6	44.13	18
7	48.58	24

From: Bender (1977), Table 5.

Bender (1977) concludes that goal attainment scoring "not only provides a means of empirically measuring progress toward goals, but assists the therapist and client in defining the specific problems the client is going to work on while he is in the program" (p. 8). We cannot argue with this point. However, in Bender's study, and in many other program evaluation studies using goal attainment scaling as the primary dependent measure, there are no attempts to demonstrate the reliability of the measurement system. This is a serious flaw in the methodology. Nonetheless, goal attainment scaling, as currently employed, is superior to mere global impressions of client functioning not anchored in a numerical rating system or operationally defined.

Summary

In this chapter, we have looked at one of the basic commitments of the clinical psychologist—research evaluation—highlighting some of the research areas studied. Although other areas are open to investigation, those we have surveyed are of great interest to the majority of clinical psychologists. Included in this review, with illustrations from each area, were discussions of the following: epidemiology, personality, psychopathology, assessment, psychotherapy evaluation, and program evaluation. In presenting illustrations from the literature, we have often been critical. Also, we have endeavored to clarify the thinking behind some of the research strategies and experimental designs.

References

Abel, G. G. Assessment of sexual deviation in the male. In M. Hersen & A. S. Bellack (Eds.), *Behavioral assessment: A practical handbook.* New York: Pergamon Press, 1976.

Adams, H. E., Doster, J. A., & Calhoun, K. S. A psychological based system of reponse classification. In A. R. Ciminero, K. S. Calhoun, & H. E. Adams (Eds.), *Handbook of behavioral assessment.* New York: John Wiley & Sons, 1977.

Adebimpe, V. A rationale for DSM-III's medical model. *American Psychologist,* 1978, *33,* 853–854.

Adebimpe, V. R., Gigandet, J., & Harris, E. MMPI diagnosis of black psychiatric patients. *American Journal of Psychiatry,* in press.

Adesso, V. J., Euse, F. J., Hanson, R. W., Hendry, D., & Choca, P. Effects of a personal growth group on positive and negative self-references. *Psychotherapy: Theory Research and Practice,* 1974, *11,* 354–355.

Agras, S., Leitenberg, H., & Barlow, D. Social reinforcement in the modification of agoraphobia. *Archives of General Psychiatry,* 1968, *19,* 423–427.

Agras, W. S., Chapin, H. N., & Oliveau, D.C. The natural history of phobia. *Archives of General Psychiatry,* 1972, *26,* 315–317.

Agras, W. S., Sylvester, D., & Oliveau, D. The epidemiology of common fears and phobias. *Comprehensive Psychiatry,* 1969, *10,* 151-156, 191-197.

Albee, G. W. *Mental health manpower trends.* New York: Basic Books, 1959.

Alford, G. S., Blanchard, E. B., & Buckley, T. M. Treatment of hysterical vomiting by modification of social contingencies: A case study. *Journal of Behavior Therapy and Experimental Psychiatry,* 1972, *3,* 209–212.

American Psychiatric Association Task Force Report. *Encounter group and psychiatry.* Washington D.C.: American Psychiatric Association, 1970.

American Psychological Association. Recommended graduate training program in clinical psychology. *American Psychologist,* 1947, *2,* 539–558.

American Psychological Association. Psychology as a profession. *American Psychologist,* 1968, *23,* 195–200.

American Psychological Association. *Standards for educational and psychological tests.* Washington, D.C.: APA, 1974.

American Psychological Association. *Careers in psychology.* Washington, D.C.: APA, 1975.

American Psychological Association. *Ethical standards of psychologists.* Washington, D.C.: APA, 1977. (a)

American Psychological Association. *Casebook on ethnical standards of psychologists.* Washington, D.C.: APA, 1977. (b)

American Psychological Association. *Directory of the American Psychological Association.* Washington, D.C.: APA, 1978. (a)

American Psychological Association. Guidelines for therapy with women. *American Psychologist,* 1978, *33,* 1122–1123. (b)

APA Monitor. Exhibit A: IQ trial. Plaintiffs take the stand. 1977, *8,* 4–5.

APA Monitor. Exhibit B: IQ trial. State witness testifies. 1978, *9,* 15, 18.

Anderson, L. S., Cooper, S., Hassol, L., Klein, D. C., Rosenblum, G., & Bennett, C. C. *Community psychology: A report of the Boston conference on the education of psychologists for community mental health.* Boston: Boston University, 1966.

Andrulis, R. S. *Adult assessment: A source book of tests and measures of human behavior.* Springfield, Ill.: Charles C. Thomas, 1977.

Anthony, E. J. Comparison between individual and group psychotherapy. In H. I. Kaplan & B. J. Sadock (Eds.), *Comprehensive group psychotherapy.* Baltimore: Williams & Wilkins, 1971.

Appelbaum, S. A. *The anatomy of change.* New York: Plenum Press, 1977.

Ascher, L. M., & Clifford, R. E. Behavioral considerations in the treatment of sexual dysfunction. In M. Hersen, R. M. Eisler, & P. M. Miller (Eds.), *Progress in behavior modification* (Vol. 3). New York: Academic Press, 1976.

Ash, P. The reliability of psychiatric diagnoses. *Journal of Abnormal and Social Psychology,* 1949, *44,* 272–276.

Association for Advancement of Behavior Therapy. *Ethical issues for human services.* New York: Author, 1977.

Ayllon, T., & Azrin, N. H. The measurement of reinforcement of behavior psychotics. *Journal of the Experimental Analysis of Behavior,* 1965, *8,* 357–383.

Ayllon, T., & Azrin, N. H. *The token economy: A motivational system for therapy and rehabilitation.* New York: Appleton-Century-Crofts, 1968.

Ayllon, T., & Michael J. The psychiatric nurse as a behavioral engineer. *Journal of the Experimental Analysis of Behavior,* 1959, *2,* 323–334.

Ayllon, T., & Roberts, M. D. Eliminating discipline problems by strengthening academic performance. *Journal of Applied Behavior Analysis,* 1974, *7,* 71–76.

Bandura, A. The ethics and social purposes of behavior modification. Paper presented at the Eighth Annual Meeting of the Association for Advancement of Behavior Therapy, Chicago, November, 1974.

Bandura, A. *Social learning theory.* Englewood Cliffs, N.J.: Prentice-Hall, 1977.

Bandura, A., & Barab, P. Processes governing disinhibitory effects through symbolic modeling. *Journal of Abnormal Psychology,* 1973, *82,* 1–9.

Bandura, A., Blanchard, E. B., & Ritter, R. The relative efficacy of desensitization and modeling approaches for inducing behavioral, affective, and attitudinal changes. *Journal of Personality and Social Psychology,* 1969, *13,* 173–199.

Bandura, A., Grusec, J. E., & Menlove, F. L. Vicarious extinction of avoidance behavior. *Journal of Personality & Social Psychology,* 1967, *5,* 16–23.

Bandura, A., Jeffery, R. W., & Gajdos, E. Generalization change through participant modeling with self-directed mastery. *Bahaviour Research and Therapy,* 1975, *13,* 141–152.

Bandura, A., & Menlove, F. L. Factors determining vicarious extinction of avoidance behavior through symbolic modeling. *Journal of Personality and Social Psychology,* 1968, *8,* 99–108.

Bard, M., & Berkowitz, B. Training police as specialists in family crisis intervention: A community psychology action program. *Community Mental Health Journal,* 1967, *3,* 315–317.

Barlow, D. H. Psychologists in the emergency room: Implications for training. *Professional Psychology,* 1974, *5,* 251–256.

Barlow, D. H., Agras, W. S., Leitenberg, H., & Wincze, J. P. An experimental analysis of the effectiveness of 'shaping' in reducing maladaptive avoidance behaviour: An analogue study. *Behaviour Research and Therapy,* 1970, *8,* 165–174.

Barlow, D. H., Becker, R., Leitenberg, H., & Agras, W. S. A mechanical strain gauge for recording penile circumference change. *Journal of Applied Behavior Analysis,* 1970, *3,* 73–76.

Barrish, H. H., Saunders, M., & Wolf, M. M. Good behavior game: Effects of individual contingencies for group consequences on disruptive behavior in a classroom. *Journal of Applied Behavior Analysis,* 1969, *2,* 119–124.

Barton, E. S., Guess, D., Garcia, E., & Baer, D. M. Improvement of retardates' mealtime behaviors by timeout procedures using multiple baseline techniques. *Journal of Applied Behavior Analysis,* 1970, *3,* 77–84.

Beck, A. T., Ward, C. H., Mendelsohn, M., Mock, J., & Erbaugh, J. An inventory for measuring depression. *Archives of General Psychiatry,* 1961, *4,* 561–571.

Becker, W. C. *Parents are teachers: A child management program.* Champaign, Ill.: Research Press, 1971.

Beels, C., & Ferber, A. Family therapy: A view. *Family Process,* 1969, *8,* 280–318.

Begelman, D. A., & Hersen, M. An experimental analysis of the verbal-motor discrepancy in schizophrenia. *Journal of Clinical Psychology,* 1973, *29,* 175–179.

Bellack, A. S. Anxiety and neurotic disorders. In A. E. Kazdin, A. S. Bellack, & M. Hersen (Eds.), *New perspectives in abnormal psychology.* New York: Oxford University Press, 1980.

Bellack, A. S., & Franks, C. M. Behavioral consultation in the community mental health center. *Behavior Therapy,* 1975, *6,* 388–391.

Bellack, A. S., Glanz, L. M., & Simon, R. Self-reinforcement style and covert imagery in the treatment of obesity. *Journal of Consulting and Clinical Psychology,* 1976, *44,* 490–491.

Bellack, A. S., & Hersen, M. *Behavior modification: An introductory textbook.* Baltimore: Williams & Wilkins, 1977. (a)

Bellack, A. S., & Hersen, M. The use of self-report inventories in behavioral assessment. In J. D. Cone & R. P. Hawkins (Eds.), *Behavioral assessment: New directions in clinical psychology.* New York: Brunner/Mazel, 1977. (b)

Bellack, A. S., & Hersen, M. Assessment and single-case research. In M. Hersen & A. S. Bellack (Eds.), *Behavior therapy in the psychiatric setting*. Baltimore: Williams & Wilkins, 1978. (a)

Bellack, A. S., & Hersen, M. Chronic psychiatric patients: Skills training. In M. Hersen & A. S. Bellack (Eds.), *Behavior therapy in the psychiatric setting*. Baltimore: Williams & Wilkins, 1978. (b)

Bellack, A. S., Hersen, M., & Lamparski, D. *Role play tests for assessing social skills: Are they valid? Are they useful?* Unpublished manuscript, 1978.

Bellack, A. S., Hersen, M., & Turner, S. M. Generalization effects of social skills training in chronic schizophrenics: An experimental analysis. *Behaviour Research and Therapy*, 1976, *14*, 391–398.

Bellack, A. S., Hersen, M., & Turner, S. M. Role play tests for assessing social skills: Are they valid? *Behavior Therapy*, 1978, *9*, 448–461.

Bellack, A. S., Hersen, M., & Turner, S. M. The relationship of role-playing and knowledge of appropriate behavior to assertion in the natural environment. *Journal of Consulting and Clinical Psychology*, 1979, *47*, 670–678.

Bellack, A. S., & Schwartz, J. S. Assessment for self-control programs. In M. Hersen, & A. S. Bellack (Eds.), *Behavioral assessment: A practical handbook*. New York: Pergamon Press, 1976.

Bellack, A. S., Turner, S. M., & Hersen, M. Social skills training for day hospital schizophrenics. Unpublished grant application, University of Pittsburgh, 1977.

Bellak, L. The Thematic Apperception Test in clinical use. In L. E. Abt & L. Bellak (Eds.), *Projective psychology*. New York: Grove Press, 1959.

Bellak, L. (Ed.). *A concise handbook of community psychiatry and community mental health*. New York: Grune & Stratton, 1974.

Bender, D. P. Evaluation of a day treatment program based on goal attainment scaling. In R. F. Luber, J. T. Maxey, & P. M. Lefkowitz (Eds.), *Proceedings of the annual conference on partial hospitalization 1977*. Boston: Federation of Partial Hospitalization Study Groups, 1977.

Bender, L. *A visual motor Gestalt test and its clinical use*. New York: American Orthopsychiatric Association, 1938.

Benjamin, A. *The helping interview*. Boston: Houghton Mifflin, 1974.

Benner, B., & Price, R. H. (Eds.), *Community mental health: Social action and reaction*. New York: Holt, Rinehart, and Winston, 1973.

Benton, A. L. *Revised visual retention tests* (Manual). New York: Psychological Corporation, 1963.

Bergin, A. E. The evaluation of therapeutic outcomes. In A. E. Bergin & S. L. Garfield (Eds.), *Handbook of psychotherapy and behavior change: An empirical analysis*. New York: John Wiley & Sons, 1971.

Bergin, A. E., & Suinn, R. M. Individual psychotherapy and behavior therapy. *Annual Review of Psychology*, 1975, *26*, 509–556.

Bernhardt, A. J., Hersen, M., & Barlow, D. H. Measurement and modification of spasmodic torticollis: An experimental analysis. *Behavior Therapy*, 1972, *3*, 294–297.

Bernstein, D. A., & Neitzel, M. T. Demand characteristics in behavior modification: The natural history of a "nuisance." In M. Hersen, R. M. Eisler, & P. M. Miller (Eds.), *Progress in behavior modification* (Vol. 4). New York: Academic Press, 1977.

Bernstein, D. A., & Paul, G. L. Some comments on therapy analogue research with small animal "phobias." *Journal of Behavior Therapy and Experimental Psychiatry,* 1971, *2,* 225–237.

Bersoff, D. N. Silk purses into sow's ears: The decline of psychological testing and a suggestion for its redemption. *American Psychologist,* 1973, *28,* 892–899.

Bersoff, D. N., & Prasse, D. Applied psychology and judicial decision making: Corporal punishment as a case in point. *Professional Psychology,* 1978, *9,* 400–411.

Betz, B. J. Experiences in research in psychotherapy with schizophrenic patients. In H. H. Strupp & L. Luborsky (Eds.), *Research in psychotherapy* (Vol. 2). Washington: D.C.: APA, 1962.

Bijou, S. W., Peterson, R. F., Harris, F. R., Allen, K. E., & Johnston, M. S. Methodology for experimental studies of young children in natural settings. *Psychological Record,* 1969, *19,* 177–210.

Bindrim, P. A report in a nude marathon. *Psychotherapy: Theory, Research and Practice,* 1968, *5,* 180–188.

Birnbrauer, J. S. Mental retardation. In H. Leitenberg (Ed.), *Handbook of behavior modification and behavior therapy.* Englewood Cliffs, N.J.: Prentice-Hall, 1976.

Blanchard, C. G., & Barlow, D. H. Psychologists and psychiatrists in a department of psychiatry. *Professional Psychology,* 1976, *7,* 331–338.

Blanchard, E. B. The relative contributions of modeling, informational influences and physical contact in the extinction of phobic behavior. *Journal of Abnormal Psychology,* 1970, *76,* 55–61.

Blanchard, E. B., & Epstein, L. H. The clinical utility of biofeedback. In M. Hersen, R. M. Eisler, & P. M. Miller (Eds.), *Progress in behavior modification* (Vol. 4). New York: Academic Press, 1977.

Blanchard, E. B., & Hersen, M. Behavioral treatment of hysterical neurosis: Symptom substitution and symptom return reconsidered. *Psychiatry,* 1976, *39,* 118–129.

Bloom, B. L. *Community mental health: A general introduction.* Monterey: Brooks/Cole, 1977.

Bolman, W. M. An outline of preventive psychiatric programs for children. *Archives of General Psychiatry,* 1967, *12,* 5–8.

Bornstein, M., Bellack, A. S., & Hersen, M. Social skills training for unassertive children: A multiple baseline analysis. *Journal of Applied Behavior Analysis,* 1977, *10,* 183–195.

Bornstein, P. H. "I" language-induced anxiety. *Psychological Reports,* 1974, *35,* 453–454.

Boulougouris, J. C., Marks, I. M., & Marset, P. Superiority of flooding to desensitization as a fear reducer. *Behaviour Research and Therapy,* 1971, *9,* 7–16.

Bowen, M. The use of family therapy in clinical practice. *Comprehensive Psychiatry,* 1966, *7,* 345–374.

Braginsky, B. M., & Braginsky, D. D. Schizophrenic patients in the psychiatric interview: An experimental study of their effectiveness at manipulation. *Journal of Consulting Psychology,* 1967, *31,* 543–547.

Brown, B. S. Foreword. In B. B. Wolman (Ed.), *The therapist's handbook: Treatment methods of mental disorders.* New York: Van Nostrand Reinhold, 1976.

Brown, W. R., & McGuire, J. M. Current psychological assessment practices. *Professional Psychology,* 1976, *7,* 475–484.

Brownell, K. D., Heckerman, C. L., & Westlake, R. J. The effect of couples training and partner cooperativeness in the behavioral treatment of obesity. Unpublished manuscript, Brown University, 1977.

Buros, O. K. (Ed.), *Tests in part II: An index to tests, test reviews, and the literature on specific tests.* Highland Park, N.J.: Gryphon Press, 1974.

Butcher, J. N., & Koss, M. P. Research on brief and crisis-oriented psychotherapies. In S. L. Garfield & A. E. Bergin (Eds.), *Handbook of psychotherapy and behavior change: An empirical analysis.* New York: John Wiley & Sons, 1978.

Butcher, J. N., & Maudal, G. R. Crisis intervention. In I. B. Weiner (Ed.), *Clinical methods in psychology.* New York: John Wiley & Sons, 1976.

Caplan, G. Types of mental health consultation. *American Journal of Orthopsychiatry,* 1963, *33,* 470–481.

Caplan, G. *Principles of preventive psychiatry.* New York: Basic Books, 1964.

Carr, A. C. Psychological deficit and psychological testing. *International Psychiatry Clinics,* 1964, *1,* 773–798.

Carver, C. S., & Glass, D. C. Coronary-prone behavior pattern and interpersonal aggression. *Journal of Personality and Social Psychology,* 1978, *36,* 361–366.

Cattell, R. B. *Manual for forms A and B: Sixteen Personality Factor Questionnaire.* Champaign, Ill.: Institute for Personality and Ability Testing, 1949.

Cautela, J. R. Behavior therapy and the need for behavioral assessment. *Psychotherapy: Theory, Research, and Practice,* 1968, *5,* 175–179.

Cautela, J. R., & Upper, D. A behavioral coding system. Presidential address presented at the seventh Annual Convention, AABT, Miami Beach, Dec., 1973.

Cautela, J. R., & Upper, D. The behavioral inventory battery: The use of self-report measures in behavioral analysis and therapy. In M. Hersen & A. S. Bellack (Eds.), *Behavioral assessment: A practical handbook.* New York: Pergamon Press, 1976.

Chapman, L. J., & Chapman, J. P. Illusory correlation as an obstacle to the use of valid psychodiagnostic signs. *Journal of Abnormal Psychology,* 1969, *74,* 271–280.

Chinsky, J. M., & Rappaport, J. Brief critique of the meaning and reliability of "accurate empathy" ratings. *Psychological Bulletin,* 1970, *73,* 379–382.

Ciminero, A. R., Calhoun, K. S., & Adams, H. E. (Eds.), *Handbook of behavioral assessment.* New York: John Wiley & Sons, 1977.

Clarizio, H. F. Stability of deviant behavior through time. In H. F. Clarizio (Ed.), *Mental health and the educative process.* Chicago: Rand McNally, 1969.

Clingman, J., & Fowler, R. L. The effects of primary reward contingency on the IQ performance of grade school children as a function of initial IQ level. *Journal of Applied Behavior Analysis,* 1976, *9,* 19–23.

Coffey, H. S. The school of psychology model. *American Psychologist,* 1970, *25,* 434–436.

Cohen, L. D. Overview: Past, present, future. *Professional Psychology,* 1974, *5,* 222–226.

Comrey, A. L. Common methodological problems in factor analytic studies. *Journal of Consulting and Clinical Psychology,* 1978, *46,* 648–659.

Cone, J. D., & Hawkins, R. P. *Behavioral assessment: New directions in clinical psychology.* New York: Brunner/Mazel, 1977.

Cooper, A., Furst, J. B., & Bridger, W. A brief commentary on the usefulness of studying fears of snakes. *Journal of Abnormal Psychology,* 1969, *74,* 413–414.

Costello, C. G. (Ed.), *Symptoms of psychopathology: A handbook.* New York: John Wiley & Sons, 1970.

Cowen, E. L. Social and community interventions. In P. Mussen & M. Rosenzweig (Eds.), *Annual review of psychology,* 1973, *24,* 423–472.

Cowen, E. L., Pederson, A., Babigian, H., Izzo, L. D., & Trost, M. A. Long-term follow-up of early detected vulnerable children. *Journal of Consulting and Clinical Psychology,* 1973, *41,* 438–446.

Cronbach, L. J. *Essentials of psychological testing.* New York: Harper & Row, 1970.

Cronbach, L. J. Five decades of public controversy over mental testing. *American Psychologist,* 1975, *30,* 1–14.

Crowne, D., & Marlowe, D. *The approval motive.* New York: John Wiley & Sons, 1964.

Curran J. P., Corriveau, D. P., Monti, P. M., & Hagerman, S. B. Self-report measurement of social skill and social anxiety in a psychiatric population. *Behavior Modification,* in press.

Curran J. P., & Gilbert, F. S. A test of the relative effectiveness of a systematic desensitization program and interpersonal skills training program with date anxious subjects. *Behavior Therapy,* 1975, *6,* 510–521.

Denner, B., & Price, R. H. (Eds.), *Community mental health: Social action and reaction.* New York: Holt, Rinehart, and Winston, 1973.

Deri, S. K. The Szondi test. In L. E. Abt & L. Bellak (Eds.), *Projective psychology.* New York: Grove Press, 1959.

Derner, G. F. Professional excellence and graduate education. *The Clinical Psychologist,* 1975, *29,* 1–3.

Derner, G. F. The education for the profession of clinical psychology and the psychology technician. *The Clinical Psychologist,* 1976, *29,* 1–2, 13.

Detre, T. P., & Jarecki, H. G. *Modern psychiatric treatment.* Philadelphia: J. B. Lippincott, 1971.

Deutsch, F., & Murphy, W. F. *The clinical interview: Therapy* (Vol. 2). New York: International Universities Press, 1955.

Dohrenwend, B. P., & Dohrenwend, B. S. Social and cultural influences on psychopathology. *Annual Review of Psychology,* 1974, *25,* 417–452.

Driscoll, J. M., Meyer, R. G., & Schanie, C. F. Training police in family crisis intervention. *Journal of Applied Behavioral Science,* 1973, *9,* 62–82.

Drotar, D. Clinical psychological practice in a pediatric hospital. *Professional Psychology,* 1977, *8,* 72–80.

Dublin, J. E. Gestalting psychotic persons. *Psychotherapy: Theory, Research and Practice,* 1973, *10,* 149–152.

Eddy, G. L., & Sinnet, E. R. Behavior setting utilization by emotionally disturbed college students. *Journal of Consulting and Clinical Psychology,* 1973, *40,* 210–216.

Education and Training Broad. *Criteria for accredidation of doctoral training programs and internships in professional psychology, Draft VI.* Washington, D.C.: APA, 1978.

Edwards, A. L. *Edwards Personality Inventory* (Manual). Chicago: Science Research Associates, 1967.

Eisler, R. M., Hersen, M., Miller, P. M., & Blanchard, E. B. Situational determinants of assertive behaviors. *Journal of Consulting and Clinical Psychology,* 1975, *43,* 330–340.

Eisler, R. M., Miller, P. M., & Hersen, M. Components of assertive behavior. *Journal of Clinical Psychology,* 1973, *29,* 295–299.

Ellenberger, H. F. A clinical introduction to psychiatric phenomenology and existential analysis. In R. May, E. Angel, & H. F. Ellenberger (Eds.), *Existence: A new dimension in psychiatry and psychology.* New York: Basic Books, 1958.

Ellis, A. Rational psychotherapy. *Journal of General Psychology,* 1958, *59,* 35–49.

Emmelkamp, P.M.G. The behavioral study of clinical phobias. In M. Hersen, R. M. Eisler, & P. M. Miller (Eds.), *Progress in behavior modification* (Vol. 8). New York: Academic Press, 1979.

Endler, N. S., & Okada, M. A multidimensional measure of trait anxiety: The S-R Inventory of General Trait Anxiousness. *Journal of Consulting and Clinical Psychology,* 1975, *43,* 319–329.

Epstein, L. H. Psychophysiological measurement in assessment. In M. Hersen & A. S. Bellack (Eds.), *Behavioral assessment: A practical handbook.* New York: Pergamon Press, 1976.

Epstein, L. H., & Hersen, M. Behavioral control of hysterical gagging. *Journal of Clinical Psychology,* 1974, *30,* 102–104.

Epstein, L. H., & Malone, D. R. Feedback influenced BMG changes in stroke patients. *Behavior Modification,* 1978, *2,* 387–402.

Epstein, L. H., Hersen, M., & Hemphill, D. P. Music feedback as a treatment for tension headache: An experimental case study. *Journal of Behavior Therapy and Experimental Psychiatry,* 1974, *5,* 59–63.

Epstein, L. H., Katz, R. C., & Zlutnick, S. Behavioral medicine. In M. Hersen, R. M. Eisler, & P. M. Miller (Eds.), *Progress in behavior modification* (Vol. 7). New York: Academic Press, 1979.

Exner, J. E. Projective techniques. In I. B. Weiner (Ed.), *Clinical methods in psychology.* New York: John Wiley & Sons, 1976.

Eysenck, H. J. The effects of psychotherapy: An evaluation. *Journal of Consulting Psychology,* 1952, *16,* 319–324.

Eysenck, H. J. (Ed.), *Behaviour therapy and neuroses.* New York: Pergamon Press, 1960. (a)

Eysenck, H. J. The effects of psychotherapy. In H. J. Eysenck (Ed.), *Handbook of abnormal psychology.* London: Pittman Medical Publishers, 1960. (b)

Eysenck, H. J. The effects of psychotherapy. *International Journal of Psychiatry,* 1965, *1,* 99–144.

Eysenck, H. J., & Eysenck, S.B.G. *Eysenck Personality Inventory* (Revised Manual). San Diego: Educational and Industrial Testing Service, 1968.

Feather, B., & Rhoads, J. Psychodynamic behavior therapy: I. Theory and rationale. *Archives of General Psychiatry,* 1972, *26,* 496–502.

Feifel, H. Death: Relevant variable in psychology. In R. May (Ed.), *Existential Psychology.* New York: Random House, 1961.

Fiester, A. R. JCAH standards for accredidation of community mental health service programs: Implications for the practice of psychology. *American Psychologist,* 1978, *33,* 1114–1121.

Filskov, S. B., & Goldstein, S. G. Diagnostic validity of the Halstead-Reitan neuropsychological battery. *Journal of Consulting and Clinical Psychology,* 1974, *42,* 382–388.

Fine, R. Psychoanalysis. In R. Corsini (Ed.), *Current psychotherapies*. Itasca, Ill.: Peacock Press, 1973.

Fo, W., & O'Donnell, C. The buddy system: Relationship and contingency conditions in a community intervention program for youth with professionals as behavior change agents. *Journal of Consulting and Clinical Psychology, 1974, 42, 163–169.*

Ford, D. H., & Urban, H. B. *Systems of psychotherapy: A comparative study.* New York: John Wiley & Sons, 1963.

Foulkes, S. F. *Therapeutic group analysis.* New York: International Universities Press, 1965.

Fox, R. E. Family therapy. In I. B. Weiner (Ed.), *Clinical methods in psychology.* New York: John Wiley & Sons, 1976.

Foxx, R. M., & Azrin, N. H. Restitution: A method of eliminating aggressive-disruptive behavior of retarded and brain-damaged patients. *Behaviour Research and Therapy, 1972, 10, 15–28.*

Foxx, R. M., & Azrin, N. H. The elimination of autistic self-stimulatory behavior by overcorrection. *Journal of Applied Behavior Analysis, 1973, 6, 1–14.*

Foy, D. W., Eisler, R. M., & Pinkston, S. G. Modeled assertion in a case of explosive rage. *Journal of Behavior Therapy and Experimental Psychiatry, 1975, 6, 135–137.*

Frank, G. Psychiatric diagnosis: A review of research. *Journal of General Psychology, 1969, 81, 157–176.*

Frank, G. *Psychiatric diagnosis: A review of research.* Oxford: Pergamon Press, 1975.

Frank, J. D. Expectation and therapeutic outcome—The placebo effect and the role induction interview. In J. D. Frank, R. Hoehn-Saric, S. D. Imber, B. L. Liberman, & A. R. Stone (Eds.), *Effective ingredients of successful psychotherapy.* New York: Brunner/Mazel, 1978.

Frank, J. D., Hoehn-Saric, R., Imber, S. D., Liberman, B. L., & Stone, A. R. *Effective ingredients of successful psychotherapy.* New York: Brunner/Mazel, 1978.

Franks, C. M. (Ed.), *Behavior therapy: Appraisal and status.* New York: McGraw-Hill, 1969.

Galassi, J. P., DeLo, J. S., Galassi, M. D., & Bastien, S. The college self-expression scale: A measure of assertiveness. *Behavior Therapy, 1974, 5, 165–171.*

Gamble, K. R. The Holtzman inkblot technique: A review. *Psychological Bulletin, 1972, 77, 172–194.*

Gambrill, E. D. *Behavior modification: Handbook of assessment, intervention, and evaluation.* San Francisco: Jossey-Bass, 1977.

Garfield, S. L. Historical introduction. In B. B. Wolman (Ed.), *Handbook of clinical psychology.* New York: McGraw-Hill, 1965.

Garfield, S. L. Research on client variables in psychotherapy. In A. E. Bergin & S. L. Garfield (Eds.), *Handbook of psychotherapy and behavior change: An empirical analysis.* New York: John Wiley & Sons, 1971.

Garfield, S. L. Research problems in clinical diagnosis. *Journal of Consulting and Clinical Psychology, 1978, 46, 596–607.*

Garfield, S. L., & Kurtz, R. Clinical psychologists in the 1970's. *American Psychologist, 1976, 31, 1–9.*

Garfield, S. L., & Kurtz, M. A study of eclectic views. *Journal of Consulting and Clinical Psychology, 1977, 45, 78–83.*

Garfield, S. L., Prager, R. A., & Bergin, A. E. Evaluation of outcome in psychotherapy. *Journal of Consulting and Clinical Psychology,* 1971, *37,* 307–313.

Geer, J. H. The development of a scale to measure fear. *Behaviour Research and Therapy,* 1965, *3,* 45–53.

Gendlin, E. T. Focusing. *Psychotherapy: Theory, Research and Practice,* 1969, *6,* 4–15.

Gendlin, E. T. Experiential psychotherapy: A short summary (and some long predictions). In O. L. McCabe (Ed.), *Changing human behavior: Current therapies and future directions.* New York: Grune & Stratton, 1977.

Glass, D. C. *Behavior patterns, stress, and coronary disease.* Hillsdale, N.J.: Lawrence Erlbaum Associates, 1977.

Glass, L., Kirsch, M., & Parris, F. Psychiatric disturbances associated with erhard seminars training: I. A report of cases. *American Journal of Psychiatry,* 1977, *134,* 245–257.

Golden, M. Some effects of combining psychological tests on clinical inferences. *Journal of Consulting Psychology,* 1964, *28,* 440–446.

Goldenberg, H. *Contemporary clinical psychology.* Monterey: Brooks/Cole, 1973.

Goldfried, M. R., & Kent, R. N. Traditional versus behavioral personality assessment: A comparison of methodological and theoretical assumptions. *Psychological Bulletin,* 1972, *77,* 409–420.

Goldfried, M. R., & Linehan, M. M. Basic issues in behavioral assessment. In A. R. Ciminero, H. E. Adams, & K. S. Calhoun (Eds.), *Handbook of behavioral assessment.* New York: John Wiley & Sons, 1977.

Goldfried, M. R., & Pomeranz, D. M. Role of assessment in behavior modification. *Psychological Reports,* 1968, *23,* 75–87.

Goldfried, M., Stricker, G., & Weiner, I. B. *Rorschach handbook of clinical and research applications.* Englewood Cliffs, N.J.: Prentice-Hall, 1971.

Goldstein, G. Organic brain syndromes and related disorders. In A. E. Kazdin, A. S. Bellack, & M. Hersen (Eds.), *New perspectives in abnormal psychology.* New York: Oxford University Press, 1980.

Goldstein, G., & Halperin, K. M. Neuropsychological differences among subtypes of schizophrenia. *Journal of Abnormal Psychology,* 1977, *86,* 34–40.

Gough, H. G. *California Psychological Inventory Manual.* Palo Alto: Consulting Psychologists Press, 1957.

Greenspoon, J., & Gersten, C. D. A new look at psychological testing: Psychological testing from the standpoint of a behaviorist. *American Psychologist,* 1967, *22,* 848–853.

Gross, L. R. Effects of verbal and nonverbal reinforcement in the Rorschach. *Journal of Consulting Psychology,* 1959, *23,* 66–68.

Guertin, W. H., Ladd, C. E., Frank, G. H., Rabin, A. I., & Hiester, D. S. Research with the Wechsler intelligence scales for adults: 1965–1970. *Psychological Record,* 1971, *21,* 289–339.

Guilford, J. P., & Zimmerman, W. S. *The Guilford Temperament Survey: Manual of instructions and interpretations.* Beverly Hills: Sheridan Supply, 1949.

Gynther, M. D., & Gynther, R. A. Personality inventories. In I. B. Weiner (Ed.), *Clinical methods in psychology.* New York: John Wiley & Sons, 1976.

Hall, C. S., & Lindzey, G. *Theories of personality* (3rd ed.). New York: John Wiley & Sons, 1978.

Hamilton, R. G., & Robertson, M. H. Examiner influence on the Holtzman inkblot technique. *Journal of Projective Techniques and Personality Assessment,* 1966, *30,* 553–558.

Hamilton, S. B., & Bornstein, P. H. Increasing the accuracy of self-recording in speech-anxious undergraduates through the use of self-monitoring training and reliability enhancement procedures. *Journal of Consulting and Clinical Psychology,* 1977, *45,* 1076–1085.

Harbert, T. L., Barlow, D. H., Hersen, M., & Austin, J. B. Measurement and modification of incestuous behavior. *Psychological Reports,* 1974, *34,* 79–86.

Harrell, T. W., & Harrell, M. S. Army General Classification Test scores for civilian occupations. *Educational and Psychological Measurement,* 1945, *5,* 229–239.

Harrower, M. Clinical psychologist at work. In B. B. Wolman (Ed.), *Handbook of clinical psychology.* New York: McGraw-Hill, 1965.

Hartley, D., & Strupp, H. H. Verbal psychotherapies. In A. E. Kazdin, A. S. Bellack, & M. Hersen (Eds.), *New perspectives in abnormal psychology.* New York: Oxford University Press, 1980.

Hathaway, S. R., & McKinley, J. C. *Minnesota Multiphasic Personality Inventory.* Minneapolis: University of Minnesota Press, 1942.

Havens, L. L. The existential use of the self. *American Journal of Psychiatry,* 1974, *131,* 1–10.

Heller, K. Interview structure and interviewer style in initial interviews. In A. W. Siegman & B. Pope (Eds.), *Studies in dyadic communication.* New York: Pergamon Press, 1972.

Hersch, C. From mental health to social action: Clinical psychology in historical perspective. *American Psychologist,* 1969, *24,* 909–916.

Hersch, C. Social history, mental health, and community control. *American Psychologist,* 1972, *27,* 749–754.

Hersen, M. Sexual aspects of Rorschach administration. *Journal of Projective Techniques and Personality Assessment,* 1970, *34,* 104–105.

Hersen, M. Self-assessment of fear. *Behavior Therapy,* 1973, *4,* 241–257.

Hersen, M. Historical perspectives in behavioral assessment. In M. Hersen & A. S. Bellack (Eds.), *Behavioral assessment: A practical handbook.* New York: Pergamon Press, 1976.

Hersen, M. Do behavior therapists use self-reports as criterional? Paper read at American Psychological Association, San Francisco, August 30, 1977.

Hersen, M. Limitations and problems in the clinical application of behavioral techniques in psychiatric settings. *Behavior Therapy,* 1979, *10,* 65–80. (a)

Hersen, M. Empirical methods in the behavior disorders. In A. E. Kazdin, A. S. Bellack, & M. Hersen (Eds.), *New perspectives in abnormal psychology.* New York: Oxford University Press, 1980.

Hersen, M., & Barlow, D. H. *Single-case experimental designs: Strategies for studying behavior change.* New York: Pergamon Press, 1976.

Hersen, M., & Bellack, A. S. *Behavioral assessment: A practical handbook.* New York: Pergamon Press, 1976. (a)

Hersen, M., & Bellack, A. S. Social skills training for chronic psychiatric patients: Rationale, research findings, and future directions. *Comprehensive Psychiatry,* 1976, *17,* 559–580. (b)

Hersen, M., & Bellack, A. S. A multiple-baseline analysis of social-skills training in chronic schizophrenics. *Journal of Applied Behavior Analysis,* 1976, *9,* 239–245. (c)

Hersen, M., & Bellack, A. S. Assessment of social skills. In Ciminero, A. R., Calhoun, K. S., & Adams, H. E. (Eds.), *Handbook of behavioral assessment.* New York: John Wiley & Sons, 1977.

Hersen, M. & Bellack, A. S. (Eds.). *Behavior therapy in the psychiatric setting.* Baltimore: Williams & Wilkins, 1978. (a)

Hersen, M., & Bellack, A. S. Staff training and consultation. In M. Hersen & A.S. Bellack (Eds.), *Behavior therapy in the psychiatric setting.* Baltimore: Williams & Wilkins, 1978. (b)

Hersen, M., Bellack, A. S., & Turner, S. M. Assessment of assertiveness in female psychiatric patients: Motoric and autonomic measures. *Journal of Behavior Therapy and Experimental Psychiatry,* 1978, *9,* 11–16.

Hersen, M., Bellack, A. S., Turner, S. M., Williams, M. T., Harper, K., & Watts, J. G. Psychometric properties of the Wolpe-Lazarus Assertiveness Scale. *Behaviour Research and Therapy,* 1979, *17,* 63–69.

Hersen, M., Eisler, R. M., Alford, G. S., & Agras, W. S. Effects of token economy on neurotic depression: An experimental analysis. *Behavior Therapy,* 1973, *4,* 392–397.

Hersen, M., & Greaves, S. T. Rorschach productivity as related to verbal reinforcement. *Journal of Personality Assessment,* 1971, *35,* 436–441.

Hersen, M., Gullick, E. L., Matherne, P. M., & Harbert, T. L. Instructions and reinforcement in the modification of a conversion reaction. *Psychological Reports,* 1972, *31,* 719–722.

Hersen, M., & Luber, R. F. Use of group psychotherapy in a partial hospitalization service: The remediation of basic skills deficits. *International Journal of Group Psychotherapy,* 1977, *27,* 361–376.

Hersen, M., Turner, S. M., Edelstein, B. A., Pinkston, S. G. Effects of phenothiazines and social skills training in a withdrawn schizophrenic. *Journal of Clinical Psychology,* 1975, *31,* 588–594.

Himelstein, P. Research with the Stanford-Binet, form L-M: The first five years. *Psychological Bulletin,* 1966, *65,* 156–164.

Hines, F. R., & Williams, R. B. Dimensional diagnosis and the medical student's grasp of psychiatry. *Archives of General Psychiatry,* 1975, *32,* 525–528.

Hinsie, L. E., & Campbell, R. J. *Psychiatric dictionary.* New York: Oxford University Press, 1970.

Hobbs, N. Mental health's third revolution. *American Journal of Orthopsychiatry,* 1964, *34,* 822–833.

Hollingshead, A. B., & Redlich, F. C. *Social class and mental illness.* New York: John Wiley & Sons, 1958.

Hollingsworth R., & Hendrix, E. M. Community mental health in rural settings. *Professional Psychology,* 1977, *8,* 232–238.

Holmes, D. S., & Tyler, J. D. Direct versus projective measurement of achievement motivation. *Journal of Consulting and Clinical Psychology,* 1968, *32,* 712–717.

Holroyd, J. C., & Brodsky, A. M. Psychologists' attitudes and practices regarding erotic and nonerotic physical contact with patients. *American Psychologist,* 1977, *32,* 843–849.

Holt, R. R. Clinical *and* statistical prediction: A reformulation and some new data. *Journal of Abnormal and Social Psychology,* 1958, *56,* 1–12.

Holt, R. R. (Eds.). *Diagnostic psychological testing* (Rev. ed.). New York: International Universities Press, 1968.

Holzberg, J. D., Knapp, R. H., & Turner, J. L. College students as companions to the mentally ill. In E. L. Cowen, E. A. Gardner, & M. Zax (Eds.), *Emergent approaches to mental health problems.* New York: Appleton-Century-Crofts, 1967.

Holtzman, W. H., Thorpe, J. S., Swartz, J. D., & Herron, E. W. *Inkblot perception and personality.* Austin: University of Texas Press, 1961.

Horowitz, M. J. A study of clinicians' judgments from projective test protocols. *Journal of Consulting Psychology,* 1962, *26,* 251–256.

Hudson, W. W., & Proctor, E. K. Assessment of depressive affect in clinical practice. *Journal of Consulting and Clinical Psychology,* 1977, *45,* 1206–1207.

Hugo, J. A., II. Abbreviation of the Minnesota Multiphasic Personality Inventory through multiple regression. Unpublished Ph.D. dissertation, University of Alabama, 1971.

Hunt, W. A. Relations with other professions. In B. B. Wolman (Ed.), *Handbook of clinical psychology.* New York: McGraw-Hill, 1965.

Jenkins, C. D., Rosenman, R. H., & Zyzanski, S. J. Prediction of clinical coronary heart disease by a test for the coronary-prone behavior pattern. *New England Journal of Medicine,* 1974, *290,* 1271–1275.

Jensen, A. R. How much can we boost IQ and scholastic achievement? *Harvard Educational Review,* 1969, *39,* 1–23.

Jones, M. C. The elimination of children's fears. *Journal of Experimental Psychology,* 1924, *7,* 383–390. (a)

Jones, M. C. A laboratory study of fear: The case of Peter. *Journal of Genetic Psychology,* 1924, *31,* 308–315. (b)

Kallman, W. M., Hersen, M., & O'Toole, D. H. The use of social reinforcement in a case of conversion reaction. *Behavior Therapy,* 1975, *6,* 411–413.

Kanfer, F. H. The many faces of self-control, or behavior modification changes its focus. Paper presented at Eighth International Banff Conference, Banff, Alberta, March, 1976.

Kanfer, F. H., & Grimm, L. G. Behavioral analysis: Selecting target behaviors in the interview. *Behavior Modification,* 1977, *1,* 7–28.

Kanfer, F. H., & Phillips, J. S. *Learning foundations of behavior therapy.* New York: John Wiley & Sons, 1970.

Kanfer, F. H., & Saslow, G. Behavioral diagnosis. In C. M. Franks (Ed.), *Behavior therapy: Appraisal and status.* New York: McGraw-Hill, 1969.

Kazdin, A. E. Response cost: The removal of conditioned reinforcers for therapeutic change. *Behavior Therapy,* 1972, *3,* 533–546.

Kazdin, A. E. *Behavior modification in applied settings.* Homewood, Ill.: Dorsey Press, 1975.

Kazdin, A. E. *The token economy.* New York: Plenum Press, 1977.

Kazdin, A. E. Evaluating the generality of findings in analogue therapy research. *Journal of Consulting and Clinical Psychology,* 1978, *46,* 673–686.

Kazdin, A. E. Basic concepts and models of disordered behavior. In A. E. Kazdin, A. S. Bellack, & M. Hersen (Eds.), *New perspectives in abnormal psychology.* New York: Oxford University Press, 1980.

Kazdin, A. K. *Research design in clinical psychology,* New York: Harper & Row, 1980.

Kazdin, A. E., & Wilson, G. T. Critieria for evaluating psychotherapy. *Archives of General Psychiatry,* 1978, *35,* 407–416. (a)

Kazdin, A. E., & Wilson, G. T. *Evaluation of behavior therapy: Issues, evidence, and research strategies.* Cambridge, Mass.: Ballinger, 1978. (b)

Kelly, E. L. Clinical psychology - 1960: Report of survey findings. *Newsletter: Division of Clinical Psychology of the American Psychological Association,* 1961, *14,* 1–11.

Kelly, G. A. The theory and techniques of assessment. *Annual Review of Psychology,* 1958, *9,* 323–352.

Kempler, W. Experiential psychotherapy with families. In J. Fagan & I. L. Shepherd (Eds.), *Gestalt therapy now.* Palo Alto: Science and Behavior Books, 1970.

Kent, G. H., & Rosanoff, A. J. A study of association in insanity. *American Journal of Insanity,* 1910, *67,* 374–390.

Kent, R. N., O'Leary, D. D., Diament, C., & Dietz, A. Expectation biases in observational evaluation of therapeutic change. *Journal of Consulting and Clinical Psychology,* 1974, *42,* 774–780.

Kessler, M., & Albee, G. W. Primary prevention. *Annual Review of Psychology,* 1975, *26,* 557–591.

Kiesler, C. A. The training of psychiatrists and psychologists. *American Psychologist,* 1977, *32,* 107–108.

Kilmann, P. R., & Sotile, W. M. The marathon encounter group: A review of the outcome literature. *Psychological Bulletin,* 1976, *83,* 827–850.

Kimmel, H. D. Pathological inhibitions of emotional behavior. In H. D. Kimmel (Ed.), *Experimental psychopathology: Recent research and theory.* New York: Academic Press, 1971.

Kincannon, J. C. Predictions of the standard MMPI scale scores from 71 items: The Mini-Mult. *Journal of Consulting and Clinical Psychology,* 1968, *32,* 319–325.

Kirk, S. A., & Therrien, M. E. Community mental health myths and the fate of former hospitalized patients. *Psychiatry,* 1975, *38,* 209–217.

Kirsch, M. A., & Glass, L. L. Psychiatric disturbances associated with erhard seminars training: II. Additional cases and theoretical considerations. *American Journal of Psychiatry,* 1977, *134,* 1254–1258.

Kleinmuntz, B. Personality tests interpretation by computer and clinician. In J. N. Butcher (Ed.), *MMPI: Research developments and clinical applications.* New York: McGraw-Hill, 1969.

Koppitz, E. *The Bender-Gestalt test for young children.* New York: Grune & Stratton, 1964.

Korman, M. National conference on levels and patterns of professional training in psychology: The major themes. *American Psychologist,* 1974, *29,* 441–449.

Korman, M. (Ed.). *Levels and patterns of professional training in psychology.* Washington, D.C.: APA, 1976.

Krebs, R. Client-centered therapy: When and how it should end. *Psychotherapy: Research and Practice,* 1972, *9,* 359–361.

Kubler-Ross, E. *On death and dying.* New York: Macmillan, 1970.

Lacey, J. I. The evaluation of autonomic responses: Toward a general solution. *Annals of the New York Academy of Sciences,* 1956, *67,* 123–164.

Lahey, B. B., & Johnson, M. S. *Psychology and instruction: A practical approach to educational psychology.* Glenview, Ill.: Scott, Foresman, 1978.

Lambert, M. J., DeJulio, S. S., & Stein, D. M. Therapist interpersonal skills: Process, outcome, methodological considerations, and recommendations for future research. *Psychological Bulletin,* 1978, *85,* 467–489.

Lang, P. J. Fear reduction and fear behavior: Problems intreating a construct. In J. M. Shlien (Ed.), *Research in psychotherapy: Vol. 3.* Washington, D.C.: APA, 1968.

Lang, P. J. The mechanics of desensitization and the laboratory study of human fear. In C. M. Franks. (Ed.), *Behavior therapy: Appraisal and status.* New York: McGraw-Hill, 1969.

Lang, P. J., & Lazovik, A. D. Experimental desensitization of a phobia. *Journal of Abnormal and Social Psychology,* 1963, *66,* 519–525.

Lang, P. J., Lazovik, A. D., & Reynolds, D. J. Desensitization, suggestibility, and pseudotherapy. *Journal of Abnormal Psychology,* 1965, *70,* 395–402.

Langer, T. S., & Michael, S. T. *Life stress and mental health.* New York: Macmillan, 1963.

Lazarus, A. A. Multimodal behavior therapy: Treating the "BASIC ID." *Journal of Nervous and Mental Disease,* 1973, *156,* 404–411.

Lazarus, A. A., & Davison, G. C. Clinical innovation in research and practice. In A. E. Bergin & S. L. Garfield (Eds.), *Handbook of psychotherapy and behavior change: An empirical analysis.* New York: John Wiley & Sons, 1971.

Lecker, S. Family therapies. In B. B. Wolman (Ed.), *The therapist's handbook: Treatment methods of mental disorders.* New York: Van Nostrand Reinhold, 1976.

Leighton, D. C. Distribution of psychiatric symptoms in a small town. *American Journal of Psychiatry,* 1956, *112,* 716–723.

Leitenberg, H. Training clinical researchers in psychology. *Professional Psychology,* 1974, *5,* 59–69.

Leitenberg, H. Review of Hersen & Bellack's *"Behavioral assessment: A practical handbook." Behavior Modification,* 1978, *2,* 137–139.

Leitenberg, H., Agras, W. S., Allen, R., Butz, R., & Edwards, J. Feedback and therapist praise during treatment of phobia. *Journal of Consulting and Clinical Psychology,* 1975, *43,* 396–404.

Levine, J., & Feirstein, A. Differences in test performance between brain-damaged, schizophrenic, and medical patients. *Journal of Consulting and Clinical Psychology,* 1972, *39,* 508–511.

Levy, M. R., & Fox, H. M. Psychological testing is alive & well. *Professional Psychology,* 1975, *6,* 420–424.

Lewandowski, D. G., & Saccuzzo, D. P. The decline of psychological testing. *Professional Psychology,* 1976, *7,* 177–184.

Lewinsohn, P. M., & Graf, M. Pleasant activities and depression. *Journal of Consulting and Clinical Psychology,* 1973, *41,* 261–268.

Lewis, S. A comparison of behavior therapy techniques in the reduction of fearful avoidance behavior. *Behavior Therapy,* 1974, *5,* 648–655.

Liberman, B. L. The maintenance and persistence of change: Long-term follow-up investigations of psychotherapy. In J. D. Frank, R. Hoehn-Saric, S. D. Imber, B. L. Liberman, & A. R. Stone (Eds.), *Effective ingredients of successful psychotherapy.* New York: Brunner/Mazel, 1978.

Liberman, R. P., & Davis, J. Drugs and behavior analysis. In M. Hersen, R. M. Eisler, & P. M. Miller (Eds.), *Progress in behavior modification: Volume 1.* New York: Academic Press, 1975.

Lick, J. R., Sushinsky, L. W., & Malow, R. Specificity of fear survey schedule items and the prediction of avoidance behavior. *Behavior Modification,* 1977, *1,* 195–203.

Lieberman, M. A., Yalom, I. D., & Miles, M. B. *Encounter groups: First facts.* New York: Basic Books, 1973.

Lindzey, G. *Projective techniques and cross-cultural research.* New York: Appleton-Century-Crofts, 1961.

Littell, W. M. The Wechsler Intelligence Scale for Children: Review of decade of research. *Psychological Bulletin,* 1960, *57,* 132–156.

Lombardo, T. W., & Turner, S. M. Use of thought-stopping to control obsessive ruminations in a chronic schizophrenic patient. *Behavior Modification,* 1979, *3,* 267–272.

Louttit, C. M., & Browne, C. G. Psychometric instruments in psychological clinics. *Journal of Consulting Psychology,* 1947, *11,* 49–54.

Lovaas, O. I., Freitas, L., Nelson, K., & Whalen, C. The establishment of imitation and its use for the development of complex behavior in schizophrenic children. *Behaviour Research and Therapy,* 1967, *5,* 171–181.

Luber, R. F. The growth and scope of partial hospitalization. In R. F. Luber (Ed.), *Partial hospitalization.* New York: Plenum, 1979.

Lubin, B. Group Therapy. In I. B. Weiner (Ed.), *Clinical methods in psychology.* New York: John Wiley & Sons, 1976.

Lubin, B., & Eddy, W. B. The laboratory training model: Rationale, method, and some thoughts for the future. *International Journal of Group Psychotherapy,* 1970, *20,* 305–339.

Lubin, R., Wallis, R., & Paine, C. Patterns of psychological tests used in the United States: 1935–1969. *Professional Psychology,* 1971, *2,* 70–74.

Luborsky, L. Perennial mystery of poor agreement among criteria for psychotherapy outcome. *Journal of Consulting and Clinical Psychology,* 1971, *37,* 316–319.

Luborsky, L., Auerbach, A. H., Chandler, M., Cohen, J., & Bachrach, H. M. Factors influencing the outcome of psychotherapy. *Psychological Bulletin,* 1971, *75,* 145–185.

Luborsky, L., Singer, B., & Luborsky, L. A comparative study of psychotherapies: Is it true that "everyone has won and all deserve prizes?" *Archives of General Psychiatry,* 1975, *32,* 995–1008.

Madsen, C. H. Jr., Becker, W. C., & Thomas, D. R. Rules, praise, and ignoring: Elements of classroom control. *Journal of Applied Behavior Analysis,* 1968, *1,* 139–150.

Mahl, G. F. Measuring the patient's anxiety during interviews from "expressive" aspects of his speech. *Transactions of the New York Academy of Sciences,* 1959, *21,* 249–257.

Malan, D. H. The outcome problem in psychotherapy research: A historical review. *Archives of General Psychiatry,* 1973, *29,* 719–729.

Mann, R. A. The behavior-therapeutic use of contingency contracting to control an adult behavior problem: Weight control. *Journal of Applied Behavior Analysis,* 1972, *5,* 99–109.

Mann, R. A. Behavioral excesses in children. In M. Hersen & A. S. Bellack (Eds.), *Behavioral assessment: A practical handbook.* New York: Pergamon Press, 1976.

Mannino, F. V., & Shore, M. F. The effects on consultation: A review of empirical studies. *American Journal of Community Psychology,* 1975, *3,* 1–21.

Marks, I. M. Behavioral treatment of phobic and obsessive-compulsive disorders: a critical appraisal. In M. Hersen, R. M. Eisler, & P. M. Miller (Eds.), *Progress in behavior modification* (Vol. 1). New York: Academic Press, 1975.

Marks, P. A., & Seeman, W. *Actuarial description of abnormal personality.* Baltimore: Williams & Wilkins, 1963.

Martin, B. *Anxiety and neurotic disorders.* New York: John Wiley & Sons, 1971.

Marwit, S. J. Communication of a tester bias by means of modeling. *Journal of Projective Techniques and Personality Assessment,* 1969, *33,* 346–352.

Marwit, S. J., & Marcia, J. E. Tester-bias and response to projective instruments. *Journal of Consulting Psychology,* 1967, *31,* 253–258.

Masling, J., & Harris, S. Sexual aspects of TAT administration. *Journal of Consulting and Clinical Psychology,* 1969, *33,* 166–169.

Maslow, A. H. Existential psychology: What's in it for us? In R. May (Ed.), *Existential Psychology.* New York: Random House, 1961.

Matarazzo, J. D. The interview. In B. B. Wolman (Ed.), *Handbook of clinical psychology.* New York: McGraw-Hill, 1965.

Matarazzo, J. D. *Wechsler's measurement and appraisal of adult intelligence.* Baltimore: Williams & Wilkins, 1972.

Matarazzo, J. D., Lubin, B., & Nathan, R. G. Psychologists' membership on the medical staffs of university teaching hospitals. *American Psychologist,* 1978, *33,* 23–29.

Matarazzo, J. D., & Wiens, A. N. *The interview: Research on its anatomy and structure.* Chicago: Aldine-Atherton, 1972.

Matarazzo, J. D., & Wiens, A. N. Speech behavior as an objective correlate of empathy and outcome in interview and psychotherapy research: A review with implications for behavior modification. *Behavior Modification,* 1977, *1,* 453–480.

Matarazzo, R. G. Research on the teaching and learning of psychotherapeutic skills. In A. E. Bergin & S. L. Garfield (Eds.), *Handbook of psychotherapy and behavior change.* New York: John Wiley & Sons, 1971.

Max, L. Breaking up a homosexual fixation by the conditioned reaction technique. *Psychological Bulletin,* 1935, *32,* 734.

May, R. Contributions of existential psychotherapy. In R. May, E. Angel, & H. F. Ellenberger (Eds.), *Existence: A new dimension in psychiatry and psychology.* New York: Basic Books, 1958.

May, R. The emergence of existential psychology. In R. May (Ed.), *Existential psychology.* New York: Random House, 1961.

McClelland, D. C. Testing for competence rather than for "intelligence." *American Psychologist,* 1973, *28,* 1–14.

McCreary, C. P. Training psychology and law students to work together. *Professional Psychology,* 1977, *8,* 103–108.

McFall, R. M., & Lillesand, D. B. Behavior rehearsal with modeling and coaching in assertion training. *Journal of Abnormal Psychology,* 1971, *77,* 313–323.

McGinnies, E. *Social behavior: A functional analysis.* Boston: Houghton Mifflin, 1970.

Mead, W. R. Feedback: A 'how to' primer for T-group participants. In R. T. Golembiewski & A. Blumberg (Eds.), *Sensitivity training and the laboratory approach: Readings about concepts and applications.* Itasca, Ill.: Peacock Press, 1977.

Meehl, P. E. *Clinical versus statistical prediction: A theoretical analysis and a review of the evidence.* Minneapolis: University of Minnesota Press, 1954.

Meehl, P. E. Wanted—A good cookbook. *American Psychologist,* 1956, *11,* 263–272.

Meehl, P. E. When shall we use our heads instead of the formula? *Journal of Counseling Psychology,* 1957, *4,* 268–273.

Mehrabian, A. Nonverbal betrayal of feeling. *Journal of Experimental Research in Personality,* 1971, *5,* 64–73.

Mehrabian, A. *Nonverbal communication.* Chicago: Aldine-Atherton, 1972.

Meichenbaum, D. H. Cognitive modification of test anxious college students. *Journal of Consulting and Clinical Psychology,* 1972, *39,* 370–380.

Meichenbaum, D. A cognitive-behavior modification approach to assessment. In M. Hersen & A. S. Bellack (Eds.), *Behavioral assessment: A practical handbook.* New York: Pergamon Press, 1976.

Meichenbaum, D. H., Gilmore, J. B., & Fedoravicius, A. Group insight versus group desensitization in treating speech anxiety. *Journal of Consulting and Clinical Psychology,* 1971, *36,* 410–421.

Melamed, B. Behavioral aproaches to fear in dental settings. In M. Hersen, R. M. Eisler, & P. M. Miller (Eds.), *Progress in behavior modification* (Vol. 7). New York: Academic Press, 1979.

Melamed, B. G., & Siegel, L. J. Reduction of anxiety in children facing hospitalization and surgery by use of filmed modeling. *Journal of Consulting and Clinical Psychology,* 1975, *43,* 511–521.

Miller, P. M. An experimental analysis of retention control training in the treatment of nocturnal enuresis in two institutionalized adolescents. *Behavior Therapy,* 1973, *4,* 288–294.

Miller, P. M., Hersen, M., Eisler, R. M., & Hilsman, G. Effects of social stress on operant drinking of alcoholics and social drinkers. *Behaviour Research and Therapy,* 1974, *12,* 65–72.

Miller, P. M., Hersen, M., Eisler, R. M., & Watts, J. G. Contingent reinforcement of lowered blood/alcoholic levels in an outpatient chronic alcoholic. *Behaviour Research and Therapy,* 1974, *12,* 261–263.

Millon, T. *Modern psychopathology.* Philadelphia: Saunders, 1969.

Millon, T., & Diesenhaus, H. I. *Research methods in psychopathology.* New York: John Wiley & Sons, 1972.

Mischel, W. *Personality and assessment.* New York: John Wiley & Sons, 1968.

Mischel, W. Direct versus indirect personality assessment: Evidence and implications. *Journal of Consulting and Clinical Psychology,* 1972, *38,* 319–324.

Mischel, W. On the future of personality measurement. *American Psychologist,* 1977, *32,* 246–254.

Montagu, J. D., & Coles, E. M. Mechanism and measurement of the galvanic skin response. *Psychological Bulletin,* 1966, *65,* 261–279.

Moos, R. H. Conceptualizations of human environments. *American Psychologist,* 1973, *28,* 652–665.

Moos, R. H. (Ed.), *Coping with physical illness.* New York: Plenum Press, 1977.

Morgan, C. D., & Murray, H. A. A method for investigating fantasies: The Thematic Apperception Test. *Archives of Neurology and Psychiatry,* 1935, *34,* 289–306.

Morganstern, K. P. Behavioral interviewing: The initial stages of assessment. In M. Hersen & A. S. Bellack (Eds.), *Behavioral assessment: A practical handbook.* New York: Pergamon Press, 1976.

Morgenstern, F. S., Pearce, J. F., & Rees,W. L. Predicting the outcome of behaviour therapy by psychological tests. *Behaviour Research and Therapy,* 1965, *2,* 191–200.

Mosak, H. H., & Dreikurs, R. Adlerian psychotherapy. In R. Corsini (Ed.), *Current psychotherapies.* Itasca, Ill.: F. E. Peacock, 1973.

Murray, E. J., & Jacobson, L. I. The nature of learning in traditional and behavioral psychotherapy. In A. E. Bergin & S. L. Garfield (Eds.), *Handbook of psychotherapy and behavior change: An empirical analysis.* New York: John Wiley & Sons, 1971.

Murray, H. A. *Thematic Apperception Test Manual.* Cambridge, Mass.: Harvard University Press, 1943.

Naranjo, C. Present-centeredness: Technique, prescription, and ideal. In J. Fagan & I. L. Shepherd (Eds.), *Gestalt therapy now.* Palo Alto: Science and Behavior Books, 1970.

National Register of Health Providers in Psychology. Council for the National Register of Health Service Providers. Washington, D.C., 1975.

Nietzel, M. T., Winett, R. A., MacDonald, M. L., & Davidson, W. S. *Behavioral approaches to community psychology.* New York: Pergamon Press, 1977.

Norman, W. T. Psychometric considerations for a revision of the MMPI. In J. N. Butcher (Ed.), *Objective personality assessment: Changing perspectives.* New York: Academic Press, 1972.

O'Connor, R. D. Modification of social withdrawal through symbolic modeling. *Journal of Applied Behavior Analysis,* 1969, *2,* 15–22.

O'Dell, S. Training parents in behavior modification: A review. *Psychological Bulletin,* 1974, *81,* 418–443.

O'Leary, K. D., & O'Leary, S. G. (Eds.). *Classroom management:The successful use of behavior modification.* New York: Pergamon Press, 1972.

Oltmanns, T. F. Selective attention to schizophrenic and manic psychoses: The effect of distraction on information processing. *Journal of Abnormal Psychology,* 1978, *87,* 212–225.

Orne, M. T. On the social psychology of the psychological experiment: With particular reference to demand characteristics and their implications. *American Psychologist,* 1962, *17,* 776–783.

Paquin, M. J. The role of psychology in government and the policy formation process. *Professional Psychology,* 1977, *8,* 349–360.

Pascal, G. R., & Suttell, B. J. *The Bender-GestaltTest: Quantification and validity for adults.* New York: Grune & Stratton, 1951.

Paul, G. F. Physiological effects of relaxation training and hypnotic suggestion. *Journal of Abnormal Psychology,* 1969, *74,* 425–437.

Paul, G. L. *Insight vs. desensitization in psychotherapy.* Stanford: Stanford University Press, 1966.

Paul, G. L., & Lentz, R. J. *Psychosocial treatment of chronic mental patients: Milieu versus social-learning programs.* Cambridge: Harvard University Press, 1977.

Perloff, R., Perloff, E., & Sussna, E. Program evaluation. *Annual Review of Psychology,* 1976, *27,* 569–594.

Perls, F. S. Four lectures. In J. Fagan & I. L. Shepherd (Eds.), *Gestalt therapy now.* Palo Alto: Science and Behavior Books, 1970. (a)

Perls, F. S. Dream seminars. In J. Fagan & I. L. Shepherd (Eds.), *Gestalt therapy now*. Palo Alto: Science and Behavior Books, 1970. (b)

Perls, F., Hefferline, R. E., Goodman, P. *Gestalt therapy*. New York: Dell, 1965.

Perls, F. One Gestalt therapist's approach. In J. Fagan & I. L. Shepherd (Eds.), *Gestalt therapy now*. Palo Alto: Science and Behavior Books, 1970.

Peterson, D. R. The Doctor of Psychology program at the University of Illinois. *American Psychologist*, 1968, *23*, 511–516.

Peterson, D. R. Is psychology a profession? *American Psychologist*, 1976, *31*, 572–581.

Pope, B., & Siegman, A. W. Relationship and verbal behavior in the initial interview. In A. W. Siegman & B. Pope (Eds.), *Studies in dyadic communication*. New York: Pergamon Press, 1972.

Raimy, V. (Ed.). *Training in clinical psychology*. New York: Prentice-Hall, 1950.

Rappaport, J., & Chinsky, J. M. Accurate empathy: Confusion of a construct. *Psychological Bulletin*, 1972, *77*, 400–404.

Reiff, R. Mental health manpower and institutional change. *American Psychologist*, 1966, *21*, 540–548.

Reisman, J. M. *Toward the integration of psychotherapy*. New York: John Wiley & Sons, 1971.

Rice, D. G., & Gurman, A. S. Unresolved issues in the clinical psychology internship. *Professional Psychology*, 1973, *4*, 403–407.

Rickers-Ovsiankina, M. A. (Ed.). *Rorschach psychology*. New York: Robert E. Krieger Publishing Company, 1977.

Rinn, R. C. Children with behavior disorders. In M. Hersen & A. S. Bellack (Eds.), *Behavior therapy in the psychiatric setting*. Baltimore: Williams & Wilkins, 1978.

Rioch, M. J. Pilot projects in training mental health counselors. In E. L. Cowen, E. A. Gardner, & M. Zax (Eds.), *Emergent approaches to mental health problems*. New York: Appleton-Century-Crofts, 1967.

Rodgers, D. A. Minnesota Multiphasic Personality Inventory. In O. K. Buros (Ed.), *The seventh mental measurements yearbook* (Vol. 1). Highland Park, N. J.: Gryphon Press, 1972.

Rogers, C. *Counseling and psychotherapy*. Boston: Houghton Mifflin, 1942.

Rogers, C. *Client-centered therapy*. Boston: Riverside Press, 1951.

Rogers, C. The necessary and sufficient conditions of therapeutic personality change. *Journal of Consulting Psychology*, 1957, *21*, 95–103.

Rogers, C. *Carl Rogers on encounter groups*. New York: Harper & Row, 1970.

Rogers, C. In retrospect: Forty six years. *American Psychologist*, 1974, *29*, 115–123.

Rogers, C. R., Gendlin, G. T., Kiesler, D. V., & Truax, C. B. *The therapeutic relationship and its impact: A study of psychotherapy with schizophrenics*. Madison: University of Wisconsin Press, 1967.

Roman, M. Community control and the community mental health center: A view from the Lincoln Bridge. In B. Denner & R. H. Price (Eds.), *Community mental health: Social action and reaction*. New York: Holt, Rinehart, and Winston, 1973.

Rorschach, H. *Psychodiagnostik*. Translated by P. Lemkov & B. Kronenberg. Berne: Verlag Hans Huber, 1921.

Rotter, J. B. Some problems and misconceptions related to the construct of internal versus external control of reinforcement. *Journal of Consulting and Clinical Psychology*, 1975, *43*, 56–67.

Rotter, J. B., & Rafferty, J. E. *The Rotter incomplete sentences blank: College form.* New York: Psychological Corporation, 1950.

Rush, A. J., & Beck, A. T. Adults with affective disorders. In M. Hersen & A. S. Bellack (Eds.), *Behavior therapy in the psychiatric setting.* Baltimore: Williams & Wilkins, 1978.

Rush, A. J., Beck, A. T., Kovacs, M., & Kollon, S. Comparative efficacy of cognitive therapy and pharmocotherapy in the treatment of depressed outpatients. *Cognitive Therapy and Research,* 1977, *1,* 17–38.

Russell, E. W., Neuringer, C., & Goldstein, G. *Assessment of brain damage: A neuro-psychological key approach.* New York: Wiley-Interscience, 1970.

Russell, R. W. Academic and applied psychology: A rapprochement. *Professional Psychology,* 1973, *4,* 232–236.

Saccuzzo, D. P., & Miller, S. Critical interstimulus interval in delusional schizophrenics and normals. *Journal of Abnormal Psychology,* 1977, *86,* 261–266.

Salzinger, K. Schizophrenia. In A. E. Kazdin, A. S. Bellack, & M. Hersen (Eds.), *New perspectives in abnormal psychology.* New York: Oxford University Press, 1980.

Sandifer, M. G., Pettus, C., & Quade, D. A study of psychiatric diagnosis. *Journal of Nervous and Mental Disease,* 1964, *139,* 350–356.

Sartre, J. P. *Existential psychoanalysis.* New York: Philisophical Library, 1953.

Sattler, J. M. *Assessment of children's intelligence.* Philadelphia: Saunders, 1974.

Schacht, T., & Nathan, P. E. But is it good for the psychologist? Appraisal and status of DSM-III. *American Psychologist,* 1977, *32,* 1017–1025.

Schafer, R. *The clinical application of psychological tests: Diagnostic summaries and case studies.* New York: International Universities Press, 1948.

Scheiderer, E. G. Effects of instructions and modeling in producing self-disclosure in the initial clinical interview. *Journal of Consulting and Clinical Psychology,* 1977, *45,* 378–384.

Schofield, W. *Psychotherapy, the purchase of friendship.* Englewood Cliffs, N. J.: Prentice-Hall, 1964.

Schulberg, H. C. Issues in the evaluation of community mental health programs. *Professional Psychology,* 1977, *8,* 560–572.

Schulberg, H. C., & Baker, F. Evaluating health programs: Art and/or science. In H. Schulberg & F. Baker (Eds.), *Program evaluation in the health fields.* (Vol. 2). New York: Human Sciences, 1979.

Scott, W. A., & Johnson, R. C. Comparative validities of direct and indirect person-personality tests. *Journal of Consulting and Clinical Psychology,* 1972, *38,* 301–318.

Shaffer, J.B.P., & Galinsky, M. D. *Models of group therapy and sensitivity training.* Englewood Cliffs, N. J.: Prentice-Hall, 1974.

Shakow, D. *Clinical psychology as science and profession: A forty-year odyssey.* Chicago: Aldine, 1969.

Shemberg, K., & Keeley, S. Psychodiagnostic training in the psychiatric setting: Past and present. *Journal of Consulting and Clinical Psychology,* 1970, *34,* 205–211.

Sherman, A. R. Real-life exposure as a primary therapeutic factor in the desensitization treatment of fear. *Journal of Abnormal Psychology,* 1972, *29,* 18–28.

Siegman, A. W., & Pope, B. The effects of ambiguity and anxiety on interviewer verbal behavior. In A. W. Siegman & B. Pope (Eds.), *Studies in dyadic communication.* New York: Pergamon Press, 1972.

Singer, E. *Key concepts in psychotherapy.* New York: Random House, 1965.

Slavson, S. R. *Analytic group psychotherapy.* New York: Columbia University Press, 1950.

Sloane, R. B., Staples, F. R., Cristol, A. H., Yorkston, N. J., & Whipple, K. *Psychotherapy versus behavior therapy.* Cambridge, Mass.: Harvard University Press, 1975. (a)

Sloane, R. B., Staples, F. R., Cristol, A. H., Yorkston, N. J., & Whipple, K. Short-term analytically oriented psychotherapy versus behavior therapy. *American Journal of Psychiatry,* 1975, *132,* 373–377. (b)

Smith, P. B. Controlled studies of the outcome of sensitivity training. *Psychological Bulletin,* 1975, *82,* 597–622.

Snyder, W. U. *Casebook of non-directive counseling.* Boston: Houghton Mifflin, 1947.

Spearman, C. "General intelligence," objectively detemined and measured. *American Journal of Psychology,* 1904, *15,* 201–293.

Spearman, C. *The abilities of man.* New York: Macmillan, 1927.

Spielberger, C. D., Gorsuch, R. L., & Lushene, R. E. *Manual for the State-Trait Anxiety Inventory.* Palo Alto: Consulting Psychologist Press, 1970.

Spitzer, R. L., Endicott, J. E., & Robins, E. Clinical criteria for psychiatric diagnosis and DSM-III. *American Journal of Psychiatry,* 1975, *132,* 1187–1192.

Spotnitz, H. Comparison of different types of group psychotherapy. In H. I. Kaplan & B. J. Sadock (Eds.), *Comprehensive group psychotherapy.* Baltimore: Williams & Wilkins. 1977.

SPSSI. Guidelines for testing minority group children. *Journal of Social Issues,* 1964, *2,* 127–145.

Srole, L., Langner, T. S., Michael, S. T., Opler, M. K., & Rennie, T.A.C. *Mental health in the metropolis* (Vol. 1). New York: McGraw-Hill, 1962.

Staples, F. R., Sloane, R. B., Whipple, K., Cristol, A. H., & Yorkston, N. J. Differences between behavior therapists and psychotherapists. *Archives of General Psychiatry,* 1975, *32,* 1517–1522.

Stern, R. S. Behavior therapy and psychotropic medication. In M. Hersen & A. S. Bellack (Eds.), *Behavior therapy in the psychiatric setting.* Baltimore: Williams & Wilkins, 1978.

Strupp, H. H. Graduate training in clinical psychology: A very personal endeavor. *The Clinical Psychologist,* 1974, *28,* 1–2.

Strupp, H. H. & Bergin, A. E. Some empirical and conceptual bases for coordinated research in psychotherapy. *International Journal of Psychotherapy,* 1969, *7,* 18–90.

Strupp, H. H., & Hadley, S. W. A tripartite model of mental health and therapeutic outcomes. *American Psychologist,* 1977, *32,* 187–196.

Sue, S. Community mental health services to minority groups: Some optimism, some pessimism. *American Psychologist,* 1977, *32,* 616–624.

Sundberg, N. D. The practice of psychological testing in clinical service in the United States. *American Psychologist,* 1961, *16,* 79–83.

Tammimen, A. W. A comparison of the Army General Classification Test and the Wechsler Bellevue Intelligence Scales. *Educational and Psychological Measurement,* 1951, *11,* 646–655.

Taplin, J. R. Crisis theory: Critique and reformulation. *Community Mental Health Journal,* 1971, *7,* 13–23.

Tate, B. G., & Baroff, G. S. Aversive control of self-injurious behavior in a psychotic boy. *Behaviour Research and Therapy,* 1966, *4,* 281–287.

Taylor, B. J., & Wagner, N. N. Sex between therapists and clients: A review and analysis. *Professional Psychology,* 1976, *7,* 593–601.

Taylor, R. E. Demythologizing private practice. *Professional Psychology,* 1978, *9,* 68–70.

Terman, L. M., & Merrill, M. A. *Stanford-Binet Intelligence Scale: Manual for the Third Revision, Form L-M.* Boston: Houghton Mifflin, 1960.

Thelen, M. H., Varble, D. L., & Johnson, J. Attitudes of academic clinical psychologists towards projective techniques. *American Psychologist,* 1968, *23,* 517–521.

Thorndike, E. L., Bregman, E. O., Cobb, M. V., & Woodward, E. *The measurement of intelligence.* New York: Teachers College, 1927.

Thorne, F. C. Eclectic Psychotherapy. In R. Corsini (Ed.), *Current psychotherapies.* Itasca, Ill.: Peacock Press, 1973.

Thurstone, L. L., & Thurstone, T. G. Factorial studies of intelligence. *Psychometric Monographs,* (No. 2). Chicago: University of Chicago Press, 1941.

Tolor, A. Diagnosing the state of the diagnostic function: An analysis of the literature. *Journal of Clinical Psychology,* 1973, *29,* 338–342.

Towbin, A. P. When are cookbooks useful? In J. R. Braun (Ed.), *Clinical psychology in transition.* Cleveland: Howard Allen, Inc. 1961.

Truax, C. B. Reinforcement and nonreinforcement in Rogerian psychotherapy. *Journal of Abnormal Psychology,* 1966, *71,* 1–9.

Truax, C., & Carkhuff, R. *Toward effective counseling and psychotherapy: Training and practice.* Chicago: Aldine, 1967.

Truax, C. B., & Mitchell, K. M. Research on certain therapist interpersonal skills in relation to process and outcome. In A. E. Bergin & S. L. Garfield (Eds.), *Handbook of psychotherapy and behavior change: An empirical analysis.* New York: John Wiley & Sons, 1971. (a)

Turner, S. M., Hersen, M., & Alford, H. Effects of massed practice and meprobamate on spasmodic torticollis: An experimental analysis. *Behaviour Research and Therapy,* 1974, *12,* 259–260.

Turner, S. M., Hersen, M., & Bellack, A. S. Effects of social disruption, stimulus interference, and aversive conditioning on auditory hallucinations. *Behavior Modification,* 1977, *1,* 249–258.

Turner, S. M., Hersen, M., Bellack, A. S., & Wells, K. C. Behavioral treatment of obsessive-compulsive neurosis. *Behavior Research and Therapy,* 1979, *17,* 95–106.

Ullmann, L. P. Behavioral community psychology: Implications, opportunities, and responsibilities. In Neitzel, M. T., Winett, R. A., MacDonald, M. L., & Davidson, W. S. *Behavioral approaches to community psychology.* New York: Pergamon Press, 1977.

Vega, A., & Parsons, O. A. Cross-validation on the Halstead-Reitan tests for brain damage. *Journal of Consulting Psychology,* 1967, *31,* 619–625.

Wade, T. C., & Baker, T. B. Opinions and use of psychological tests. *American Psychologist,* 1977, *32,* 874–882.

Wahler, R. G., & Leske, G. Accurate and inaccurate observer summary reports: Reinforcement theory interpretation and investigation. *Journal of Nervous and Mental Disease,* 1973, *156,* 386–394.

Waite, R. R. The intelligence test as a psychodiagnostic instrument. *Journal of Projective Techniques.* 1961, *25,* 90–102.

Walk, R. D. Self ratings of fear in a fear-invoking situation. *Journal of Abnormal and Social Psychology,* 1956, *22,* 171–178.

Wallace, J., & Sechrest, L. Frequency hypothesis and content analysis of projective techniques. *Journal of Consulting Psychology,* 1963, *27,* 387–393.

Wallen, R. Gestalt therapy and gestalt psychology. In J. Fagan & I. L. Shepherd (Eds.), *Gestalt therapy now.* Palo Alto: Science and Behavior Books, 1970.

Watkins, J. G. Psychotherapeutic methods. In B. B. Wolman (Ed.), *Handbook of clinical psychology.* New York: McGraw-Hill, 1965.

Watson, C. G., & Klett, W. G. Predictions of WAIS IQ's from the Shipley-Hartford, the Army General Classification Test and the Revised Beta Examination. *Journal of Clinical Psychology,* 1968, *24,* 338–341.

Watson, J. B., & Rayner, R. Conditioned emotional reactions. *Journal of Experimental Psychology,* 1920, *3,* 1–14.

Watson, R. I. A brief history of clinical psychology. *Psychological Bulletin,* 1953, *50,* 321–346.

Wechsler, D. A standardized memory scale for clinical use. *Journal of Psychology,* 1945, *19,* 87–95.

Wechsler, D. *The measurement and appraisal of adult intelligence.* Baltimore: Williams & Wilkins, 1958.

Wein, K. S., Nelson, R. O., & Odom, J. V. The relative contributions of reattribution and verbal extinction to the effectiveness of cognitive restructuring. *Behavior Therapy,* 1975, *6,* 459–474.

Weiner, I. B. Individual psychotherapy. In I. B. Weiner (Ed.), *Clinical methods in psychology.* New York: John Wiley & Sons, 1976.

Weiner, I. B. Approaches to Rorschach validation. In M. A. Rickers-Ovsiankina (Ed.), *Rorschach Psychology.* New York: Robert E. Krieger Publishing Company, 1977.

Weiss, R. L., & Birchler, G. R. Adults with marital dysfunction. In M. Hersen & A. S. Bellack (Eds.), *Behavior therapy in the psychiatric setting.* Baltimore: Williams & Wilkins, 1978.

Wells, K. C., Hersen, M., Bellack, A. S., & Himmelhoch, J. Social skills training for unipolar depressive females. Paper presented at the annual meeting of the Association for Advancement of Behavior Therapy, Atlanta, 1977.

Whitaker, D. S. & Lieberman, M. A. *Psychotherapy through the group process.* New York: Atherton Press, 1965.

Wildman, R. W., & Wildman, R. W., II. The psychologist as a ward administrator: 1975. *Professional Psychology,* 1976, *7,* 371–376.

Wolberg, L. R. *The technique of psychotherapy,* New York: Grune & Stratton, 1967.

Wolf, A., & Schwartz, E. K. *Psychoanalysis in groups.* New York: Grune & Stratton, 1962.

Wolpe, J. *Psychotherapy by reciprocal inhibition.* Stanford: Stanford University Press, 1958.

Wolpe, J. *The practice of behavior therapy.* New York: Pergamon Press, 1969.

Wolpe, J., & Lazarus, A. A. *Behavior therapy techniques.* New York: Pergamon Press, 1966.

Woods, P. J. (Ed.). *Career opportunities for psychologists.* Washington, D.C.: APA, 1976.

Woodworth, R. S. *Personal Data Sheet.* Chicago: Stoelting, 1920.

Yalom, I. D., & Lieberman, M. A. A study of encounter group casualties. *Archives of General Psychiatry,* 1971, *25,* 16–30.

Yerkes, R. M. (Eds.). Psychological examining in the United States Army. *Memoirs of the National Academy of Sciences,* 1921, *15,* 1–890.

Yoakum, C. S., & Yerkes, R. M. *Army mental tests.* New York: Holt, Rinehart, and Winston, 1920.

Zax, M., & Cowen, E. L. Early identification and prevention of emotional disturbance in a public school. In E. L. Cowen, E. A. Gardner, & M. Zax (Eds.), *Emergent approaches to mental health problems.* New York: Appleton-Century-Crofts, 1967.

Zax, M., & Cowen, E. L. *Abnormal psychology: Changing conceptions.* New York: Holt, Rinehart, and Winston, 1976.

Zax, M., & Specter, G. A. *An introduction to community psychology.* New York: John Wiley & Sons, 1974.

Zubin, J. But is it good for science? *The Clinical Psychologist,* 1977, *31,* 1, 5–7.

Zubin, J., Eron, L. D., & Schumer, F. *An experimental approach to projective techniques.* New York: John Wiley & Sons, 1965.

Zuckerman, M., Bone, R., Neary, R., Mangelsdorff, D., & Brustman, B. What is the sensation seeker? Personality trait and experience correlates of the Sensation-Seeking scales. *Journal of Consulting and Clinical Psychology,* 1972, *39,* 308–321.

Zuk, G. H. Family therapy. *Archives of General Psychiatry,* 1967, *16,* 71–79.

Author Index

Subject Index